# THE GUINNESS BOOK OF
# AIR
# WARFARE

| ARBY | BARH | HIST |
|------|------|------|
|      | ✓    |      |
| MTID | CTMOB | GAML |
|      |      |      |
|      | OMB  | COTT |
|      |      |      |
| MELB | SWAV | WILL |

| BARH  |  | MELB  |       |
|-------|--|-------|-------|
| BASS  |  | SAWST |       |
| COMB  |  | SWAV  |       |
| COTT  |  | WATB  |       |
| FULB  |  | WILL  |       |
| GAML  |  |       |       |
| GSHEL |  | CSMOB | 10/97 |
| HIST  |  | CTMOB |       |
| LINT  |  | SMOBC |       |

# THE GUINNESS BOOK OF

# AIR
# WARFARE

## Robert Jackson

U.S. AIR FORCE

GUINNESS PUBLISHING

*Acknowledgement*

Not for the first time, the author is greatly indebted to his friend Alan B. Todd and his copious aviation files for assistance in his researches.

*Picture Credits*

Most illustrations supplied by the author; also:

Archiv für Kunst und Geschichte, Berlin    Associated Press
British Aerospace    Bundesministerium der Verteidigung
Flight International    Fotokhronika Tass    ECP Armées
Hawker Siddeley Aviation    Imperial War Museum    Lufthansa
Ian MacDonald (Photographs) Ltd    North American Aviation Inc
Royal Air Force Official Crown Copyright    Thames Television

*Title page illustration*

*The North American F-100 Super Sabre, the first truly supersonic aircraft to enter USAF service.*

*Editor:* Beatrice Frei
*Design and Layout:* Stonecastle Graphics Ltd.

First published in 1993 by Guinness Publishing Ltd.
This Publication Copyright © Guinness Publishing Ltd., 1993
33 London Road, Enfield, Middlesex.

Typeset in Palatino and Gill Sans by Ace Filmsetting Ltd, Frome
Printed and bound in Great Britain by The Bath Press, Bath

A catalogue record for this book is available from the British Library.

ISBN 0–85112–701–0

# Contents

# Introduction

Over the centuries, virtually every major technological advance known to mankind has found an application in warfare. As far as it is known – although this is something of a grey area, for most of our knowledge of the scientific inventions of the ancient civilizations that bordered the Mediterranean was lost forever with the destruction of the Library of Alexandria – the Chinese were the first to invent primitive flying machines in the form of kites, and according to documented history it was the Chinese who were the first to use them in war. In 206 BC, the Chinese general Han Hsin used a kite to calculate the distance between his forces and the palace of Wei Yang Kong, situated in the town he was besieging, and in AD 549 the defenders of the town of King Thai, besieged by enemy forces, used kites to send out calls for help to neighbouring villages, using a form of signalling not unlike semaphore. Chinese man-lifting kites, described by the Venetian explorer Marco Polo in the 14th century, may have been used for military observation purposes, but there is no firm documentation of this.

Four centuries later, when François Pilâtre de Rozier became the first man to be carried aloft in a tethered Montgolfier hot-air balloon on 15 October 1783, at least one man who witnessed the event was convinced that balloons had a military potential. On 21 November 1783 – by coincidence, the day on which de Rozier and the Marquis d'Arlandes made the world's first aerial journey in a free-flying balloon – Benjamin Franklin, then serving as American envoy to France, observed that an army could employ balloons for functions such as 'elevating an engineer to take a view of an enemy's army, works, etc, conveying intelligence into or out of a besieged town, giving signals to distant places, or the like'. In January the following year, he wrote that the balloon's potential in warfare was 'of great importance, and what may possibly give a new turn to human affairs. . . . Five thousand balloons, capable of raising two men each, could not cost more than five ships of the line; and where is the prince who can afford so to cover his country with troops for its defense as that ten thousand men descending from the clouds might not in many places do an infinite deal of mischief before a force could be brought together to repel them?'

It would be many years before Franklin's prophetic vision of military aviation became a reality in his native North America. In the meantime, it was France who found a practical military application for the balloon, as a powerful Allied coalition sought to destroy the embryo armies of the Republic in the wake of the French Revolution.

# 1
# MILITARY AND NAVAL AVIATION 1794–1914

## 1794

*2 April* The world's first military aviation unit, La Première Compagnie d'Aérostiers Militaires under the command of Captain Coutelle, was formed at Chalais-Meudon near Paris by decree of the Committee of Public Safety. The company's first balloon was the *Entreprenant*. Its envelope was constructed by a team of republican seamstresses in the main hall of nearby Meudon manor. Today, Chalais-Meudon is the site of France's national Air Museum.

*2 June* The *Entreprenant* was deployed to Meubeuge, Belgium, for use by the French Republican Army against the Austrians. The first operational ascent was made on *26 June* when Captain Coutelle carried out a series of observations of Austrian forces manoeuvring on the battlefield at Fleurus. Coutelle was airborne for a total of ten hours and was accompanied later in the day by the French commander, General Jourdan. Their observations made a decisive contribution to the French victory. The hydrogen-filled *Entreprenant* had been hauled from Meubeuge to Fleurus, a distance of about 40 miles (64 km), in a fully inflated condition. Two balloon companies were eventually attached to the Republican Army, but were disbanded in 1799. No more than four balloons were ever operational. The two-man crew transmitted messages to the ground by means of semaphore, luminous balls hung on the basket or written information slid in sandbags down the mooring cable. One balloon was deployed to Egypt during Napoleon's campaign of 1798.

## 1841

During the Seminole War that took place in this year, when the US Army was engaged in a protracted fight with the Seminole Indians in the Florida Everglades, Army Colonel John Sherburne suggested to Secretary of War Joel Poinsett that balloons might be sent up at night to detect Seminole campfires, so that the Indian camps could be pinpointed and attacked by infantry columns. The idea was rejected out of hand by General W.K. Armistead, the US commander in Florida.

## 1846

During the war between the United States and Mexico (which arose out of a dispute over the ownership of New Mexico) a Pennsylvania balloonist named John Wise suggested using a balloon to drop 'a thousand percussion bombshells' on the fort of San Juan de Ulloa at Veracruz, whose gun batteries were holding up the advance on Mexico City of American forces under General Winfield Scott. The idea was ignored by the War Department, and the fort eventually succumbed to a land assault.

## 1849

*22 August* Austrian forces, laying siege to Venice, launched unmanned hot-air balloons, each carrying a 30 lb (14 kg) explosive charge and time fuze, towards the city. The plan misfired when adverse winds carried many of the balloons back into the Austrian positions, where they exploded. The Venetians capitulated on 28 August.

# 1859

**10 June** The French balloonist Eugène Godard began a series of tethered ascents in a Montgolfier-type hot-air balloon to observe Austrian troop movements during the Battle of Solferino. His operations lasted until **24 June**, when the Austrians were defeated by French and Sardinian forces.

# 1861

## The American Civil War
**20 April** A week after the outbreak of hostilities, Ohio aeronaut Thaddeus S.C. Lowe, preparing for a transatlantic attempt, took off from Cincinnati on a practice flight and landed at Unionville, South Carolina, in Confederate-held territory. Lowe was at first thought to be a spy, but later recognized and released. Lowe immediately offered his services and those of his balloon, *Enterprise*, to President Abraham Lincoln. On **18 June** he carried out a demonstration in Washington, during which he transmitted a telegraph message from the balloon to President Lincoln. The President instructed a reluctant General Winfield Scott, commander of the Union Army, to employ Lowe's services in developing balloons for military use. Meanwhile, aeronaut John Wise had once again volunteered his services, and this time his offer was accepted. Another aeronaut, James Allen, was also enlisted and both were placed at the disposal of Brigadier General Irvin McDowell, commanding the main US field army. The first operational ascent was made by James Allen on **19 June** and, although early operations were beset by mishaps, Wise succeeded in observing Confederate lines and obtained useful reconnaissance information on **24 July**, following the Union Army's defeat in the first Battle of Bull Run. Several days later, however, Wise's balloon broke free of its moorings and had to be shot down. Disillusioned, Wise became a cavalry officer.

**2 August** Thaddeus Lowe and the men of his embryo balloon corps received orders to build the US Army's first balloon, the *Union*. Lowe made his first operational ascent in this balloon on **24**

*September*, using his aerial telegraph to direct artillery fire.

**1 October** The first American Army Balloon Corps was officially formed under the command of Thaddeus S.C. Lowe, Chief Aeronaut of the Army of the Potomac, with a complement of 50 men. By the end of the year the Corps had five balloons, the *Constitution*, *Intrepid*, *Union*, *United States* and *Washington*. Two more, the *Excelsior* and *Eagle*, were added to the strength early in 1862. From November 1861, a converted coal barge, the *G.W. Parke Custis*, was used to transport and tow observation balloons during operations along the Potomac River; this may be said to have been the world's first aircraft carrier.

# 1862

**31 March** Control of the Balloon Corps was transferred to the Quartermaster Corps, a move that led to increasingly severe logistical and administrative difficulties. Though successful in the field, the Balloon Corps never had a proper place in the Union Army's command structure; the aeronauts were never given ranks, they received inadequate and infrequent pay, and the Corps' horses and wagons were often commandeered by the Quartermaster Corps.

Despite the problems, the Balloon Corps proved its worth time and again, especially in directing artillery fire. In *May–June 1862*, the *Intrepid*, *Washington* and *Constitution* were used in support of General George B. McClellan's Peninsula Campaign, notably at the Battle of Seven Pines (Fair Oaks). Their observation activities always attracted heavy enemy fire, but none was lost through enemy action. The Confederate forces operated one balloon briefly in the spring of 1862. It was manufactured from silk dresses donated by Southern ladies, but because the only gas supply was in Richmond, Virginia, it had to be inflated there and then towed to the front by train or boat. The American Army Balloon Corps, on the other hand, had portable hydrogen-making equipment. On **11 December 1862** one of Lowe's balloons was used to assist Union forces in their successful crossing of the river Rappahannock, prior to the costly Battle of Fredericksburg.

# 1863

**7 May** The American Army Balloon Corps was transferred again, this time to the Corps of Engineers, and a 40 per cent salary cut was imposed. Lowe resigned in protest, and the Balloon Corps was disbanded. Lowe himself had made over 3000 operational ascents over the past two years. It would be three decades before the US Army once again showed an interest in military aviation.

# 1865

**18 March** War broke out between Paraguay and an international coalition comprising Argentina, Brazil and Uruguay. Observation balloons were used extensively in this bitter and bloody conflict, which ended on 1 March 1870 with the devastation of Paraguay.

# 1870

## The Franco-Prussian War

From September 1870 to January 1871, 66 balloon flights were made out of Paris, under siege by Prussian forces, to unoccupied territory. The balloons carried a total of 110 passengers, more than 2½ million letters, and carrier pigeons to fly back to Paris bearing despatches. The first flight, on 23 September 1870, was made by Jules Duroug, carrying despatches. After a three-hour flight over Prussian-held territory, he landed at Evreux. The early flights from Paris were made by skilled aeronauts, but later missions were undertaken by French Navy personnel, specially trained for the task. Five balloons and their occupants were captured by the enemy; of the others, two were lost in the Atlantic and one came down in Norway, after a flight of 14 hr 40 min. The flights ceased on 28 January 1871.

While the balloon flights out of Paris – the first airlift in history – had been something of an epic, it was clear that the venture would have been a greater success if the aeronauts had been able to steer their craft. The experience gave impetus to the idea of building a dirigible balloon – an airship.

# 1878–79

Great Britain entered the field of military aeronautics with the establishment of an Army Balloon Equipment Store at Woolwich in 1878, the year in which the War Office allocated £150 for the construction of a balloon. Captain J.L.B. Templer of the Middlesex Militia, a qualified aeronaut and the owner of a balloon named *Crusader*, and Captain H.P. Lee of the Royal Engineers were placed in charge of development work. Templer therefore became the first British air commander, and his *Crusader* the first balloon to be used by the British Army, in 1879. The first British military aeronauts were Lieutenant G.E. Grover and Captain F. Beaumont, both of the Royal Engineers, who had been attached to the American Army Balloon Corps in 1862–3. The first British Army balloon, using coal gas fuel and named *Pioneer*, was constructed in 1879. It cost £71 from the initial allocation of £150.

# 1880

At intervals during the year, Frenchman Arthur Batut carried out experiments in aerial photography, using kites. Air photographs had been taken previously, notably by the American Army Balloon Corps during the Civil War, but this was the first time anyone tried to devise a systematic technique.

**24 June** The British Army used a man-carrying observation balloon for the first time during military manoeuvres at Aldershot, Hampshire.

# 1884

**26 November** A balloon unit attached to the Royal Engineers left England to take part in an expedition to Bechuanaland. The balloon created an enormous impression. In the words of one native chief: 'If the first white men who came into this country had brought a thing like that, and demanded that we should worship and serve them, we should have done so. The English have indeed great power.' The expedition reached Cape Town on 19 December. A second Royal Engineers balloon accompanied an expedition to the Sudan, leaving England on **15 February 1885**.

# 1892

The Royal Engineers Balloon Depot was given a permanent base at Aldershot and a school of ballooning founded there. The factory produced its first balloons in 1893. A second balloon factory was established at South Farnborough, Hampshire, in 1894.

# 1897

**14 October** The French inventor and aviation pioneer Clement Ader attempted to demonstrate his *Avion No. 3* at Satory, Versailles, before Ministry of War officials. On 9 October 1890 Ader had achieved the first short 'hop' in a man-carrying aeroplane, the *Eole*, but this had not been a sustained and controlled flight. The French War Ministry allocated 650 000 gold francs to further development work that was to have led to a two-seater aircraft capable of carrying a bomb load of 165 lb (75 kg). This was to have been based on his *Avion No. 3*, which in the event crashed in strong wind conditions after a brief uncontrolled flight at Satory. The report of the military commission was unfavourable and Ader abandoned his work, which was a pity. His aircraft designs were powered by heavy steam engines; had he waited until lighter petrol engines became available, he might have become the first man to make a genuine powered flight.

# 1898

**25 March** Theodore Roosevelt, Assistant Secretary of the US Navy, recommended to the Secretary that he appoint two officers 'of scientific attainments and practical ability' who, with representatives from the War Department, would examine Professor Samuel P. Langley's flying machine and report upon its practicability for use in war. Langley's flying machine was a steam-powered model with a 14 ft (4.25 m) wing span and was capable of a sustained flight of up to 4200 ft (1280 m). The resulting Army–Navy report expressed a general sentiment in favour of supporting Langley in further experimentation. The War Department allocated a grant of $50 000 to Langley to build a full-scale, powered and manned flying machine.

**May** Following the outbreak of the war between the United States and Spain over the latter's brutal domination of Cuba, a US 'Balloon Company' was sent to the Caribbean island in support of an American expeditionary force. In fact, the balloon company comprised 27 men and a single balloon owned by a carnival aeronaut named William Ivy, who had been hired by General Adolphus Greely, commander of the US Signal Corps. Ivy was given the rank of sergeant and was sent to Cuba with Signal Corps Lieutenant-Colonel Joseph Maxfield. They arrived with a damaged balloon and no hydrogen generator. Ivy repaired the balloon, filled it with bottled hydrogen, and after several tentative ascents used it to confirm the presence of the Spanish fleet in Santiago harbour on **30 June**. The next day, he and Maxfield helped direct artillery fire and observe the Spanish positions during the American assault on San Juan Hill. Towards the end of the day the balloon, with only Ivy aboard, was badly holed by enemy fire and dropped into the water. Ivy survived and lived until 1955, with the dubious distinction of having become the first pilot in history to be shot down in war.

# 1899–1900

## The Boer War

*December* A Royal Engineers balloon detachment under Captain Jones carried out observations during the Battle of Magersfontein. The balloon was sent up to the front by railway and could have been used for aerial reconnaissance of the enemy's trenches before the battle started, but the British commander, Lieutenant-General Lord Methuen, neglected to issue the necessary orders, with the result that his forces were committed to action with no real knowledge of the enemy's trench systems. The British suffered heavy casualties, which would certainly have been heavier still if balloon observation had not detected enemy movements during the battle itself. Observation balloons were also used during the siege of Ladysmith, and to reconnoitre the terrain ahead of the British advance on Pretoria in May–June 1900. The activities of the British 'war balloons' persuaded some senior British officers that aerial reconnaissance was a valuable asset, although others remained convinced that scouting by cavalry remained the best method.

# EARLY MILITARY AVIATION: THE MARCH OF PROGRESS

THE first decade of the 20th century saw amazing advances in the development of heavier-than-air flying machines, and also some significant steps forward in techniques that would play a major part in the development of air fighting. On **13 November 1907**, for example, a Frenchman named Paul Cornu made the world's first free, untethered, manned helicopter flight at Coquainvilliers, near Lisieux, his primitive machine – known as the 'flying bicycle' – hovering one foot clear of the ground for 20 seconds. It would be many years before the dream of vertical flight became a practical reality, but it was a beginning.

The aircraft's role as a potential war machine was demonstrated several times in 1910. On **19 January**, Lieutenant Paul Beck released sandbags, representing bombs, over Los Angeles from an aeroplane flown by the pioneer aviator Louis Paulhan, and on **30 June** Glenn H. Curtiss dropped dummy bombs from a height of 50 ft

(15 m) in an area representing the shape of a battleship, marked by buoys on Lake Keuka. The feasibility of discharging firearms from an aircraft was also demonstrated on **20 August 1910**, when Lieutenant Jacob Earl Fickel of the US Army fired a 0.30-inch calibre rifle from a Curtiss biplane at a ground target at Sheepshead Bay, New York. More significantly in terms of future development, a German named August Euler had filed a patent some weeks earlier for a device enabling a fixed machine gun to be fired from an aeroplane.

There was another event of significance on **27 August 1910**, when James McCurdy, a Canadian, sent and received messages from a Curtiss 'Golden Flyer' piloted by E.W. Pickerill via an H.M. Horton wireless set at Sheepshead Bay, NY. The age of airborne wireless telegraphy, which was to play such a vital part in the efficiency of future military air operations, was born.

# 1903

*June* A quarter-scale model of Samuel P. Langley's proposed aeroplane, powered by a petrol engine designed by Charles Manly, an engineering student from Cornell, became the world's first aeroplane powered by a petrol engine to achieve sustained flight. The development programme was still funded by the US War Department.

**7 October** Langley's full-size aircraft, the *Aerodrome*, with a span of 48 ft (14.6 m) and powered by a 52 hp Manly-Balzer petrol engine, was catapulted from the deck of a barge on the river Potomac with Charles Manly at the controls. It fouled the launcher and dropped into the river. A second attempt, on **8 December**, met with similar failure and the US Government withdrew its support from the project.

**17 December** Wilbur and Orville Wright achieved the world's first sustained and controlled flight in a heavier-than-air machine powered by a petrol engine at Kill Devil Hill, North Carolina. Four

flights were made in all that day, the last one covering 852 ft (260 m) and lasting 59 seconds. The Wright *Flyer*, powered by a 12 hp four-cylinder water-cooled engine, was entirely a private venture and had no military or government funding.

# 1905

**17 October** During a flight in the dirigible *Lebaudy II*, French aeronauts Richard and Bois dropped dummy bombs and took photographs of various objectives in a demonstration for military observers.

**19 October** *Lebaudy II* made an observation flight over the military stronghold at Toul in a mission lasting 2 hr 31 min and covering 31 miles. The crew, Juchmès, Rey and Voyer, were accompanied by General Pamard. On **24 October** the airship made a flight from Toul with the French War Minister, M. Berteaux, on board. *Lebaudy II* was subsequently purchased by the French Army and was the first of a line of Lebaudy military airships.

Germany's Parseval I *non-rigid airship carried out simulated attacks on a fort near Koblenz in October 1909.*

# 1907

**1 August** Brigadier General James Allen, commanding the US Army Signal Corps, signed a confidential War Department directive, establishing the Aeronautical Division of the Signal Corps – the first permanent air service in American history.

**10 September** Britain's first Army airship, the Dirigible No. 1 *Nulli Secundus*, made its first flight from Farnborough golf course. The crew were Colonel John Capper, RE, commandant of the Balloon Factory, Captain W.A. de C. King, the Balloon Factory's adjutant, and Samuel F. Cody, the first man to make a powered flight in Britain, who had been commissioned to install the ship's 50 hp Antoinette engine and to design the gondola and steering gear. The airship flew for 1000 yd (914 m). The airship was destroyed in a storm on **5 October** after flying over London and was rebuilt as the *Nulli Secundus II*.

career. Count Ferdinand von Zeppelin's prototype rigid airship, the LZ.1, had first flown over Lake Constance on **2 July 1900**; the first Zeppelin ordered by the German Army was LZ.4, but this crashed after escaping from its moorings on 5 August 1908 and LZ.3 was pressed into service instead before it could begin a planned series of operational trials.

**30 October** The German non-rigid airships *Parseval I* and *Gross-Basenach II*, together with the German Army Zeppelin Z.2 (LZ.5), carried out a simulated attack on a fort near Koblenz during military manoeuvres. Major von Parseval was the leading designer of non-rigid airships in Germany before World War I, beginning work in 1906. In all, 27 were built. The Parseval was the first airship to be successfully exported, several being supplied to foreign services – including one to the Royal Navy.

# 1909

**3 July** The German Army formally took delivery of its first Zeppelin rigid airship, the LZ.3, at Metz. It was used as a training airship for most of its

# 1910

**10 February** The French Army took delivery of its first aircraft, a Wright biplane, at Satory near Versailles. General Roques, in charge of military

aviation, launched a campaign to recruit pilots; the artillery provided three men, the infantry four, and the cavalry rejected the request with disdain! The first French military pilot to receive his brevet was Lieutenant Felix Camerman, who was subsequently promoted to command the aviation school at Chalons.

**9 June** France's Aéronautique Militaire carried out its first operational mission when Lieutenant Féquant and his observer, Captain Marconnet, flew from Chalons to Vincennes and took aerial photographs. Their aircraft was a two-seater Blériot.

**September** For the first time, French military aircraft – two Henry Farmans, a Sommer and a Blériot, all two-seaters, took part in large-scale manoeuvres with the French Army in Picardy, operating with the 2nd Corps. Later, two more Farmans, a Blériot and a Wright were attached to the 9th Corps for similar exercises. The results encouraged General Roques to order more aircraft. By the end of the year the French Army had 29 military aircraft (Blériots, Breguets, Farmans, Antoinettes and Voisins) and 39 pilots.

**October** The German Army received the first of seven aircraft on order, all Etrich *Taube* types. A training school for military pilots had already been set up during the summer of 1910 at Döberitz; the first German military pilot to receive his brevet was *Leutnant* Richard von Tiedemann, a Hussar officer, who flew solo on **23 July 1910**.

**14 November** Eugene B. Ely, a civilian pilot, became the first aviator ever to fly from a ship, his Curtiss Golden Flyer taking off from a platform built over the bow of the American cruiser USS *Birmingham*. Ely tried to take off before the vessel was properly under way in Hampton Roads, Virginia; his aircraft dipped and struck the water, damaging its propeller, but Ely maintained control and landed safely at Willoughby Spit after a flight of 2½ miles (4 km).

# 1911

**7 January** The first trials with live bombs were undertaken at San Francisco, California, by Lieutenant Myron S. Crissy and Philip O. Parmalee in a Wright Type B biplane. Further trials were carried out on 15 January.

**16 January** The first photographic reconnaissance mission in the United States was carried out by

G.E.M. Kelly and W. Brookins, in a Wright biplane.

**18 January** At 11.01 a.m., Eugene Ely, in a Curtiss Golden Flyer, landed on a platform specially built over the stern of the armoured cruiser USS *Pennsylvania* at anchor in San Francisco Bay. At 11.58 a.m. he took off and returned to Selfridge Field, San Francisco, having completed the earliest demonstration of the adaptability of aircraft to shipboard operations.

**26 January** The first successful hydroaeroplane flight was made by Glenn Curtiss at North Island, San Diego. This important step in adapting aircraft to naval needs was witnessed by Lieutenant T.G. Ellyson, who assisted in preparing for the test. The aircraft was a standard Curtiss biplane, fitted with triple floats arranged in tandem.

**1 February** Glenn Curtiss made two successful flights from the water at San Diego, with a single main float in place of the triple floats used in earlier tests. In a further trial on **17 February**, he taxied his biplane alongside the USS *Pennsylvania* at anchor in San Diego Harbour, was hoisted aboard, returned to the water by ship's crane and then took off for the return flight to base.

**23 March** The Belgian Army founded its first Military Aviation School at Brasschaet.

**1 April** The Air Battalion of the Royal Engineers was formed at Larkhill, Wiltshire, under the command of Major Sir Alexander Bannerman. It consisted of two companies: No. 1 (Airship, Balloon and Kite) and No. 2 (Aeroplanes). The establishment of the Battalion was fixed at 14 officers and 176 men, but it was some time before full strength was attained. The Battalion had three airships, the *Beta*, *Gamma* and *Delta*, and an assortment of aircraft described as 'an antique Wright which had originally belonged to C.S. Rolls; a somewhat antique and very dangerous Blériot; "The Paulhan", a type no longer sold by Paulhan, a de Havilland, a Henri Farman, four Bristols and a Howard Wright'.

**22 May** Britain's first rigid airship, the Vickers R.1 (the *Mayfly*), was brought from her hangar at Barrow-in-Furness and moored in the open in readiness for trials. She was destined never to fly; in September, she broke her back during handling and was scrapped. The airship had been intended for service with the Royal Navy.

**1 July** Glenn Curtiss demonstrated the A-1 floatplane, the first aircraft built for the US Navy, taking off from and alighting on Lake Keuka at Hammondsport, N.Y. The flight lasted five min-

utes, the aircraft rising only to 25 ft (8 m). Three more flights were made later in the day, two by Lieutenant T.G. Ellyson, USN. On *3 July* he became the first naval aviator to make a night flight, flying the A-1 from Keuka to Hammondsport and alighting without the aid of lights.

*10 September* The French 6th and 7th Army Corps, each supported by 25 aircraft, began a week of intensive manoeuvres on France's eastern frontier. Originally scheduled to take place in central France, the exercises were switched to the country's frontier with Germany, following a rise in political tension between the two countries. It was the first time that aircraft had been used as part of a military show of strength.

*22 October* Following Italy's declaration of war on Turkey over a dispute involving the Italian occupation of Cyrenaica and Tripolitania, Captain Carlo Piazza, commanding the Italian Expeditionary Force's air flotilla, carried out a reconnaissance of Turkish positions between Tripoli and Azizzia in a Blériot XI. The flight marked the first use of an aeroplane in war.

*December* The Royal Navy's first flying school was officially established at Eastchurch, Kent, with six Short biplanes loaned by Frank McClean, a pioneer of the Royal Aero Club. The first four RN pilots had actually begun flying training in March 1911. The role of the Royal Navy's aviators in time of war was defined: their primary task would be reconnaissance, but they would also be required to search for submarines, to locate mine-fields, to act as spotters for naval guns, and 'to ascend from a floating base'.

Sometime during 1911 – the exact date is not recorded – an Italian airman, Captain Guidoni, became the first pilot to release a torpedo from an

**Above:**
*The* Beta *and* Gamma *airships were in service when the Air Battalion of the Royal Engineers was formed at Larkhill, Wiltshire, on 1 April 1911.*

**Below:**
*Britain's first attempt at rigid airship design – the ill-fated Vickers No. I or Mayfly.*

*The hazards of early aviation: a Sopwith biplane comes to grief on the bank of Chingford reservoir, Essex.*

aeroplane (a Farman biplane). The torpedo weighed 352 lb (160 kg).

# 1912

**10 January** Lieutenant Charles R. Samson, RN, became the first British naval officer to fly from a ship, taking off from a platform mounted on the bows of the battleship HMS *Africa* in a Short S.38 biplane. The ship was moored at Sheerness.

**10 March** During operations in North Africa, two Italian Army airships, the P.2 and P.3, carried out a reconnaissance over Turkish positions and their crews dropped several grenades, but without inflicting any damage. On **13 April**, during another reconnaissance mission, they remained airborne for 13 hours, their crews spotting for Italian artillery. Several more missions were flown by the two ships before they were withdrawn in June. Some of the later bombing missions were highly successful, the airships' crews breaking up concentrations of Arab tribesmen with well-directed grenades. The P.2 and P.3 were small non-rigid craft, designed by an engineer named Forlanini.

**13 April** The Royal Flying Corps was constituted by Royal Warrant. A scheme for the organization of the RFC, approved by the Committee of Impe-

rial Defence, was prepared by Brigadier General D. Henderson, Captain F.M. Sykes and Major D.S. MacInnes.

**13 May** The Royal Flying Corps was formed, absorbing the Royal Engineers Air Battalion and the Naval Air Organization. The new Corps included a Military Wing, a Naval Wing, a Central Flying School, a Reserve, and the Royal (formerly Army) Aircraft Factory at Farnborough. The Military Wing (Captain F.M. Sykes) was to comprise a Headquarters, seven aeroplane squadrons, one airship and kite squadron, and a Flying Depot, Line of Communications (later renamed Aircraft

*The Army Tractor Biplane, built by the Royal Aircraft Factory, became the BE.2a – first in a long line of distinguished military aircraft.*

Park). Nos. 1, 2 and 3 Sqns formed on 13 May 1912, No. 4 in September 1912, No. 5 in August 1913, No. 6 in January 1914 and No. 7 in May 1914. The first four squadrons were equipped with a miscellany of the aircraft types then available.

*June* The German Naval Airship Division was formed under *Korvettenkapitän* Friedrich Metzing, and Nordholz, near Cuxhaven, developed as an airship base. The first complete naval airship crew began training on *1 July* at Fuhlsbüttel in the Zeppelin passenger airship *Viktoria Luise.*

*2 June* The first trials in the United States with an aircraft armed with a machine gun began on this date. The aircraft was a Wright B flown by Lieutenant Thomas de Witt Milling at College Park, Maryland, and the gunner was Captain Charles de Forest Chandler of the US Army Signal Corps, who was armed with a Lewis gun.

*September* An airship and 24 aircraft participated in the British Army manoeuvres held in East Anglia, flying a total of 7855 miles (12 641 km). A memorandum issued by the Director of Military Operations at the War Office stated: 'There can no longer be any doubt as to the value of airships and aeroplanes in locating an enemy on land and obtaining information which could otherwise only be obtained by force. . . . Though aircraft will

*The* Viktoria Luise *rigid Zeppelin airship was used to train the Imperial German Navy's first airship crews in the summer of 1912.*

probably have several uses in war, their primary duty is searching for information.

*3 October* A recoilless aircraft gun designed by Commander Cleland Davis, USN, was given initial tests at the Naval Proving Ground, Indian Head. The gun was intended to fire a large-calibre shell from an aircraft.

*12 November* The US Navy's first successful launch of an aircraft by catapult was made at the Washington Navy Yard by Lieutenant T.G. Ellyson in a Curtiss A-3.

*18 December* Lieutenant J.H. Towers, USN, completed a series of tests (begun on 26 October) to determine the feasibility of spotting submarines from the air. He reported that the best altitude for observation was about 800 ft (240 m) and that submarines could be detected when running a few feet below the surface. The trials were held in Chesapeake Bay, with further trials on *6 January 1913* by the entire aviation element of the US Navy, this time at Guantanamo Bay, Cuba, where the water was clearer.

# 1913

**March** An Experimental Branch of the Military Wing, RFC, was formed under Major H. Musgrave to deal with ballooning, kiting, wireless telegraphy, photography, meteorology, bomb-dropping, musketry, gunnery and artillery co-operation developments.

**5 March** The US Army Signal Corps' Aeronautical Division issued Field Order No. 1, establishing the First Aero Squadron at Galveston Bay, Texas City, under Captain Charles Chandler. The Aeronautical Division's sole Wright biplane was joined by a Curtiss D, a Burgess H and a Martin TT seaplane. The First Aero Squadron remained at Galveston then moved early in 1914 to San Diego, California, where the Signal Corps Aviation School was formed.

**10 May** Didier Masson, a supporter of General Alvarado Obregon, became the first airman to drop bombs on an enemy warship when he attacked Mexican gunships in Guaymas Bay, Gulf of California.

**30 November** (Date imprecise). In what must have been the world's first air combat, Phillip Radar and Dean I. Lamb, each flying in support of a rival Mexican faction, exchanged revolver shots over Naco. No hits were registered.

**Top:**
*Experiments with machine guns mounted on aircraft began well before the outbreak of World War I, as this experimental Grahame-White biplane of 1912 shows.*

**Above:**
*The Bristol Tractor Biplane of 1912 had a distinctive four-wheel undercarriage and was an efficient design. Bristol later specialized in monoplanes.*

# 1914

*The Clement-Bayard series of non-rigid airships were used by the French for observation purposes prior to World War I.*

**January** French aviators operating from Tunis carried out a series of attacks on dissident Moroccan tribesmen using grenades, Danish-made Aasen 6.6 lb (3 kg) bombs and bundles of steel darts. The explosives were dropped on rebel camps and caravans, the darts on cavalry concentrations.

**20 April** A US Navy aviation detachment of three pilots, 12 enlisted men and three aircraft, under the command of Lieutenant John H. Towers, sailed from Pensacola on board the USS *Birmingham* to join Atlantic Fleet forces operating off Tampico in the Mexican crisis. The next day, a second detachment from Pensacola comprising one pilot, three student pilots and two aircraft, commanded by Lieutenant (jg) P.N.L. Bellinger, embarked in the USS *Mississippi* and sailed for Mexican waters to assist in military operations at Veracruz. In the days that followed, Lieutenant Bellinger, flying an AB-3 flying boat and an AH-3 floatplane, photographed the harbour at Veracruz and made a search for mines. On **2 May** Bellinger, with Ensign W.D. Lamont as observer, flew the first mission in direct support of ground troops as US Marines, encamped near Tejar, reported being under attack and requested the aviation unit at Veracruz

to locate the attackers. On **6 May**, the Curtiss AH-3 floatplane, flown by Bellinger with Lieutenant (jg) R.C. Saufley as observer, was hit by rifle fire over enemy positions in the vicinity of Veracruz. The aviation detachment was stood down from active operations on **19 May** as the crisis diminished.

**1 July** The Naval Wing of the Royal Flying Corps re-formed as the Royal Naval Air Service.

**28 July** A 14 in (35.6 cm) torpedo weighing 810 lb (367 kg) was dropped at the Royal Naval Air Station, Calshot, by a Short Seaplane flown by Squadron Commander Arthur Longmore, RN. The main float crossbars were bent upwards to allow the torpedo to be slung between the floats clear of the water, and the aircraft was fitted with a quick-release mechanism designed by Flight Lieutenant D.H. Hyde-Thompson.

**1 August** Germany declared war on Russia.

**3 August** Germany declared war on France and invaded Belgium.

**4 August** Britain declared war on Germany.

# 2
# THE 1914–18 WAR

## 1914

**4 August** The German thrust into Belgium was supported by a small number of *Taube*-type aircraft, carrying out reconnaissance. Similar missions were also flown by Belgian aircraft (type not identified) over the German spearheads east of Liège. The aircraft were fired on, but no damage was sustained.

**6 August** The German Army Zeppelin Z.6 (LZ.21) dropped 440 lb (200 kg) of bombs on Liège. The airship was hit by anti-aircraft fire and was destroyed on crash-landing near Bonn.

**11 August** The first mission under war conditions was flown by a German Navy Zeppelin; L.3 located a Dutch battleship and four destroyers off Terschelling during a reconnaissance flight from Fuhlsbüttel.

**13 August** Nos. 2, 3, 4 and 5 Sqns of the Royal Flying Corps deployed to France with 64 aircraft, 105 officers and 775 other ranks in support of the British Expeditionary Force, initially assembling in the Amiens area. The deployment was completed within 48 hours. A temporary RNAS flying base was also set up at Ostend and seaplane patrols initiated between that location and Westgate, Kent, to protect the troopships carrying the BEF to France.

**14 August** Lieutenant Césari and Corporal Prudhommeaux of the *Aviation Militaire*, flying a Blériot XI, bombed the German airship sheds at Metz-Frescaty. During a second similar mission, flown on **18 August**, French aviators claimed to have destroyed three enemy aircraft and an airship on the ground, but this was unconfirmed.

**17 August** The Zeppelin L.3 reconnoitred the Skagerrak on the Naval Airship Division's first long war flight, 600 miles (960 km) round trip.

**19 August** The first RFC reconnaissance flight of the war was made from Maubeuge, Belgium, by Captain P. Joubert de la Ferte of No. 3 Sqn, in a Blériot, and Lieutenant G.W. Mapplebeck of No.

4 Sqn in a BE 2. The RFC suffered its first loss of the war on **22 August** when an Avro 504 of No. 5 Sqn, piloted by Lieutenant V. Waterfall, was shot down by enemy rifle fire over Belgium.

**22 August** On the Eastern Front, the German Army airship Schütte-Lanz SL.2 made a reconnaissance flight on a line Kholm–Lublin–Krasnik in support of Austrian ground forces. The information brought back by the airship played a vital

*Airships were to play a major role throughout World War I. This photograph shows a naval SS-type non-rigid patrol dirigible with its car converted from the fuselage of a BE.2 biplane.*

# ORDERS OF BATTLE, AUGUST 1914
# THE GERMAN AND ALLIED
# MILITARY AIR ARMS

IN August 1914 the heavier-than-air component of the German Imperial Air Service comprised 246 aircraft, 254 pilots and 271 observers. There were 33 *Feldflieger Abteilungen* (Field Flight Sections), each with six aircraft, and eight *Festungflieger Abteilungen* (Fortress Flight Sections), each with four aircraft. The former came under the direct operational control of the Army, one being assigned to each individual Army headquarters and one to each Army Corps, while the latter had the task of protecting fortress towns along Germany's frontiers. About half the aircraft were Etrich *Taube* (Dove) types, which in the years leading up to the war were built in large numbers by several firms, including Albatros, Gotha, Rumpler and DFW. The unarmed *Taube* monoplane had a top speed of 60 mph (96 km/h). Other types in service, all biplanes, were the AEG B.II, Albatros B.II, Aviatik B.I and B.II, and the DFW B.I. At the outbreak of war, the German Army possessed five Zeppelin airships, numbered Z.4 to Z.9, while the German Navy's Airship Division as yet had only one, the L.3.

France's *Aviation Militaire* had at its disposal 132 aircraft, with a further 150 in reserve, the latter mostly assembled at Saint-Cyr. The first-line aircraft were divided between 24 *Escadrilles*, each having six machines on average, although the number varied somewhat. Five were equipped with Maurice Farmans (MF 2, 5, 8, 16 and 20); four with Henry Farmans (HF 1, 7, 13 and 19); two with Voisins (V 14 and 21); one with Caudrons (C 11); one with Breguets (Br 17); seven with Blériots (Bl 3, 9, 10 and 18, and also Bl C2, 4 and 5, the last three being attached to cavalry units); two with Deperdussins (D4 and D6); one with REPs (REP 15) and one with Nieuports (N 12). All these units were tasked with reconnaissance and were assigned to the five French field armies engaged on the Western Front. In addition, the French Army had 15 non-rigid airships, mostly of Astra-Torres or Clément-Bayard design.

The Royal Flying Corps, at least on paper, had 180 aircraft of all types on its inventory; in fact, many of these were elderly training types, and of the total only 84 were really airworthy. The five RFC squadrons already formed at the start of hostilities operated a miscellany of aircraft that included Blériot XIs, Henry Farmans, Maurice Farmans, Royal Aircraft Factory BE.2s and 2as, Sopwith Tabloids, Avro 504s and BE.8s. No. 1 Sqn had lost its aircraft in May 1914, these having been allocated to the other squadrons; No. 1 had been briefly redesignated the Airship Detachment RFC, but had re-formed with heavier-than-air craft when the RFC's airships had been turned over to the RNAS in July 1914. It was still under training when war broke out. Of the other squadrons, Nos. 2 and 4 were completely equipped with BE.2s, No. 3 had Blériots and Henry Farmans, and No. 5 had Henry Farmans, Avro 504s and BE.8s.

The Royal Naval Air Service had 71 aircraft, of which 31 were seaplanes, and seven airships. The landplanes were a mixture of various types, but Short Brothers were becoming firmly established as the main seaplane suppliers, with 17 of their machines in service. The available aircraft were based at a series of air stations along the east coast of Britain, from the Channel to Scotland. These stations were within flying distance of one another, enabling the RNAS to mount overlapping coastal patrols.

The other main belligerents in August 1914, Russia and Austria, were poorly equipped in terms of aircraft. The Russian Imperial Air Service had 24 aircraft, 12 airships and 46 observation balloons. The most promising design in Russia at this time was the *Ilya Mourometz*, by Igor Sikorsky. This, the world's first four-engined bomber, had flown early in 1914, and ten examples were on order for the Air Service at the outbreak of war, a number later increased to 80.

The Austrian Air Service had 36 aircraft, one airship and ten balloons. The aircraft were mostly *Taube* types. The small Austrian aviation industry did not really develop until the summer of 1915, when it underwent a rapid expansion following Italy's entry into the war.

*The Avro 504 was widely used in World War I, first for bombing and reconnaissance and then as a trainer. This example crashed after stalling on the approach to land at Netheravon, Wiltshire.*

part in ensuring an Austrian victory at the Battle of Krasnik the following day. Air reconnaissance also played a key role in securing the crushing German victory at the Battle of Tannenberg in East Prussia, which began on 26 August.

The Zeppelin Z.8 was shot down by a French 75 mm gun battery commanded by Lieutenant Quiquandon.

*24 August* The French airship *Dupuy-de-Lome* was mistakenly fired on by French troops at the Place de Reims and crashed at Courcy after being hit several hundred times. One crew member, Lieutenant Jourdan, was killed. In the early weeks of the war, ground forces tended to fire indiscriminately at anything in the air. From September, the belligerents began to apply national insignia to their aircraft, and ground forces were given rudimentary instruction in aircraft recognition.

*25 August* German Army airship Z.9 (LZ.25) dropped nine bombs on the Belgian town of Anvers, killing or wounding 26 people and damaging the palace where the Belgian royal family was in residence. The attack was widely condemned as an atrocity.

This day saw the first aerial encounters preceding the Battle of the Marne. An enemy two-seater was forced to land after being 'buzzed' by three BE 2s of No. 2 Sqn, RFC; one of the British pilots, Lieutenant H.D. Harvey-Kelly, landed nearby and, with his observer, chased the enemy crew into a wood before setting fire to the German aircraft and taking off again. In a separate incident, Lieutenant de Bernis, the observer of a French aircraft piloted by Roland Garros, fired six or seven shots at two enemy Albatros aircraft, with no visible result.

*28 August* Zeppelin Z.5 (LZ.20) was hit by Russian ground fire which put her steering gear out of action. Drifting helplessly, she dropped two bombs, which killed 23 Russians, before coming down in a wood. The Russians captured the whole crew with the exception of the commander, *Hauptmann* Grüner, who had been killed by small arms fire.

*30 August* An Etrich *Taube*, attached to the German IX Corps and flown by *Leutnant* von Hiddessen, dropped four small bombs near the Gare de l'Est, Paris, killing one civilian and injuring four others. He also dropped a message calling on the Paris garrison to surrender. Between this date and 12 October the *Tauben* made ten attacks on the French capital, 16 aircraft dropping 56 bombs – none of which weighed more than 10 lb (4.5 kg) – killing 11 people and injuring 47.

**1 September** In the Far East, Farman seaplanes of the Imperial Japanese Navy, operating from the seaplane tender *Wakamiya Maru* and armed with improvised bombs made from naval shells, attacked and sank a German minelayer at Kiaochow Bay, China. The first Japanese officers had learned to fly in Europe in 1910, and Japan had declared war on Germany on 23 August 1914.

**15 September** For the first time, the RFC made operational use of wireless telegraphy during artillery observation. Two BE.2s of No. 4 Sqn were involved, piloted by Lieutenants D.S. Lewis and B.T. James, both of whom were later killed. The RFC also made first operational use of aerial photography during the Battle of the Aisne, which opened on 13 September.

**24 September** The German Army airship Z.4 (LZ.16) dropped 14 bombs on Warsaw from an altitude of 9000 ft (2745 m). The Zeppelin was commanded by *Hauptmann* von Quatz.

**5 October** A Voisin pusher biplane of *Escadrille VB24*, armed with a Hotchkiss machine gun and flown by Lieutenant Joseph Frantz (pilot) and Corporal Quénault (observer) shot down a German Aviatik two-seater near Reims. The crew of the Aviatik, both of whom were killed when their aircraft crashed in flames, were Wilhelm Schlichting (pilot) and *Oberleutnant* Fritz von Zangen. Corporal Quénault fired 47 rounds at the Aviatik, which was the first aircraft in history to be shot down and destroyed by another. Frantz survived the war, as did Quénault, and added two more Aviatiks to his score in May 1915. He died in September 1979 in Paris, Quénault in Marseille in April 1958.

*The Imperial Russian Air Service, engaged from the earliest days of World War I, was equipped with a miscellany of aircraft. The type shown is a Morane Type N of the 19th Sqn.*

**8 October** The first successful British air raid on Germany was mounted by Squadron Commander D.A. Spenser-Grey and Flight Lieutenant R.L.G. Marix of the Eastchurch RNAS Squadron, flying Sopwith Tabloids from an advanced base at Antwerp. Each aircraft carried a small load of 20 lb (9 kg) Hales bombs, and their targets were the airship sheds at Düsseldorf and Cologne. Grey failed to find his target in bad visibility and dropped his bombs on Cologne's central railway station; Marix bombed the Zeppelin shed at Düsseldorf and destroyed it, together with Zeppelin Z.9 (LZ.25). Both pilots returned but Marix, whose aircraft had been damaged by gunfire, was forced to land 20 miles (30 km) from Antwerp. An earlier raid on Düsseldorf and Cologne, by five BE.2s of No. 2 Sqn RNAS on **22 September**, had been frustrated by bad weather; only Flight Lieutenant C.H. Collet found the sheds at Düsseldorf, but his three Hales bombs failed to explode.

**19 October** Zeppelin L.5 (*Oberleutnant-zur-See* Hirsch) made a reconnaissance flight over the North Sea to within 60 miles (96 km) of Great Yarmouth as a preliminary to a raid on the British coast by German naval forces.

**October/November** Important decisions were taken affecting the organization of the *Aviation Militaire*. From now on, all scouting (fighter) units were to be equipped with Morane-Saulnier monoplanes; reconnaissance units were to have Maurice

# EARLY TYPES OF BOMB

THE bombs available to both sides at the outbreak of hostilities in August 1914 were very rudimentary devices. The standard German bomb in the early months of the war was the so-called Carbonite type; the smallest weighed 10 lb (4.5 kg) and the heaviest 110 lb (50 kg). They were pear-shaped, pointed, and had a propeller-actuated pistol. Instead of fins, they were stabilized by a kind of inverted tin cap, attached to the tail of the bomb by stays. The Germans also used a hand-thrown grenade-type projectile weighing 1.75 lb (800 gr), but this was too small to be effective.

The weapon initially available to the Royal Naval Air Service, which pioneered strategic bombing in its early raids on the Imperial German Navy's Zeppelin sheds, was the 20 lb (9 kg) Marten Hale bomb, which contained a 4.5 lb (2 kg) charge of Amatol (a mixture of TNT and ammonium nitrate) and which exploded on impact. It was armed by a fuzing mechanism activated by a small propeller behind the tail fins which started to revolve when the missile was dropped. The RNAS also used a small number of 100 lb (45 kg) bombs produced by the Royal Arsenal, Woolwich, but these were not provided with adequate safety devices and were danger-ous to their users. Trials were also carried out with an incendiary bomb consisting of a light casing holding 2 gal (9 l) of petrol; these were fitted with a cartridge which detonated when the bomb was dropped and ignited the liquid.

Such primitive bombs were used by the Royal Flying Corps too, whose pilots also employed flechettes. These were pointed and fluted steel darts about 5 in (13 cm) long, which were dropped from canisters containing about 500 from an optimum height of 5000 ft (1500 m) and attained the velocity of a rifle bullet by the time they reached the ground. They were intended to be effective against troop and cavalry concentra-tions, but in practice they were virtually useless.

The early bombs used by France's *Aviation Militaire* were little more than modified 75 mm or 155 mm artillery shells. The 75 mm weapon, which weighed 20 lb (9 kg), proved reasonably effective as an anti-personnel weapon and was usually released from a height of 6500 ft (2000 m).

# AIRCRAFT ARMAMENT, 1914

WHEN the RFC, RNAS and France's *Aviation Militaire* went to war in August 1914, there was no longer any doubt that the machine gun provided the obvious solution to the question of aircraft armament; this had already been demonstrated in trials in Britain, France and the United States in the years leading up to the outbreak of hostilities. There were several problems to be overcome, however, before the solution became a practical reality.

Firstly, machine guns could be fitted only to the sturdier of the types then in service; on other aircraft, the weight penalty was unacceptable. There was also the problem of aiming and firing any sort of gun, as pilot and observer were surrounded by a considerable wing area, with its attendant struts and bracing wires, and seated either behind or in front of a large and vulnerable wooden propeller.

Nevertheless, the RFC and RNAS quickly adopted the 27 lb (12 kg), American-designed Lewis gun as standard armament for its observation aircraft – particularly the 'pusher' types in which the observer, who sat in front of the pilot, had a large cone of fire upwards, downwards and to either side. In the beginning the gun mounting was usually devised by the observer to suit himself. The French selected the Hotchkiss, which like the Lewis was air-cooled; a belt-fed weapon, it initially proved too inflexible for the observer and so a drum feed was adopted. The Germans chose the lightweight Parabellum MG 14, a modification of the water-cooled Maxim; this also had a drum magazine.

# WIRELESS TELEGRAPHY AND AIR PHOTOGRAPHY, 1914

SOME of the first practical experiments with airborne wireless telegraphy were carried out by the Royal Engineers during the British Army manoeuvres of 1912, when the non-rigid airships *Gamma* and *Delta* transmitted signals that were received up to 35 miles (56 km) away. Much valuable W/T development was carried out by Major Herbert Musgrave, who was made head of the Experimental Branch of the Military Wing of the RFC in 1913, and by Lieutenants D.S. Lewis and B.T. James, both of the Royal Engineers, who by June 1914 were able to communicate with each other in the air. The Naval Wing (later RNAS) had also been experimenting with wireless telegraphy, and by the outbreak of war, 16 of its seaplanes had been fitted with lightweight equipment of French design for communication with shore stations. The radio traffic at this stage was one way, from air to ground; it would be some time before the difficulties of reception by aircraft were overcome. In the RFC, pioneering work with W/T was carried out mainly by No. 3 Sqn, and it was this unit that carried out trials under operational conditions. However, early airborne W/T equipment was bulky and unreliable, and visual signalling by strips, panels and other devices remained the primary means of communication between observation aircraft and artillery in the first months of the war.

No. 3 Sqn, under the energetic and far-seeing Captain H.R.M. Brooke-Popham, also pioneered aerial photography. Because of a lack of funds, its officers had to buy their own cameras and adapt them for aerial work by trial and error. Just before the outbreak of war they succeeded in producing a complete set of photographs covering the defences of the Isle of Wight and the Solent.

The original cameras were of the folding type with bellows and loaded with plates. They were cumbersome to handle in the air, especially in cold weather, and produced poor results. In the autumn of 1914 Major W.G.H. Salmond made a study of the French photographic organization, which was more advanced than any other, and as a result of his report an experimental photographic section was formed with Lieutenants J.T.C. Moore-Brabazon and C.D.M. Campbell, Sergeant F.C.V. Laws and Second Air Mechanic W.D. Corse. These four men set about designing a new, effective air camera and completed their task in less than two months. While they were doing so, the first successful photographic reconnaissance was carried out in January 1915, when pictures were taken of some brick stacks south of the La Bassée Canal. These revealed a new German trench and contributed greatly to the success of an Allied attack that went in on 6 January. From now on, aerial photography was to be a vital factor in operations on all fronts; its importance was such that the need to protect photographic reconnaissance aircraft brought about the requirement for fighter escorts, which in turn was to give enormous impetus to the development of air fighting as a whole.

Farmans; Caudron biplanes were to be assigned to artillery observation units; and a bomber force was to be created, based on Voisin biplanes. The force was to be expanded to comprise 46 army co-operation units and 16 bomber units. The first of these, GB 1, was formed on **23 November**.

**21 November** Three Avro 504s of the RNAS, flying from Belfort and piloted by Squadron Commander E.F. Briggs, Flight Lieutenant J.T. Babington and Lieutenant S.V. Sippe, bombed the Zeppelin sheds at Friedrichshafen. Each aircraft carried four 20 lb (9 kg) bombs. A gas tank was set on fire and the Zeppelin L.7 (LZ.32) slightly damaged. Briggs was wounded in the head and forced to land after his aircraft was badly damaged by machine gun fire; he was taken prisoner, but later escaped.

**24 December** Aircraft of the RNAS were launched by seaplane carriers in the German Bight to attack Nordholz; only one found the target in bad weather and no damage was inflicted on the German Navy's Zeppelin sheds there. Zeppelins L.5 and L.6 took off to attack the British surface forces. L.6 (von Buttlar) dropped one bomb on the carrier *Empress* but missed the target; L.5 (Hirsch) dropped two bombs on the submarine E.II off Norderney, also with no effect.

**24 December** A Friedrichshafen FF 29 seaplane of the Imperial German Navy's *Seeflieger Abteilung* 1 (Seaplane Unit No. 1) and piloted by *Oberleutnant-zur-See* Stephan Prondzynski, with *Fähnrich-zur-See* von Frankenburg as his observer, dropped the first bomb on British soil, forming a crater 10 ft (3 m) across and 4 ft (1.2 m) deep in the garden of Thomas A. Terson, an auctioneer living near Dover Castle. There were no casualties and little damage. On **25 December** the same aircraft and crew dropped two bombs near Cliffe railway station, Kent. The FF 29 was intercepted by a Vickers Gunbus of No. 7 Sqn RFC (2nd Lieutenant M.R. Chidson and Corporal Martin) and several bursts were fired at it, but it got away.

# 1915

**19 January** The Imperial German Navy's Airship Division made its first successful attack on the British Isles, a previous attempt (on 13 January) having been called off because of adverse weather. Three airships, L.3, L.4 and L.6, took off from Nordholz and Fuhlsbüttel, but L.6 turned back with engine trouble. L.3 (Fritz) and L.4 (von Platen-Hallermund) crossed the Norfolk coast at about 8 p.m. and nine bombs were dropped in the Great Yarmouth area by L.3, killing two people and injuring three others. L.4 bombed several targets in Norfolk, including King's Lynn, where it dropped seven high explosive bombs and an incendiary, killing two people and injuring 13. The RFC flew its first ever night defence sorties against the raiders, but the two aircraft involved, both Vickers FB 5s, failed to intercept. As a result of this raid, a small number of RFC airfields around London remained at readiness to combat night attacks; the RNAS already had an air defence scheme, with a screen of aircraft between Grimsby and London to intercept airships flying from northern Germany, and between London and Dungeness to cope with aircraft flying from Belgian bases.

**25 January** The German Army Parseval airship PL.19 (*Oberleutnant* Maier) was shot down in the Baltic by a Russian battery commanded by Lieutenant Pankratov. The crew of seven were taken prisoner.

**12 February** The RNAS mounted its biggest air attack of the war so far when a force of 34 aircraft of all types, led by Wing Commander C.R. Samson, attacked several targets along the Belgian coast. This was followed by a second raid on **16 February**, when 40 RNAS aircraft attacked enemy gun positions, the locks of the canal between Bruges and the sea, and craft in Zeebrugge harbour. This second raid was made in conjunction with a diversionary attack by French airmen on the German airfield at Ghistelles. No British aircraft were lost through enemy action in these two raids.

**15 February** Four-engined *Ilya Mouromets* bombers of the Imperial Russian Air Service's *Eskadra Vozdushnikh Korablei* (Squadron of Flying Ships) went into action for the first time, one of the aircraft attacking a target in Poland. The pilot was Captain Gorshkov. In a further raid on **6 March**, the same pilot dropped ten 35 lb (15.8 kg) bombs on Willenburg during a mission lasting four hours.

**17 February** Zeppelin L.3 (Fritz) crash-landed on the Danish island of Fano and was destroyed by its crew. L.4 (von Platen-Hallermund) also crash-landed on the Danish coast at Blaavands Huk after engine failure in gale conditions; four crew were lost when the ship rebounded into the air and drifted out over the North Sea.

**4 March** Zeppelin L.8 (*Kapitän Leutnant* Beelitz) took off from Gontrode (Belgium) in an attempt to raid England. It was hit by machine gun fire over Nieuport and crashed near Tirlemont in the early hours of 5 March. One crew member (Bense) was killed.

**10 March** Start of the British offensive at Neuve Chapelle, an attack based – for the first time in history – on maps prepared solely from intelligence gathered by aerial photographic reconnaissance. As the offensive got under way, the RFC launched the first tactical air bombing offensive, intended to delay the progress of enemy reinforcements. Aircraft of the 2nd Wing attacked the Menin junction and Courtrai railway station, while the 3rd Wing attacked the railway stations at Lille, Douai and Don, using bombs of 25 lb (11 kg) and 100 lb (45 kg). The RFC squadrons had been organized into Wings in November 1914, the Wings being attached to Army Corps.

**20 March** German Army Zeppelins LZ.29 (Z.10) and LZ.35 (Frichs and Corsby) bombed Paris. Z.10 was hit by French anti-aircraft fire and crash-landed near St Quentin. The Schütte-Lanz airship SL.2 bombed Compiègne.

Throughout March, Short and Sopwith seaplanes operating from HMS *Ark Royal*, the first vessel in the world to be completed as an aircraft carrier, flew intensively in support of operations against

Turkish forces in the Dardanelles. The aircraft carried out general reconnaissance, directed naval gunnery and spotted for mines.

*1 April* Roland Garros, flying a Morane Type N monoplane armed with a nose-mounted Hotchkiss machine gun firing through the propeller disc, shot down an Albatros two-seater. The propeller was fitted with deflector blades designed by Panhard and refined by Garros' mechanic, Jules Hué. It was the first time that an aircraft had been destroyed by another mounting a fixed, forward-firing machine gun.

*13 April* Zeppelin LZ.35 was hit by anti-aircraft fire and crash-landed near Maria Aeltre, Belgium. The airship was destroyed by gale-force winds.

*14 April* Zeppelin L.9 (Mathy) dropped bombs on mining villages north of the River Tyne during the night, injuring two people. A Bristol TB 8 from RNAS Whitley Bay failed to intercept. (The TB 8's gunner was a young Australian named Bert Hinkler, who later became a pilot and became famous for the first solo flight to Australia in 1928.)

*15 April* Zeppelins L.5 (Böcker) and L.6 (von Buttlar) made night attacks on Lowestoft and Maldon. L.7 (Peterson) flew over Norfolk but failed to find its target in the blackout. All three ships returned safely, although L.6 was damaged by rifle fire.

*16 April* In the first sortie against England by a

# GERMAN AIRSHIP TACTICS

SUCH was the weight of propaganda surrounding the German airship raids on Britain that it is for this type of operation that the Zeppelin is best remembered. However, throughout the war, the primary task of the Naval Airship Division was reconnaissance. Far more could undoubtedly have been achieved if the German Navy had exploited its airships to the full. Capable of remaining airborne for 100 hours, with a range of 3000 miles (4800 km), the airships might have wrought havoc on Allied convoys in the North Atlantic had they been used for scouting in conjunction with submarines.

Zeppelin tactics over the British Isles usually involved climbing to a height where the airship could exploit favourable easterly winds as it crossed the coastline. The Zeppelins could only fly in good weather and at night, provided there was little or no moonlight. The engines would be switched off as the airship approached the target area, making it virtually impossible to detect from the ground unless illuminated by searchlights.

The Zeppelin design was steadily improved as the war progressed. The last generation, which made its appearance in 1918 with L.70 (LZ.112), could carry a bomb load of 8000 lb (3630 kg) on raids over Britain; this was roughly the same as the average load carried by the Avro Lancaster bomber in World War II. These outstanding airships had an operational ceiling of 22 970 ft (7000 m) and a maximum speed of 81 mph (130 km/hr). They were powered by up to seven Maybach engines.

Of the 115 Zeppelin airships built by the end of the war, 22 were broken up at the end of their useful lives; nine were handed over to the Allies after the Armistice; seven were sabotaged by their own crews; 17 were destroyed in the air by aircraft or AA guns; 19 were damaged in the air and wrecked on landing; seven landed in enemy or neutral territory; eight were destroyed in their sheds by enemy attack; and 26 were lost in accidents. Some 380 aircrew – about 40 per cent of the number trained – were killed on active service.

The hardships and losses suffered by the Naval airship crews were overshadowed by those experienced by their counterparts in the Army Airship Service, at least in the early part of the war. Many of the missions they flew were suicidal, the airships operating at low level over enemy troop concentrations despite the hideous vulnerability of the hydrogen-filled gas cells to small arms fire. The Army made extensive use of Schütte-Lanz airships, despised by the Navy because of the vulnerability of their plywood structures and poor performance; their top speed was only 53 mph (85 km/hr) and operational ceiling 7875 ft (2400 m). Most of the 22 Schütte-Lanz airships built were used on the Eastern Front. Eight were employed by the German Navy.

# THE SYNCHRONIZED MACHINE GUN

THE year 1915 saw a major revolution in air fighting tactics with the development of technology that enabled machine guns to fire forwards through the propeller disc. 'Synchronization' meant, quite simply, relating the rate of fire of a machine gun to the rate of revolution of a propeller so that the bullets missed the advancing and retreating blades. Experiments to this end had been carried out before the war in France and Germany by Raymond Saulnier of Morane-Saulnier and Franz Schneider of LVG, and Schneider had in fact patented a primitive synchronization device in 1913. An updated version was installed in an LVG E.VI monoplane early in 1915, but the aircraft was destroyed in an accident and no further examples were built.

In France, despite encouraging early tests, Raymond Saulnier was unable to raise development funds from the authorities and resorted to the cheaper and more basic method of fitting steel wedge-shaped deflector plates to the propeller blades so that any bullet striking them would be diverted harmlessly. In March 1915 this device was tested operationally by Roland Garros of *Escadrille* MS.23, a noted pre-war aviator who had been seconded to assist Saulnier with his experiments. In less than three weeks he destroyed five enemy aircraft flying a Morane-Saulnier monoplane, but on 19 April 1915 he was forced to land behind enemy lines after his aircraft was hit by ground fire. He failed to set fire to the Morane, which was examined by German technical officers.

The Germans copied the idea, but trials proved disappointing. Whereas French bullets had a copper coating, German bullets, which were plated with chrome, shot the propeller blades to pieces.

The French device was shown to Anthony Fokker, the Dutch designer who – having been turned down by the British and the French – was building aircraft for Germany. Fokker quickly realized that the deflector-plate idea was too dangerous to be really successful; severe vibrations set up when the bullets struck the plates would inevitably, in time, shake loose the engine mounting. The Dutchman therefore set about designing a simple engine-driven system of cams and push-rods which operated the trigger of a Parabellum machine gun once during each revolution of the propeller. In effect, the propeller fired the gun. (Much of the design work on this gear, in fact, was carried out by three members of Fokker's engineering staff, Heber, Leimberger and Lübbe.)

The mechanism was successfully demonstrated on a Fokker M5K monoplane. This was given the military designation E.I, and so became the first of the Fokker monoplane fighters. It was to be February 1916 before RFC aircraft equipped with similar interrupter gear, designed by Vickers, reached the squadrons in Flanders.

German Army aeroplane, an Albatros B.II dropped five small bombs near Sittingbourne, Kent, and five incendiaries near Canterbury. The aircraft, from *Feldflieger Abteilung* 41, was fired on by an anti-aircraft battery at Faversham, but escaped undamaged. (Reports that German Army *Tauben* had raided Britain in October 1914 were unsubstantiated, although often quoted.)

**3 May** Zeppelin L.9 (Mathy) sighted four British submarines on the surface off Terschelling and attacked one of them, the E.5, with four 110 lb (50 kg) bombs. The airship also dropped five bombs on the submarine D.4 half an hour later. Both attacks were unsuccessful.

**26 May** 18 Voisin 3 aircraft of *Groupe de Bombardement* GB 1, flying from Malzeville near Nancy, set out to bomb the Badische Anilin und Soda Fabrik at Ludwigshafen, which was producing poison gas (first used against the Allies at Ypres on 22 April 1915). One aircraft was forced down with engine trouble; the remainder bombed the factory with 87 bombs from 5000 ft (1520 m). It was the beginning of the *Aviation Militaire*'s strategic air offensive against industrial targets in the Ruhr.

**31 May** German Army airship LZ.38 (*Hauptmann* Linnarz) bombed London for the first time, dropping 3000 lb (1360 kg) of explosives, killing seven people and injuring 35. The attack caused nearly £19 000 worth of damage. Fifteen air defence sorties failed to intercept.

**7 June** German Army Zeppelin LZ.37 (von der

Haegen) was attacked by Flight Sub-Lieutenant R.A.J. Warneford of No. 1 Sqn RNAS, flying a Morane-Saulnier Parasol from Dunkirk. The airship, together with LZ.38 and LZ.39, had set out from Bruges to bomb London. Warneford shadowed LZ.37 from Ostend to Ghent, being kept at bay by heavy defensive fire, then made a single pass over the airship and dropped six 20 lb (9 kg) bombs on it. The airship exploded and fell in flames on the convent of Grand Béguinage de Sainte-Elisabeth, killing two nuns and two children. One member of the Zeppelin crew survived. Warneford was awarded the Victoria Cross, but was killed a few days later in a crash. Of the other two Zeppelins, LZ.38 was forced to return to her shed at Évère with engine trouble; she had been there only a matter of hours when she was destroyed in a bombing attack by two RNAS pilots, Flight Lieutenant J.P. Wilson and Flight Sub-Lieutenant J.S. Mills.

**8 June** Returning from a bombing mission, the Italian dirigible M-2 (Felice di Pisa) was shot down in flames by an Austrian seaplane flown by G. Kissing and H.R.F. Gronenwald.

**1 July** Leutnant Kurt Wintgens of *Feldflieger Abteilung* 6b became the first pilot to shoot down an enemy aircraft with a machine gun synchronized to fire through the propeller disc. He was flying a Fokker E.I *Eindecker* monoplane, newly arrived at the front for operational trials, when he encountered a French Morane single-seater in the Verdun sector. The Frenchman dived to attack, but Wintgens took evasive action, got on the Morane's tail and shot it down.

**25 July** The first RFC fighter unit, No. 11 Sqn, arrived in France. The squadron was equipped with the two-seater Vickers FB.5 'Gunbus' and was the first specialized fighter squadron ever formed, having received its first FB.5s in *January 1915*.

**9–10 August** Zeppelins L.9, L.10, L.11, L.12 and L.13 set out to attack London and the Humber. L.9 (Loewe) bombed Goole, Yorkshire, killing 16 people; L.10 (Wenke) bombed Eastchurch; L.11 (von Buttlar) jettisoned its bombs in the sea off Lowestoft; L.12 (Peterson) bombed Dover; and L.13 (Mathy) turned back short of the British coast with engine trouble. L.12 was hit by the Dover guns and made a forced landing in the Channel. It was towed to Ostend by a torpedo-boat, surviving attacks by RNAS aircraft en route, but the ship's forward section exploded and burned during the dismantling process.

**12–13 August** Zeppelin L.10 (Wenke) bombed

Harwich, causing insignificant damage. L.11 (von Buttlar) reached the British coast but returned to base without dropping any bombs, flying through a violent thunderstorm en route.

**12 August** Flight Commander C.H.K. Edmonds of the RNAS, flying a Short 184 seaplane from the seaplane carrier *Ben-my-Chree*, a converted Isle of Man packet on station in the Dardanelles, sighted a 5000-ton (5080-tonne) Turkish supply vessel off Gallipoli. Descending to 15 ft (4.57 m) over the water, Edmonds released his torpedo from 300 yd (274 m) and scored a direct hit. Despite being informed later that the ship had already been disabled by a British submarine, the E14, Edmonds was the first pilot to carry out an air attack using a torpedo dropped from an aircraft. On *17 August* he repeated his exploit and torpedoed the middle one of three transport ships off Ak Bashi Liman, leaving her on fire. On that day, Flight Commander G.B. Dacre, flying another Short 184 from the *Ben-my-Chree*, had to alight in the Straits with engine trouble, but then saw an enemy tug which he torpedoed while taxying. He then managed to take off and returned to the seaplane carrier.

**17 August** Zeppelin L.10 (Wenke) bombed the north-east London suburbs of Leyton and Wanstead Flats, killing ten people and injuring 48. L.11 (von Buttlar) dropped 62 bombs on Ashford and Faversham, Kent. (On *3 September* L.10, with *Kapitän-Leutnant* E. Hirsch in command, exploded during a training flight from Nordholz. All 19 crew were killed.)

**25 August** Caproni Ca 32 aircraft of the *Corpo Aeronautico Militare* carried out the first Italian bombing raid of the war against the Austro-Hungarian Empire. The Ca 32 was designated Ca 2 in military service. The Italians carried out a sustained bombing offensive against the Austro-Hungarians, most operations being flown at night.

**25 August** 50 out of 62 aircraft of *Groupes de Bombardement* GB 1, 2 and 3 despatched to attack steel works and blast furnaces at Dillingen, successfully bombed the target, only one failing to return. GB 1, 2, 3 and 4 were now concentrated on Malzéville, but despite the success of their operations, the French GHQ was losing faith in the value of strategic bombing and the promising Malzéville force was broken up in September, the *escadrilles* being reassigned to tactical duties.

**7 September** London was raided by German Army airships LZ.74 and SL.2. LZ.74 bombed Cheshunt and dropped one incendiary on the City of London; SL.2 dropped its bombs on the docks at Millwall, Deptford, Greenwich and Woolwich.

# BOMBING TACTICS, 1915

**B** Y THE late summer of 1915, thanks to its considerable experience of attacking German industrial targets, the French *Aviation Militaire* had succeeded in formulating well-thought-out tactics for mounting large-scale daylight strategic raids. The first aircraft to take off was always that of the Group Commander, who led the formation throughout the mission; his machine was distinguished by pennants carried on the rear centre struts. Once the formation had made rendezvous well behind the lines, and out of the immediate sight of the enemy, the Group Commander fired off a series of signal flares and then set course for the target at optimum cruising speed, the rest of the aircraft formating on him as closely as was practicable. Over the target the formation made its bombing run downwind, increasing its groundspeed and therefore minimizing the length of time spent in the defended area; individual aircraft usually attacked from varying heights to make the task of the anti-aircraft gunners more difficult. These tactics were soon adopted, with certain variations, by the Royal Flying Corps.

## Bomb Sights

Apart from an understandable desire to get clear of the target area with the minimum delay, one reason for bombing downwind was the primitive nature of the bomb sights in use at the time, which had no mechanism for computing crosswind bombing angles. The Central Flying School Bomb Sight, used by the RFC and RNAS, was typical. Based on an earlier sight devised by an American, Lieutenant Riley Scott, it was developed by Lieutenant R.B. Bourdillon of the CFS Experimental Flight and Lieutenant L.A. Strange. Known as the CFS 4B bomb sight, it had a timing scale which enabled the pilot, with the aid of a stopwatch, to measure his ground speed by taking two sights of one object. A movable foresight was then set on the timing scale to correspond with the time interval, recorded in seconds on the stopwatch between the two sightings; this gave the correct angle for bomb release.

---

On its way back to base, the latter airship made a forced landing near Berchem Ste Agathe, Belgium, and was badly damaged.

**9 September** Zeppelins L.9 and L.13 raided the British Isles. L.9 (Loewe) bombed Skinningrove iron works on the North Yorkshire coast; L.13 (Mathy) caused damage amounting to over half a million pounds in London. One of the bombs weighed 660 lb (300 kg) – the biggest dropped on Britain so far.

**23 September** Nos. 2 and 3 Wings of the RFC, plus aircraft of No. 12 (HQ) Sqn, began the first intensive series of air interdiction operations in support of the Allied offensive at Loos, Belgium. In the five days between 23 and 28 September, the RFC dropped 82 100 lb (45 kg), 163 20 lb (9 kg) bombs and a number of small incendiaries on enemy rail communications in the Lille–Douai–Valenciennes triangle. In these and subsequent attacks up to 13 October, the railway lines were damaged in 16 places, five trains were partially wrecked, a signal box was destroyed and sheds at Valenciennes set ablaze. The deepest penetration behind enemy lines was 36 miles (57 km).

*October* During this month, the Fokker *Eindecker* began to establish a definite measure of air superiority over the Western Front, even though only 55 aircraft of this type were in service by the month's end. Groups of four *Eindecker* began to fly together in *Kampfeinsitzer Kommandos* (KEK), forerunners of the permanent *Jagdstaffeln* (fighter squadrons) that were to be formed in 1916. A primitive 'early warning' system was devised with the front-line anti-aircraft batteries, which fired 'pointer' bursts at Allied aircraft crossing the lines so that the KEKs could intercept.

*13–14 October* England was raided by five German Navy Zeppelins. L.11 (von Buttlar) dropped its bombs on villages in Norfolk; L.15 (Breithaupt) bombed the area north of the Strand, London; L.13 (Mathy) bombed the village of Shalford and Woolwich Arsenal; L.14 (Böcker) bombed the suburbs of Croydon and L.16 (Peterson) attacked the town of Hertford. Despite heavy anti-aircraft fire and attempts at interception by British fighters, all the airships returned safely to base. The attacks killed 71 people and injured 128.

# 1916

**14 January** Following severe losses inflicted on Allied aircraft by the Fokker *Eindecker* patrols, HQ RFC ordered that its reconnaissance machines were to be escorted by at least three scouts (fighting aircraft), and that if one of the escorts became detached the mission was to be abandoned. For the first time in air warfare, one side had gained air supremacy and therefore held the initiative.

**29 January** Paris was attacked for the second time by German Army Zeppelins LZ.77 and LZ.79. French airmen made 42 sorties, but failed to intercept.

**30 January** Paris was again bombed by Zeppelin LZ.79. Soon after the attack, the airship was shot down at Mainveaux (Belgium) by the French pilot Jean de Lesseps.

**30 January** The RFC established Brigade formations in which each field army was allotted two Wings grouped as a Brigade, one for routine Army Corps work and the other for fighting, bombing and long-range reconnaissance.

**31 January–1 February** Nine Zeppelins – L.11, L.13, L.14, L.15, L.16, L.17, L.19, L.20 and L.21 – attacked Liverpool and targets in the Midlands, killing 70 people and injuring 113. On the way home L.19, with three engines out of action, came down in the North Sea and the British trawler *King Stephen* refused to pick up the crew. *Kapitän Leutnant* Odo Loewe and the other 15 crew members were drowned.

**7 February** No. 24 Sqn RFC – the first ever RFC squadron to be equipped with single-seat fighters – arrived at St Omer, France, with Airco DH 2 aircraft, its primary purpose being to combat the 'Fokker Scourge'. The DH 2 eventually equipped nine RFC squadrons and probably did more than any other Allied aircraft to overcome the Fokker menace.

**21 February** German Army Zeppelins LZ.77 and LZ.95 set out with two others to bomb railroad junctions near Verdun. LZ.77 (*Hauptmann* Horn) was hit by French gunners and crashed in flames at Revigny, leaving no survivors. LZ.95 was also hit and crashed at Namur. The battle for Verdun, which began on this day, saw intense air activity as the *Aviation Militaire* went on the offensive against German observation aircraft and the Germans sought to protect the latter by increasing their fighting patrols.

**11 March** Following a raid on the New Mexico town of Columbus by an outlaw gang led by Pancho Villa, the recently ousted dictator of Mexico, General John J. Pershing was ordered to lead an expedition south to capture the bandit. The expedition was supported by eight Curtiss JN-2s and JN-3s of the First Aero Squadron, which in the next five months flew 346 hours on 540 courier and reconnaissance missions. Two aircraft were lost in accidents.

**21 March** The *Escadrille Americaine* (N.124), later known as the *Escadrille Lafayette*, was formed around a nucleus of American volunteers in the *Aviation Militaire* and equipped with Nieuport 11 aircraft.

**31 March** Zeppelins L.13, L.14, L.15, L.16 and L.22 attacked London, Stowmarket, Thameshaven, Brentwood and Cleethorpes. L.15 (Breithaupt) was intercepted by a BE.2c of No. 19 Sqn RFC flown by 2nd Lieutenant A. de B. Brandon and, severely damaged by anti-aircraft fire and Brandon's Ranken darts came down in the Thames Estuary at Knoch Deep. One crew member was drowned, 17 taken prisoner.

**15 April** In the first use of aircraft for delivering food and supplies, RFC and RNAS aeroplanes carried 13 tons of stores into Kut el Amara, besieged by the Turks. Four BE.2s of No. 30 Sqn RFC, and three Short floatplanes, a Voisin and a Henry Farman of the RNAS were allotted to the task. Operations continued – under considerable harassment by Fokker monoplanes – until 29 April, when the Kut garrison surrendered.

**4 May** The Italian dirigible M-4 (G. Pastine), returning from a raid on Austrian positions, was shot down in flames near Gorizia by two Brandenburg C.Is and a Fokker E.III.

**4 May** Zeppelin L.7, shadowing British naval forces off the island of Sylt, was shot down by gunfire from cruisers. Eleven dead, seven prisoners.

**5 May** Army Zeppelin LZ.85 (Scherzer) made a forced landing near Salonika after being hit by anti-aircraft fire. The crew were taken prisoner after setting fire to the airship.

**11 May** The British Government created an Air Board under the presidency of Lord Curzon to discuss matters of general policy in relation to the air, and in particular combined operations of Naval and Military Air Services, and also to make recommendations on the types of aircraft required.

**31 May** In the first use of an aircraft during a major fleet battle, Flight Lieutenant F.J. Rutland and his observer, Assistant Paymaster G.S. Trewin, flying a Short seaplane, shadowed units of the German High Seas Fleet in the opening phase of the Battle of Jutland and radioed position reports to the seaplane carrier HMS *Engadine*. German Naval Zeppelins, scouting for the High Seas Fleet, were unable to play an important part in the battle because of poor visibility.

**1 July** The opening phase of the Battle of the Somme. In all, 27 RFC squadrons, comprising 421 aircraft and four kite balloon squadrons with 14 balloons, were assigned to support the various British Army Corps committed to the battle. All Corps squadrons, with the exception of No. 3, which flew Moranes, were equipped with BE 2cs. Escort for the Corps aircraft on their reconnaissance tasks was carried out by the Army Wings equipped with FE 2s and DH 2s, which also undertook offensive sweeps. The battle saw the operational debut (on 3 July) of the Sopwith 1½ Strutter, the first British operational aircraft with a machine gun firing through the propeller. A two-seater, it also had a Lewis gun mounted in the rear cockpit. The first unit to receive the 1½ Strutter at the front was No. 70 Sqn. The *Aviation Militaire*'s main air commitment to the battle, in support of General Fayolle's Sixth Army, comprised *Escadrilles* N.3, 26, 73 and 103 of *Groupe de Combat* 12, together with *Escadrilles* N.37, 62 and 65, temporarily attached. All were equipped with Nieuports. The Allies succeeded in establishing air superiority over the Somme battleground with their new aircraft types and, to counter this, the German High Command ordered the formation of *Jagdstaffeln* – fighter squadrons – which were to be stationed on the most active areas of the front. The *Jagdstaffel*, which on average was equipped with 14 fighter aircraft, was the brainchild of the brilliant German tactician Oswald Boelcke. By the end of August seven were in operation; this number increased to 15 in September and 33 by the end of 1916. The *Jagdstaffeln*, or *Jastas* for short, were equipped initially with the Fokker E.III monoplane, and later in 1916 with Albatros D.Is and D.IIIs and Halberstadt D.IIs.

**3 July** Sopwith 1½ Strutters of No. 3 Wing, RNAS, attacked petrol storage facilities at Mulheim in conjunction with the *Aviation Militaire*'s *Groupe de Bombardement* 4. The operation marked the beginning of a joint Anglo-French bombing initiative, first discussed on 1 May 1916.

**15 July** A Middle East Brigade was formed in Egypt under Brigadier General W.G.H. Salmond, concentrating RFC units in Macedonia, Mesopotamia, Palestine and East Africa under one command.

**19 August** Zeppelins of the German Naval Airship Division flew in support of German warships operating in the North Sea, carrying out long-range reconnaissance over an arc stretching from the Norwegian coast to Scotland, Tynemouth and the Humber. L.30 (von Buttlar) was hit and slightly damaged by shellfire from the armed trawler *Ramexo*. During this operation the L.31 (Mathy) worked in conjunction with the submarine U-53 – a foretaste of the co-operation between aircraft and U-boats that was to become established practice during World War II.

**29 August** The United States Naval Flying Corps was formed, with an establishment of 150 officers and 350 enlisted men. Provision was also made for the formation of a Naval Reserve Flying Corps.

**2 September** Schütte-Lanz airship SL.11 (*Hauptmann* W. Schramm) was shot down in flames at Cuffley by Lieutenant W. Leefe Robinson, RFC, of No. 39 Sqn. All 16 crew were killed. SL.11 was part of a force of 16 Army and Navy airships which set out to raid England; it was the last time that Army airships appeared over the British Isles. The loss of SL.11 marked a turning point in the strategic air offensive against the British Isles; from now on, the air defences became more effective and enemy airship losses began to mount.

**15 September** British tanks went into action for the first time at Flers, during the Somme battle, and were supported by observation aircraft of Nos. 7 and 34 Sqns, RFC. It was the first example of co-operation between aircraft and armour.

**15 September** The French submarine *Foucault*, operating in the Adriatic, was bombed and sunk by an Austrian Lohner flying boat – the first submersible craft to fall victim to air attack.

**22 September** 12 German Naval Zeppelins attacked London and the Midlands. L.33 (Böcker), severely damaged by Lieutenant A. de B. Brandon of No. 39 Sqn RFC and by AA fire, crash-landed in a field near Little Wigborough, Essex, and was set on fire by its crew, all 22 of whom were taken prisoner. L.32 (Peterson) was shot down in flames near Billericay, Essex, by 2nd Lieutenant Frederick Sowrey, also of No. 39 Sqn. All 22 crew were killed.

**1 October** 11 German Naval airships set out to raid England; three turned back in bad weather. L.31 (*Kapitän Leutnant* Henrich Mathy) was attacked over London by a BE 2c of No. 39 Sqn, RFC, flown by 2nd Lieutenant W.J. Tempest, and fell in flames at Potters Bar, Essex. All 19 crew were killed.

# THE AIR DEFENCE OF GREAT BRITAIN, 1916

ON 30 May 1916, the German Naval Airship Division received the first of a new class of Zeppelin, the L.30. These airships were 649 ft (198 m) long and had an operational ceiling of 17 700 ft (5400 m). They were powered by six 240 hp Maybach engines, giving them a maximum speed of 64 mph (103 km/hr), and carried a defensive armament of up to ten machine guns, although in practice, to save weight, only two were normally fitted.

The L.30 class could carry a five-ton war load, made up of star shells, incendiary and explosive bombs. The star shells, used for target illumination, could be fuzed to burst at any height and, on bursting, released a parachute to which was attached a magnesium flare. They were thrown out by hand from the side windows of the control car.

All the other bombs were hung along the corridor of the airship and were released electrically from the pilot's car. The explosive bombs weighed 110, 220 and 660 lb (50, 100 and 300 kg) and were pear-shaped, containing the same type of explosive charge as that used in German naval shells, mines and torpedoes. Incendiary bombs were cylindrical, 15.75 in (40 cm) long and were filled with a charge of solid carburetted hydrogen and thermite paste. The exterior of the bombs was covered in fibre soaked in resin.

Because the Zeppelin presented so vast a target, the favoured method of attack was from above, using small bombs, either the 20 lb (9 kg) Hale or the 16 lb (7 kg) incendiary designed at the Royal Laboratory, Woolwich, but there were alternative weapons. One was the *Ranken Dart*, devised by Engineer Lieutenant Francis Ranken, RN. Originally used by the RNAS, and also adopted by the RFC, the dart weighed about one pound and consisted of an iron-pointed metal tube containing high explosive and black powder. The tail unit embodied spring-loaded vanes which opened and locked into position when they engaged the Zeppelin's envelope after the head had penetrated inside, and at the same time activated a detonator rod. The dart, held fast in the envelope, would then burst into flames, igniting the gas from the airship's ruptured cells. The darts were carried in batches of 24, which could be released all at once or in small groups.

Another anti-Zeppelin weapon was the *Fiery Grapnel*, which was carried in pairs attached to a BE.2c. The idea was to approach the Zeppelin from right angles with the grapnel trailing behind, then to leap over the intended victim and allow the weapon to engage its envelope, whereupon an explosive charge would ignite leaking hydrogen.

The problem with these devices was that, because of the Zeppelin's superior rate of climb, it was usually difficult, if not impossible, for an attacking aircraft to get above it. The answer, clearly, was to be able to attack from any position, including below, using explosive bullets.

Such bullets had existed for some years. One had been invented by a New Zealander, John

12 *October* 34 French bombers (Breguets and Farmans) and 21 British (Sopwith 1½ Strutters of No. 3 Wing RNAS) set out to attack the Mauser rifle factories at Oberndorff. Many crews failed to find the target because of dense cloud, and the factory was bombed by about 20 aircraft. The raid was escorted by Nieuport 17s of the Lafayette *Escadrille*, but the limited range of these aircraft prevented them from remaining with the bombers in the target area. The French lost seven aircraft, the RNAS two. After this attack, the Farman 'pushers' were withdrawn from daylight operations. The raid underlined the hazard of sending unescorted bombers by daylight into defended areas – a lesson that would be re-learned at great cost in World War II.

28 *November* German Naval Zeppelins attacked targets in north-east England. L.34 (*Kapitän Leutnant* Max Dietrich) was shot down off the coast by 2nd Lieutenant I.V. Pyott of No. 36 Sqn RFC, flying a BE 2c from Seaton Carew, soon after bombing targets in the vicinity of West Hartlepool; all 20 crew were killed. L.21 (*Kapitän Leutnant* Frankenburg) was also destroyed by two RNAS pilots (Flight Lieutenant Egbert Cadbury and Flight Sub-Lieutenant E.L. Pulling) flying BE 2cs from Great Yarmouth. The airship was also inter-

Pomeroy, in 1908 and he had offered it without success to the British Government in 1914; it was only in 1916, after he had written to the British Prime Minister, David Lloyd George, that the Munitions Inventions Department agreed to sponsor development. In August 1916, a 500 000-round order was placed for the RFC.

The Admiralty had shown more interest in an explosive bullet designed in 1915 by Flight Lieutenant F.A. Brock, which was ordered for both the RNAS and RFC. A phosphorus incendiary bullet devised by a Coventry engineer, J.F. Buckingham, was also ordered, so that by June 1916 GHQ Home Forces were able to issue a recommended scale of armament for home defence aircraft, as follows:

BE.2c: Four HE bombs or one box of Ranken Darts, one Lewis gun mounted to fire upwards through the top wing trailing edge cut-out and three to five drums of ammunition. (Aircraft flown as a single-seater.)

BE.12: One box of Ranken Darts, one Lewis gun with three to five drums of ammunition, ten Le Prieur rockets. (The invention of a French naval officer, these were mounted on the outer interplane struts and fired electrically. They proved effective against observation balloons on the Western Front, but were never fired on home defence operations.)

FE.2b: Four HE bombs or one box of Ranken Darts, one Lewis gun for the observer with at least seven drums of ammunition.

With minor variations – the HE bombs were discarded later in 1916 – this combination remained the standard anti-Zeppelin armament for the remainder of the war.

cepted by Flight Sub-Lieutenant G.W.R. Fane, but his gun jammed.

**12 December** The Army Council approved the expansion of the RFC to 106 active squadrons and 95 reserve squadrons. Two night-flying squadrons were added later.

*Combat over Flanders; a German pilot falls from his blazing Albatros D.V. Many pilots, lacking parachutes, jumped clear of stricken aircraft to escape a fiery death.*

# 1917

**Note:** Air activity on the Western Front was almost non-existent during January 1917 because of severe weather conditions.

**23 February** The French non-rigid airship *Pilâtre de Rozier* (*Capitaine* L. Prêcheur) was shot down and its crew killed. Following its loss, the French Military Command decided to withdraw all dirigibles from service at the front. The surviving craft were turned over to the French Navy for anti-submarine and convoy protection duties.

**23 February** The first RFC unit specifically assigned to night bombing operations, No. 100 Sqn, was formed at Hingham, Norfolk. It moved to France in March, where it was equipped with FE 2bs.

**16 March** Southern England was raided by German Naval Zeppelins L.35, L.39, L.40, L.41 and L.42. After dropping its bombs on Kent, L.39 (*Kapitän Leutnant* Koch) was carried as far as Compiègne by a gale. Shortly after dawn it was subjected to a 15-min AA barrage and was finally shot down in flames by a battery commanded by Capitaine Galibert. All 17 crew were killed. One of the other Zeppelins, L.35, broke its back on landing at Dresden and was out of action until 14 June.

**1–7 April** During the first week of the month that was to go down in history as 'Bloody April', the RFC lost 75 aircraft in action. The aircraft and tactics of the German *Jagdstaffeln* were superior, and new RFC pilots were being sent to the front with as little as 17½ hours' flying experience. By the middle of 'Bloody April' the average life expectancy of an RFC pilot in France had dropped to two months. The fierce air battles of early April

preceded the Battle of Arras, which began on 9 April. By the end of the month the RFC and RNAS had lost over 150 aircraft and 316 aircrew, the French and Belgians 200 aircraft. The Germans lost 370 aircraft along the whole front, 260 of them in the British sectors.

**6 April** The United States declared a state of war with Germany. At this time the US Army Aviation Section had fewer than 300 aircraft, none of them combat types, and only 35 qualified pilots. The US Navy and Marine Corps had 54 aircraft, 48 officers and 239 enlisted men.

**21 April** The British non-rigid airship C.17, operated by the Royal Navy, was shot down in flames by two Brandenburg floatplanes (Kastner and Meyer) from Zeebrugge, Belgium.

**3 May** For the first time, RFC aircraft made coordinated low-flying machine gun attacks (from

# BOMBER DEVELOPMENT, 1917

IMPERIAL Russia, with its giant *Ilya Mouromets* series of aircraft, was the first of the belligerents to recognize the potential of the heavy bomber. Heavily armed with up to eight defensive machine guns, the four-engined IMs flew 450 missions and dropped 65 tons of bombs for the loss of only three aircraft in three years of operational flying, before the October Revolution of 1917 brought an end to their activities. Had it not been for persistent technical troubles and the constant problem of obtaining spares, the big bombers might have had a much greater influence on the air war on the Eastern Front than was actually the case.

Italy was the next country to introduce heavy bombers, and by 1917 the standard type was the Caproni Ca 33, a three-engined design which had an endurance of three and a half hours and which could carry a 1000 lb (450 kg) bomb load. These aircraft carried out many strategic operations against targets on the Adriatic coast, including the city and seaport of Trieste and the naval bases at Kotor, Pola and Sebenico. Strategic operations virtually ceased early in November 1917, when the Germans overran the Capronis' main base at Pordenone following the Italian defeat at Caporetto. One Ca 33 unit, the 18th *Gruppo*, operated on the Western Front in the spring of 1918.

France's efforts in 1917 concentrated on the

production of the excellent Breguet 14 medium bomber, broadly the equivalent of Britain's DH.4. The British, however, also set about building up an effective heavy bomber force, the Handley Page 0/100 of 1916 being joined the following year by an improved variant, the 0/400. For the duration of the war the two mounted what was virtually a round-the-clock offensive against enemy targets, the 0/100s switching to night attacks while the higher-performance 0/400s carried out more hazardous daylight raids.

In 1917 the Germans had several formidable heavy bombers at their disposal, notably the Gotha G.IV and G.V and the Friedrichshafen G.III. In the summer of 1917 the latter joined the Gotha G.V in carrying out a series of night air attacks on British depots and installations in the Dunkirk area, inflicting substantial damage. It was for their air raids on Britain, however, that the Gothas achieved notoriety, and at the end of the year they were joined by an even more formidable heavy bomber, the four-engined Zeppelin Staaken R.IV. In 1917–18 raids by these aircraft had a profound psychological effect on the civilian population of southern England. Moreover, they compelled the British air defences – by now enjoying growing success against the Zeppelin airships – to revise their tactics almost completely.

# THE FIRST BATTLE OF BRITAIN: DEFENCE AGAINST THE BOMBERS, 1917

ON 19 July 1917, with the Gotha raids on London a frequent occurrence, Lieutenant-General J.C. Smuts – a member of the British War Cabinet who had led a committee specially appointed to examine the problems of air defence – submitted his report. It recommended, amongst other things, that all the resources of the London Air Defence Area (LADA) be placed under the command of one man, whose sole duty would be to organize the defences and co-ordinate them during air attacks. The man duly appointed was Major-General E.B. Ashmore, an artillery officer and a qualified pilot.

As a first step in the reorganization programme, three extra fighter squadrons were immediately allocated to LADA, and in August a 'gun barrier' was set up to the east of London, on the Gothas' approach routes. The Home Defence Group fighter squadrons of the RFC and RNAS developed new tactics to counter the raiders; 'readiness' was signified by three short klaxon bursts, whereupon pilots and mechanics ran to their aircraft and wheeled them from their sheds. The engines were started up and the pilots sat in their cockpits, awaiting further orders. On the 'patrol' order, aircraft climbed in formation to their allotted areas unless ordered for some special patrol, and thereafter acted in accordance with ground signals. In practice, most of the damage to the attacking Gothas was caused by coastal defence flights of the RNAS and by coastal AA batteries; the RFC squadrons, patrolling London's inner ring of defences, had few opportunities to engage the enemy.

In September 1917 the Gothas switched to night attacks, confronting the air defences with a new set of problems. A new balloon barrage on the northern and eastern perimeter of London was planned; this comprised 20 'aprons' each of three balloons, flying at 500 yd (457 m) intervals and linked with cables from which steel wires, 1000 ft (305 m) long, hung vertically every 25 yd (22.86 m). The balloons' operating height was 7500 ft (2286 m), later increased to 9500 ft (2895 m). The first 'apron' was deployed in October 1917, but only nine more were in operation by the summer of 1918. In conjunction with the balloon barrage, the London Metropolitan Area was divided into squares under a new anti-aircraft defence system. Raiding aircraft would be tracked by sound locators as they passed from square to square, and AA batteries would concentrate their barrage, known as a 'curtain', in the appropriate sector. By the end of October 1917, 90 such 'curtains' were operational in the London area.

In all, 24 Gothas were shot down or were lost in the sea during operations against targets in Britain. A further 36 were destroyed in landing accidents.

50–300 ft/15–90 m) on enemy troops in direct support of the British infantry offensive at Arras.

**14 May** The German Naval Zeppelin L.22 (Lehmann) was shot down in flames off Texel by a Curtiss H-12 Large America flying boat (Flight Lieutenant Galpin and Flight Sub-Lieutenant Leckie) from RNAS Great Yarmouth, Norfolk. All 21 crew were killed.

**20 May** The German submarine U-36 was attacked and sunk in the North Sea by a Large America flying boat piloted by Flight Sub-Lieutenant C.R. Morrish, RNAS. This was the first German submarine to be sunk by an aircraft.

**25 May** 21 Gotha G.IV aircraft of *Kagohl* 3 (*Kampfgeschwader der Obersten Heeresleitung*, or German High Command Bomber Wing) attacked Folkestone in the first major raid by aeroplanes on the British mainland. The original attack plan, with London as the primary target, was frustrated by bad weather. The raid, which was carried out in the early evening, killed 95 civilians and injured 195 in the Folkestone area. More than 70 home defence aircraft were sent up to intercept, but only two contacts were made, and the results were inconclusive. The Gothas were intercepted near the Belgian coast by nine Sopwith Pups of Nos. 4 and 9 Sqns RNAS from Dunkirk, and one bomber was reported shot down.

***June*** In the course of the month, *Jagdstaffeln* 4, 6, 10

The men who became the scourge of the Flanders skies: pilots of Jasta 11. Manfred von Richthofen is in the cockpit of an Albatros D.III.

Albatros D.III of Manfred von Richthofen's Jagdstaffel at Donai – March 1917.

and 11 were merged into a single *Jagdgeschwader* (Fighter Wing) under the leadership of *Rittmeister* (Cavalry Captain) *Freiherr* (Baron) Manfred von Richthofen, commander of *Jasta* 11. Although patrols were still flown at *Jasta* strength, von Richthofen could now, in response to an increase in Allied air activity, concentrate a large number of fighter aircraft in any particular sector of the front. Moreover, the *Jagdgeschwader* was highly mobile and could be switched quickly from one part of the front to another in support of ground operations. To counter the threat posed by the *Jagdgeschwader* in the summer of 1917, the RFC and *Aviation Militaire* were forced to adopt a policy of concentrating their best fighter squadrons and pilots in opposition to von Richthofen wherever his squadrons appeared. These élite units were the cradle of the leading Allied fighter aces of 1917. The first encounters between the Richthofen *Jagdgeschwader* and the RFC occurred during the Battle of Messines, which opened on **7 June 1917**.

**13 June** 18 Gotha G.IVs (out of 20 despatched) of *Kagohl* 3 carried out the first formation bombing raid on London, killing 162 people and injuring

432. The air defences sent up 92 sorties, but failed to destroy any of the attackers. The first attack on London by an aeroplane had in fact taken place on 28 November 1916, when a solitary LVG C IV (Brandt and Ilges) flew over the capital at 13 000 ft (3960 m) in broad daylight and dropped several small bombs near the Admiralty, injuring 12 people.

*14 June* Zeppelin L.43 (*Kapitän Leutnant* Kraushaar) was shot down off Ameland by a Curtiss H-12 (Flight Sub-Lieutenants Hobbs and Dickey) from RNAS Felixstowe. All 24 crew were killed.

*16 June* High-altitude raid on southern England by Zeppelins L.41, L.42, L.44 and L.48. The latter was attacked by a BE 12 flown by a Canadian pilot, Lieutenant L.P. Watkins, and shot down in flames over Holly Tree Farm, Theberton, Suffolk. Fourteen crew were killed, including the commander, *Korvettenkapitän* Viktor Schütze, who had recently taken command of the Naval Airship Service. There were three survivors. The BE 12 belonged to 'A' Flight of No. 37 Sqn RFC.

*7 July* 22 Gotha G.IVs made a second daylight attack on London, killing 57 people and injuring 193. The air defences flew 108 sorties; one Gotha was shot down after being attacked by several fighters and three others were wrecked on land-

*The Albatros D.V fighter, developed from the excellent D.III series, reached its peak of service in the autumn of 1917.*

ing after sustaining severe damage. Two defending fighters were also shot down (one by friendly AA fire) and their crews killed.

*11 July* This date marked the beginning of an intense period of air activity on the Western Front prior to the launching of a major Allied offensive (the Third Battle of Ypres) on the last day of the month. At this time the combined strength of the RFC, RNAS, *Aviation Militaire* and the small Belgian Air Corps was 852 aircraft, of which 360 were fighters; the German strength was 600 machines, of which 200 were fighters. When the ground offensive began, much of the Allied air effort was switched to attacks on enemy airfields and infantry columns with light bombs as well as machine guns.

*1 August* The German Army began the process of disbanding its Airship Service. Most of the surviving airships were dismantled, but two late-model craft, the six-engined LZ.113 and LZ.120, were handed over to the Navy.

*2 August* Squadron Commander E.H. Dunning, RN, carried out the first ever landing by an aircraft

# AIRCRAFT CARRIER DEVELOPMENT, 1917

IN 1917, the Royal Navy was a long way ahead of the rest of the world in the development of vessels that could truly be defined as aircraft carriers – in other words, fitted with flight decks from which landplanes were able to operate. The first such ship was the light battle-cruiser HMS *Furious*, laid down shortly after the outbreak of war. Launched on 15 August 1916, she was fitted initially with a flight deck forward of her superstructure, but was eventually completed with a continuous flight deck and hangar accommodation for 14 Sopwith 1½-Strutters and two Sopwith Pups, although by early 1918 she had been re-equipped with Sopwith Camels. She was also fitted with

workshops, electrically-operated lifts from her hangar to the flight deck and a primitive form of arrester gear comprising strong rope nets suspended from cross pieces.

A similarly-equipped vessel, HMS *Cavendish*, was commissioned in October 1918 and renamed HMS *Vindictive*, but her operational career was limited to a brief foray in support of the Allied Intervention Force in North Russia and the Baltic in 1919–20. The most important development was centred on three new carriers, all fitted with unbroken flight decks: the 10850-ton HMS *Hermes*, HMS *Argus* and HMS *Eagle*. Of the three, only HMS *Argus* joined the Fleet before the end of hostilities.

on a ship under way when he touched down in a Sopwith Pup on the deck of the converted light cruiser HMS *Furious*. The ship was steaming at 26 knots into a wind of 21 knots. On **7 August**, Dunning was killed when his aircraft stalled and went over the side as he attempted to repeat the exploit.

**5 August** A London Air Defence Area was created under Major General E.B. Ashmore, three RFC squadrons equipped with Sopwith Pups and Camels being formed specifically for operations against the Gotha daylight bombing raids.

**17 August** A Report on Air Organization drawn up by a committee under the presidency of Lieutenant General J.C. Smuts was presented to the British War Cabinet. It recommended the creation of an Air Ministry 'to control and administer all matters in connection with air warfare of every kind and that the new Ministry should proceed to work out the arrangements for the amalgamation of the two Services (the RFC and RNAS) and for the legal constitution and discipline of the new Service.... The day may not be far off when aerial operations with their devastation of enemy lands and destruction of industrial and populous centres on a vast scale may become the principal operations of war, to which the older forms of military and naval operations may become secondary and subordinate'. This important and far-sighted document marked the first step along the road that was to lead, in the following year,

to the creation of the first independent air force in the world – the Royal Air Force.

**21 August** Zeppelin L.23 (*Oberleutnant-zur-See* Dinter) was shot down off the Jutland coast by a Sopwith Pup launched from a turret platform on the light cruiser HMS *Yarmouth*, the first vessel to be so modified. The Pup was flown by Flight Sub-Lieutenant B.A. Smart, who afterwards landed close to the destroyer HMS *Prince*. He was picked up safely, although his aircraft was lost. By the end of the year, all British battle cruisers and light cruisers were equipped to launch their own aircraft.

**22 August** Three out of ten Gothas attacking Margate, Ramsgate and Dover were shot down by the British defences. It was the last daylight raid on the British Isles; from September 1917, the German bombers switched to night attacks.

**2 September** Two unidentified aircraft, possibly twin-engined AEGs of *Kagohl* 4, which had been engaged in night attacks on Allied targets in France and Belgium, dropped 14 bombs on Dover, signalling the start of a night offensive against the British Isles by heavier-than-air machines.

**3 September** Four Gotha G.IVs made a night attack on Chatham, killing 132 people and injuring 96. This was *Kagohl* 3's first night raid on England. Sixteen air defence sorties failed to make contact with the enemy.

3 *September* Personnel of the US 1st Aero Squadron arrived in France and Brigadier General William L. Kenly was appointed Chief of Air Service within the American Expeditionary Force. It had already been decided that American pursuit pilots would fly French types.

4 *September* Nine Gothas of *Kagohl* 3 attacked London by night, killing 19 and injuring 71. One Gotha crashed at sea, probably the victim of AA fire. In the next raid, on 24 *September*, 13 Gothas attacked London; none of the bombers was lost, but five air defence fighters were written off in accidents. Attacks on London were an almost nightly occurrence during the last week of September 1917, and on the last night of the month a new German bomber type made its appearance: the Zeppelin (Staaken) R Type, known as the *Riesenflugzeug* (giant aircraft), which was capable of carrying a 2200 lb (1000 kg) bomb load.

1 *October* The General Officer Commanding the Royal Flying Corps in France was informed that enemy raids on England were interrupting munitions production and was asked to take immediate action against German objectives which could be reached by British bombers flying from Nancy.

5 *October* The Palestine Brigade of the Royal Flying Corps was formed to provide air support for the forthcoming offensive against the Turks by General Sir Edmund H.H. Allenby. The Brigade's four squadrons were equipped with BE.2es, RE 8s, Bristol Fighters and Vickers Bullets.

11 *October* No. 41 Wing RFC (Lieutenant Colonel C.L.N. Newall) was formed at Bainville-sur-Madon to bomb industrial targets in Germany in response to the Gotha raids on Britain. Its three squadrons were No. 55, equipped with De Havilland DH 4s for the day bombing role, No. 100 with FE 2bs and No. 16 RNAS with Handley Page 0/100s.

19 *October* 13 Zeppelins were prepared for the last great airship raid on the British Isles: L.41, L.42, L.44, L.45, L.46, L.47, L.49, L.50, L.51, L.52, L.53, L.54 and L.55. A crosswind prevented two of them, L.42 and L.51, from leaving their sheds; the others, led by Peter Strasser, commanding the German Navy's airship operations, set course for targets in the Midlands. L.44 (Stabbert) was shot down by French guns over Chennevières: 18 dead, no survivors. L.45 (Kolle) made a forced landing at Sisteron and was set on fire by its crew, all 17 of which were taken prisoner. L.49 (Gayer) was brought down at Bourbonne-les-Bains under repeated attacks by the *Aviation Militaire*'s N.152 'Crocodiles' *Escadrille* (Lafargue, de la Marque,

Denis, Gresset and Lefèvre) and its 19 crew made prisoner. L.50 (Schwonder) hit the ground during a rapid descent at Montigny-le-Roy; part of the ship, with four men still inside, took to the air again and was lost over the Mediterranean, the other 16 crew being captured. L.55 (Flemming) was destroyed on returning from the raid at Tiefenort, Germany. Because of the great height at which the Zeppelins flew over England, and because the defences were ordered to remain 'covered' in case gun flashes and searchlights gave away the positions of targets, the attack was remembered as the 'Silent Raid'. The loss of five Zeppelins in one night was the biggest disaster suffered by the German Naval Airship Service.

24 *October* 16 FE 2bs of No. 100 Sqn and nine 0/100s of No. 16 RNAS Sqn carried out No. 41 Wing's first night raid, attacking steelworks at Saarbrücken-Burback and railyards between Falkenburg and Saarbrücken. Two 0/100s failed to return. No. 55 Sqn's DH 4s had already carried out daylight attacks on 17 and 21 October, losing one DH 4 and claiming four enemy fighters destroyed.

28 *October* Two RFC squadrons – No. 28 (Sopwith Camels) and No. 34 (RE 8s) – were sent to Italy to support the Italian offensive at Caporetto. They were followed by two more Camel-equipped squadrons, Nos. 45 and 66.

9 *November* Attacks by aircraft of the RFC Palestine Brigade on the main ammunition dump and railhead of the Turkish Eighth Army at El Tine, Gaza, caused widespread panic among hostile troops. The commander of the German air contingent supporting the Turks stated that 'This did more to break the heart of the Eighth Army and to diminish its fighting strength than all the hard fighting that had gone before.'

20 *November* The Battle of Cambrai opened. During the attack, RFC aircraft dropped bombs from low level on anti-tank guns and strongpoints to clear a path for advancing British tanks – an early example of the *Blitzkrieg* tactics that would later be developed into a fine art by the Germans in World War II.

21 *November* Zeppelin L.59 (Bockholt) left Jamboli in Bulgaria with a crew of 22 to ferry supplies and ammunition to German forces in East Africa. On 22 November, beyond Khartoum, the airship was recalled and returned to Jamboli after 95 hr 35 min in the air, having covered a record distance of 4200 miles (6720 km).

11 *December* The British coastal airship C.27, based at Pulham, Norfolk, was attacked by three

Brandenburg W.12 floatplanes from Zeebrugge and shot down in flames into the North Sea in less than two minutes. Its final destruction was credited to *Oberleutnant* Friedrich Christiansen. After its loss, no further British dirigible flights were made in areas which could be reached by German aircraft.

# 1918

**2 January** The Air Ministry was formed in London. The first Air Council was established the next day, with Lord Rothermere as Secretary of State for Air. Major General Sir Hugh Trenchard was appointed Chief of the Air Staff later in the month; he was succeeded as GOC RFC France by Major General J.M. Salmond.

**26 January** In an experiment designed to provide fighter escort for German airships, an Albatros D.III fighter was successfully released from Zeppelin L.35 at an altitude of 4600 ft (1400 m). The technique was not adopted operationally.

**28 January** No. 44 Sqn RFC achieved the first unqualified victory at night between aeroplanes when two of its Sopwith Camels (Captain G.H. Hackwill and 2nd Lieutenant C.C. Banks) shot down a Gotha bomber attacking London. A Bristol Fighter of No. 39 Sqn also attacked a Staaken Giant, but was shot down by defensive fire; the crew survived.

**1 February** No. 41 Wing RFC was redesignated VIII Brigade and tasked with independent strategic bombing operations against Germany.

**18 February** The first American fighter squadron from the continental United States, the 95th Aero (Pursuit) Squadron, arrived in France. It was joined later by the 94th Aero Squadron, the two units forming the First Pursuit Group. It was equipped with Nieuport Scouts.

**1 March** The airship station at Paimboeuf, where several US Navy personnel had been on duty with the French since November 1917, was taken over by American forces and commissioned as a Naval Air Station under the command of Lieutenant Commander L.H. Maxfield. The French non-rigid dirigible Astra-Torres AT-1 was also taken over from the French and made its first flight under AS Navy control on 3 March. In all, 18 French airships were assigned to American control before the end of hostilities.

**10 March** Zeppelin L.59 (Bockholt) dropped 14 000

lb (6350 kg) of bombs on Naples, returning to Jamboli after a flight of 37 hr 10 min. On **20 March** this airship left Jamboli to attack Port Said, Egypt, but aborted because of strong headwinds and returned to base after a flight of 52 hr 23 min; on a second attempt, on **7 April**, L.59 caught fire and exploded over the Straits of Otranto with the loss of all 23 crew. The cause of the accident was probably a petrol fire.

**12–20 March** Air activity on the Western Front, particularly opposite the sectors held by the British, increased dramatically. By the third week of March the Germans had air superiority on the Somme, with 730 aircraft, including 326 fighters, opposing 579 RFC machines, of which 261 were fighters. Opposite the French sectors the Germans had a further 367 aircraft of all types; the *Aviation Militaire* had some 2000 aircraft of all types in service at this time, but no accurate figure exists for the numbers deployed in any given sector. By 16 March, there were clear indications that the Germans were concentrating their best *Geschwader* to the south of Lille, the normal operating area of von Richthofen's *Jagdgeschwader* 1. On the evening of 20 March, RFC reconnaissance aircraft returned with the intelligence that enemy troops in the front line opposite the British Third and Fifth Armies were being relieved by fresh units, a sure sign that a major attack was about to develop. Many of the new units had been reassigned from the Eastern Front, where hostilities between Russia and the Central Powers had ceased following the Treaty of Brest–Litovsk, concluded on 2 March 1918.

**21 March** German offensive opened on the Western Front, with 56 divisions attacking. Bad weather hampered air activity, and by nightfall 17 RFC squadrons had been compelled to evacuate their airfields, which were in danger of being overrun.

**23 March** Air activity intensified in clearing weather, with up to 70 aircraft engaged in air combats over the battle area. During the next six days the RFC and RNAS carried out many low-level bombing and strafing attacks on enemy forces, causing great disruption and confusion. At night, the offensive against enemy supply lines was continued by the FE 2bs of Nos. 101, 102 and 83 Sqns. Ground attack operations in Picardy were also carried out by the *Aviation Militaire*, in particular by GC 12 *Cigognes* and GC 19. By the end of the month, thanks to stubborn resistance on the ground and continual air attacks, the enemy advance had lost its impetus. It was the first time that the large-scale use of tactical air power had made a decisive contribution to the outcome of a major battle.

**Above:**
*Crews of No. 22 Sqn pose in front of a Bristol Fighter on 1 April 1918, the day the RAF came into being.*

**Below:**
*The two-seat Bristol Fighter despite early reservations went on to become one of Britain's most successful fighter aircraft of World War I.*

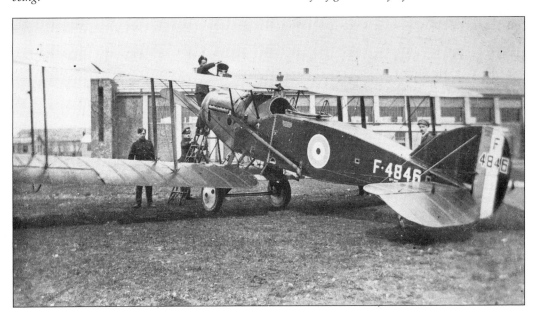

*1 April* The Royal Air Force was formed by the amalgamation of the Royal Flying Corps and the Royal Naval Air Service. A female branch of the new Service, the Women's Royal Air Force, was also formed on the same day.

*11 April* The US I Corps Observation Sqn (Salmson 2As) flew its first operational mission over the front. This was the first time a US squadron had operated independently; the 103rd Pursuit Sqn had been formed from the Lafayette *Escadrille* on 18 February 1918, but was still under French control.

*18 April* The US First Pursuit Group (94th Aero Sqn) carried out its first war patrol in the Champagne sector (Captain David Petersen, Lieutenant Reed Chambers and Lieutenant Edward Rickenbacker). On a second patrol that day, Lieutenants Alan Winslow and Douglas Campbell destroyed two enemy fighters, an Albatros D.V and a Pfalz D.III – the Group's first victories.

*21 April* Manfred von Richthofen, the top scoring fighter pilot of World War I with 80 victories, was shot down and killed near Corbie. Credit for his death was variously claimed by Captain Roy Brown of No. 209 Sqn RAF and by Australian machine gunners of the 24th Machine Gun Company (Sergeant C.B. Popkin and Gunner R.F. Weston) and the 53rd Battery, 14th Australian Field Artillery Brigade (Gunners W.J. Evans and R. Buie). The controversy still remains unresolved. The German General Ludendorff stated that the psychological impact of von Richthofen's loss was equivalent to the loss of 30 divisions.

During April, the Germans switched the focus of their offensive on the Somme to the Ypres–Armentières sector, north of the Lys, with the object of breaking through to the vital supply ports of Calais and Boulogne. Again, the offensive was blunted by stubborn resistance on the ground and by sustained air attacks. The final German attack, halted before Amiens, took place on *24 April*.

*1 May* The 1st Air Division was formed within the *Aviation Militaire* for the strategic bombing role. It comprised the *Groupement Ménard* (*Escadre de Combat* 1 and *Escadre de Bombardement* 2) and the *Groupement Féquant* (*Escadre de Combat* 2 and

*Spoils of victory: British airmen examine the machine guns from the Fokker Dr.1 triplane in which Baron Manfred von Richthofen was shot down.*

*Escadre de Bombardement* 13). Both fighting groups had a collective total of 50 Breguet 14 bombers and 130 fighters (SPAD VII or XIII), the latter having the task of escorting the bombers to and from their objectives.

*2 May* The British SS *Zero* class non-rigid dirigible Z-29 sighted a periscope off Folkestone and directed surface forces to the scene, resulting in the destruction of UB-31.

*13 May* The Independent Air Force, RAF (Commander, Major General Sir Hugh Trenchard as from 6 June) was formed, the first time that an Air Force had been created for the express purpose of conducting a war without reference or subordination to Army or Navy Commands. The role of the IAF was to operate by day and night against industrial targets in Germany and enemy airfields. Its nine squadrons were equipped with DH 4s, DH 9s, DH 9As, Handley Page 0/400s and FE 2Bs, with one squadron of Sopwith Camels for escort work.

*18 May* German Gotha bombers carried out a night raid on No. 12 Ordnance Depot at Blarges, France, destroying 6000 tons of British Army ammunition. Fifteen more Gothas also attacked a railway bridge over the Canche estuary; some of

*The Breguet XIV, seen here in post-war civilian colours, was an excellent light bomber that equipped the majority of France's Escadrilles de Bombardement at the war's end.*

their bombs fell on the nearby military hospital at Etaples, killing 182 patients and injuring 643. On the following night, the Gothas attacked No. 20 Ordnance Depot at Seigneville, destroying 5600 tons of ammunition, including 69 million small-arms rounds. Had these attacks taken place some weeks earlier, when the British field commanders were desperate for supplies of ammunition to sustain their battered and retreating armies, they might have contributed directly to a German breakthrough on the Somme.

*19 May* 28 Gothas and three Giants attacked London. Defending fighters shot down three Gothas, AA guns destroyed two, and a sixth crashed in Essex after suffering engine failure. It was the heaviest loss sustained by the German Flying Corps over England in the war.

*6 June* The Independent Force, RAF, carried out its first operational mission. Ten DH 4s of No. 55 Sqn bombed factories, the railway station and barracks at Koblenz, and five DH 9s of No. 99 Sqn attacked rail targets at Thionville. Eleven DH 9s had been sent out, but half were forced to turn back with engine trouble – a recurring problem with this type.

**12 June** The first US bomber unit of the American Expeditionary Force, the 96th Aero Sqn, carried out its first operational mission, an attack on rail communications at Dommary-Baroncourt. Formed on 18 May 1918, the squadron was equipped with Breguet 14s.

The renewal of trench warfare that followed the failure of the German spring offensives of 1918 made heavy demands on the observation squadrons of both sides, for there were entirely new trench systems to be registered and artillery emplacements to be accounted for. The RE 8s of No. 3 Sqn, Australian Flying Corps, were particularly effective during this period. On 6 and 7 June they were responsible for the elimination of 17 German gun batteries, entrenched in the woods along the Somme between Sailly Laurette and Etinahem, by directing accurate counter-battery fire.

**4 July** No. 3 (Australian) Sqn and No. 9 Sqn RAF joined forces in a major supply drop to the 4th Australian Division. While No. 3 Sqn bombed and strafed enemy positions at Hamel before dawn to cover the sound of the advancing Australian infantry, No. 9 Sqn began operations at first light, its 12 RE 8s dropping 93 boxes containing 111 600 rounds of ammunition to the Australian forward troops. The drops were made from 200 ft (60 m) and two REs were shot down by enemy gunfire.

**17 July** Two flights of Sopwith Camels led by Captain W.D. Jackson and Captain B.A. Smart took off from the aircraft carrier HMS *Furious* to attack the Zeppelin sheds at Tondern. All six aircraft, each of which carried two 50 lb (22 kg) bombs, made successful attacks. Two sheds and an ammunition dump were hit and set on fire, and Zeppelins L.54 and L.60 were destroyed. Two British pilots regained the carrier; three more landed in Denmark in bad weather and the other crashed in the sea and was drowned.

**18 July** French, British and American air squadrons joined forces to stem a major German offensive east and west of Reims (Second Battle of the Marne). Throughout the heavy fighting that followed, the Allied airmen maintained pressure on enemy airfields, forcing the *Jagdgeschwader* on to the defensive. By 21 July, the Germans were once again in retreat across the Marne.

**August** During this month, the Royal Air Force introduced offensive fighter 'sweeps' on the West-

ern Front, usually with Sopwith Camel squadrons flying at 10 000 ft (3000 m), SE.5 squadrons at 14 000 ft (4200 m) and Bristol Fighter squadrons providing top cover at 18 000 ft (5500 m).

**6 August** Zeppelins L.53, L.56, L.65 and L.70 carried out the last raid of the war on Britain. L.70 (von Lossnitzer) was shot down in flames by Major Egbert Cadbury and Captain Robert Leckie in a DH.4 and fell in the sea near King's Lynn, Norfolk. The 22 dead included Peter Strasser, head of the German Naval Airship Service.

**8 August** A major Allied offensive was launched east of Amiens. In the preceding week the Allied air forces made numerous attacks on enemy airfields, particularly those occupied by the *Schlachtstaffeln*. Casualties among the low-flying squadrons were high, reaching 23 per cent. This phase also witnessed bitter air fighting, with heavy losses on both sides. In the week 5–11 August the RAF alone claimed 177 enemy aircraft destroyed for the loss of 150 of their own.

**11 August** Zeppelin L.53 (Proelss) was shot down off Ameland by Lieutenant Stuart Culley, flying a Sopwith Camel launched from a lighter towed behind the destroyer HMS *Redoubt*. One member of the Zeppelin's crew survived, baling out at 19 000 ft (5790 m).

**September** Throughout the month, Allied air power continued to operate at maximum effort in support of renewed Allied offensives towards the Hindenburg Line, the last German line of defence. Between 11 and 15 September, a massive concentration of 1483 fighter, bomber and observation aircraft – the largest of the entire war – was employed during the battle for the Saint-Mihiel salient under the command of General William Mitchell of the US Air Service.

**21 September** RAF aircraft, in support of General Allenby's campaign in Palestine, attacked and destroyed the retreating Turkish Seventh Army at Wadi el Fara. Of this attack, T.E. Lawrence wrote: 'It was the RAF which had converted the Turkish retreat into a rout, which had abolished their telephone and telegraph connections, had blocked their lorry columns, scattered their infantry units.'

**27 September** The Allied assault on the Hindenburg Line began. Prior to this, German night bombers made determined attempts to attack Allied supply depots in the rear and suffered heavy losses, mainly at the hands of No. 151 Sqn RAF's Sopwith Camels, which were tasked with night fighting.

**1–2 October** In a two-day operation, Nos. 82 and 218 Sqns RAF (FK.8s and DH.9s) joined with

# PARACHUTES: THE VEXED QUESTION

**A**LTHOUGH balloon observers were equipped with parachutes from the early days of the war, the failure to issue parachutes to flying personnel caused much unnecessary suffering and loss of life. In the beginning, primitive parachutes were bulky and heavy, and to wear them would have imposed an unacceptable weight penalty, as well as restricting the pilot's movements. But by 1918, more powerful engines and improved parachute design had done away with such objections, and the RAF's doctrine that the wearing of parachutes would be detrimental to the aggressive spirit of its pilots was frankly nonsensical; exactly the opposite would have been true. The Germans, suffering increasingly heavy losses in action and anxious to conserve their remaining pool of pilots and observers, began to issue parachutes in the summer of 1918, to their allies as well as to their own personnel. The first recorded instance of a pilot escaping from an aircraft, and surviving, occurred on 22 August 1918, when Lieutenant Frigyes Hefty of the 42nd Fighter Squadron, Austro-Hungarian Air Corps, jumped from his burning Albatros D.III after a fight with Italian Hanriots over the Piave River; he made a heavy landing, but suffered no serious injury.

Belgian air units in dropping 13 tons of rations to French and Belgian troops in the Houthulst Forest, whose reserves were exhausted. The rations were packed in bags of earth to prevent damage and the airdrop was entirely successful.

*12 October* Zeppelins L.63 and L.65 carried out a short reconnaissance over the German Bight; it was the last flight by rigid airships under war conditions. As the Germans fell back from the Hindenburg Line in October, much of the Allied air effort was devoted to attacks on road junctions, railway stations and other bottlenecks. The German Flying Corps continued to fight fiercely, if spasmodically, and to inflict losses on the Allied day bombers, although their own losses were far from light. The last intense air engagements of the war were fought over the British sector between **4** and **11 November**, the RAF claiming 68 enemy aircraft destroyed for the loss of 60 of their own.

*11 November* At 11.45 a.m., an RE.8 observation aircraft of No. 15 Sqn RAF landed at Auchy. Its crew, Captains H.L. Tracy and S.F. Davison, reported that no enemy aircraft had been seen. British troops were in Mons, where the British Expeditionary Force's long retreat had started more than four years earlier, and anti-aircraft fire was nil. The Armistice came into effect 15 minutes later.

*The Pfalz D.XII was a fast, manoeuvrable fighter that did not enter service until September 1918, too late to influence the course of the air war.*

# 3

# THE TROUBLED YEARS OF PEACE 1918–38

## Russia and the Baltic, 1918–20

In the summer of 1918, while the conflict in Europe still raged, contingents of British, French, Japanese – and, later, American – troops landed on Russian soil. Ostensibly, their purpose was to guard Allied war stores from capture by the Germans in a Russia that was now torn by civil war, but it was not long before they became directly embroiled in the bitter struggle between the embryo Bolshevik armies and the so-called 'White' Russian forces, loyal to the Tsar.

In both north and south Russia, Allied land operations were supported by small RAF contingents. In September 1918, a Royal Air Force flight of eight DH.4s arrived by sea at the north Russian port of Archangel'sk and quickly moved up to a primitive airfield at Bakaritsa to operate in support of Allied operations on the river Dvina. At Bakaritsa, the RAF personnel discovered several Nieuport 17s and Sopwith 1½-Strutters, still in

crates, part of a batch supplied to Imperial Russia in the previous year and apparently overlooked by the Bolsheviks, who had recently been driven out of the area. These aircraft were quickly assembled and, together with the DH.4s, were used to form two squadrons, Nos. 2 and 3 (numbers which bore no relation to those of normal RAF units). No. 2 Sqn was commanded by Major Charles R. Carr, RAF, and the other by an expert Russian airman named Alexander Kazakov, who had been Commanding Officer of the 19th Sqn, Imperial Russian Air Corps. The two squadrons went into action in November 1918 against the Bolshevik units that were pressing the Dvina Force.

Late in November, the pilots received a welcome addition to their equipment in the shape of six Sopwith Camel fighters, and it was while flying one of these that Kazakov, in January 1919, shot down the first Bolshevik aircraft – a seaplane – to be destroyed by the Allied Expeditionary Force. Enemy aircraft, in fact, were very scarce in this sector, a fact that enabled the Allied pilots to carry out their task, albeit with poor equipment and under difficult conditions, in fairly routine fashion. At this stage the numerical strength of the 'Workers' and 'Peasants' Air Fleet – the future Soviet Air Force – stood at not more than 150 aircraft. Most of them were British and French types – Farmans, Spads, Nieuports, Caudrons, Morane-Saulniers and Sopwith 1½-Strutters – most of them in poor shape. There were also some Albatros D.IIIs, Fokker E Types, Halberstadt CL.IIs and LVGs, left behind by the Germans in the Ukraine. All the serviceable aircraft were divided between 36 squadrons, most of which had only

*Rare photograph of Sopwith Snipes, unit unidentified, at an airfield in southern Russia, 1919.*

two or three machines. The few aircraft that were available to the Reds in the north were quickly neutralized by attacks on enemy aerodromes.

In south Russia, the RAF deployed No. 47 Sqn from Amberkoj in Greece to Ekaterinodar in April 1918, and No. 221 Sqn, together with 'A' Flight of No. 17 Sqn, from Mudros to Petrovsk in December. The function of Nos. 221 and 17 Sqns, both of which were equipped with DH.9s, was to bomb the Bolshevik bases on the Caspian and provide air support for the Royal Navy, which was operating a small armada of vessels in the area. By May 1919, following a series of limited air–sea actions against the Bolsheviks, the whole of the Caspian with the exception of Astrakhan was in Allied hands.

No. 47 Sqn comprised three flights, two equipped with DH.9 and 9A bombers and one with Sopwith Camels, all of them war-weary. In March 1919, the squadron moved to Beketovka to lend direct support to White Russian ground operations, carrying out reconnaissance, ground attack and escort work, and in May the pilots were ordered to step up their operations and destroy as many enemy aircraft as possible in support of the White Russian advance on Tsaritsyn. Attacks centred on Urbabk airfield, where several Red air units were based, and the squadron mounted a series of ground attack operations in the Tsaritsyn area. By the end of the month, No. 47 Sqn's aircrews had accounted for some 20 enemy aircraft in air engagements.

The squadron flew intensively during the summer months of 1919, carrying out attacks on enemy cavalry formations and river traffic. In September it moved to Kotluban, from where it continued attacks on the enemy's lines of communication. It was now the sole RAF unit operating in south Russia, No. 221 Sqn having disbanded on 1 September. In October No. 47 Sqn lost its identity, becoming known simply as 'A' Detachment, RAF.

By the last week of October the Red forces were advancing on all fronts. The RAF Detachment was earmarked to carry on the fight in support of General Mai-Maevsky's White Volunteer Army,

*De Havilland DH.9 light bombers were widely used by the RAF detachments in Russia and by White Russian squadrons.*

engaged in bitter fighting around Kharkov, but both men and machines were swept up in the chaos of retreat and the Detachment was disbanded, the crews making their way to Rostov. They were evacuated in March 1920, after destroying their few remaining aircraft.

The evacuation of the Allied intervention forces left the Red Air Fleet in undisputed mastery of the sky on all fronts. The élite of the White Russian pilots were dead; those who were left were outclassed by the Red pilots, many of whom had now developed a high degree of skill. It was widely rumoured that some Red formations were led by German mercenaries, and although this was never confirmed, Allied pilots reported that Red air combat tactics in some sectors during 1919–20 were reminiscent of those employed by the wartime German Flying Corps.

Nevertheless, the White ground attack squadrons continued to inflict severe casualties on enemy ground forces in the Crimea during the last major battles of the Civil War in the summer of 1920. In one extraordinary incident in July, the White Russian air commander, General Tkatchov – leading a flight of six DH.9s – fought an inconclusive battle with his opposite number in the Red Air Fleet, Piotr Mesheraup, who was flying a Nieuport. This is believed to be the only occasion in the history of air fighting when the commanders of two opposing air arms met in combat.

In the summer of 1919, a Royal Navy task force entered the Baltic to operate in defence of the neutrality of the Baltic States, which were being subjected to the ravages not only of the Bolsheviks, but also of German mercenary *Freikorps* units. The primary task of the British naval force was to keep the Russian Baltic Fleet penned up in its base at Kronshtadt, at the eastern end of the Gulf of Finland. A Royal Air Force contingent commanded by Squadron Leader D.G. Donald and equipped with a miscellany of aircraft that included Sopwith Camels and 1½-Strutters, Short Seaplanes and Griffins, was transported to the area by the air-craft carriers *Vindictive* and *Argus* and placed ashore on rudimentary airstrips.

During their early operations, the RAF aircraft were employed mainly on reconnaissance and anti-submarine patrols from their principal base at Biorko, but on 30 July 1919 the naval force commander, Admiral Cowan, decided to mount an attack on Kronshtadt to pre-empt a possible Russian naval sortie against his ships. A mixed force of 11 aircraft carried out the raid, dropping ten 112 lb (50 kg) and six 65 lb (29 kg) bombs on the depot ship *Pamyat Azova* and a neighbouring dry dock. The crews reported five direct hits and two large fires started. All the aircraft returned safely, despite heavy gunfire from ships and shore batteries.

During August 1919, eight daylight and two night bombing raids were carried out in addition to routine patrols, and on the night of 17/18 August all serviceable aircraft – now reduced to eight – carried out a diversionary raid in conjunction with a highly successful and daring torpedo attack by coastal motor boats (CMBs) of the Royal Navy on Russian warships in Kronshtadt. Having dropped their bombs, the aircrews strafed searchlight and gun crews while the CMBs made their torpedo run. Subsequent reconnaissance showed that the *Pamyat Azova* and two battleships had been sunk, leaving only a handful of destroyers to oppose the British naval presence.

Air operations against Kronshtadt ceased on 11 December 1919, when the naval base became icebound. During their five months of active service in the Baltic the RAF aircraft had flown a total of 837 operational hours. Of the original 55 aircraft deployed, 33 had been lost: three were shot down, nine force-landed in the sea, seven crashed on take-off and 14 deteriorated beyond repair owing to the climatic conditions. The British presence in the Baltic was withdrawn on 2 February 1920, when Estonia signed a peace treaty with the Bolshevik government.

# Policing an Empire: Command and Control from the Air, 1919–30

In March 1921, at a time when the Royal Air Force was faced with the possibility of almost complete extinction in the wake of savage post-war defence cuts, a conference was held in Cairo under the presidency of Winston Churchill, who was then Secretary of State for the Colonies, with the Chief of Air Staff, Air Chief Marshal Sir Hugh Trenchard, at his right hand. The conference was attended by the civil and military administrators of the British protectorates and mandates throughout the Middle East, and to them Churchill and Trenchard proposed a novel scheme: that the policing of troubled areas, particularly in Mesopotamia and the North-West Frontier of India, be carried out by designated squadrons of the RAF, reducing ground forces to the necessary minimum.

The effectiveness of the aircraft as a peace-keeping instrument had already been demonstrated in 1919 in Somaliland, where for 17 years the Dervish leader, Mohammed bin Abdullah Hassan – nicknamed the 'Mad Mullah' – had been fomenting unrest. A force of 12 DH.9s, under the command of Group Captain Robert Gordon and known as 'Z Force', had been shipped out to Berbera in HMS *Ark Royal*, and in three weeks of sustained operations alongside the Camel Corps and the King's African Rifles they had succeeded in overthrowing the Mullah completely.

So the novel scheme was adopted – although not without a good deal of opposition initially – and it was decided to implement it in Mesopotamia (renamed Iraq in September 1921) and in Jordan. The RAF assumed responsibility for internal and external security in these two countries in 1922 and its garrison in Iraq was raised to eight squadrons. Five of these were stationed at Hinaidi: they were No. 1 (Sopwith Snipes), No. 6 (Bristol Fighters), No. 30 (DH.9As), No. 45 (Vickers Vernons) and No. 70 (Vickers Vimys), exchanged for Vernons in November 1922. No. 8 Sqn with DH.9As was at Basra, No. 55 with DH.9As at Mosul and No. 84 with DH.9As at Shaibah.

The air policing method was simple enough in principle. If a local political officer or the police reported a disorder that was beyond their control, the offenders would be summoned to appear for trial in a court of law. If they refused, or continued their criminal activities, a warning would be dropped telling them that unless they submitted, their village would be bombed and subsequently blockaded by air until the required submission was forthcoming. An aircraft would duly appear over the now-deserted village on the stated date and bomb it, and in the days that followed further light attacks would be made, possibly with delayed-action bombs scattered around the area of the village. Almost without fail, this method produced a submission within a very short time; the villagers, already living at poverty level, could not afford to have their routine interrupted for long. Once the offenders had surrendered, a small force of police or troops, supported by medical personnel, would be flown in to restore order, tend to the sick and wounded and help restore the bombed village to habitable standard. After the system had been in force for some time, a mere threat of action was usually all that was necessary to persuade offenders to turn themselves in.

Sometimes, however, the RAF squadrons in Iraq were called upon to deal with more serious disturbances. At the end of 1922, for example, the Turks – now beginning to recover from their earlier defeats and humiliation under the energetic leadership of Mustapha Kemal – began to create trouble among the tribes in Kurdistan, and in September 1922 they established an outpost on Iraqi territory 40 miles (64 km) from Kirkuk. This was attacked by RAF aircraft and the Turks expelled. In 1923, in the same area, the RAF also operated against a Kurdish leader named Sheikh Mahmoud, who had begun plotting with his Turkish neighbours with a view to creating an independent Kurdistan. When the British received intelligence that Mahmoud was about to launch a general uprising, they airlifted reinforcements and supplies into the Kirkuk area and bombed Mahmoud's headquarters at Sulaimaniya, forcing him to retreat into the mountains. He surfaced at intervals over the next seven years, but the RAF kept him effectively bottled up until, in 1930, the Iraqi Army moved against him and defeated him, driving him into exile for good.

Policing work by the RAF squadrons in Iraq continued, and in January 1928 another major emergency arose when areas of southern Iraq and Kuwait were threatened by a fanatical Islamic group called the Akhwan. An air and ground operation was mounted against them, the units involved being known as Akforce; its primary task was to deny the use of waterholes to the raiders and then to throw them back across the

*The Bristol F.2B Fighter equipped several RAF overseas squadrons in the years after World War I. These examples, belonging to No. 6 Sqn, are pictured over Iraq in the early 1920s.*

Persian border. Akforce HQ was established at Ur, and the DH.9As of Nos. 55 and 84 Sqns were detached to desert airstrips to operate in conjunction with armoured car sections. Air supply was undertaken by No. 70 Sqn, which had begun to re-equip with Vickers Victorias. Fuel for the DH.9As was the main commodity transported by No. 70 Sqn, each Victoria carrying 56 four-gallon (18.2 l) drums on a typical sortie. By the time the operation ended with the withdrawal of the raiders on 29 May, the Victorias had airlifted 1192 passengers and 517 tons of freight, the air and ground crews operating in appalling conditions of extreme heat, often accompanied by dust storms.

In India, bombing and reconnaissance operations against rebel tribesmen on the North-West Frontier had been a frequent undertaking ever since No. 31 Sqn had first arrived there with a mixture of BE.2cs and Henry Farmans at the end of 1915. By the end of 1919 the RAF's air strength in India had increased to six squadrons, Nos. 20, 31, 48 and 114 with Bristol Fighters, No. 99 with DH.9As and No. 97 with DH.10s; these were incorporated in an India Group, with its HQ at Raisina (later New Delhi). Between them, this handful of squadrons had the formidable task of policing some 27 000 square miles of some of the world's most barren and inhospitable terrain, peopled by several millions of the world's hardiest, cruellest and most

experienced guerrilla fighters. For this purpose the RAF had, in the summer of 1922, 70 aircraft – on paper. The reality was somewhat different. Of that total, only seven were airworthy; the remainder were grounded either through a critical shortage of spares or because they were simply worn out. The problem was so serious that Air Vice-Marshal Sir John Salmond was sent out to India to investigate matters and he subsequently reported that the RAF in India at that time was non-effective as a fighting force. Steps were taken to set matters right, but it was to be six years before the India squadrons were provided with better equipment.

It says much for the skill and dedication of the RAF ground crews, working in dreadful conditions with the limited equipment available, that the RAF was never unable to meet the Army's request for tactical support in its operations along the Frontier. Sometimes, operations were undertaken solely by the RAF units, and as a result, the authorities in India came to rely more on air action that was independent of costly, and often unwieldy, movements on the ground.

There was a good example of this policy in March 1925, when 16 DH.9As of Nos. 27 and 60 Sqns were flown up to the outpost airstrip at Miramshah, 120 miles (193 km) from Kohat,

under the command of Wing Commander R.C.M. Pink, Officer Commanding No. 2 (Indian) Wing, for operations against Mahsud tribesmen in South Waziristan. Operations HQ were at Tank and the Bristol Fighters of No. 5 Sqn were flown there from Kohat to support the DH.9s. For seven weeks, beginning on 9 March, the DH.9As carried out sustained bombing operations against the Mahsud strongholds in the mountains, each bombing raid usually being accompanied by strafing attacks. On 1 May, the rebel leaders sought an honourable peace and the short air campaign known as 'Pink's War' came to a close. The cost to the RAF had been one DH.9A of No. 27 Sqn, which was shot down by ground fire on 21 March; the crew received fatal burns and died shortly afterwards. (Contrary to popular myth, aircrew who came down in rebel territory were usually well treated. On one occasion, a flight lieutenant who suffered a broken leg was carried 40 miles (64 km) to hospital by Afridi tribesmen, some of the most hostile in the whole area. They were so impressed by his courage and fortitude that they sent a deputation to Shah Hospital every week to check on his progress.)

*The Westland Wapiti was an effective Army co-operation aircraft between the wars. This aircraft, serving in India, belonged to the Risalpur Wing (Nos. 11 and 39 Sqns).*

*This striking photograph shows a formation of Westland Wapitis over the River Indus, c. 1930.*

One of the more celebrated operations carried out by the RAF in India occurred at the end of 1928. On 14 November, a rebellion broke out against the ruler of Afghanistan; thousands of tribesmen went on the rampage throughout the country's southern provinces and the British Legation, situated two and a half miles outside Kabul, was trapped between loyalist and rebel forces. Between 23 December and 25 February 1929, the Vickers Victorias of No. 70 Sqn evacuated 586 civilians from the Legation, together with 41 tons of baggage. DH.9As of Nos. 27 and 60 Sqns were also involved in the operation. In all, the RAF aircraft flew 57 438 miles (92 435 km) through very severe winter weather and at altitudes of up to 10 000 ft (3048 m) in mountainous terrain to achieve their objective.

The RAF was by no means alone in using its resources to police the outposts of empire; the French, Italians and Spanish all made extensive use of air power in helping to quell uprisings in North Africa during the 1920s. The difference was that the RAF applied a specific policy to its air policing operations, designed to minimize the loss of life and damage to property, in particular holy places. Other nations showed fewer scruples; the Italians, for example, made liberal use of chemical weapons during their North Afri-

*With the splendour of Mount Everest in the background, this Hawker Hart is flying round the 22 000 ft (6705 m) peak of Nanga Parbat in the Himalayas.*

can operations. The RAF's air policing role in Iraq and India in the 1920s and 1930s may have been of a temporary nature, but it showed a succession of wavering governments that the Service had a definite part to play in maintaining the stability of the Empire. Most importantly of all, it assured the future of the RAF itself.

# The World's Leading Air Arms, 1920–30

## The Royal Air Force

It has already been mentioned that the RAF's new role of policing the Empire greatly helped to maintain its status as an independent force. Yet its continued independence was mainly due to the determination of the Chief of the Air Staff, Sir Hugh Trenchard, who fought off continual attempts by the Admiralty and the War Office to subordinate British air power to the Army and Navy. The squabble often reached a petty level; in 1919, for example, the Army and Navy refused to allow the RAF to use their officer ranks, so Trenchard invented new ones. The new RAF rank titles – Pilot Officer, Flying Officer and so on, up to Marshal of the Royal Air Force – officially came into being on 4 August 1919.

By 1921 the strength of the RAF was at a very low ebb. Apart from training establishments, there were only four army co-operation squadrons and one fighter squadron in the United Kingdom, five squadrons in Egypt, four in Iraq, four in India and one in the Far East, not counting a handful of floatplane or flying boat squadrons for maritime reconnaissance and coastal patrol.

In April 1922, however, a defence sub-committee recommended that the strength of the RAF be greatly increased, and the government gave its approval to the formation of 52 new squadrons, totalling some 500 aircraft – later increased to 600 – for home defence. The re-equipment programme lacked both urgency and funds, and by the end of 1923 there were still only 11 fighter squadrons in the United Kingdom, equipped predominantly with ageing Sopwith Snipes. These were eventually replaced by three new fighter designs, the Hawker Woodcock, Gloster Grebe and Gloster Gamecock, but by the late 1920s the RAF's fighter squadrons had begun to standardize on a more advanced biplane, the Armstrong Whitworth Siskin IIIA.

The sweeping disarmament measures of 1919, and the disbandment of the Independent Force, had left the RAF without a single home-based bomber squadron. By the end of 1923 there were six, five equipped with DH.9As and one with Vickers Vimys, and three more Vimy-equipped units formed in the following year. Two other units, Nos. 15 and 22 Sqns, although nominally bomber squadrons, were used for trials work at the Aeroplane and Armament Experimental Establishment, RAF Martlesham Heath.

The RAF's light bomber strength received a boost in October 1925 with the formation of the first four Auxiliary Air Force bomber squadrons, all equipped with DH.9As. In 1926 two new light bombers made their appearance; the first was the Fairey Fawn, which equipped five squadrons but was not a success, having a performance inferior to that of the DH.9A, and the other was the Fairey Fox, a very successful design which, because of financial constraints, equipped only one squadron. Other new bomber types to enter service by the end of the decade were the Handley Page Hyderabad heavy bomber, which was developed from the W.8b commercial airliner, the Handley Page Hinaidi four-seat heavy night bomber, the Boulton Paul Sidestrand twin-engined medium day bomber, and the Hawker Horsley, which filled the dual role of torpedo bomber and day bomber.

By the end of the 1920s the RAF also had at its disposal six army co-operation squadrons, equipped with Bristol F.2Bs, and a Fleet Air Arm – established in April 1924 – comprising six Fleet Fighter Flights equipped with Fairey Flycatchers, two Fleet Spotter Flights with Westland Walrus, Blackburn Blackburn and Avro Bison aircraft, four Fleet Reconnaissance Flights with Fairey IIIDs and Parnall Panthers, and three Fleet Torpedo Flights with Blackburn Darts. Although adminis-

A Hawker Hind light bomber of No. 83 Sqn, RAF Scampton, in the late 1930s. Had it not been for crash rearmament schemes, the RAF would have gone to war in 1939 equipped with types such as this.

**Above:**
*The RAF pioneered the use of long-range flying boats between the wars. This Short Singapore III of No. 203 Sqn was based at Basra, Iraq.*

**Below:**
*Hawker Hart light bombers of No. 142 Sqn flying over the Canal Zone, 1936.*

tered by the RAF, the Fleet Air Arm came under the operational control of the Royal Navy when embarked. There were also four maritime patrol squadrons, three with Supermarine Southamptons and one with Fairey IIIDs (the latter at Kalafrana, Malta).

## The *Aviation Militaire*

In November 1918, France's *Aviation Militaire* possessed 3222 first-line aircraft in 247 *escadrilles*. By 1 January 1920, the number of *escadrilles* had been reduced to 135, grouped into regiments. There were three fighter regiments each with nine *escadrilles*, three bomber regiments each with 12 *escadrilles*, and nine observation regiments each with eight *escadrilles*. Two more regiments were in Morocco and Algeria.

From the end of 1923, following some administrative reorganization, the force was expanded to 186 *escadrilles*. There were two fighter regiments with Nieuport-Delage NiD-29s and Spad 81s, two day bomber regiments with Breguet 14B2s and Breguet 19s, two night bomber regiments with twin-engined Farman F-60s, three long-range reconnaissance regiments with Breguet 14A2s and Breguet 19A2s, and four observation regiments with a variety of types, notably Potez 15s. Almost the whole emphasis, operationally, was on army co-operation; fighter aircraft had the primary task of escorting observation machines, as they had done during the war, and there was no attempt to develop a specialized strategic bombing force.

Although France retained a sizeable air arm compared to other European nations, it was not particularly modern, even though a number of new combat aircraft types made their appearance after 1924. It was not until 1928, when France became aware that the Germans – debarred by the Treaty of Versailles from possessing a military air arm – were nevertheless building up a substantial sporting and commercial aviation network, with a large reserve of pilots and fast 'postal' aircraft that could all too clearly be modified for military use, that French public opinion began to clamour for the armed forces to be strengthened. This led, in September 1928, to the formation of an Air Ministry, which was to be responsible for both civil and military aviation in France and her colonies. It was the first step towards establishing a modern air arm that would no longer be a mere auxiliary of the land forces. State funds were made available to aircraft constructors, and a system was evolved whereby every new prototype was thoroughly evaluated at the Villacoublay test centre and then subjected to stringent operational trials

*The Bloch 200 was a good French bomber design of the early 1930s, but suffered from a lack of speed. Most had been withdrawn by the outbreak of World War II.*

*Like Britain, France developed flying boats for military use. One of them was the huge Breguet Bizerte, which policed France's colonial sea routes in the 1930s.*

in the hands of experienced military pilots. It was a scheme that should have worked well; instead, it was to suffer from the maladministration of successive governments in the 1930s, each of which had different ideas about the priorities of French military aviation.

## The *Regia Aeronautica*

During World War I, Italy's *Corpo Aeronautica Militare* had relied heavily on French-designed combat aircraft, with the exception of bombers and naval types. The first Italian-produced fighters did not enter service until 1918. At the time of the Armistice, 1683 aircraft were in first-line Italian service. Afterwards, there was a period of decline that lasted until 1923, when the *Regia Aeronautica* came into being and the aircraft industry became geared up to meet the military aviation demands of Benito Mussolini's new fascist government. Inspired by dreams of creating a new Roman Empire, one of Mussolini's foremost aims was to build up Italy's military forces to formidable strength. Italy was, in fact, the first of the European powers to begin a determined policy of rearmament, and the aviation industry, building on the lessons of World War I, produced a number of practical combat aircraft designs which gave excellent service throughout the 1920s. During the insurrection in Libya in the middle of the decade, the *Regia Aeronautica* showed itself to be very efficient in the tactical role, but its success in this campaign – and also during the invasion of Ethiopia in 1935 – created an entirely false impression of its true capabilities.

## The Red Air Fleet

The expansion of the Soviet Union's military aviation resources began in 1922, with clandestine German help. Under the terms of an agreement negotiated between Leon Trotsky, the Soviet Commissar for War, and General von Seeckt, commander of the German *Reichswehr*, hundreds of German personnel were secretly sent to the Soviet Union to build aircraft production facilities and to train Soviet personnel. Several joint German–Soviet military exercises were held, involving the widespread use of aircraft; the lessons that emerged enabled the Red Air Fleet planners to draw up a manual of air fighting, based largely on the tactics evolved by the Germans during the war.

At Fili, near Moscow, an aircraft factory was established under the direction of Hugo Junkers, and Andrei N. Tupolev was appointed as chief designer. In 1927, after designing a number of general-purpose types, Tupolev produced the ANT-4, a twin-engined bomber and reconnaissance aircraft known as the TB-1 in Red Air Force service; it was the progenitor of an unbroken line of Tupolev bombers that continues to this day. The following year saw the appearance of the I-4, an all-metal sesquiplane fighter conceived by Tupolev, Pavel O. Sukhoi and Vladimir Petlyakov; it was ordered into quantity production. The most successful Soviet fighter designer of the period, however, was Nikolai N. Polikarpov, who in 1927

produced a new single-seat fighter, the I-3. It was followed by the R-5, an excellent reconnaissance biplane that was subsequently built in large numbers, and the I-5, a single-seat biplane fighter with exceptional manoeuvrability and an armament of four machine guns. It was Polikarpov who was to dominate the Soviet fighter scene throughout the 1930s.

Before these new types reached fruition, the Red Air Force continued to depend on foreign combat aircraft. The de Havilland DH.9 and 9A featured prominently in assisting the Red Army to put down the insurrections that flared up in various parts of the Soviet Union during the 1920s, and in 1929 aircraft of this type also flew in support of the Far Eastern Army under Marshal Blukher, which was in action against Chinese forces on the Manchurian border.

## The United States Army Air Corps

The US Army Air Service, under the command of General William Mitchell, had ended the war with 45 squadrons, 740 aircraft, 800 pilots and 500 observers. From May 1918 it had enjoyed a brief period of autonomy, but in June 1920 it came back under direct command of the US Army. In that year, Congress cut defence spending and reduced the USAAS to 27 squadrons, instead of the 87 which had been planned.

Luckily, among the 9050 personnel who remained in 1920, there was a hard core of young officers who had come out of the war convinced that a strong air arm was vital to the future of America's defences. Foremost among them was General 'Billy' Mitchell, who, with others, strongly advocated the creation of an independent air force on the lines of the RAF. Like Trenchard in Britain, Mitchell met with enormous opposition from the Army and the Navy. The Navy, in particular, saw its battleships as the nation's first line of defence; the possibility that they could be made obsolete by bombers, as Mitchell claimed, seemed preposterous. Mitchell's persistent lobbying – in which he became something of a celebrity – caught the attention of Congress, and pressure was brought to bear on the reluctant Navy to allow Mitchell a chance to prove his claim that Air Service bombers could sink a battleship.

Beginning on 21 June 1921, trials were carried out off the Virginia Capes. On that day the German submarine U-117 was sunk by 12 bombs dropped from Navy F5Ls at 1100 ft (335 m). On the 29th, Navy aircraft located the radio-controlled battleship *Iowa* 1 hr 57 min after being alerted of her

*The Lockheed YP-24 was that company's first attempt to produce a modern fighter aircraft. A two-seater, it fell victim to the 1929 depression and was cancelled by the US Army Air Corps in 1931.*

approach somewhere within a 25 000 mile$^2$ (64 750 km$^2$) area, and attacked her with dummy bombs. On 13 July, Army bombers sank the German destroyer G-102, and on the 18th the light cruiser *Frankfurt* went down under the combined effect of 74 bombs delivered by Army and Navy aircraft. Tests against the German battleship *Ostfriesland* began on 20 July, when Army, Navy and Marine Corps aircraft dropped 52 bombs, and ended the next day when Army bombers sank her with eleven 1000 and 2000 lb (450–900 kg) bombs. The significance of the tests was hotly debated and became a bone of contention between a generation of Army and Navy air officers. The one firm conclusion that could be drawn was that aircraft, in unopposed attack, could sink capital ships.

Despite this, bomber development in the 1920s was slow. The aircraft that sank the *Ostfriesland*, the Glenn Martin MB-2 (a derivative of the MB-1, produced as a successor to the Handley Page 0/400, which was built under licence in the USA at the end of the war) remained in service until 1928, when it was gradually replaced by the Keystone LB series of bomber aircraft.

In December 1925 a special board convened by President Calvin Coolidge rejected the idea of a separate air force, but recommended that the Air Service be upgraded to Corps status, with the appointment of an Assistant Secretary of War for Air. On 2 July 1926 Congress passed the Air Corps Act, creating the US Army Air Corps, with an increased budget designed to bring USAAC strength to 1800 aircraft within five years. In fact, 12 years were to pass before that target was reached.

In 1925, out of a total of 1400 aircraft available on paper, only 78 were pursuit (fighter) types and 59 were bombers; the remainder were training, observation and general-purpose aircraft. The USAAC's first pursuit aircraft to be built in any numbers was the Curtiss P-1, which led to the P-6 Hawk; together with the Boeing PW-9, it formed the backbone of the USAAC's fighter strength throughout the 1920s. Variants of both types were also supplied to the US Navy.

## Japan

The early 1920s saw the establishment of Kawasaki, Mitsubishi and Nakajima as the 'big three' of Japan's embryo aircraft industry, whose early development work relied heavily on aid from Britain, the USA, France and Germany. In 1923, the German Dr Richard Vogt (later of Blohm und Voss) became chief designer for Kawasaki, and he was responsible for designing a two-seat general-purpose biplane, the KDA-2, which entered service with the Imperial Japanese Army in 1928 as the Type 88. The Mitsubishi design team was led by Herbert Smith, formerly of the Sopwith company, and in 1922 developed the Mitsubishi B1M, the first Japanese aircraft designed for the torpedo attack role. It remained in production until 1933, by which time 442 had been built for the Imperial Japanese Navy and 48 for the Army. Its replacement was the Mitsubishi B2M1, a metal structure torpedo-bomber-reconnaissance aircraft which was actually designed by Blackburn Aircraft Ltd and which entered service in 1932 as the Navy Type 89.

One of the first nationally-designed fighters to enter service with the Japanese Army Air Force was the Nakajima Type 91, evolved to meet a requirement issued in 1927. The JAAF also evaluated the Curtiss P-1C, although this did not measure up to performance requirements. Deliveries of the Type 91 began in 1931, replacing the French-designed Nieuport-Delage NiD 29C in Army service; this type had been built under licence by Nakajima, who produced a total of 608.

By the beginning of the 1930s, therefore, Japan was no longer dependent on aircraft of foreign design, or on the foreign designers and engineers who had helped to sustain her military aircraft production. During the decade that followed, Japanese military aviation development passed virtually unnoticed by the rest of the world, which remained ignorant of the fact that Japan was producing military aircraft which were the equal of, and in some cases superior to, those produced by the western nations.

# The Rise of the *Luftwaffe*

When Adolf Hitler and the Nazi Party rose to power in Germany in January 1933, and embarked on an open programme of rearmament, the first problem they had to consider – insofar as the creation of a modern air arm was concerned – was that Germany was still disarmed and vulnerable and therefore faced with the real prospect of a preventive war, waged by her neighbours to stop her resurrection as a military power. It was this consideration, more than any other, that dictated the structure of the future *Luftwaffe*. France was Hitler's greatest fear, and France had a large army. The Germans, therefore, had no real choice in deciding whether their air force was to built around a nucleus of strategic bomber aircraft, as was Britain's, or a nucleus of tactical ground support aircraft, as was France's. Attractive though the strategic option might seem in terms of political advantage, what the Germans needed, if they were to resist any possible military action by the French, was a strong tactical air force that could be assembled quickly and equipped with the most modern combat aircraft Germany's industry could produce.

The whole machinery of the new air arm had to be built from scratch. Given the facts that no German air force survived from the 1914–18 War, except as a secret planning staff within the army, and that the aviation industry was geared entirely for civil aircraft production, the development of the *Luftwaffe* was an enormously complex task. That it succeeded was hardly due to Hermann Göring, the *Reich* Air Minister who became Commander-in-Chief of the *Luftwaffe* in March 1935; a fine pilot who had commanded the Richthofen *Geschwader* in its latter days, Göring nevertheless remained almost entirely ignorant of the leading principles of airpower application throughout his career. The real driving force was Erhard Milch, State secretary in the new Air Ministry, who possessed a thorough knowledge of the capabilities of the German aircraft industry and who had excellent political connections within the *Reich*. Milch had left the military after the war and become the head of *Lufthansa*; this fact, together with his arrogance, later brought him into conflict with *Luftwaffe* officers who had remained professional soldiers during the difficult years of the Weimar Republic.

One of the leading priorities of the new regime was airfield construction. New airfields sprang up all over Germany, often with scant regard to the nature of the foundations on which they were built or to the surrounding terrain. Many were little more than grass strips that turned to mud during periods of heavy rain. Those that did have concrete runways later proved inadequate to ac-

**Top:**
*The Junkers Ju 52, developed as a civil airliner in the early 1930s, subsequently served as a bomber in Spain and as Germany's most widely-used transport aircraft of World War II.*

**Above:**
*The Junkers G.24 light transport also provided the German industry with much experience in all-metal aircraft design.*

commodate future generations of advanced combat aircraft, and it was often impossible to extend the runways because of the local topography.

As far as military aircraft construction was concerned, the designer Ernst Heinkel rapidly moved into a leading position, thanks to his willingness to design and build every type of aircraft required by the crash re-equipment programme. In the early 1930s Heinkel produced the He 45 light bomber, the He 46 tactical reconnaissance aircraft and the He 51 fighter, all of which formed the backbone of the new *Luftwaffe's* tactical units; he also built the He 50, which served in the dive-bombing role until the introduction of the Junkers Ju 87 *Stuka*, the He 59 and He 60 floatplanes, and the He 72 Kadett, which became one of the *Luftwaffe's* most important primary trainers. He was also responsible for the He 70 fast commercial airliner, which, although a failure when adapted for military purposes, nevertheless contributed much to the development of Heinkel's most famous design, the He 111 bomber.

By the end of 1933 the *Luftwaffe's* requirements for the next generation of combat aircraft were clearly

*The big Junkers G.38 was the biggest landplane in the world when it entered* Lufthansa *service in 1931 and might have formed the basis for future strategic bomber designs – but the new* Luftwaffe *was only interested in tactical aircraft.*

defined, and within the next two years prototypes of aircraft such as the Messerschmitt Bf 109, Junkers Ju 88 and Dornier Do 17 were making their appearance. By 1939 these aircraft would make the *Luftwaffe* technically the best-equipped air arm in the world, and yet in its command and control system there were severe limitations. The overemphasis on tactics and operations was at the expense of other spheres like logistics, intelligence, signals, training and air transport. Moreover, some senior *Luftwaffe* operational commanders were ex-Army officers who had never piloted an aircraft, let alone led a squadron or wing; in the RAF and USAAC, this would have been unthinkable. In the early, critical years of World War II, the appointment of wrong commanders to key positions was to cost the *Luftwaffe* dearly.

**Below:**
*Developed as a fast mail aircraft, the Heinkel He 70 had beautiful aerodynamic lines. Some were used in the Spanish Civil War.*

**Bottom:**
*The four-engined Blohm und Voss Ha 139 seaplane, shown here on a catapult launcher, was used briefly in the minesweeping role early in World War II.*

# The Quest for Performance

In the two decades following the end of World War I, the major air arms of the world all took part in record-breaking exercises that pushed range, endurance, altitude and speed to the limits of known technology. Such exercises were to have a profound effect on the development of future combat aircraft, some of which were directly descended from machines produced specifically for record-breaking purposes.

In the early days, the US Navy was at the forefront of range and endurance flying; on 27 May 1919 a Curtiss NC-4 flying boat of the US Navy's Seaplane Division One, commanded by Lieutenant-Commander A.C. Read, became the first to make a transatlantic flight, arriving in Lisbon Harbour after flying from Newfoundland via the Azores. Just under three weeks later, though, the honour of making the first non-stop Atlantic crossing fell to two RAF officers, Captain John Alcock and Lieutenant Arthur Whitten Brown, in a converted Vickers Vimy, while on 6 July 1919 the British military rigid airship R.34 completed the first east–west transatlantic flight. But it was the US Navy which, in 1924, successfully completed the first round-the-world flight, using Douglas DT-2 biplanes which were externally similar to those in service as torpedo-bombers; apart from bringing well-deserved honour to the crews, and praise for their flying and navigational skills, this epic voyage brought home a number of lessons which were to make their mark on the design of future aircraft and equipment. One such lesson was that wood and fabric were far from suitable materials for use in wing and float structures under hot and humid conditions; another was that the flight would not have been possible without massive support and organization, with US warships carrying spares, fuel and technicians positioned all along the route. Logistical support of long-range air operations was something in which the Americans, over the next 20 years, would come to excel.

While American long-range flying boats opened up the Pacific air routes from the late 1920s, and the Royal Air Force blazed a trail across the British Empire, French airmen were steadily making inroads into Africa, carrying out aerial surveys and setting up desert airstrips along the embryo mail routes which were to prove of inestimable value during World War II, when air reinforcements for the Middle East had to fly to the Suez Canal Zone across the African continent from Takoradi, on the Gold Coast.

All these operations were valuable in that they led to a great improvement in long-range navigational techniques – particularly significant in the case of the RAF, with its emphasis on long-range strategic bombing – and logistical support. But as far as high-performance combat aircraft were concerned, the real advances came as a result of the ongoing search for improved speed and altitude performance.

The key to the whole matter was the high-performance aero-engine, and in this respect it seemed that the Americans and French had established commanding positions in the years immediately after World War I. In 1920–23, racing variants of the Nieuport-Delage 29 fighter, fitted with a 320 hp Hispano-Suiza engine, improved on the world absolute air speed record seven times, as well as capturing numerous trophies, while in 1923 Curtiss CR-3 biplanes, powered by 400 hp Curtiss D.12 engines, achieved first and second places in the coveted Schneider Trophy contest.

These foreign successes spurred leading British aero-engine manufacturers into re-examining their engine design philosophy. From the Rolls-Royce stable came the Kestrel, which represented a considerable advance over the Curtiss D.12 and was selected to power the RAF's highly successful Hawker Hart light bomber and Hawker Fury fighter. The Kestrel in its ultimate form – the Kestrel V – went on to be developed into the PV.12, the prototype of the engine that was to play such an enormous part in World War II – the Rolls-Royce Merlin. Ironically, it was an imported Rolls-Royce Kestrel that powered the prototype of Germany's most famous fighter, the Messerschmitt Bf 109.

As far as radial engines were concerned, British efforts in the immediate post-war years had not been particularly successful. The first generation of post-war British fighters – types such as the Siskin, Grebe and Flycatcher – were powered by the Armstrong Siddeley Jaguar, a heavy, complex and cumbersome two-row radial that suffered from a short running life and lubrication problems. The situation improved in 1925, with the introduction of the Bristol Jupiter; this powered the nimble little Gloster Gamecock, the first really viable British fighter of post-war design, and the later Bristol Bulldog. Its successor, the Mercury, was installed in the RAF's last biplane fighter, the Gloster Gladiator.

In 1929 the Schneider Trophy was won outright for Britain by a Supermarine S.6 racing seaplane, powered by a Rolls-Royce 'R' engine of 1900 hp. The success of this engine was a powerful factor in persuading the Directorate of Technical Development that Rolls-Royce had established a firm lead in the design of high-performance liquid-cooled powerplants, and in 1934 their PV.12 was approved for installation in a new monoplane fighter then being developed by the Hawker Aircraft Company, the Fury Monoplane – later to be called the Hurricane. Similarly, it was the PV.12 that was chosen to power Supermarine's monoplane fighter design, based on the S.6 racer – the aircraft that was to become the incomparable Spitfire.

In the United States, despite the success of the liquid-cooled Curtiss D.12, aero-engine manufacturers – notably Wright and Pratt & Whitney – concentrated on the development of radial engines for the future generation of combat aircraft.

Both firms were to make an outstanding contribution to military aviation in World War II, producing engines that achieved a remarkable reputation for reliability – a vital factor in the Pacific Theatre, where operations involved long hours of over-water flying. On the other hand, the US in-line engine that was in production at the end of 1939 – the Allison V-1710, which powered the Curtiss

P-40 and early variants of the North American P-51 Mustang – was unreliable. In fact, it was replaced in later versions of the Mustang by the Packard-built Rolls-Royce Merlin, and the result was an exceptional combination of engine and airframe.

In Germany, aero-engine development progressed rapidly during the early 1930s, with four main companies involved: Daimler-Benz, Junkers, BMW and Siemens-Halske. The first two built inverted 12-cylinder liquid-cooled engines and the other two air-cooled radials. The Daimler-Benz engine was also designed to take a 20 mm gun fitted in the V formed by the cylinder blocks and firing through the hollow shaft of the propeller reduction gear. This arrangement produced an unexpected spin-off in that the supercharger had to be repositioned and it proved impracticable to fit the carburettor to it in the normal way. The designers tried several variations, but in the end dispensed with the carburettor altogether and instead used a multi-point fuel injection system spraying directly on to the cylinders. The result was that the Daimler engine continued to perform well during all combat manoeuvres – unlike the Rolls-Royce Merlin, which tended to cut out because of a negative 'g' effect on the carburettor float chamber when the aircraft was inverted or when the pilot put the nose down to dive on an enemy.

# Aircraft Armament

For 15 or more of the 20 years that separated the two world wars, the concept of the traditional fighter layout died hard. In the early 1930s the world's leading air arms were still equipped with open-cockpit biplane or high-wing fighters, armed with two rifle-calibre machine guns mounted to fire through the propeller disc. The only large-calibre machine gun in general use in the late 1930s was the 0.50-inch gun mounted in some American fighters and its 12.7 mm or 13 mm equivalent fitted in a few Continental designs such as the Italian Fiat CR.32.

The problem of air armament was well summarized by Squadron Leader Ralph Sorley of Flying Operations 1 (FO 1) in the British Air Ministry, who led a vigorous campaign that led to

the RAF's new monoplane fighters, the Spitfire and Hurricane, being fitted with eight 0.303-inch machine guns.

'The choice lay between the 0.303 gun, the 0.50 gun and a new 20 mm Hispano gun which was attracting the attention of the French, and in fact of other countries in Europe who could obtain knowledge of it from them. During 1934 this gun was experimental and details of its performance and characteristics were hard to establish. On the other hand, designs of better 0.303 guns than the Vickers had been tested over the preceding years with the result that the American Browning from the Colt Automatic Weapon Corporation appeared to offer the best possibilities from the point of view of rate of fire.

'Our own development of guns of this calibre had been thorough but slow, since we were in the throes of economizing, and considerable stocks of old Vickers guns still remained from the First War. The acceptance of a new gun in the numbers likely to be required was a heavy financial and manufacturing commitment. The 0.50-inch on the other hand had developed little, and although it possessed a better hitting power the rate of fire was slow and it was a heavy item, together with its ammunition, in respect of installed weight . . . the controversy was something of a nightmare during 1933–34. It was a choice on which the whole concept of the fighter would depend, but a trial staged on the ground with eight 0.303s was sufficiently convincing and satisfying to enable them to carry the day.'

While the RAF opted for an armament of eight 0.303 guns – which would be replaced by four 20 mm Hispano cannon from 1941 – the Americans decided to standardize on an armament of up to six 0.50-inch guns in their new generation of monoplane fighters. The Germans, Italians, Russians, French and Japanese all settled for a mixed armament of cannon and machine guns, a combination that would be retained throughout much of the 1939–45 war. Although each variation had its commendable points, it was the all-cannon armament, with its greater range and striking power, that would emerge as the best option.

# The Sino-Japanese Wars

On 18 September 1931, for reasons which still remain obscure – although the Japanese claimed that the Chinese had blown up part of the South Manchuria Railway – fighting broke out at Mukden between Chinese and Japanese forces. This incident was to lead, step by step, to the Japanese conquest of the whole of Manchuria. Air operations during this period were carried out by the Imperial Japanese Army, using mainly Mitsubishi Type 87 light bombers, Kawasaki Type 88 reconnaissance aircraft and Nakajima Type 81 fighters, with which they had little difficulty in establishing superiority over the Chinese. The occupation of Manchuria – renamed Manchukuo by the Japanese – signalled the beginning of a major aircraft modernization and expansion programme.

In July 1937 the Japanese launched a full-scale invasion of China, quickly capturing urban centres along the Chinese coast and pushing rapidly along the Yangtse River as Chinese forces retreated westward. During the initial period of operations, the Imperial Japanese Army left the brunt of the air fighting to the Navy, limiting their activity to air support of ground operations along the Manchukuo border while new units were formed.

The Imperial Japanese Navy was well placed to conduct offensive air operations. Its first-line squadrons were now equipped with Mitsubishi A5M monoplane fighters, its carrier-based attack squadrons with the Yokosuka B4Y bomber and its land-based bomber squadrons with the twin-engined Mitsubishi G3M. Within a week of the start of hostilities, the latter aircraft, operating from Kanoya and Kisarazu, were carrying out the world's first trans-oceanic bombing attacks on Chinese targets.

In August 1937, following the conclusion of a non-aggression pact between China and the Soviet Union, the Soviet Central Committee agreed to supply quantities of aircraft and equipment for use by the Chinese Central Government. The first contingent of Soviet Air Force personnel arrived in China during the last week of September, and by the beginning of 1938 there were over 350 Russians serving in the country.

The total included 80 Soviet Air Force fighter pilots. Although their task was ostensibly to give flying instruction to Chinese crews converting to Russian aircraft types, their real purpose was to fly four squadrons of Polikarpov I-152 (I-15 bis) fighters in combat against the Japanese. Two squadrons of SB-2 bombers also arrived at the same time, and they, too, were manned by Russian crews. Operational flying began almost immediately from bases in the vicinity of Nanking, the Chinese capital, which by that time was coming under heavy Japanese air attack. In January 1938, two of the I-15 squadrons were pulled out of the front line and replaced by two fresh units operating I-16s, which proved able to meet the Japanese A5M2 fighters on more equal terms. The Soviet contingent was commanded by Lieutenant Colonel Stepan P. Suprun.

Meanwhile, Chinese units had begun to receive the first of the 400 I-152s and I-16s promised by the Soviet Government, and Russian-trained Chinese pilots were flowing through the flying and technical schools at Nanchang, Langchow and Hami at a fast rate – so fast, in fact, that many of them were far from ready to take on the highly skilled Japanese aircrews in combat. Nevertheless, they were immediately sent into action in the defence of Nanking, replacing the Soviet Air Force squadrons. That was in mid-November. Four weeks later, their pilots completely outclassed by the Japanese, the Chinese squadrons defending Nanking had been decimated and had to be withdrawn to Nanchang, leaving the capital naked to air attack.

The Russian squadrons, meanwhile, had regrouped near Langchow, where a new batch of crews had arrived to start their four-month tour of duty in China. There was little air activity on either side during the spring of 1938, but in April and May Japanese reconnaissance aircraft began to appear in increasing numbers over Langchow and other places in north-west China, where the combat aircraft being supplied by Russia were assembled. The first heavy air raids on these centres were carried out late in May and continued for five weeks, heavy losses being inflicted on the attacking Mitsubishi G3M bombers – which had a poor defensive armament and which were outside fighter cover – by the defending fighters.

Two months later, in July 1938, a major clash occurred between Soviet and Japanese forces after Russian troops occupied a ridge near Lake Khasan on the Soviet–Manchurian border. The Japanese claimed that the ridge was theirs and attacked the Russian positions in strength on 29 July, capturing it. During the bitter fighting that followed, four squadrons of TB-3 heavy bombers, escorted by I-152s, repeatedly pounded the Japanese positions. While Soviet infantry and tanks fought their way back towards the ridge, several squadrons of I-16s and I-152s strafed ahead of them, and waves of SB-2s took over from the TB-3s and continued to pound the summit of the ridge. The Japanese were unable to hold on, and by nightfall the ridge was once again in Russian hands. Japanese attacks the next day were also broken up by Soviet aircraft, about 180 of which were committed to the battle.

On 11 May 1939 the Japanese, anxious to avenge their defeat at Lake Khasan, launched a major offensive into Mongolian territory at Khalkhin-Gol. There was sporadic air fighting during the opening weeks of the battle, with aircraft used for bombing and strafing by both sides. The battles of August, however, were to be marked by the biggest air confrontation the world had seen since the 1914–18 War.

During July, the Japanese assembled a total of 475 aircraft of all types in Manchuria, including considerable numbers of Mitsubishi A5M and Nakajima Ki-27 fighters. There were also some bomber squadrons equipped with Mitsubishi Ki-21s, fast twin-engined bombers which had entered service with the Japanese Army Air Force the previous year and which were later to be known by the Allied code-name of *Sally*. The Russians, meanwhile, had been pouring troops and equipment into Mongolia, and the First Army Group – commanded by General Georgi K. Zhukov, who was to achieve fame during World War II – was rapidly deployed along the disputed frontier. At his disposal, at the end of July, Zhukov had 580 aircraft operated by both Soviet and Mongolian squadrons. The total included 125 SB-2s, 25 TB-3s, 150 I-16s, 200 I-15s and I-152s, and 80 transport and reconnaissance aircraft of various types. The I-15s had already clashed with Japanese fighters on several occasions, and had proved inferior to the Nakajima Ki-27; during subsequent operations they were relegated mainly to the ground-attack role, leaving the I-16s and I-152s to engage the enemy.

During August, four of the Red Air Force squadrons exchanged their I-15s for the more modern I-153, with a retractable undercarriage, and the appearance of these aircraft over the Khalkhin-Gol took the Japanese fighter pilots by surprise, especially as the Russian pilots evolved tactics which were deliberately designed to mislead the enemy. They would approach the combat area with their undercarriages lowered, giving the impression that they were slower I-15s or I-152s and inviting the Japanese to attack. The Ki-27s suffered heavy losses before their pilots realized what was happening.

Combats over the Khalkhin-Gol sometimes involved as many as 200 aircraft. The Japanese usually emerged the worse from these encounters; although the Ki-27 could hold its own against the I-153 and was superior to the I-152, it was outclassed in speed and firepower by its most frequent opponent – the I-16, which the Japanese nicknamed *Abu* (Gadfly).

Figures of the air losses sustained by both sides are vague and conflicting. The Russians were reported to have lost 145 aircraft of all types between 11 May and 15 September, when a cease-fire was arranged; the Japanese are said to have lost 600, 200 of them during the last ten days of fighting, but these figures seem over-optimistic. What is certain is that very heavy aircraft losses were suffered by both sides, and particularly by the Japanese. Although there had not been a great deal of difference in terms of skill between Russian and Japanese pilots, the Russian tactics had been better. So had the armament of their aircraft – four machine guns mounted in both the I-16 and I-153, compared to the twin MGs carried by the Ki-27 and A5M.

The air battles over the Khalkhin-Gol produced an interesting and novel incident. On 20 August 1939, five I-16s, led by Lieutenant N.I. Zvonarev and armed with RS-82 air-to-ground rocket projectiles, fired their salvoes of these at a formation of Japanese aircraft and brought down two of them. It was the *first fighter-to-fighter engagement with rocket projectiles*. (Le Prieur rockets in World War I had been used against balloons only.)

Apart from an International Air Squadron comprising British, Dutch and American volunteers and equipped with a motley collection of outclassed aircraft – whose activities ceased when

their base at Hankow was destroyed in 1938 – Russian personnel and aircraft formed the bulwark of China's air defences between 1937 and 1940, although they were withdrawn in August that year following the signing of the non-aggression treaty between the Soviet Union and Germany, Japan's ally.

The Japanese Army Air Force's poor showing in the fighting against the Russians, and the clear superiority of Russian equipment and tactics, led the Japanese High Command to consider the USSR as the principal potential enemy, and equipment planning was influenced by the requirement to be prepared for a renewed conflict on the Manchukuo–Siberia border. New combat aircraft were developed to carry out tactical missions in cold weather, so that they were poorly suited to long overwater missions among the Pacific islands in the war of 1941-45. The Imperial Japanese Navy, on the other hand, bore the brunt of long-range operations against Chinese targets, the aircraft industry developing bombers for missions at extreme range and also a fighter capable of escorting them to the target and back. The result was one of the finest fighter aircraft of all time, the Mitsubishi A6M *Zero*.

By the end of 1939 the Japanese Naval Air Arm was probably the most efficient, highly-skilled striking force in the world. Five aircraft carriers – the *Kaga, Akagi, Ryujo, Soryu* and *Hiryu* – were in service, and two more, the *Shokaku* and *Zuikaku*, were building.

# Air War Over Spain, 1936–39

When civil war broke out in Spain in July 1936 there were some 200 military aircraft in the country, most of them obsolete or obsolescent types. Most of these remained in the hands of the *Fuerzas Aereas Españolas*, the air arm of the Republican Government, and only a very few found their way to the Nationalist commanders, General Franco in North Africa and General Mola in northern Spain.

It was the Nationalists who were the first to receive substantial aid from overseas. On 26 July 1936, Franco sent emissaries to Adolf Hitler, who

promised German support for the Nationalist cause, and by the end of the month 85 *Luftwaffe* personnel and six Heinkel He 51 fighters sailed from Hamburg, bound for Cadiz. The ship also carried spare parts for 20 Junkers Ju 52 bomber-transports, which had reached Spain by way of Italy. They were used to transport thousands of Nationalist troops from North Africa to the Spanish mainland, each grossly overladen Ju 52 making up to seven trips a day. Further air re-inforcements for the Nationalists came in August, with the arrival of nine Italian SM.81 bombers and an initial batch of Fiat CR.32 fighters.

Meanwhile, the Soviet Government had been making plans to assist the Republicans by supplying arms and military advisers. By the end of October 1936, 30 Polikarpov I-15 fighters had arrived in Spain, along with 150 Russian personnel. The group included 50 fighter pilots under the command of Colonel Yakob Shmushkievich, who was known as 'General Douglas' throughout Russia's commitment in Spain, and it was in their hands that the I-15 – dubbed *Chato* (Snub-nose) by the Spaniards – made its operational debut on the Madrid front.

The I-15s' first combat over Spain took place on 4 November 1936, when ten fighters, all flown by Russian pilots, attacked an Ro 37 reconnaissance aircraft of the Italian Legion over the Manzanares river. The Ro 37 escaped, but two Fiat CR.32s escorting it were shot down.

The first Russian type to see action over Spain, however, was not the well-tried I-15, but an aircraft which had entered service with the Red Air Force only a matter of weeks before the first batch

*Personnel of the* Kondor Legion *examining a captured Polikarpov R-Z army co-operation aircraft during the Spanish Civil War.*

arrived at Cartagena in mid-October; the fast, twin-engined Tupolev SB-2 bomber. For weeks the SB-2s, which were used for both bombing and reconnaissance, roved virtually at will over Nationalist territory. To deal with them the Nationalist fighter pilots had to evolve a completely new set of tactics; these involved flying standing patrols at 16 500 ft (5029 m) over the front line. As soon as an SB-2 was sighted, the fighter pilots would build up speed in a dive – their only hope of catching the Russian aircraft.

The third Russian aircraft type to enter service in Spain was the Polikarpov I-16 fighter, which went into battle on 15 November 1936, providing air cover for a Republican offensive against Nationalist forces advancing on Valdemoro, Sesena and Equivias. The I-16 – nicknamed *Mosca* (Fly) by the

Republicans and *Rata* (Rat) by the Nationalists – proved markedly superior to the Heinkel He 51. It was also faster than its most numerous Nationalist opponent, the Fiat CR.32, although the Italian fighter was slightly more manoeuvrable and provided a better gun platform. Apart from that, the Nationalists' tactics were better; the Republicans tended to stick to large, tight, unwieldy formations that were easy to spot and hard to handle. During the early stages of their commitment, both I-15s and I-16s were used extensively for ground attack work, but the responsibility for most missions of this kind was gradually undertaken by the fourth Russian type to enter combat in Spain – the Polikarpov R-Z *Natasha*, the attack version of the R-5 reconnaissance biplane.

Meanwhile, as the Russians continued to step up their aid to the Republicans, increasing numbers of German personnel had been arriving in Spain on the Nationalist side. Their presence was kept a closely-guarded secret. *Luftwaffe* personnel posted for a tour with the Condor Legion – as the German contingent was known – reported to a secret office in Berlin where they were issued with civilian clothing, Spanish currency and papers. They then left for Döberitz, where they joined a *Kraft durch Freude* (Strength through Joy) tour ostensibly bound for Genoa via Hamburg.

The main body of the Condor Legion sailed for Spain during the last days of November 1936. It consisted of three fighter squadrons equipped with He 51s, four bomber-transport squadrons operating Junkers Ju 52/3ms, a reconnaissance squadron equipped with Heinkel He 70s, a seaplane squadron operating He 59s and He 60s, six anti-aircraft batteries, four signals companies and one repair section. After settling in, the Legion began a series of bombing raids on Mediterranean ports held by the Republicans, but the Ju 52s encountered severe icing difficulties over the Sierra Nevada and were later transferred to Melilla in Spanish Morocco, from where they made attacks across the straits. One of the most active elements of the Condor Legion was *Jagdgruppe* J/88, comprising the three He 51-equipped squadrons. However, the Heinkel fighter's limitations soon became apparent; it proved incapable of intercepting the Republican SB-2 bombers even under the most favourable conditions and was forced to avoid combat with I-15s and I-16s. By the spring of 1937 the He 51 could no longer carry out its task as a fighter without suffering unacceptable losses, and from March onwards, fitted with bomb racks, it was confined to close support duties.

Throughout the spring of 1937 the Republicans, thanks to the influx of Soviet aircraft, retained air superiority over the vital Madrid battlefront. They had concentrated some 200 I-15s, I-16s, R-Zs and SB-2s in the Madrid area, and the five fighter squadrons assigned to the Jarama sector inflicted heavy losses on the Nationalist Ju 52 units engaged there. Following the failure of the Nationalist offensive at Jarama, the Republican Air Arm was substantially reorganized, with many of the I-15 and I-16 squadrons which had hitherto been staffed exclusively by Russian personnel now being turned over to the Spaniards. The first all-Spanish I-16 unit was *Grupo* 21, which began to exchange its Breguet XIXs for *Ratas* just in time to take part in the final stage of the Republican counter-attack. The other I-16 squadron which featured prominently in the strafing attacks on the Nationalists was a Red Air Force unit based at Barajas, which was also the base of the Voluntary International Squadron commanded by André Malraux and equipped with I-15s.

By the summer of 1936 there were 13 Republican fighter squadrons – six of I-16s and seven of I-15s – opposing eleven Nationalist, ten of which were equipped with Fiat CR.32s. The 11th Nationalist fighter squadron, the Condor Legion's 1 *Staffel*, J/88, had just received the first examples of a combat aircraft which was to become one of the most famous fighters of all time: the Messerschmitt Bf 109. The Bf 109 ultimately equipped three Nationalist squadrons.

In July 1937 bitter fighting raged in the Brunete sector, on the extreme left of the Nationalist Madrid Army Corps, following a massive attack by Government forces. Some of the biggest air battles of the war raged over the front, with large formations of Republican fighters patrolling the battle area. One of the I-15 squadrons began operations as a night-fighter unit during this period, although it also continued to fly daylight missions. By 25 July the battle for Brunete was virtually over, with the town firmly in Nationalist hands; their victory was made all the more noteworthy by the fact that the Republicans had retained air superiority throughout, the Nationalists having laboured under the dual handicap of inferior numbers and, for the most part, worn-out aircraft.

In August 1937 the Nationalists concentrated most of their air force in the north, in support of their army's offensive against Santander, and during two weeks of fighting the Republicans lost almost the whole of their fighter force in this sector, two squadrons of *Ratas* and two of *Chatos*. However, when the Republicans launched a new offensive at Belchite, on the Aragon front, there were still plenty of aircraft to support it, and here the Nationalists suffered a reverse. Despite this, Franco's forces were victorious on the northern front, where the final Nationalist offensive began in October 1937. By the end of the month the Republican fighter force had been virtually destroyed, only four aircraft – three I-15s and one I-16 – surviving the air battles and ground attacks. The loss of the Republican fighter strength in the north was critical, for it gave the Nationalists overall air superiority for the first time, with 15 fighter squadrons against twelve. This was demonstrated during the battle of Teruel, which raged from December 1937 until February 1938, when packs of Nationalist fighters roved deep into enemy territory with orders to seek out the Republican formations and engage them in combat. Thanks to these tactics, the Republicans were forced on to the defensive right from the start.

By the spring of 1938 the Nationalists were on the offensive everywhere and now air superiority was firmly in their grasp. To add to the Republicans' problems, Soviet personnel were being withdrawn from Spain in growing numbers, the Russian-manned squadrons being progressively handed over to the Spaniards as Soviet crews were recalled. The battles of the summer of 1938 saw the struggle in the air intensify, with losses on both sides, but the Nationalists never lost their superiority. For the first time, the Condor Legion's Me 109s were operating at their full strength of three squadrons, now using a tactical formation devised in the preceding months and known as the *Schwarm* (swarm). This comprised four aircraft, made up of two sections of two known as the *Rotte*, a word having numerous military meanings such as company and file, but best translated in this context as pair. The aircraft were positioned about 650 ft (200 m) apart, the four assuming a formation that resembled the tips of the fingers when spread out flat and controlled with the aid of FuG 7 radio telephony equipment. This loose formation, which enabled one fighter to protect another's tail, was found to be ideal for aerial combat and was to bring the *Luftwaffe* tactical air superiority in the early months of World War II.

*Aircraft of the* Kondor Legion *stage a victory flypast over Barcelona, March 1939.*

The Spanish Civil War, which ended in March 1939 with the surrender of Madrid to Franco's forces, brought the Germans immeasurable experience in air combat tactics – experience which their allies, the Italians, somehow failed to assimilate. The Italians, like the Republicans, persisted in operating in large, unwieldy formations that left little room for individual action, and paid the price in terms of losses.

It was in Spain, too, that the Germans tested their new generation of bomber types, the Heinkel He 111 and the Dornier Do 17, and also the Junkers Ju 87 *Stuka* dive-bomber, whose limited operations in Spain laid the foundations of the *Blitzkrieg* (lightning war) close support tactics that were to prove so effective in Poland and the Battle of France. The He 111s, Do 17s and the Italian SM.79 bombers, because of their relatively high performance, suffered light losses during daylight operations, with the result that both German and Italian designers paid little attention to defensive armament. It was an omission that was to cost the *Luftwaffe* and *Regia Aeronautica* dearly when they came up against the RAF's eight-gun fighters.

# 4
# THE SECOND WORLD WAR 1939–45

## THE POLISH CAMPAIGN, SEPTEMBER 1939

WHEN, shortly after 4 a.m. on 1 September 1939, it was reported that German reconnaissance aircraft were flying over Polish territory, the news came as no surprise to the Polish General Staff. Political unrest during the previous months following the Germans' denunciation of their 1934 non-aggression treaty with Poland, coming as it did in the wake of the Nazi annexation of Czechoslovakia, had given the Poles ample notice of Hitler's intention to invade, and plans to resist an invasion had already been in force for several weeks.

On 29 August all Polish operational squadrons had been moved from their peacetime bases to specially prepared secret airfields. But the defensive preparations came too late. Because of high-level bungling and the firm belief of the Polish High Command that a major European war was unlikely to begin before 1941 or 1942, plans for the expansion and modernization of the Polish Air Force had been delayed time and again, with the result that when Poland did go to war it was without modern aircraft or reserves and with critical shortages of fuel, spares and ammunition.

The last pre-war expansion scheme had been approved by the Polish Government in 1936 – to be put into effect in 1941. It envisaged a total of 78 operational squadrons with 642 first-line aircraft and 100 per cent reserves. The force was to consist of 15 interceptor squadrons, each with ten fighters; ten twin-engined heavy fighter squadrons with ten aircraft each; 14 light bomber-reconnaissance squadrons, each with ten aircraft; 21 bomber squadrons, each with six aircraft; and 18 army co-operation squadrons, each with seven aircraft.

Home-produced combat aircraft were to be the backbone of the force, and Poland's new types were as good as any in the world. They were to include 300 P-50 *Jastrzeb* (Hawk) fighters, 300 P-46 *Sum* (Swordfish) bombers, 180 P-37 *Los* (Elk) medium bombers, 200 LWS-3 *Mewa* (Gull) army cooperation aircraft, a number of twin-engined *Wilk* (Wolf) heavy fighters and dive-bombers, and some 200 training aircraft.

Then came the blow; the government announced cuts in the military budget, and the whole expansion scheme was placed in peril. Air Force Commander General Rayski resigned, and his post was taken over by General Kalkus, who immediately cancelled the order for the 300 *Jastrzebs* on the grounds that the prototypes had proved to be badly underpowered, and ordered more obsolete PZL P-11s to make up for the deficiency.

During 1939, the maximum monthly output of the Polish aircraft industry was about 160 machines; with careful planning and shift work, the figure could have been doubled at any time. Yet right up to the outbreak of war, Poland's newest and largest factory – PZL WP-2 at Mielec, which was capable of producing 450 aircraft a year – employed only a skeleton staff engaged in completing a handful of *Los* bombers transferred from another factory. Incredibly, combat aircraft were still being exported to

# 1939

**1 September** 04.45 a.m.: three Junkers Ju 87B *Stukas* of III/*Stuka-Geschwader* 1 (StG 1), flying from Elbing, made a low-level attack on the steel bridges spanning the River Vistula at Dirschau. The bridges were to have been seized by the German 7th Paratroop Division, but the planned air drop was frustrated by fog. The *Stukas'* task was to destroy strongpoints from which detonation charges would be fired by Polish engineers. The

---

Bulgaria, Turkey and Romania while the Polish Air Force desperately needed new machines.

At the end of August 1939, the Polish Air Force possessed some 436 operational aircraft and a personnel strength of 15 000 men. In the spring of 1939 the first-line units had been reorganized around a combat nucleus consisting of a pursuit and a bomber brigade under the direct command of the Commander-in-Chief of the Polish armed forces, the remainder being split up among the six Polish Army regions. The Pursuit Brigade, whose main task was the defence of Warsaw, was equipped with four squadrons of P-11C fighters and one squadron of even older P-7As; eight more P-11C and two more P-7A squadrons served with the Army Air Force. The Bomber Brigade operated four and a half squadrons of *Los* bombers – a total of 36 aircraft – and five squadrons of *Karas* (Carp) light bombers.

In the event of a German invasion, plans had been laid to rush British and French squadrons to Poland's aid; apart from helping indirectly by bombing targets in Germany, the RAF was to send 10 Fairey Battle light bombers and a squadron of Hawker Hurricane fighters to Polish bases, while the French planned to send five bomber squadrons.

But the expected help never arrived. The overwhelming swiftness of the German *Blitzkrieg* destroyed all hope of that.

On 31 August 1939, the *Luftwaffe* Order of Battle against Poland included 648 bombers, 219 dive-bombers, 30 ground-attack aircraft and 210 fighters, together with 474 reconnaissance, transport and miscellaneous types, divided between *Luftflotten* 1 and 4.

---

three aircraft dropped three 550 lb (250 kg) and twelve 110 lb (50 kg) bombs on their targets. The *Luftwaffe's* first mission of the war was only a partial success, as one of the bridges was blown soon afterwards. The raid was led by *Oberleutnant* Bruno Dilley. An hour later, the strongpoints were attacked again by a flight of Dornier Do 17Z bombers of III/*Kampfgeschwader* 3 (KG 3) from Heiligenbeil.

As the morning fog cleared, 36 Henschel Hs 123 ground-attack biplanes of II/*Lehrgeschwader* 2 (LG 2) bombed and strafed Polish positions in the village of Pryzstain. This was the first instance in World War II that the *Luftwaffe* carried out direct support operations in conjunction with ground forces.

Sixty Heinkel He 111s of I and III/KG 4 dropped 48 tons of bombs on airfields in the Cracow area. Later, further attacks on these targets were made by Ju 87 *Stukas* of StG 1 and Dornier Do 17s of KG 76 and KG 77. The bombers were escorted by Messerschmitt Bf 110s of I/*Zerstörergeschwader* 76 (ZG 76). In another attack, *Stukas* of StG 2 encountered PZL P.11C fighters of the Polish Air Force's 111/2 *Dyon* (squadron) which had taken off to intercept the Heinkels of KG 4. One P.11C was shot down by a *Stuka*; another P.11C (Lieutenant W. Gnys) destroyed two Dornier Do 17s of KG 77.

In the afternoon, a Polish cavalry brigade, advancing towards the German frontier from Wielun, was heavily attacked by *Stukas* of StG 1 and StG 2, followed by Dornier Do 17s of KG 77. The destruction of the cavalry brigade was complete after 90 sorties.

By the end of the first day's fighting, the Polish Pursuit Brigade had claimed 14 enemy aircraft destroyed, but the Brigade had lost half its effective strength.

**2 September** Continued attacks by *Stukas* inflicted further heavy losses on Polish ground forces. Airfields in the Deblin area were attacked by 88 Heinkel He 111s of KG 4 and Bf 110s of ZG 76. Following the airfield attacks, various *Luftwaffe* units struck at lines of communication, supply and ammunition dumps and also bombed Polish harbour installations, warships and coastal batteries. Polish fighters registered some successes, but continued to sustain unacceptable losses.

At about noon, 18 *Karas* light bombers of the 64th and 65th *Dyon* attacked concentrations of German armour on the northern front. Seven *Karas* were shot down and three more were destroyed on landing.

**3 September** 11 a.m.: Great Britain declared war on Germany.

5 p.m.: France declared war on Germany.

**4 September** Polish fighter aircraft destroyed a number of German army co-operation aircraft in the Lodz sector, but 11 P.11s were shot down in combats with Messerschmitt Bf 109s of I/ZG 2.

The 1st and 4th Panzer Divisions suffered severe dislocation as a result of attacks by *Los* bombers of the Polish Bomber Brigade, followed by *Karas* bombers of the 21st, 22nd and 55th *Dyon*. Between 2 and 5 September the Bomber Brigade mounted nine major attacks on German armour and supply columns, but no fighter cover was available and the bombers suffered crippling losses.

**6 September** At the end of the first week of fighting, Polish fighter pilots had claimed 105 victories, 63 by army units and 42 by the Pursuit Brigade. Their own losses were 79 fighters.

**9–12 September** With the German armies about to complete a pincer movement around the Polish capital, Warsaw, the Poles launched a final counter-attack on the River Bzura, aimed at the exposed flank of the German 8th Army. As the threat developed, General von Rundstedt, commanding Army Group South, called for a maximum air effort. Between 9 and 12 September, massed dive-bomber attacks were launched from forward airstrips. The impetus of the Polish attack was halted by the destruction of bridges over the Bzura and then its main elements broken up by two days of concentrated air attacks by *Stukas*, Heinkels, Dorniers and Henschel Hs 123s. The 200 000 troops of the Army of Poznan were isolated, surrounded and subjected to almost continual air attack until their surrender on 19 September.

**12 September** From this date onwards, the *Luftwaffe* began withdrawing large numbers of bombers, dive-bombers and fighters from Poland in readiness for possible future operations in the west.

**13 September** The *Luftwaffe* carried out the first phase of 'Operation Seaside' (*Unternehmen Seebad*), the mass attack on Warsaw. A total of 183 bombers and *Stukas* attacked the north-west district of the city, causing severe damage.

**14/15 September** Final air defence sorties were flown over Warsaw by the 'Deblin Group', a unit composed of PZL P-7 fighters, the surviving P.11Cs and the prototype PZL P-24, whose pilot (Lieutenant Hwyk Szczesny) destroyed two enemy bombers.

**17 September** In accordance with a secret German–Soviet agreement on the partition of Poland, Soviet forces invaded the country from the east. Airfields in that sector were strafed by Russian fighter-bombers. The final German aircraft destroyed by a Polish pilot during the campaign was shot down by Lieutenant Tadeusz Koc.

**18 September** The remnants of the Polish Air Force were evacuated to Romania. Among the aircraft that got away were 39 *Los* and 15 *Karas* bombers; these were impressed by the Romanian Air Force and later, ironically, fought on the side of Germany during the invasion of Russia. Thirty-eight fighter aircraft, many of them damaged and only just airworthy, were also evacuated.

A total of 327 aircraft were lost by the Polish Air Force during the campaign. Of these, 260 were lost in action; air-to-air combat losses were around 70, the remainder being destroyed on the ground. Aircrew losses were 234.

The *Luftwaffe*, for its part, lost 285 aircraft, of which about 90 were claimed by anti-aircraft fire. Polish fighter pilots claimed 126 victories, but in view of the overall German loss figure their actual score must have been much greater. In addition, over 200 German aircraft were so badly damaged that they had to be withdrawn from operations. The campaign revealed that German bombers were deficient in armour plating and defensive armament, and steps were taken to remedy this – although the resulting extra weight led to a notable decrease in performance, particularly in the case of the Dornier Do 17.

**25 September** Beginning at 8 a.m., and following the dropping of propaganda leaflets urging the garrison of Warsaw to surrender, 400 bombers – including eight *Stukagruppen* – attacked the city in relays. Thirty Junkers Ju 52s were also employed as makeshift bombers, their crews shovelling incendiary bombs through the open loading doors. By the end of the day, 500 tons of high explosive and 72 tons of incendiaries had been dropped on Warsaw, whose garrison surrendered on 27 September. On the same day the garrison at Modlin also capitulated, the town having been subjected to severe air raids for 36 hours. The last organized Polish resistance ended on 5 October.

While the Polish campaign developed, Britain prepared for war.

**2 September** The first echelon of the AASF – ten squadrons totalling 160 Fairey Battle light bombers – deployed to French airfields. It was followed by the Air Component of the BEF, comprising four squadrons of Lysanders, four of Blenheims, two of Hurricanes and two of Gladiators. Two more Hurricane squadrons were also deployed to provide fighter support for the AASF.

**3 September** Following Britain's declaration of war on Germany, a Bristol Blenheim of No. 139 Sqn, RAF Wyton, carried out a photographic reconnaissance of the German naval base at Wilhelmshaven – the RAF's first operational sortie over Germany in World War II.

**3/4 September** The first *Nickel* (leaflet-dropping) operation was flown by the RAF over Germany, three Whitleys of No. 51 Sqn and seven of No. 58 Sqn dropping over 6 million leaflets (13 tons) over Hamburg, Bremen and the Ruhr. Three aircraft made emergency landings in France with engine trouble.

**4 September** Five Blenheims of No. 107 Sqn and five of No. 110, RAF Wattisham, attacked German warships at Wilhelmshaven; hits were registered on the battleship *Admiral Scheer* but the bombs failed to explode. Five Blenheims failed to return (FTR), all shot down by flak. Later, Wellingtons of Nos. 9 and 149 Sqns made an inconclusive attack on warships in the Elbe estuary. Two of No. 9 Sqn's aircraft FTR, one being shot down by *Unteroffizier* Alfred Held in a Bf 109 of III/JG 77 from Nordholz. It was the *Luftwaffe*'s first victory against the RAF.

**5 September** An Avro Anson of No. 500 Sqn, RAF Detling, made the first attack of the war on a U-Boat in the North Sea, claiming a possible kill.

**Above:**
*RAF Bomber Command's first operations over Germany involved leaflet dropping. Here, an airman loads a bundle of propaganda leaflets into the chute aboard a Whitley of No. 102 Sqn.*

**Below:**
*A Bristol Blenheim IV of No. 139 Sqn RAF, the first unit to make a reconnaissance flight over German territory in World War II.*

# THE 'PHONEY WAR'
# SEPTEMBER 1939–APRIL 1940

THE term 'phoney war' was coined by a United States Senator. He was referring to the apparent stalemate on the Western Front in the closing months of 1939. For the air forces of both sides, however, it was anything but. Before September was out, reconnaissance aircraft were suffering losses and major air battles were developing over the Maginot Line, France's static line of defence along her eastern frontier, as the *Luftwaffe* began a sparring match with the RAF and the *Armée de l'Air* that was to be halted, albeit temporarily, by the onset of winter.

On 3 September 1939, the *Luftwaffe* mustered some 1300 aircraft on Germany's western frontier in *Luftflotten* 2 and 3. These included 336 Messerschmitt Bf 109Ds and 109Es in 26 *Jagdstaffeln*, 180 Bf 109Cs, 109Ds and 110s in five *Zerstörergruppen*, and 280 medium bombers in nine *Kampfgruppen*. There were also about 100 Junkers Ju 87s organized in three *Stukagruppen*, while 26 more fighter squadrons, some of them newly formed, were based deeper in Germany for air defence.

In September 1939, France's fighter aviation was beginning to shake off the shackles of obsolescence which had bound it for so long, although the process of expansion and modernization was painfully slow. Effective first-line strength was less than 400 machines; this total included 225 Morane-Saulnier MS 406s,

rugged cannon-armed monoplanes which equipped four *Escadres de Chasse*. In terms of all-round performance, the Morane was inferior to its British and German counterparts, the Hawker Hurricane and Messerschmitt Bf 109E.

The *Armée de l'Air*'s other first-line type was an American fighter, the Curtiss Hawk 75A. By the beginning of September 1939 100 of these were operational with two *Escadres de Chasse*. French pilots spoke highly of the Hawk's handling qualities; it had a longer range and climbed faster than the Morane 406, although its armament of three machine guns left a lot to be desired. Two new fighter types, the Bloch 151 and the Dewoitine 520, were eagerly awaited, but it would be the end of the year before the first of these – the Bloch – became operational.

The French bomber force was totally ill-equipped to wage modern warfare. Of the 399 bombers in service, only five – Lioré et Olivier LeO 451s – could be classed as modern. Most of the bomber groups were equipped with obsolete, fixed-undercarriage types such as the Bloch 200 and Amior 143; apart from the LeO 451, the only French medium bomber with a retractable undercarriage was the Bloch MB 210,

*The Bloch 151 fighter was about to enter service with the* Armée de l'Air *on the outbreak of World War II.*

# FINLAND'S AIR WAR

ON 30 November 1939, as Allied and German fighter pilots sparred with one another in the early engagements of the Western Front's 'Phoney War', a savage conflict broke out in the far north between the Soviet Union and Finland. The small Finnish Air Force operated a miscellany of combat aircraft, the most modern of which were 31 Dutch-built Fokker D.XXI monoplanes with fixed, spatted undercarriages; the other 120 or so available aircraft included Fokker C.Xs and C.VEs, Blackburn Ripon floatplanes, Junkers K.43s and Bristol Bulldogs.

Against these, the Red Army Air Force had four bomber and two fighter brigades totalling about 750 aircraft. The bomber and reconnaissance units were equipped with SB-2s, TB-3s, DB-3s, Polikarpov R-5s and R-Zs; the main equipment of the fighter units was the I-15 and I-152, with only a small number of I-153s and I-16s. Because of their conviction that there would be no serious opposition from the Finns, the Russians had not thought it necessary to commit their more modern fighter types to the battle.

Despite the odds against it, the Finnish Air Force proved a formidable opponent, just as the Finnish Army did on the ground. By mid-December the Russian offensive had been halted and the Red Air Force, its casualties mounting, switched its attacks from towns and communications to Finnish airfields, whereupon the Finns began operating from frozen  s.

Early in the new year a Swedish volunteer squadron, *Flygflottilj* 19, joined the Finns in action; equipped with 12 Gloster Gladiators and four Hawker Harts, it operated from a frozen lake at Kemi.

Although over 150 targets in Finland were repeatedly bombed by the Red Air Force, the latter completely failed to achieve its primary objective, which was the neutralization of a large part of the Finnish war effort. Because of the inefficiency of their navigation and poor bombing accuracy, the Russians persisted in daylight attacks until the very end of the campaign, and it cost them dearly. By the time an armistice brought the 'Winter War' to an end on 12 March 1940, 280 Russian aircraft had been shot down by Finnish and Swedish fighters, and a further 314 had been destroyed by anti-aircraft fire. Against this staggering total the Finns lost only 62 aircraft in combat, although 69 more were so badly damaged that they could no longer operate.

The Soviet–Finnish War was notable for one thing: the first large-scale use of airborne forces. On several occasions, commandos and saboteurs were dropped behind the Finnish lines, and two airborne brigades were used in action against the Mannerheim Line – Finland's principal defensive line – and in attacks on Petsamo in the far north. The airborne assaults lacked both planning and cohesion, and could not be considered successful.

shot down a Heinkel He 111. The day's operations confirmed the value of the fighter defence sector scheme.

**29 November** A Heinkel He 111 of KG 26 crash-landed in a field near Haddington, Lothian, after repeated attacks by Spitfires of Nos. 602 and 603 Sqns, R⁁ urnhouse. This was the first enemy ll on the British mainland in the 1939–4  War. Both enemy gunners were killed, the pilot wounded and the navigator unhurt.

**3 December** 24 Vickers Wellingtons of Nos. 38, 115 and 149 Sqns set out to attack German warships in the Heligoland Bight. During the attack, a bomb which had become hung up dropped away and scored a direct hit on a German AA battery on

shore; this is believed to be the first British bomb to fall on Germany in World War II, albeit accidentally. All the bombers returned to base.

**12 December** RAF Bomber Command inaugurated offensive patrols against enemy seaplane bases on the islands of Sylt, Borkum and Norderney as a countermeasure against minelaying operations off the British coast by Heinkel He 115 floatplanes. These offensive patrols were undertaken at first by Whitleys, and later by Hampdens.

**14 December** 12 Wellingtons of No. 99 Sqn took off from Newmarket to attack the German cruisers *Nürnberg* and *Leipzig*, which had been damaged by a British submarine and were limping back to the Jade Estuary. The bombers were intercepted

# SELF-SEALING FUEL TANKS

ONE of the most important lessons absorbed by the *Luftwaffe* from its experiences in the Spanish Civil War was the extreme vulnerability of light alloy aircraft fuel tanks to bullets and shell fragments. In the worst case, red-hot ammunition might ignite the layer of fuel vapour above the liquid, causing explosion and fire; at best, fuel might be lost at such a rapid rate that the aircraft would be forced down. The German response to the problem was to construct fuel tanks of compressed cellulose fibre with 2 mm thick walls and an outer covering comprising a series of layers; 3 mm of chrome leather, 3 mm of unvulcanized rubber, two layers of lightly vulcanized rubber 0.5 mm thick and an outer layer of highly vulcanized rubber, 3 mm thick. When the tank wall was pierced and fuel ran out, a chemical reaction occurred, causing the layer of unvulcanized rubber to swell up and seal the hole. In September 1939 only the *Luftwaffe* was equipped with self-sealing tanks; the RAF suffered a series of tragic and unnecessary losses before it, too, learned the lesson.

by Bf 109s of II/JG 77 and five were shot down, a sixth crash-landing at Newmarket. Despite this disaster, further daylight attacks against German naval forces were authorized.

*18 December* 24 Wellingtons of Nos. 9, 37 and 149 Sqns were despatched with orders to patrol the Schillig Roads, Wilhelmshaven and the Jade Estuary and to attack any warships sighted. The bombers were detected by two experimental German *Freya* radar stations on Heligoland and Wangerooge, and soon afterwards were attacked by Bf 109s and Bf 110s of JG 26, JG 77 and ZG 76. Twelve Wellingtons were shot down. At the subsequent post-mortem, it was established that some of the bombers had caught fire very quickly after being hit, and as a result priority was given to the fitting of self-sealing fuel tanks to No. 3 Group's

*Vickers Wellington bombers suffered heavy casualties in early daylight attacks on German naval bases. Photograph shows aircraft of No. 9 Sqn.*

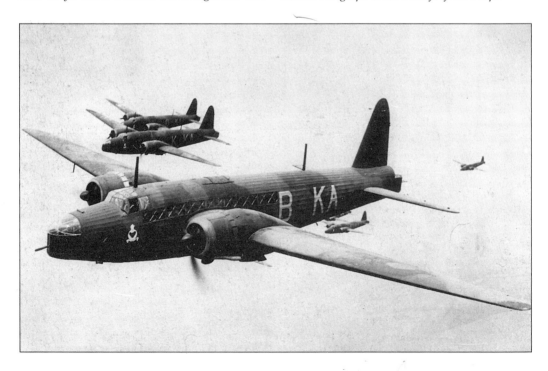

Wellington force. As a result of this raid, daylight armed reconnaissances in the Heligoland Bight area were suspended and emphasis placed on the development of night bombing techniques. Nos. 3 and 5 Groups (Wellingtons and Hampdens) were ordered to take part in *Nickel* operations to give their crews night flying experience.

# 1940

**1 January** The RAF introduced coded IFF (Identification Friend or Foe) signals to identify Bomber, Coastal and Fighter Command aircraft. VHF (Very High Frequency) installations were also completed in eight selected sectors. Service operational trials of VHF radio had been held at RAF Duxford in October 1939.

**11 January** A Messerschmitt 108 communications aircraft, carrying a *Luftflotte* 2 staff officer to a conference in Cologne, went off course and landed in Belgium. The staff officer carried the operational plans for a German offensive on the West-

*HM King George VI inspects Hurricanes of No. 85 Sqn and Gladiators and Blenheims of the BEF Air Component in France during the 'Phoney War' period.*

ern Front. The documents were examined by Allied intelligence experts, who concluded that they were fakes.

**12/13 January** Whitleys of No. 77 Sqn, operating from an advanced base at Villeneuve, dropped leaflets for the first time over Prague and Vienna.

By the end of January, 14 Hudsons and one Sunderland of RAF Coastal Command had been fitted with ASV (Air to Surface Vessel) Mk I radar detection sets. Although the development of ASV radar had begun in the 1930s, as a natural progression of the work undertaken by Robert Watson-Watt and other scientists on RDF (ships were detectable on an experimental set fitted to a Handley Page Heyford bomber in 1936), it was not until 1940 that real strides began to be taken in refining and evaluating ASV techniques and equipment. In December 1939 the first airborne radar detection of a submarine was made off Gosport at an unrecorded but very short range.

In January and February 1940, operations everywhere in north-west Europe and the North Sea area were severely hampered by bad weather. Bomber and Coastal Commands continued to carry out armed reconnaissances over the North Sea and there were a few attacks on enemy shipping, with inconclusive results. Then, as the weather began to clear in March, there was a sharp increase in aerial activity on both sides.

**1 March** Two Dornier Do 17 reconnaissance aircraft were destroyed within minutes of each other by French pilots of GC II/7 and GC III/6.

**7/8 March** For the first time, leaflets were dropped over Poznan, Poland, by a Whitley of No. 77 Sqn, operating from Villeneuve.

**11 March** A Bristol Blenheim of No. 82 Sqn, RAF Watton, piloted by Squadron Leader M.V. Dunlap, attacked and sank the submarine U-31, which was surprised on the surface in the Schillig Roads.

**16 March** A small force of *Luftwaffe* bombers attacked Scapa Flow. Some bombs again fell on the island of Hoy, this time killing a civilian. By way of retaliation, Bomber Command was authorized to carry out its first bombing attack against an enemy land target: the seaplane base of Hörnum, on the island of Sylt. Hitherto, attacks had been restricted to the bombing of flarepaths on the water.

**19/20 March** 26 Whitleys of Nos. 10, 51, 77 and 102 Sqns and 15 Hampdens of Nos. 44, 50, 61 and 144 Sqns, out of a total force of 50 aircraft despatched, attacked the German seaplane base at Hörnum. Whitley Mk V N1380 'R–Robert' (Squadron Leader J.C. Macdonald) of No. 102 Sqn became the first RAF bomber to attack a German land target in World War II. The aircraft flew singly to the target and bombed from levels varying between 1000 and 10 000 ft (305–3050 m), dropping 40 500 lb (225

kg), 84 250 lb (112 kg) bombs and 1200 incendiaries. One Whitley FTR. Post-attack reconnaissance revealed no damage to the target, and this led to a serious reappraisal of Bomber Command's night navigation and bombing techniques.

During the last days of March, enemy air activity over the Western Front was devoted mainly to reconnaissance, although packs of fighters patrolled the front line and became increasingly aggressive. Sometimes, two or three squadrons of Messerschmitts carried out sweeps over French territory as far as Metz or Nancy. Long-range Messerschmitt Bf 110 fighters were now appearing in increasing numbers; these usually stayed up very high and only engaged in combat when pressed by Allied fighters. The indications were that the *Luftwaffe* was experimenting with new battle formations and offensive tactics.

**4 April** A Blenheim reconnaissance aircraft of No. 139 Sqn reported a large concentration of German warships and merchant vessels assembled in the Schillig Roads. Six Blenheims of No. 2 Group were despatched to attack them, but without result. Further air reconnaissance the next day revealed that the ships had gone.

**6 April** Air reconnaissance reported major units of the German Fleet, including the battle cruisers *Scharnhorst* and *Gneisenau*, assembling at Wilhelmshaven. Bomber crews returning from *Nickel* operations over north-west Germany reported sighting convoys of vehicles, headlights full on, heading towards the north German ports.

**7 April** Blenheim crews on armed reconnaissance over the North Sea sighted an enemy cruiser and four destroyers. The warships were shadowed, and a few minutes later the main body of the German Fleet was located about 76 miles (122 km) NNW of Horns Reef. The Blenheims attacked a cruiser, believed to be either the *Scharnhorst* or *Gneisenau*, but with no result. A squadron of Wellingtons sent out that afternoon failed to locate the warships, and further sorties were frustrated by bad weather.

**8 April** A Short Sunderland of No. 204 Sqn, RAF Sullom Voe (Shetland Islands), located and reported the crusier *Hipper* and four destroyers heading for Trondheim.

**9 April** A Sunderland of No. 204 Sqn confirmed that German naval forces had entered Trondheimsfjord. A third Sunderland of No. 204 Sqn, despatched to check on enemy naval activity near Oslo, failed to return. There was no longer any doubt that the German invasion of Norway had begun.

*Fairey Battles of No. 88 Sqn, flanked by Curtiss Hawk 75As of GC I/5 over France, early 1940. The Battles suffered appalling losses during the Battle of France.*

# The Norwegian Campaign
## April–June 1940

*9 April* 6.15 a.m.: In the first phase of Operation *Weserübung* (Weser Crossing), German paratroops were dropped on key points in Denmark, including Aalborg airfield, by Junkers Ju 52 transports. Other paratroops were dropped later in the morning on the Norwegian airfields of Oslo–Fornebu and Stavanger–Sola. The transport aircraft were escorted by Messerschmitt Bf 110s of ZG 76, which were engaged by Gloster Gladiators of the Norwegian Army Air Force. The Gladiators, completely outclassed, suffered heavy losses and the survivors were withdrawn to the north. Most were written off while attempting to land on frozen lakes.

In conjunction with the airborne landings, *Luftwaffe* bombers and dive-bombers attacked Norwegian airfields and also strongpoints commanding Oslo Fjord. Towards noon, units of the British Fleet off Bergen were attacked by 41 Heinkel He 111s of KG 26 and 47 Junkers Ju 88s of KG 30. The battleship HMS *Rodney* was hit by a 1000 lb (450 kg) bomb, which failed to explode; the cruisers HMS *Devonshire*, HMS *Southampton* and HMS *Glasgow* were damaged, and the destroyer HMS *Gurkha* was sunk west of Stavanger.

*10 April* Seven Blackburn Skua dive-bombers of No. 800 Sqn, Fleet Air Arm, and nine of No. 803 Sqn, operating from Hatston in the Orkney Islands, attacked and sank the German cruiser *Königsberg* in Bergen harbour. One Skua FTR.

*11 April* Three Wellingtons of No. 115 Sqn, temporarily operating under RAF Coastal Command, attacked Stavanger–Sola airfield – the first British attack on a mainland target. The bombers were escorted by two Blenheim IVs of No. 254 Sqn, Coastal Command. One of the other Wellingtons which did not attack Stavanger was shot down by enemy fighters.

*11/12 April* 23 Whitleys and 20 Hampdens were despatched to attack shipping between Kiel Bay and Oslo. One Whitley scored a direct hit on what was apparently an ammunition ship; it blew up.

*12 April* 36 Wellingtons, 24 Hampdens and 23 Blenheims were despatched to attack shipping at Stavanger in the RAF's biggest bombing operation so far. Six Hampdens and three Wellingtons FTR, and the Germans admitted the loss of five fighters.

*13/14 April* First minelaying operation by the RAF: 15 Hampdens of No. 5 Group (Nos. 44, 49, 50, 61 and 144 Sqns) were despatched to lay mines off the Danish coast. Twelve claimed successful sorties, two aborted and one FTR.

*15–24 April* During this period, Stavanger–Sola airfield was attacked 16 times by aircraft of Bomber Command, Coastal Command and the Fleet Air Arm. One of the best-executed raids was carried out on 17 April by 12 Blenheims of No. 107 Sqn; the bombers attacked in two formations, the first bombing from high level and the second from low level ten seconds later. Minelaying operations continued, and naval operations in Narvik fjord were covered by Fleet Air Arm fighters: Skuas of Nos. 800 and 803 Sqns, and Sea Gladiators of No. 802 Sqn. The latter operated from the carrier HMS *Glorious*, recalled from the Mediterranean. Oslo–Fornebu airfield was also attacked on several occasions by Whitleys, the only Bomber Command aircraft with sufficient range to reach this target.

*24–28 April* In support of land operations by an Anglo-French expeditionary force at Namsos and Andalsnes, 18 Gloster Gladiators of No. 263 Sqn flew off the carrier HMS *Glorious* and began operations from a frozen lake at Lesjaskog. The Gladiators shot down four He 111s and a He 115, but most were destroyed on the ground when the frozen lake was bombed and the squadron was evacuated on 28 April.

*7 May* First operational use of a 2000 lb (900 kg) bomb, dropped by a Bristol Beaufort of RAF Coastal Command near a German cruiser anchored off Norderney.

*22 May* Eight Gladiator IIs of No. 263 Sqn, flying off HMS *Glorious*, arrived at Bardufoss near Narvik to provide air support for the Allies' second Norwegian Expedition. Six more Gladiators flew in the next day.

*26 May* 15 Hawker Hurricanes of No. 46 Sqn flew to Bardufoss from HMS *Glorious* to provide further air support for the Norwegian Expedition. By 28 May, the combined force of Gladiators and Hurricanes had destroyed 19 enemy aircraft; the final tally at the end of the campaign was 36, by which time the RAF fighter force had been reduced to eight Gladiators and ten Hurricanes.

**2 June** The surviving Hurricanes and Gladiators provided air cover for the Expeditionary force, now being evacuated from Narvik under heavy air attack. These operations, during which the RAF fighters claimed their final victories, lasted until first light on **8 June**, when the two squadrons were ordered to embark their remaining aircraft on HMS *Glorious*. All landed-on safely, despite the fact that none of the Hurricane pilots had taken part in deck landing practice, but on the homeward passage the aircraft carrier was intercepted and sunk by the German cruisers *Scharnhorst* and *Gneisenau*. Of the RAF pilots on board, only two – Squadron Leader K.B.B. Cross and Flight Lieutenant Jameson – survived.

# *Blitzkrieg*: The Campaign in the West May–June 1940

**10 May** Between dawn and dusk on 10 May 1940, in support of the German land offensive against France and the Low Countries, the *Luftwaffe* flew more than 1000 individual bombing sorties against targets in France, Belgium and Holland. During the morning, 400 Heinkel He 111s, Dornier Do 17s and Junkers 88s attacked 72 airfields, 47 of them in northern France, in an attempt to wipe out a large proportion of the Allied air forces on the ground. In fact, the *Luftwaffe* failed to achieve more than a fraction of its objectives during this opening phase; in the Northern Zone of Air Operations, only four Allied aircraft were destroyed on the ground in the initial onslaught and 30 or so damaged, while in the Eastern Zone the only real result was obtained by the Dornier Do 17s of KG 2, which destroyed five Amiot 143s of GB II/34 and two RAF Hurricanes. In the course of the day, French fighter pilots claimed 49 victories, including 42 bombers; the BEF Air Component claimed 36 German bombers destroyed, while the AASF's Hurricane squadrons claimed six enemy aircraft shot down. The RAF claims, however, are impossible to verify as most of the squadron records were subsequently lost in the evacuation from the continent.

At first light on 10 May, German airborne forces in 41 DFS 230 assault gliders, towed to their objectives by Ju 52 transports, secured the Belgian fortress of Eben Emael, commanding the Albert Canal south of Maastricht, and the strategic bridges over the River Maas at Vroenbhoven and Veldwezelt. Other airborne operations included the capture by German paratroops of the Moerdijk and Dordrecht bridges in Holland, the seizure of the bridges over the Maas at Rotterdam by special forces carried to the target in He 59 floatplanes, and the securing of strategic crossroads on the Franco–Luxembourg–Belgian border by special forces transported in 123 Fieseler *Storch* aircraft. During the first day of the invasion, the *Luftwaffe* carried out 75 attacks on Belgian airfields, destroying one-third of the Belgian Air Force's first-line strength.

In Holland, paratroops seized the airfield at Waalhaven in the wake of a heavy bombing attack by 27 Heinkel He 111s of II/KG 4, while other German troops were brought in by Ju 52s which landed on the beaches near The Hague. The Ju 52 transports suffered heavily during these operations, accounting for 157 of the 304 aircraft of all types lost by the *Luftwaffe* on 10 May. Heavy losses were also suffered by the Netherlands Army Aviation.

Because of political indecision, the French bomber force was not committed to action on 10 May, but enemy forces in Holland were attacked by 33 Blenheims of No. 2 Group, RAF Bomber Command, which lost three aircraft. In the early afternoon, 32 Fairey Battles of the AASF were despatched to attack enemy columns advancing through Luxembourg. Thirteen Battles failed to return, falling victim to the German mobile 20 mm *Flakvierling* (quadruple AA) batteries. Ten more Battles were shot down by fighters later in the afternoon.

**10/11 May** Eight Whitleys of Nos. 77 and 102 Sqns attacked enemy communications in Germany west of the Rhine – the first raid by the RAF on mainland Germany.

**11 May** Eight Fairey Battles of Nos. 88 and 218

# THE BOMBING OF ROTTERDAM

O N 14 May 1940, Rotterdam city centre was destroyed by a German air attack. The action, which cost the lives of 814 Dutch civilians, caused a huge outcry in neutral countries and provided the Allies with valuable propaganda. In fact, the attack might have been avoided had it not been for an unfortunate chain of circumstances.

By the time 100 Heinkel He 111s of KG 54 took off from their airfields in the Bremen area to carry out the attack, a Dutch delegation was on its way to Rotterdam to discuss surrender terms. General Rudolf Schmidt, commanding the German 39th Corps, who had orders to avoid unnecessary casualties among Dutch

civilians, had sent a signal to *Luflotte* 2 calling off the raid; unfortunately, various delays meant that by the time the signal was received, the Heinkels were already approaching the Dutch border. To complicate matters further, the radio operators on board the bombers had closed down their stations and taken up combat stations in the under-fuselage machine gun blisters, so that radio signals failed to reach them. German ground forces fired red flares as an abort signal as the bombers approached Rotterdam, but these were invisible in dust and haze until the first 57 aircraft had released their bomb loads. The remaining Heinkels returned to base with their bombs still on board.

Sqns attempted to attack enemy columns in Luxembourg. Seven Battles FTR. No. 114 (Blenheim) Sqn, AASF, was virtually annihilated on the ground in a low-level raid by Dornier Do 17s. Enemy armoured columns were attacked by ten LeO 451 bombers of GB I/12 and II/12, one of which FTR, and eighteen Breguet 693s of GBA I/54 and II/54, eight of which FTR. The bridges at Vroenhoven, Veldwezelt and Briedgen were attacked by nine Fairey Battles of the Belgian Air Force's 5/III/3 squadron; six were shot down before reaching the target. The bridges were attacked in turn by the LeO 451s of GB I/12 and II/12, which lost one aircraft, and twelve Blenheims of Nos. 21 and 110 Sqns RAF, which lost four.

**11/12 May** Lines of communication in Germany were attacked by 18 Whitleys and 18 Hampdens of RAF Bomber Command; the airfield of Bonn–Hangelar was attacked by the Amiot 143s of GB I/34 and II/34, the first French night bombing raid of the campaign.

**12 May** In an attack on the Maas bridges, four out of five Fairey Battles of No. 112 Sqn RAF were shot down. Flying Officer D.E. Garland and Sergeant T. Gray were later posthumously awarded the first air Victoria Crosses of World War II.

Curtiss Hawks of the *Armée de l'Air* surprised a formation of Junkers Ju 87 *Stukas* bombing a French armoured column in the Ardennes and destroyed 16 of them. This was perhaps the first real demonstration of the dive-bomber's vulnerability in the face of determined fighter opposition.

Seven out of nine Blenheims of No. 139 Sqn RAF, attempting to attack an enemy armoured column near Tongeren, were shot down by enemy fighters. Before dark, 42 Blenheims of No. 2 Group were despatched to bomb bridges in the Maastricht–Tongeren area; 11 aircraft FTR.

**13–14 May** German forces broke through the French front at Sedan. Between 3 p.m. and 4 p.m. on 14 May, the entire force of available AASF Battles and Blenheims was despatched against pontoon bridges and troop columns in this sector. Out of 71 aircraft involved, 39 were shot down by flak and fighters. It was the highest loss in an operation of similar size ever sustained by the RAF. At dusk, 28 Blenheims of No. 2 Group attacked the pontoons; six FTR.

**15–20 May** With the AASF and the French day bomber force shattered, the brunt of the Allied bombing offensive against the Meuse bridgeheads had to be borne by the home-based squadrons of RAF Bomber Command. At 11 a.m. on 15 May 12 Blenheims of No. 2 Group attacked enemy columns in the Dinant area, while 150 French fighters flew patrols in relays over the battlefront. Sixteen more Blenheims, escorted by 27 French fighters, made an attack at 3 p.m. on bridges in the Samoy region and also on enemy armour. Four Blenheims FTR. By nightfall on 15 May the British Air Forces in France had lost 205 aircraft: 86 Battles, 39 Blenheims, 9 Lysanders and 71 Hurricanes. RAF Bomber Command, principally No. 2 Group, had lost a further 43.

On the night of 15/16 May RAF Bomber Command's strategic air offensive against Germany began with the despatch of 99 aircraft – 39 Wellingtons, 36 Hampdens and 24 Whitleys – to industrial targets in the Ruhr. No aircraft was lost through enemy action, but a Wellington of No. 115 Sqn crashed into high ground near Rouen.

On 17 May the Blenheims of No. 2 Group sustained their heaviest loss to date when 12 aircraft of No. 82 Sqn were detailed to attack tanks and troops near Gembloux. Ten were shot down by fighters and one by ground fire.

By 19 May the rapid German advance to the line of the Scheldt in the north – held by the BEF – had become a direct threat to the bases of the Air Component, and orders were given to begin the evacuation of what was left of its squadrons. The first to leave, on 19 May, were three of the seven fighter squadrons – Nos. 3, 32 and 79. They were followed the next day by Nos. 85, 87, 607 and 615, and by the majority of the Lysanders. Of the 261 Hurricanes committed to the battle – replacement aircraft included – only 66 were evacuated; 74 had been lost on operations, the remainder having been either destroyed on the ground or abandoned because there were not enough pilots to fly them home. Beginning on 20 May, RAF fighter operations over the battlefield were carried out by the Hurricanes and Spitfires of No. 11 Group Fighter Command, operating from bases in southern England.

**22 May** Seven Westland Lysanders of No. 16 Sqn, Army Co-operation Command, dropped supplies to the besieged garrison at Calais and also bombed enemy positions on the coast. On the following day, the Squadron attacked gun positions near Boulogne, while Lysanders of No. 2 Sqn dive-bombed enemy concentrations north of Calais. Further supply drops to both Calais and Boulogne were carried out by these two units and also by Nos. 16, 26 and 613 Sqns. By the time these operations ceased in the first week of June, more than 30 Lysanders had been lost.

**23–24 May** Spitfires and Messerschmitts met in combat for the first time over the French coast. In two days of air fighting No. 92 Sqn, operating from RAF Hornchurch, claimed the destruction of six Bf 109s and 17 Bf 110s for the loss of four Spitfires, although these claims were later found to have been greatly exaggerated. The hectic nature of air combat always made an accurate assessment of enemy aircraft destroyed a difficult task.

**26 May** Following the fall of Calais and Boulogne,

Dunkirk remained the only North Sea port still open for the evacuation of Allied troops, and from 26 May it was subjected to very heavy air attack. British fighter cover over Dunkirk was provided by 16 first-line squadrons drawn from Air Vice-Marshal Keith Park's No. 11 Fighter Group, operating principally from the airfields of Biggin Hill, Manston, Hornchurch, Lympne, Hawkinge and Kenley. This standing cover of 16 squadrons was frequently rotated, those which suffered a high rate of attrition being sent north for a rest and replaced by fresh units drawn from Nos. 12 and 13 Groups, so that, in fact, 32 fighter squadrons in all participated in the nine days of Operation Dynamo, as the Dunkirk evacuation was code-named. No more than 16, however, were committed at any one time, for Air Chief Marshal Sir Hugh Dowding, the AOC-in-C RAF Fighter Command, was anxious to preserve his fighter strength to meet the major air battles anticipated over England in the months to come.

**27 May** 300 German bombers, escorted by 550 fighter sorties, attacked Dunkirk and vessels offshore. RAF fighters carried out 23 patrols, using 287 available aircraft. During the course of the day, 14 Spitfires and Hurricanes were lost, but the RAF claimed the destruction of 38 enemy aircraft – including two Bf 109s and three He 111s shot down by the Boulton-Paul Defiants of No. 264 Sqn, newcomers to the battle. The Defiant bore some resemblance to the Hurricane head-on and was frequently mistaken as such by *Luftwaffe* pilots during these early encounters, but they soon got the measure of it and the squadrons using it were decimated thereafter. *Kampfgeschwader* 2 and 3 suffered heavily in the day's action, losing 23 Dornier Do 17s and 70 aircrew.

**28 May** No. 11 Group flew 11 squadron patrols in the Dunkirk sector, with 321 individual fighter sorties, and claimed the destruction of 23 enemy aircraft for the loss of 13 of their own number. On the following day the Group carried out nine patrols, with formations of between 25 and 44 fighters providing air cover for the BEF. They intercepted three out of five major attacks launched by the *Luftwaffe* that day, but all the raids were heavily escorted by fighters and the RAF could not succeed in breaking them up. The RAF lost 16 aircraft, the *Luftwaffe* 14.

**31 May** In the course of eight fighter sweeps in the Dunkirk sector, No. 11 Group destroyed 17 enemy aircraft. On this day, Wellingtons of No. 3 Group and Blenheims of No. 2 Group carried out attacks on enemy positions in support of Allied forces holding the Dunkirk perimeter. Hudsons and Ansons of RAF Coastal Command and aircraft of the Fleet Air Arm also participated in operations over Dunkirk.

*3 June* By this, the last day of the Dunkirk evacuation, the RAF squadrons committed to the battle over the beaches and beyond had carried out 171 reconnaissance, 651 bombing and 2739 fighter sorties. Combat losses for the RAF during the nine-day period were 177 aircraft destroyed or severely damaged, including 106 fighters. By 4 June, Fighter Command had suffered such attrition over Dunkirk that its first-line strength was reduced to 331 Spitfires and Hurricanes, with only 36 fighters in reserve. *Luftwaffe* losses during this period were 240 aircraft of all types along the whole Franco-Belgian front, of which 132 were lost in the Dunkirk sector.

On 3 June the *Luftwaffe* launched Operation Paula, an attack by 500 bombers and fighters of *Luftflotten* 2 and 3 on airfields and communications in the Paris area. Attacks on 13 French airfields resulted in the destruction of only 16 aircraft on the ground, with six runways temporarily put out of action. Twenty-two railway stations and junctions and 15 factories were also hit, killing 254 civilians and injuring 652. In the course of 243 sorties, French fighter pilots destroyed 26 enemy aircraft, losing 17 of their own in air combat.

*5 June* In the course of 438 sorties in suppport of ground forces resisting a German offensive on the Somme, French fighter pilots claimed the destruction of 40 enemy aircraft for the loss of 15 of their own. French bombers and assault aircraft – including some drawn from *Aéronavale* (Naval Air) units – flew 126 sorties and dropped 60 tons of bombs. As well as the French commitment, the AASF's Battle squadrons, redeployed to new airfields and with a total strength of about 70 aircraft, together with 250 aircraft of RAF Bomber Command, made repeated attacks on the enemy's lines of communication on and after 5 June.

*7/8 June* Berlin was bombed for the first time by a French *Aéronavale* aircraft – Farman 223 *Jules Verne* of *Escadrille* B.5. Taking off from Bordeaux-Mérignac, the aircraft approached its target via Denmark and the Baltic and dropped several bombs on the German capital from 5400 ft (1650 m). They exploded in the suburbs and damaged a factory. The return flight was made across Germany and the Rhine, the aircraft landing at Orly at dawn after being airborne for 13½ hours. Two nights later, the *Jules Verne* dropped bombs in the vicinity of the Heinkel aircraft factory at Rostock.

*10 June* Italy declared war on Great Britain and

France. The air war in the south was fought mainly between the *Regia Aeronautica* and the *Aéronavale*, which had 132 serviceable aircraft in the Mediterranean Maritime Zone.

*11/12 June* 36 Whitleys of No. 4 Group, drawn from Nos. 10, 51, 58, 77 and 102 Sqns, were despatched to bomb Italian targets, having refuelled in the Channel Islands. Twenty-three aircraft aborted because of bad weather; ten claimed attacks on the primary target, the Fiat works in Turin, two more bombed Genoa and one FTR.

*13 June* Four Chance-Vought 156F bombers of *Escadrille* AB 3, *Aéronavale*, attacked an Italian submarine off Albenga. Five bombs were dropped and the submarine was thought to have been damaged. That afternoon, another 156F of AB 3 was shot down by a Fiat CR.42 of Hyères. Earlier, Italian bombers had attacked Karouba, destroying three Loire 70s of *Escadrille* E3 on the ground.

*15 June* 23 Fiat BR.20 bombers, escorted by 15 Fiat CR.42 fighters, attacked French airfields in Provence. They were intercepted by Bloch 151s of AC 3 and Dewoitine D.520s of GC III/6. Six Chance-Vought 156Fs of AB 3 were destroyed on the ground and four Bloch 151s were shot down. Five Fiat CR.42s were destroyed in combat, four of them – together with a Fiat BR.20 – being shot down by one Dewoitine pilot, *Sergent-Chef* Le Gloan.

On 15 June the remnants of the RAF Hurricane Squadrons in France were ordered to cover the final evacuation of British forces from ports still held by the Allies. Nos. 1, 73 and 242 Sqns were given the task of defending Nantes, Brest and St Nazaire, while Nos. 17 and 501 Sqns were assigned to St Malo and Cherbourg. The squadrons were ordered back to the UK on 18 June; the last to leave were Nos. 1 and 73 Sqns, which had been the first to arrive in France in 1939.

*15/16 June* Eight Wellingtons of Nos. 99 and 149 Sqns were despatched from Salon, near Marseille, to bomb the Ansaldo factory in Genoa, but only one claimed to have made a successful attack. On the following night, 14 Wellingtons out of 22 despatched bombed Genoa and Milan; all aircraft returned safely. The Wellingtons returned to the UK immediately after this operation.

The fighting in France had cost the RAF a total of 1029 aircraft, of which 299 belonged to the AASF and 279 to the Air Component. Over 1500 personnel were killed, wounded or missing.

*18–20 June* The *Armée de l'Air* ordered all fighter groups with aircraft of sufficient range to fly to

French bases in North Africa. The five Curtiss Hawk groups – GC I/4, II/4, I/5, II/5 and III/2 – evacuated 146 aircraft; about 160 Dewoitine D.520s were also evacuated. The final fighter missions of the campaign up to the armistice of 25 June were flown by Bloch 152s and Morane 406s.

**24 June** As far as may be ascertained, the last operational sortie by the *Armée de l'Air* was flown in the afternoon of 24 June by 11 LeO 451s of *Groupement* 6, which attacked enemy pontoon bridges between Moirans and Grenoble. About 180 LeO 451s were evacuated to North Africa before or after the armistice.

The Battle of France cost the *Armée de l'Air* and *Aéronavale* 892 aircraft (508 fighters, 218 bombers and 166 reconnaissance). Aircrew losses were 1493. Actual losses in combat were 513 aircraft; the remainder were destroyed on the ground by enemy action, or lost as the result of accidents.

The Allied air forces claimed the destruction of 1735 enemy aircraft, a figure that was greatly exaggerated. Combat losses admitted by the *Luftwaffe* totalled 534 aircraft, although this does not include aircraft which were written off through severe battle damage or those lost accidentally.

# The Battle of Britain

In June 1940, while the Battle of France was still being fought, the *Luftwaffe* had begun to turn its attention to targets in the United Kingdom. From 5 June, small numbers of bombers attacked 'fringe' targets on the east and south-east coasts of the United Kingdom. These attacks lasted for about eight weeks and caused little significant damage; their main purpose was to provide the *Luftwaffe* with operational and navigational experience. On 30 June, *Reichsmarschall* Hermann Göring, the Commander-in-Chief of the *Luftwaffe*, issued a general directive, setting out the aims of the planned air assault on Britain. The *Luftwaffe's* main target was to be the Royal Air Force, with particular reference to its fighter airfields and aircraft factories; as long as Fighter Command remained unbeaten, the *Luftwaffe's* first priority had to be to attack it by day and night at every opportunity, in the air and on the ground, until it was destroyed. Only then would the *Luftwaffe* be free to turn its attention to other targets, such as the Royal Navy's dockyards and operational harbours, as a preliminary to invasion. Early in July, as a first step towards meeting this objective, Göring authorized his bombers to begin attacks on British convoys in the Channel, the twofold object being to inflict serious losses on British shipping and to bring RAF Fighter Command to combat. So began the first phase of what was to become known as the Battle of Britain.

**10 July** 26 Dornier Do 17s, escorted by five fighter *Staffeln*, were despatched to attack a large convoy off Dover. The attack was intercepted by 30 RAF fighters, which destroyed eight enemy aircraft for the loss of one Spitfire. Falmouth was attacked by 63 Junkers Ju 88s, whose bombs damaged railways, ships at anchor and a munitions factory and caused 86 casualties.

**11 July** In a day of heavy air fighting over the Channel, the RAF shot down 15 enemy aircraft engaged in convoy attacks. British losses were six aircraft. In similar operations during the next seven days, the *Luftwaffe* lost a further 30 aircraft, the RAF 13.

**19 July** Six Boulton Paul Defiants of No. 141 Sqn were destroyed in a single encounter with Bf 109s south of Folkestone. After this, No. 141 Sqn played no further part in the daylight phase of the battle. During the day, Fighter Command lost ten fighters against four *Luftwaffe* aircraft destroyed.

**25 July** The *Luftwaffe* adopted a change of tactics, sending out strong fighter sweeps to bring the RAF fighters to battle before launching its bomber attacks. As a result, 60 Ju 87 *Stukas* of *Fliegerkorps* VIII were able to bomb a convoy with impunity while the fighters of No. 11 Group were on the ground refuelling. Later in the day, the convoy was attacked by 30 Ju 88s, escorted by 50 Bf 109s. The attacks continued until 6.30 p.m.; 15 RAF fighter squadrons were engaged, losing six Spitfires against German losses of 16.

*31 July* In four weeks of operations, the *Luftwaffe* had sunk 40 000 tons of British shipping, including three destroyers. Combat losses during the month's air fighting were *Luftwaffe* 190, RAF 77. On *15 July*, RAF Bomber Command had begun attacks on enemy shipping and barge concentrations in North Sea and Channel ports, as well as on enemy airfields in occupied France and the Low Countries; these attacks were to continue on a regular basis until the end of October.

*8 August* After a week of relative inactivity, the *Luftwaffe* launched very heavy attacks on a westbound Channel convoy, the first since 25 July, off Dover and Wight. The Germans lost 21 aircraft, including eight Ju 87 *Stukas*, and the RAF lost 15.

*11 August* In the morning, 165 German bombers escorted by Bf 109s and Bf 110s made heavy attacks on Portland and Weymouth. Eight RAF fighter squadrons intercepting in mid-Channel were engaged by the Messerschmitts, allowing the bombers to slip through. There were also separate attacks on a Channel convoy. The day's losses – the highest so far – were 35 German aircraft and 30 British. Total losses since 1 July were now 274 *Luftwaffe*, 124 RAF.

*12 August* As a preliminary to the main air offensive, bomb-carrying Bf 109s and Bf 110s of *Erprobungsgruppe* 210, together with Ju 88s of KG 51 and KG 54, attacked several radar stations on the south coast, putting the one at Ventnor on the Isle of Wight out of action and damaging three others. While these attacks were in progress, Do 17s of KG 2 raided the airfield at Lympne with 100 lb (45 kg) bombs, causing some damage; a convoy

*Waiting for battle: RAF fighter pilots at readiness, July 1940.*

in the Thames estuary was also bombed by *Stukas*. In the afternoon, RAF Manston was attacked and temporarily put out of action by *Erprobungsgruppe* 210, while enemy bombers struck at Hawkinge and again at Lympne, causing heavy damage to both airfields. By nightfall on 12 August, *Luftflotten* 2 and 3 had sent 300 bombers against British targets; the *Luftwaffe* had lost 27 aircraft, the RAF 20.

**13 August** The start of Operation *Adler Angriff* (Eagle Attack), the air offensive against England. H-Hour at 7.30 a.m. was postponed because of bad weather, but the Dorniers of KG 2 failed to receive the order and set out over the Channel without fighter escort. They were attacked over the Thames estuary and five bombers were shot down, although the remainder caused heavy damage to Sheerness and Eastchurch. In the afternoon, Ju 87s of *Stukageschwader* 77, escorted by Bf 109s of JG 27, set out to attack RAF airfields over Portland. They were engaged over the coast by Spitfires of No. 609 Sqn and five *Stukas* were shot down. Soon afterwards, Ju 88s bombed Southampton harbour and the airfields of Middle Wallop and Andover. Over Kent, fighters of No. 11 Group were heavily engaged against *Stukas* of VIII *Fliegerkorps*, which had carried out heavy attacks on several airfields. The hardest hit was Detling, which was bombed by 86 *Stukas*. At the close of the day, the *Luftwaffe* had flown 485 sorties, mostly against RAF airfields; three had been badly damaged, but none was a fighter base. The *Luftwaffe* lost 34 aircraft; the RAF's loss was 13 aircraft and 7 pilots. On the next day *Luftwaffe* operations were frustrated by bad weather; only one major raid was carried out by Bf 110s of *Erprobungsgruppe* 210, which attacked Manston. Dover, Middle Wallop and Sealand were also attacked by small numbers of enemy aircraft. The defences claimed 19 enemy aircraft; the RAF lost 4.

**15 August** This was the heaviest day's fighting of the entire battle. In the morning, 40 *Stukas* of II *Fliegerkorps*, escorted by a similar number of Bf 109s, attacked Lympne and Hawkinge airfields, causing severe damage ro the former. At the same time, aircraft of *Luftflotte* 5 from Norway and Denmark launched a major attack on the north of England. Flying from Stavanger, 63 He 111s of KG 26, escorted by 21 Bf 110s of ZG 76, made landfall on the Northumbrian coast and were intercepted by Spitfires and Hurricanes of Nos. 41, 72, 79, 605 and 607 Sqns, which destroyed eight Heinkels and six Bf 110s for the loss of one Spitfire. Forty Junkers Ju 88s, attempting to attack airfields in Yorkshire, were engaged by Nos. 73 and 616 Sqns

and six were shot down, although the attack badly damaged RAF Driffield and destroyed several Whitley bombers on the ground. In the afternoon, the airfields of Eastchurch and Rochester were heavily bombed by the Dornier Do 17s of KG 3 and severe damage was caused to the Shorts aircraft factory at the latter, setting back production of the Stirling heavy bomber by several months. Eleven RAF fighter squadrons were scrambled to intercept the incoming raids, but these became involved with the massive enemy fighter escort. In addition, the airfield of Martlesham Heath was severely damaged by bomb-carrying Messerschmitts of *Erprobungsgruppe* 210 and put out of action for 36 hours. At 5 p.m., a mixed formation of Junkers Ju 87 *Stukas* and Junkers Ju 88s, again under heavy escort – about 200 aircraft in all – attempted to attack airfields on the south coast. They were engaged by 14 fighter squadrons and suffered very heavy losses. In the evening, 23 Messerschmitts of *Erprobungsgruppe* 210 bombed Croydon, south London, in mistake for RAF Kenley and destroyed 40 training aircraft on the ground. Six Bf 110s and a Bf 109 were shot down by Hurricanes of Nos. 32 and 111 Sqns and Spitfires of No. 66 Sqn. This brought the day's combat losses for the *Luftwaffe* to 71 aircraft, mostly bombers and Bf 110s. The RAF's loss was 28.

**16 August** On this day, the *Luftwaffe* attacked eight RAF airfields in the south, but half of these were training or Fleet Air Arm establishments. Forty-six training aircraft were destroyed in an attack on Harwell, and the radar station at Ventnor was attacked again. In an air action near Southampton, Flight Lieutenant J.B. Nicolson of No. 249 Sqn remained in his burning Hurricane to shoot down a Bf 110 before baling out, and was subsequently awarded the Victoria Cross – Fighter Command's only recipient of this medal. In the afternoon, poor weather frustrated attempts by the *Luftwaffe* to make further attacks on RAF airfields; nevertheless, air combats during the day, mostly in the morning, cost the *Luftwaffe* 44 aircraft and the RAF 22.

**18 August** Following another spell of bad weather, the *Luftwaffe* launched a series of heavy attacks on the important sector stations of Kenley and Biggin Hill. Kenley was badly hit, and its operations room put out of action. In the afternoon, a strong force of bombers attacked the airfields at Ford, Gosport and Thorney Island. The aircraft involved were the *Stukas* of VIII *Fliegerkorps*, and they ventured over the coast with inadequate fighter escort. They were engaged by the Hurricanes of No. 43 and the Spitfires of No. 152 Sqns, which destroyed 16 of their number. Total *Luftwaffe* combat loss was 60 aircraft; the RAF lost 35 fighters. The Hurricanes of No. 1 (Canadian) Sqn saw action for the first time on this day.

**19 August** On the personal orders of Hermann Göring, Ju 87 *Stukas* were withdrawn from the daylight battle over England. The fighters of *Luftflotte* 3 were ordered to move to new airfields in the Pas de Calais in order to extend their range to the utmost limit, and to fly close escort to the bombers – a move that frittered away their tactical advantage. From **19 to 23 August** inclusive air action was confined to skirmishing as both sides rested and regrouped; during this period, the *Luftwaffe* lost 27 aircraft, the RAF 11 fighters.

**24 August** After four days of cloud and rain, the *Luftwaffe* resumed heavy attacks on Fighter Command airfields, especially on Manston, which by midday had ceased to function. Hornchurch and North Weald airfields were heavily bombed, as was Portsmouth naval base. The *Luftwaffe* lost 30 aircraft during the day, the RAF 24. Among the RAF's losses were five Defiants of No. 264 Sqn, scrambled to intercept an attack on Manston. That night, during attacks on targets in the London area, some bombers of KG 1 made a navigational error and dropped bombs on London itself – an act that was to have a far-reaching effect on the future conduct of the battle.

**25 August** Heavily-escorted formations of bombers attacked Portland, Weymouth and Warmwell airfield. The attack on Warmwell was broken up by the Hurricanes of No. 17 Sqn and the airfield suffered only minor damage. Dover was heavily attacked in the early evening. In the day's fighting, the *Luftwaffe* lost 20 aircraft, the RAF 16.

**25/26 August** RAF Bomber Command attacked Berlin for the first time, aiming at industrial targets in the city by way of reprisal for the previous night's raid on London. The attack was hampered by thick cloud. Of the 81 aircraft despatched (Wellingtons, Whitleys and Hampdens of Nos. 3, 4 and 5 Groups) 29 claimed to have bombed Berlin. Six aircraft, all Hampdens, FTR; three ditched in the sea and their crews were rescued.

**26 August** From 11 a.m., No. 11 Group fought a running battle between Canterbury and Maidstone against 50 German bombers escorted by 80 fighters. In this action, No. 616 Sqn lost five out of 12 Spitfires, No. 264 Sqn lost three more Defiants, and No. 1 (Canadian) Sqn three Hurricanes, but an attempted raid on Biggin Hill was broken up. All available squadrons were committed to intercept a further attack by 40 Do 17s of KG 2 and KG

*The Dornier Do 17, badly under-armed, suffered heavily at the hands of the RAF's fighters.*

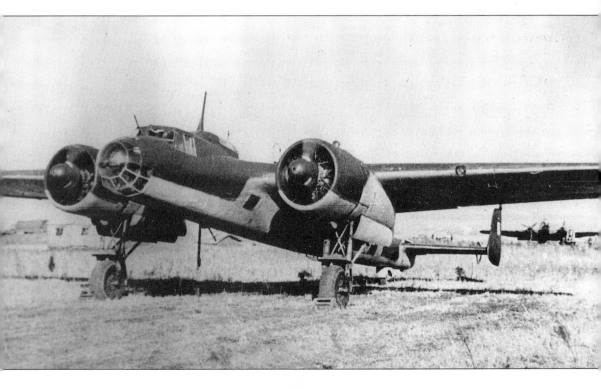

3 on Debden and Hornchurch airfields, escorted
by 120 fighters; the latter were compelled to withdraw through lack of fuel and the bombers suffered heavily. A third major attack, by 50 He 111s
escorted by 107 fighters, was intercepted by three
RAF squadrons and eight enemy aircraft were
destroyed for the loss of four British. This marked
the last major daylight operation by KG 3 for three
weeks. Total losses for the day were 34 German,
27 British. RAF Fighter Command was now under
immense strain.

*28 August Luftwaffe* attacks resumed after a day of
poor weather, two heavily escorted bomber formations crossing the Kent coast soon after 9 a.m.
Eastchurch airfield was badly damaged. No. 264
Sqn lost four more Defiants in action; after this,
the Defiant was withdrawn from daylight operations. In three operational sorties No. 264 Sqn had
lost 12 aircraft, with 14 pilots and gunners killed.
Rochford was damaged in an attack by 30 Dorniers.
The day's losses were 26 *Luftwaffe*, 17 RAF.

*28/29 August* This marked the beginning of much
heavier night raids by the *Luftwaffe*. The Germans
flew some 340 sorties against Merseyside and
other targets. In 600 night sorties flown so far by
*Luftflotte 3*, the enemy had lost only seven aircraft.

*29 August* The *Luftwaffe* launched 700 fighter sorties over southern England in an attempt to draw
Fighter Command into battle, but the RAF did not
respond. This led the Germans into the erroneous
belief that fighter supremacy had been achieved.
Twelve German aircraft were lost against nine
British.

*30 August* The day began with a fighter sweep
across Kent by 50 Bf 109s; again, the RAF did not
respond. A major attack by 150 bombers, escorted
by Bf 110s, was broken up by fighters of No. 11
Group. From 1 p.m. onwards, successive waves of
bombers and their escorts crossed the coast at 20
minute intervals. A hit on the electricity grid
temporarily disabled seven radar stations. Biggin
Hill was severely damaged, and control of its
Sector operations transferred to Hornchurch. The
Vauxhall works at Luton were attacked and 53
people killed. During the day, Fighter Command
flew 1054 sorties, losing 20 aircraft (eight of them
Spitfires of No. 222 Sqn) against the *Luftwaffe's* 24.
Liverpool was heavily attacked during the night
by 130 bombers.

*Hurricanes of No. 601 Sqn on patrol. Note the 'tail
end charlie' weaving below and behind the number
four aircraft. This kind of tight formation cost RAF
Fighter Command many lives before better tactics
were evolved.*

*31 August* The *Luftwaffe* once again attempted to draw Fighter Command into battle by sending over high-flying fighter sweeps. Later, 13 fighter squadrons were scrambled to intercept 200 raiders approaching the Thames Estuary. Fighters of No. 12 Group broke up an attack on RAF Duxford, and intercepted another on Debden in time to prevent severe damage. Croydon, Biggin Hill and Hornchurch were all badly hit. Casualties during the day's fighting were heavy, the *Luftwaffe* losing 28 aircraft and the RAF 24. Liverpool was attacked during the night by 160 bombers.

*1 September* Fighter Command's pilot losses were now acute; new pilots were reaching operational squadrons with only 20 hours' experience of Spitfires and Hurricanes, and many did not survive their first sortie. At 11 a.m., 120 bombers attacked Biggin Hill, Eastchurch and Detling. In the afternoon, the *Luftwaffe* launched two major fighter sweeps over southern England; under cover of this diversion, a small number of Do 17s made a low-level attack on Biggin Hill, wrecking the Sector Operations Room and all communications. Bristol, south Wales, the Midlands and Merseyside were attacked during the night. Losses during the day were *Luftwaffe* five, RAF 15 (the latter including five Spitfires of No. 85 Sqn, bounced on the climb by Bf 109s and 110s).

*2 September* Several airfields, including Biggin Hill, Lympne, Detling, Eastchurch (three times), Hornchurch (twice) and Gravesend, were heavily attacked, together with the aircraft factory at Rochester and Brooklands aerodrome, adjacent to the vital Hawker and Vickers factories. Fighter Command maintained standing patrols over the Sector airfields during the day. The *Luftwaffe* lost 26 aircraft, the RAF 23. Merseyside, the Midlands, Manchester and Sheffield were attacked after dark.

*3 September* The airfield attacks continued, North Weald being very severely damaged. The *Luftwaffe* and Fighter Command each lost 16 aircraft. Adolf Hitler moved the target date for the invasion of England (Operation Sea Lion) from 15 to 21 September. *Generalfeldmarschall* Albert Kesselring, commanding *Luftflotte* 2, expressed his belief that the RAF was down to its last few dozen fighters; Hugo Sperrle of *Luftflotte* 3 believed that Fighter Command had up to 1000 aircraft left.

*4 September* The *Luftwaffe* launched heavy attacks on British aircraft factories in addition to the continuing airfield raids. Twenty Bf 110s attempting to attack the Hawker factory at Brooklands were severely mauled by nine Hurricanes of No. 253 Sqn, losing six aircraft. The remaining 110s attacked the Vickers factory in error, killing 88

people, injuring over 600 and halting production of the Wellington bomber for four days. The RAF lost 18 fighters, the *Luftwaffe* 21 aircraft. Hitler threatened retaliation for the growing Bomber Command offensive against Germany.

*5 September* Over a period of eight hours 22 German formations attacked RAF airfields and the oil storage tanks at Thameshaven. The RAF lost 20 aircraft, the *Luftwaffe* 23.

*6 September* Attacks on airfields, aircraft factories and oil storage facilities continued, Thameshaven being set on fire again. Coastal Command's Photographic Reconnaissance Unit reported steadily growing numbers of invasion craft in the Dutch, Belgian and French Channel ports; Bomber Com-

mand stepped up its night offensive against these targets. The British ordered Invasion Alert No. 2 – attack probable within three days. Combat losses on 6 September were *Luftwaffe* 34, RAF 22. For the first time, a Polish fighter squadron (No. 303 Sqn, RAF Northolt) was committed to the battle. Fighter Command was now very close to exhaustion; on the week between 24 August and 6 September, the RAF had lost 103 pilots killed and 128 badly wounded – almost one-quarter of available trained pilots. Losses were now beginning to exceed replacements.

**7 September** The *Luftwaffe* high comand, under pressure from Hitler and influenced by Kesselring, switched the weight of its attacks to London in the belief that an all-out assault on the capital would force Fighter Command to commit its last reserves to the battle. Beginning at 5 p.m. and lasting until dawn the next day, 625 bombers pounded the London docks area in successive waves, killing 488 civilians. The code-word *Cromwell* – invasion imminent – brought the British defences to the highest level of readiness and action stations. Losses in combat were *Luftwaffe* 38, RAF 28.

**8 September** Attacks on London resumed after dark and continued at intervals during the night.

*The Hurricane could absorb a lot of battle damage and still survive. This fighter of No. 615 Sqn was the victim of an exploding cannon shell.*

In desultory fighting during the day, the *Luftwaffe* lost 13 aircraft, the RAF four.

**9 September** Enemy bombers attacked Southampton and targets in the Thames Estuary. A major raid on London by 200 bombers was frustrated by fighters of Nos. 11 and 12 Groups; jettisoned bombs caused widespread damage in the suburbs, killing 412 people. Combat losses during the day were RAF 15, *Luftwaffe* 25.

**10 September** Very slight air activity due to cloud and rain. London, south Wales and Merseyside were bombed at night. Combat losses were *Luftwaffe* three, RAF one, but eight Heinkel He 111s were destroyed and two badly damaged in a Bomber Command attack on II/KG 4's airfield at Eindhoven, Holland.

**11 September** The *Luftwaffe* attacked four airfields, and London, Southampton and Portsmouth. The Germans lost 24 aircraft, the RAF 27 – plus two Blenheims of No. 235 Sqn, shot down while escorting Fairey Albacores of the Fleet Air Arm in a bombing raid on Calais harbour. In the day's operations No. 1 (Canadian) Sqn and No. 41 Sqn, climbing to intercept a raid, were bounced by enemy fighters and lost 12 aircraft between them.

**12 September** Rain hampered air activity. Air reconnaissance revealed enemy invasion barge concentrations were still growing. No Fighter Command combat losses were recorded on this day; the *Luftwaffe* lost three aircraft.

**13 September** The *Luftwaffe* made a number of small-strength daylight raids on London, followed by night attacks, and lost four aircraft. Fighter Command lost two, including a Blenheim of the Fighter Interception Unit that FTR from a night sortie over the Channel.

**14 September** Attacks were made on south London and coastal radar stations. The *Luftwaffe* lost eight aircraft in combat, the RAF 11.

**15 September** On this day, the climax of the battle, the *Luftwaffe* launched 200 bombers against London in two waves. When the first wave attacked, such was the fighter opposition by Nos. 11 and 12 Groups that Fighter Command had no squadrons in reserve. If the second wave had come immediately, its bombers would have caught the Spitfires and Hurricanes on the ground, but it was two hours before this wave attacked, and by that time the fighter squadrons were ready for it. A total of 148 bombers got through to bomb London, but 56 were shot down and many more suffered severe battle damage. The RAF's loss was 26 fighters. This day, which was known to the *Luftwaffe* as

'Black Thursday', was later designated *BATTLE OF BRITAIN DAY*.

**16 September** Slight air activity in cloud and rain, mainly in the south-east and East Anglia, followed by night attacks on London, the Midlands and Merseyside. The *Luftwaffe* lost eight aircraft and the RAF two, one of which ran out of fuel while chasing a Ju 88 over the Channel.

**17 September** Bad weather once more reduced air operations, although there were a number of fighter sweeps over southern England. During the night, RAF Bomber Command despatched 194 aircraft to attack the Channel ports; 84 barges were sunk at Dunkirk alone. During the day the *Luftwaffe* lost eight aircraft, Fighter Command five. On the orders of Adolf Hitler, Operation Sea Lion was postponed indefinitely; British intelligence intercepted a secret German signal, ordering the dismantling of German invasion air transport facilities in Holland.

**18 September** The *Luftwaffe* resumed attacks on oil storage facilities in the Thames Estuary and suffered heavily, losing 16 aircraft – nine of them Ju 88s of KG 77, destroyed in a combat lasting only minutes. RAF Fighter Command lost 12 fighters. The Germans began to disperse their invasion fleet in an attempt to reduce damage caused by British bombing.

**20 September** After a lull caused by bad weather on the 19th, the *Luftwaffe* sent heavy fighter sweeps probing towards London. The RAF and *Luftwaffe* each lost seven aircraft.

**21–22 September** There was very slight activity on these two days, and most of that was confined to night operations. Losses were 11 German aircraft.

**23 September** There were numerous combats on this day, as the Germans sent more fighter sweeps over the Thames Estuary. The *Luftwaffe* lost 13 aircraft, the RAF 11.

**24 September** Messerschmitt Bf 110s of *Erprobungsgruppe* 210 made a hit-and-run attack on the Woolston Spitfire factory at Southampton, killing 98 employees. In this and other small raids, the *Luftwaffe* lost nine aircraft, the RAF seven.

**25 September** The Germans resumed their attacks on aircraft factories. The Bristol aircraft factory at Filton was badly damaged, with over 300 civilian casualties, in an attack by 58 He 111s of KG 55. The day's operations cost the *Luftwaffe* 13 aircraft (five in the Filton raid) and the RAF five.

**27 September** Following a night of heavy air raids on the south and Midlands, the *Luftwaffe* launched

**Top:**
*A* Luftwaffe *reconnaissance photograph showing oil storage tanks ablaze on the Thames estuary.*

**Above:**
*The cost: the blazing remains of a Messerschmitt Bf 109.*

# THE BLITZ ON BRITAIN, 1940–41

T HE Battle of Britain had ended in a narrow victory for RAF Fighter Command, but the ordeal of Britain's cities was only just beginning.

On the night of *14/15 November 1940*, 450 German bombers wiped out the heart of Coventry, the main bomber stream following a pathfinder unit, *Kampfgruppe 100*, that navigated its way to the target along a radio beam. Night after night, during the winter of 1940–41, the pattern was to be repeated as the night bombers pounded London, the Midlands, Lancashire, Merseyside, South Wales, Tyneside, Plymouth, Exeter, Southampton, Bristol and many other targets. The RAF was virtually powerless to stem the onslaught; Fighter Command's night-fighter defences were primitive, and the majority of the early successes were achieved by pilots flying Spitfires and Hurricanes, which were day fighters. One pilot, Flight Lieutenant R.P. Stevens, flying Hurricanes with Nos. 151 and 253 Sqns, destroyed 14 enemy bombers at night during 1941.

The mainstay of the RAF's embryo night-fighter force in the summer of 1940 was the Bristol Blenheim Mk 1F, which was completely unsuited to night operations and which was slower than some of the bombers it was supposed to catch; it was fitted with only the most primitive form of AI (Air Interception Radar). It was during trials with this equipment by the Fighter Interception Unit on *22/23 July 1940* that a Blenheim, flown by Flying Officer Geoffrey Ashfield, registered the first AI kill, shooting down a Dornier Do 17 of II/KG 3 into the Channel.

In August 1940, two squadrons of Boulton Paul Defiants – Nos. 141 and 264 – which had just been withdrawn from the day battle

following severe losses, were assigned to the night-fighter role. Both squadrons saw their first real night actions during the second week of September, when the *Luftwaffe* stepped up its night attacks on London; on the night of the 15/16 two Heinkel He 111s were shot down by Defiants of No. 141 Sqn 'B' Flight, operating from Biggin Hill. Early in November, No. 141 Sqn moved to Gravesend to guard the approaches to London, while No. 264 Sqn operated north of the Thames. Other Defiant squadrons joined the night-fighter force in the weeks that followed; the first was No. 307 (Polish) Sqn, which formed at Jurby in the Isle of Man and moved to Squires Gate to defend Merseyside early in 1941. By the spring of that year, five more Defiant squadrons had been formed: Nos. 85, 96, 151, 255 and 256. All were active during the *Luftwaffe*'s night offensive against the major British cities in the early months of 1941, but claims were few.

The RAF's night-fighter force began to score its first real successes with the operational debut, in September 1940, of the Bristol Beaufighter. Fast and heavy, this twin-engined aircraft had a formidable armament of four cannon and six machine guns; moreover, it was big enough to carry the early, bulky Mk IV AI radar without sacrificing other weight in fuel and firepower. The first squadrons to receive Beaufighters were No. 25 at North Weald, No. 29 at Digby, No. 219 at Catterick, No. 600 at Hornchurch and No. 604 at Middle Wallop. No. 219 Sqn scored the first confirmed Beaufighter kill on the night of 25/26 October, when Sergeant Hodgkinson and Sergeant Benn (observer) destroyed a Do 17. The first kill following a radar interception was registered on the night of 19/20 November by a No. 604 Sqn

a series of strong daylight raids, starting with an attack on London by bomb-carrying Bf 110s. The latter suffered heavily, LG 1 alone losing seven aircraft. A second attack on London by 55 Junkers Ju 88s of KG 77 ended in disaster when the bombers failed to rendezvous with their Bf 109 escort; 15 Ju 88s were shot down, and enemy fighters coming belatedly to the bombers' rescue were also badly mauled. In an attack on Filton, fighters of No. 10 Group destroyed four Bf 110s of *Erprobungsgruppe* 210. The day's combat losses

were *Luftwaffe* 49, RAF 28. (Losses in the previous day's operations were *Luftwaffe* eight, RAF seven.)

**28 September** The day saw sporadic raids on southern England by small formations of bombers under heavy escort. The *Luftwaffe* lost ten aircraft and the RAF 18, mostly Hurricanes.

**29 September** Reduced air operations over London and East Anglia; Liverpool was also attacked by daylight from the west. The *Luftwaffe* lost six aircraft and the RAF five.

crew, Flight Lieutenant John Cunningham and Sergeant J. Phillipson, who shot down a Ju 88.

January 1941 saw the establishment of a network of Ground Controlled Interception (GCI) stations along the south and east coasts of England. From these stations, controllers were able to steer the night-fighters to within a mile or so of their target, at which point the airborne radar took over to complete the interception. On 15/16 April 1941, Flight Lieutenant Cunningham and his observer destroyed three enemy aircraft in a single night with the aid of GCI.

On the night of 19/20 April 1941, the *Luftwaffe* launched a massive attack on London. Over 700 bombers were despatched, of which 24 were shot down by the defences. On 3/4 May, a force of 298 bombers struck at Liverpool, which had suffered ten major night raids since 28 August 1940 and many more smaller ones; the city sustained severe damage, particularly in the docks area, where an ammunition ship was hit and blew up.

The main German night offensive ended on 16/17 May with a major raid on Birmingham. There was a minor raid on Liverpool on 29 May, and on the 31st some incendiaries fell on the docks. A few of the 90 aircraft despatched to Liverpool and Bristol on 31 May strayed far to the west – possibly as a result of countermeasures jamming their navigational aids – and dropped their bombs on Dublin, killing 28 people and seriously injuring 87. Manchester had a sizeable raid on 1 June, and that same night HE bombs again damaged the dock areas of Liverpool.

After that, the night raids on Britain tailed away to insignificant levels. Early in June 1941, the bulk of the *Kampfgeschwader* in western Europe were moved east, to take part in the invasion of the Soviet Union.

**30 September** A day of heavy air activity, beginning with an attempted attack on London by 200 enemy aircraft in two waves. The attack was intercepted by 12 fighter squadrons and most of the raiders were turned back over Kent with heavy losses. An attack on the Westland aircraft factory at Yeovil was also beaten off. The day's operations cost the *Luftwaffe* 45 aircraft, the RAF 17.

**1–7 October** The beginning of October saw a change in the *Luftwaffe*'s tactics. Attacks on southern England were now made by formations of bomb-carrying Messerschmitts operating at high altitude, rather than by heavily-escorted bomber formations. To counter these new methods, No. 11 Group instituted high-level standing patrols on a line covering Biggin Hill – Maidstone – Gravesend. The main bomber force of the *Luftwaffe* now operated almost exclusively at night against British targets; London was bombed by an average of 150 bombers on every night of October except one. On **7 October** ZG 76 suffered heavily while escorting an attack on Yeovil, losing seven Bf 110s. In operations 1–7 October the *Luftwaffe* lost 78 aircraft, the RAF 30.

**12 October** On the orders of Adolf Hitler, the following directive was circulated to the German armed forces: 'The Führer has decided that from now until the spring, preparations for Sea Lion shall be continued solely for the purpose of maintaining political and military pressure on England. Should the invasion be reconsidered in the spring or early summer of 1941, orders for a renewal of operational readiness will be issued later. In the meantime, military conditions for a later invasion are to be improved.' Air losses in the battle over England, 8–12 October inclusive, were *Luftwaffe* 33 aircraft, RAF 28.

**15 October** A morning attack on London by Bf 109 fighter-bombers wrecked the approach to Waterloo station and temporarily closed the railway lines. Factories on the south bank of the Thames were badly hit, and in the evening a major attack wrecked parts of the docks, Paddington, Victoria, Waterloo and Liverpool Street stations. Civilian casualties were 512 killed, with 11 000 made homeless. *Luftwaffe* losses 13–15 October were 16 aircraft, 12 of them on the 15th. The RAF lost 19, 15 of them on the 15th.

**16–24 October** Continued attacks by high-flying fighter-bombers, operating in streams or in massed raids. The biggest German losses during this period were on 16 October, when they lost ten aircraft against the RAF's one, and on the 18th, when they lost 11 for no RAF losses. Total casualties 16–24 October were *Luftwaffe* 59, RAF 16.

**25 October** For the first time, England was attacked by Italian aircraft: 16 Fiat BR.20 bombers which carried out an inconclusive night raid on Harwich. These aircraft belonged to the *Corpo Aereo Italiano*, established on Belgian airfields on 22 October 1940 at the request of the Italian leader Benito Mussolini (a move agreed to with great reluctance by the Germans). Fiat BR.20s of the 13° and 43° *Stormo* carried out eight night attacks on

**Above:**
*Even as the threat of invasion receded after the RAF's victory, aircraft of Bomber Command continued to attack barges and naval installations in occupied Europe. Photograph shows a Handley Page Hampden being bombed-up.*

**Below:**
*Although the Hurricane destroyed more enemy aircraft in the Battle of Britain, the Supermarine Spitfire, with its clean aerodynamic lines, captured the public's imagination.*

east coast towns before the end of 1940, but only three daylight raids were attempted. These were escorted by Fiat CR.42s and Fiat G.50s of the 56° *Stormo*, but the Italians suffered heavily at the hands of the RAF's fighters. In all, between 25 October and 31 December 1940, the *CAI* despatched 97 bomber and 113 fighter sorties against east coast targets.

**27 October** Seven RAF airfields were attacked by fighter-bomber formations or individual tip-and-run raiders, forcing Fighter Command to fly 1007 defensive sorties.

**29 October** Further heavy fighter-bomber attacks on RAF airfields and coastal targets. The *Luftwaffe*'s combat loss of 20 aircraft included five Bf 109s of JG 51, bounced by RAF fighters as a result of good tactical planning. From now on, because of increasingly bad weather and the fact that the *Luftwaffe* had exhausted its tactical options, the daylight offensive against Britain began to peter out. Although daylight incursions would continue for the rest of the year, weather permitting, to all intents and purposes the Battle of Britain was over. The *Luftwaffe* had been rebuffed, its tactical advantages ruined by inept political and military decisions. Losses for the period 25–31 October inclusive were: *Luftwaffe* 75, RAF Fighter Command 37.

# Mediterranean Theatre
# June 1940–May 1941

## 1940

**11 June** In the first wartime operation of the Italian *Regia Aeronautica*, 35 Savoia-Marchetti S.79 bombers of the 2°, 11° and 41° *Stormi*, escorted by Macchi C.200s of the 6° *Gruppo*, attacked Hal Far airfield and the seaplane depot of Kalafrana on the island of Malta. One S.79 was slightly damaged by one of four Gloster Sea Gladiators that formed the island's only fighter defence. By the end of the day Malta had been attacked seven times; no Italian aircraft was lost. Also on 11 June, 26 Bristol Blenheims of Nos. 44, 55, and 113 Sqns made a dawn bombing and strafing attack on the Italian airfield at El Adem, Libya. Three aircraft FTR (A/A fire). The attack was repeated later in the day and in all 18 enemy aircraft were destroyed on the ground.

**14 June** The first air combat between British and Italian aircraft took place over North Africa when seven Gloster Gladiators of No. 33 Sqn, Mersa Matruh, attacked a Caproni Ca 310 escorted by three Fiat CR.32s; the Caproni and one of the Fiats were shot down.

**20 June** The first night raid on Malta was carried out by six S.79s of the 34° *Stormo*.

**22 June** The first Italian loss over Malta occurred during the afternoon, when a lone S.79 of the 34° *Stormo*, on a reconnaissance mission, was shot down by two Gloster Sea Gladiators. During the night, the port of Alexandria – the base of the British Mediterranean Fleet – was bombed by S.81s of the 39° *Stormo*, operating from Rhodes.

**3–4 July** Fairey Swordfish aircraft of No. 820 Sqn from the carrier HMS *Ark Royal*, escorted by Blackburn Skuas of No. 803 Sqn, carried out attacks on French warships at Mers-el-Kebir and Oran as part of the plan to destroy the French Mediterranean Squadron. In the Oran attack,

*Important installations in the Suez Canal Zone were well defended, as this AA barrage over Alexandria illustrates.*

the Swordfish torpedoed the French flagship *Dunkerque* and put her out of action. The escorting Skuas were engaged by Morane 406 and Curtiss Hawk 75A fighters of GC I/10 and two were shot down.

**5 July** Swordfish aircraft, operating from an Egyptian airfield, sank the Italian destroyer *Zeffiro* and the 4000-ton freighter *Manzoni*, as well as badly damaging the destroyer *Euro* and the 15000-ton troopship *Liguria*, in a torpedo attack on Tobruk harbour.

**8 July** Units of the Mediterranean Fleet were subjected to high-level attacks by 72 Italian bombers, which hit and damaged the cruiser HMS *Gloucester*. The attacks continued at intervals for five days and some raids were intercepted by Sea Gladiators from the carrier HMS *Eagle*, which claimed five S.79s destroyed for no loss. During this period, Swordfish aircraft from HMS *Eagle* carried out several abortive torpedo attacks on heavy Italian surface units and also torpedoed and sank the destroyer *Leone Pancaldo* and a tanker in the Sicilian harbour of Augusta (on 9 July).

**18 July** Gibraltar was bombed for the first time by three S.82s, which made a second attack on the 25th. The aircraft used HE and so-called 'FF' torpedo bombs, which were retarded by parachute. This was released when the missile hit the water, and a propeller driven by compressed air came into action. These weapons were generally unreliable.

Following preliminary skirmishing between British Dominion and Italian air forces in East Africa, the campaign in this area began in earnest with an Italian offensive into British Somaliland. The Italians initially enjoyed air superiority, with a bombing force comprising nine *Gruppi* of Caproni Ca 133s, four *Gruppi* of Savoia S.81s and *Gruppo* of S.79s, supported by five *Gruppi* of Fiat CR.32 and CR.42 fighters. The RAF's bomber force comprised Nos. 14, 47 and 223 Sqns with Vickers Wellesleys, supported by the Blenheim IV Fs of No. 203 Sqn. These were later reinforced by Gloster Gladiator fighters, Blenheim I bombers and by Junkers Ju 86 and Fairey Battle bombers of the South African Air Force; the South Africans also employed some Gladiators and a few Hawker Hurricanes. Free French units equipped with Martin 167 reconnaissance-bombers also took part. By January 1941 the RAF had nine squadrons in East Africa and the SAAF eight. The campaign lasted until June 1941, and ended in a complete Allied victory.

**15 August** First operation by Italian torpedo-bombers: an abortive attack by five S.79s of the *Reparto Speciale Aerosilurante* (Special Torpedo-Bomber Unit) on ships in Alexandria harbour.

**September** With air reconnaissance indicating that the Italian forces in Libya were about to launch a major offensive towards the Egyptian frontier, Blenheims of No. 202 Group began attacks on Tobruk harbour and enemy airfields. As the enemy columns advanced along the coast road they were subjected to increasingly heavy air attack and, as their lines of communication lengthened, this had a telling effect. The Italian advance was halted several miles east of Sidi Barrani, before they were in sight of the British defences at Mersa Matruh.

**4 September** Swordfish aircraft of Nos. 813, 815, 819 and 824 Sqns, operating from the carriers HMS *Illustrious* and HMS *Eagle*, attacked enemy airfields in the Dodecanese islands, notably Maritza on Rhodes. Four of the 13 Swordfish from HMS *Eagle* were shot down by Fiat CR.42s.

**17 September** Italian torpedo-bombers registered their first success when an S.79 of the 278[a] *Squadriglia* topedoed the cruiser HMS *Kent*, putting her out of action for a year. Two more warships, HMS *Liverpool* and HMS *Glasgow*, were also disabled by this unit before the end of the year.

**20 September** Hurricane fighter-bombers carried out their first mission in the Mediterranean Theatre; aircraft of No. 261 Sqn, Malta, attacked targets in Sicily.

**26 September** The first air reinforcements arrived in Egypt by the newly-created ferry route across Africa from Takoradi on the Gold Coast; five Hurricanes and one Blenheim reached Abu Sueir, the fighters being allocated to No. 274 Sqn.

**9 October** The Western Desert Air Force (Air Vice-Marshal Arthur Coningham) was formed to conduct future air operations in North Africa, with its HQ at Maaton Bagush. Air Vice-Marshal Longmore now had at his disposal three squadrons of Wellington bombers (Nos. 37, 38 and 70), five squadrons of Blenheims (Nos. 11, 39, 45, 55 and 113), three squadrons of Hurricanes (Nos. 33, 73 and 274) and one Gladiator squadron (No. 112). There were also three squadrons equipped with Army Co-operation Westland Lysanders: Nos. 3 and 6 RAAF, and No. 208 RAF. Taking advantage of the delay in the Italian offensive, the British land forces commander, General O'Connor, planned to launch a counter-offensive, the success of which would largely depend on the application of tactical air power.

*8 November* Units of the British Mediterranean Fleet, operating in the Ionian Sea, were heavily attacked by the *Regia Aeronautica*. The attacks were broken up by Fairey Fulmar fighters of No. 806 Sqn from HMS *Illustrious*, which claimed ten enemy aircraft for no loss to themselves.

*11 November* 21 Fairey Swordfish of Nos. 815 and 819 Sqns, HMS *Illustrious*, attacked heavy units of the Italian Fleet at Taranto naval base. Twelve of the Swordfish were armed with torpedoes, the others carried flares for target illumination, and bombs for use against oil installations on shore. The attack was brilliantly successful. The 26 622-ton battleship *Conte di Cavour* was so badly damaged that she took no further part in hostilities; her sister ship, the *Caio Duilio*, had to be beached and was out of action for six months; while the 35 000-ton *Littorio* was disabled for four months. At one stroke, the Italian battle fleet had been reduced from six to three capital ships at a crucial point in the Mediterranean war, and for the loss of only two Swordfish. It was the first real demonstration of the aircraft carrier as a means of exer-

cising flexible, mobile sea power rather than as a mere adjunct to the fleet, and it was to have a profound effect on the conduct of future naval air operations.

*15–30 November* Blenheims and Wellingtons of the Western Desert Air Force stepped up attacks on targets deep behind enemy lines; Blenheims and Lysanders, under heavy fighter escort, also provided complete reconnaissance coverage of the Italian front line south of Sidi Barrani. These sorties often met with strong opposition, mainly from Fiat CR.42s, but the RAF Hurricanes and Gladiators established a definite measure of air superiority. On 20 November, for example, nine Hurricanes and six Gladiators engaged 60 CR.42s and destroyed seven for no loss.

*9–16 December* The British counter-offensive

*This reconnaissance photograph shows Italian warships heavily damaged amid oil slicks in Taranto Harbour after the Fleet Air Arm attack of 11 November 1940.*

# THE GREEK CAMPAIGN
# OCTOBER 1940–MAY 1941

ON 28 October 1940, Italian forces invaded Greece from Albania, which Italy had overrun in April 1939. Great Britain was obliged to contribute to the defence of the Balkan countries in the event of such an invasion, and although the Greek Government declined an offer of British ground forces for fear of provoking a German reaction, the British offer of air support was eagerly accepted. The first squadron to be deployed was No. 30, with a mixture of Blenheim bombers and fighters; this was given the task of defending Athens, and by the end of November 1940 it had been joined by two more Blenheim squadrons, Nos. 84 and 211, and a squadron of Gladiators, No. 80. In December, No. 112 Sqn's Gladiators also arrived in Greece and were deployed to Larissa in the central region; No. 80 Sqn went to Paramythia in the north-west to support the Greek army on the Albanian frontier, while the Blenheim squadrons were deployed to Elevsis and Menidi, close to Athens. From time to time, during the moon periods, the bomber force was assisted by small numbers of Wellingtons, detached from squadrons in the Canal Zone.

Air operations over Greece were severely hampered by bad weather. Nevertheless, by the end of the year, the Gladiator pilots of No. 80 Sqn had claimed the destruction of 40 enemy aircraft for the loss of 6 of their own, and although the claim was probably exaggerated there is no doubt that the Gladiators established a measure of air superiority during those winter months. On 9 February 1941, 14 Gladiators of No. 80 Sqn, led by Flight Lieutenant M. St J. Pattle, engaged 40 Fiat G.50 fighters and shot down 4 of them without loss. Pattle, a South African, was credited with the destruction of 30 enemy aircraft – and possibly more – during operations in Egypt and Greece; he was killed on 20 April 1941, while commanding No. 33 Sqn.

By the end of February 1941, all three fighter squadrons in Greece were re-equipping with Hurricanes, and these operated alongside the remaining Gladiators. On 28 February, 16 Hurricanes and 12 Gladiators were patrolling at 14 000 ft (4270 m) when they encountered 50 Italian Fiat G.50s and Fiat CR.42s. In the course

of the battle – which lasted for nearly two hours, with pilots of both sides breaking off to land and refuel before returning to the fray – the RAF fighters destroyed 27 of the enemy for the loss of only one Gladiator. There was no doubting the accuracy of the RAF's claim, for the demise of each Italian aircraft was witnessed and confirmed by the Allied ground forces.

Early in 1941, the RAF air commitment in Greece was reinforced by the arrival of Nos. 11 and 113 Sqns with Blenheims, and No. 33 with Hurricanes. The Lysanders of No. 208 Sqn were also ordered to move across, and while their move was under way, the Germans entered the battle for Greece. On 6 April, 27 German divisions, of which seven were armoured, struck simultaneously in eastern Macedonia and also drove into Yugoslavia at seven points.

At the time of the German invasion, the Royal Yugoslav Air Force had 38 Hurricane Mk Is on charge, 18 with the 51st Fighter Sqn of the 2nd Regiment at Sarajevo, 14 with the 33rd Fighter Sqn of the 4th Regiment at Zagreb, and six with the 34th Fighter Sqn of the 4th Regiment. Some of these were destroyed on the ground during the initial *Luftwaffe* attacks, but the survivors fought on for a week against hopeless odds. Unfortunately no record of their operations exists, although it is known that in one regrettable incident over Belgrade, the Hurricanes became involved in a dogfight with Bf 109s belonging to their own side (the RYAF had 73 of the German fighters) and a number of each type was shot down in error. By 14 April, with their bases on the point of being overrun, the Yugoslav pilots destroyed their remaining aircraft and escaped to Greece.

After seizing their principal objectives in Yugoslavia, the Germans launched an all-out offensive in Greece, where British troops had now been committed, with the full support of *Luftflotte* 4. Faced with overwhelming enemy air superiority, it was not long before the RAF commander, Air Vice-Marshal J.H. D'Albiac, was compelled to withdraw what remained of his effective strength to the Athens area to provide air cover for an inevitable evacuation.

By 19 April, the four Hurricane squadrons in

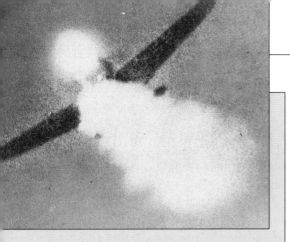

Greece could muster no more than 22 serviceable aircraft, and a few days later all but seven of these were destroyed in low-level strafing attacks; the survivors were evacuated to Crete. With this blow, Allied air resistance over the Greek mainland virtually ceased.

On 1 May 1941, the last Commonwealth forces were evacuated from the Greek mainland, and 30 000 Allied troops worked desperately to prepare the island of Crete to meet an enemy invasion. The island's entire air defence force consisted of 14 fighters – the surviving RAF Hurricanes from Greece, together with four Sea Gladiators and three Fairey Fulmars of the Fleet Air Arm. Most were destroyed on the ground, and on 18 May the remnants were evacuated to Egypt. Some sorties were flown over Crete by Hurricanes from Egypt, fitted with long-range tanks, but the time they could spend over the island was minimal.

The Luftwaffe forces committed to the invasion of Greece comprised 430 bombers, 180 fighters, 700 transport aircraft and 80 gliders. The numbers of aircraft available to Luftflotte 4 had been swollen by the transfer of Fliegerkorps X from Sicily to Greece, a move that brought a much-needed respite to the battered island of Malta.

The German attack on Crete began on 20 May with very heavy bombing, followed by the landing of airborne forces, and it was not long before the ill-equipped defenders were hard pressed. The Royal Navy, operating off the island without air cover, suffered dreadfully from dive-bomber attacks, losing three cruisers and six destroyers sunk; two battleships, an aircraft carrier, six cruisers and seven destroyers suffered more or less severe damage.

By the end of May, the battle for Crete was over, with about half the island's defenders killed or captured. But the German airborne forces had also taken tremendous punishment; Crete was their last major operation of the war.

*The Bf 109F could be outfought, as this photograph of one going down in flames shows.*

opened in the Western Desert. The squadrons of the Desert Air Force now switched their attacks to troop concentrations and supply columns. Relentless pressure was maintained, and by 16 December the last of the Italian forces had been driven back across the Egyptian border. With the enemy in full retreat, Desert Air Force bombers attacked airfields and supply dumps, while fighters provided air cover for the ground forces and also for Royal Navy warships that were shelling troop concentrations north of the Bardia–Tobruk road.

**20 December** Beginning on this date, units of Luftflotte 2 were transferred to Sicily for air operations against Malta. The forces available initially included 53 Junkers Ju 87s of I and II/St.G.2, together with 12 Ju 87s of St.G.1. By the beginning of January the Luftwaffe strength on Sicily was 141 aircraft, operating under Fliegerkorps X, whose headquarters had been transferred from Norway.

# 1941

**8 January** RAF Wellington bombers operating from Malta raided Naples, now the headquarters of the Italian fleet, and badly damaged the battleship *Giulio Cesare*, with the result that both she and the *Vittorio Veneto* were withdrawn to Genoa in the north. This attack served to underline the strategic importance of Malta as an offensive base.

**9–11 January** The *Regia Aeronautica* and *Fliegerkorps* X mounted heavy attacks on a convoy of four merchant ships sailing from Gibraltar to Malta and escorted by warships of Force H, the Royal Navy task force that included HMS *Illustrious*. On 10 January the latter was seriously damaged by Ju 87s of St.G. 1 and 2, which also set ablaze the cruiser HMS *Southampton* (later abandoned and sunk by the British). HMS *Illustrious* was hit again later in the day by a Ju 87 of the Italian 237ª *Squadriglia*. After temporary repairs at Valletta the carrier sailed for the USA for more extensive repair work and was out of action for several months. Her air group was left behind on Malta, and the Fulmars of No. 806 Sqn took part in the defence of the island until March, when they embarked on the carrier HMS *Formidable*. From 11–19 January, Valletta harbour was subjected to very heavy attacks by Ju 87s and Ju 88s, attempting (unsuccessfully) to finish off the disabled *Illustrious*.

**21 January** The Desert Air Force mounted its biggest effort to date in support of an attack on Tobruk by Dominion forces. The port fell within 48 hours. By 7 February the British offensive in North Africa had achieved a brilliant success; the Italian Tenth Army had been utterly destroyed.

**February** Units of the newly-formed German *Afrika Korps* (General Erwin Rommel) began ferrying to North Africa. The initial German build-up was supported by about 110 aircraft, including He 111s of II/KG 26 (which had been operating from Benghazi since mid-January), a *Gruppe* of St.G.3 and Bf 110s of ZG 26.

**10 February** Six Whitleys of No. 58 Sqn, deployed to Malta, dropped 38 officers and men of No. 11 Air Service Battalion at Tragino in southern Italy in an attempt to destroy the aqueduct there. The aqueduct was blown up, but the paratroops were captured as they made their way to the coast for evacuation by submarine. Two more Whitleys made a diversionary attack on Foggia; one force-landed in enemy territory.

**9 March** The aircraft carrier HMS *Formidable* joined the Mediterranean Fleet via the Cape of Good Hope; her air group comprised the Fairey Albacores of No. 826 Sqn and the Fulmars of No. 803 Sqn (later to be joined by the Fulmars of No. 806 Sqn from Malta).

**28 March** Aircraft of HMS *Formidable*'s air group, together with Blenheims from Egypt, attacked Italian naval units off Cape Matapan. Torpedoes hit the battleship *Vittorio Veneto*, which escaped, and the cruiser *Pola*, which was sunk by Force H warships together with two heavy cruisers and two destroyers detached to escort her. This crippling blow against the Italian Fleet was achieved at the cost of one Albacore destroyed.

**31 March** Opening of the *Afrika Korps* offensive towards Tobruk. British Commonwealth forces, depleted by the needs of the Greek campaign, were soon in retreat. By 15 April, Tobruk had been surrounded and Axis forces had crossed the Egyptian frontier at Halfaya. At this time, again because of the deployment of squadrons to Greece, British air strength in Cyrenaica had been reduced to three squadrons of Hurricanes and one of Blenheims, supported by three squadrons of Wellingtons from the Canal Zone and one from Malta.

**April–May** RAF units in Iraq operated against rebel forces led by Rashid Ali, which had seized power and besieged RAF Habbaniyah. The attackers were held off by aircraft of No. 4 Flying Training School, mainly Hawker Audaxes and Airspeed Oxfords, supported by Wellingtons and Blenheims. On 2 May, No. 4 FTS flew 193 bombing and strafing sorties, losing four aircraft, and subsequently attacked the retreating enemy columns. The revolt had limited *Luftwaffe* support, a small number of Bf 110s and He 111s, flown to a Syrian base from Crete. Several of these aircraft were destroyed by Gladiators of No. 94 Sqn before the revolt collapsed at the end of May.

# The German Offensive in Russia June–December 1941

**22 June** The first German air operations over the Soviet Union, excluding reconnaissance flights, were carried out from 3.15 a.m. by 30 Heinkel He 111s of KG 2, 3 and 53. Operating in flights of three, they attacked Soviet airfields close to the frontier with fragmentation bombs. Throughout the remainder of the day, Soviet airfields and other installations were subjected to heavy attacks by 510 bombers and 290 dive-bombers, supported by 440 Bf 109s and 40 Bf 110s. Four *Luftflotten* were involved in the assault: *Luftflotte* 1 (Army Group North), 2 (Army Group Centre), 4 (Army Group South) and 5 (Northern Norway). Soviet losses in the day's operations were 1489 aircraft destroyed on the ground and 322 in the air; the *Luftwaffe's* loss was 35. It was the greatest victory every achieved in a single day by one air force against another.

The invasion caught the Soviet High Command (*Stavka*) completely unawares and it was not until 10 a.m. that the Soviet Air Force began operations. These were almost totally lacking in coordination, and communications with ground forces were virtually non-existent. Priority on this and subsequent days was given to attacks on German armoured and mechanized columns, a task in which the Russian bombers suffered appalling losses. On the Western Front alone (there were five Soviet fronts in all, Northwestern, Western, Southwestern, Southern and Northern) the Russians lost 528 aircraft on the ground and 210 in the air on 22 June.

**25 June** In one of the few successful operations during the initial phase, 236 bombers of the Soviet 2nd, 41st, 55th and 5th (Composite) Air Divisions, escorted by 224 fighters, bombed 19 airfields in northern Norway and Finland in an attempt to frustrate attacks on Leningrad. The Russians claimed 41 aircraft destroyed or damaged.

**1 July** To minimize aircraft losses, most Soviet air operations were now flown at high and medium levels, small bomber formations operating under heavy fighter escort. The number of night operations increased, with bombers of the Long-Range Aviation (ADD) carrying out small-scale attacks on Königsberg, Danzig, Bucharest, Constanta and Ploesti. The priority early in July also switched to airfield attacks.

**10 July** German and Finnish forces of Army Group North began a major offensive against Leningrad. In the 22 days of fighting before the offensive was halted, the Soviet Air Force flew 16 567 sorties. Soviet fighters over the besieged city developed new tactics involving 'attack' and 'cover' groups. Older aircraft such as the I-16 and I-153 formed the attack groups, which engaged enemy bombers, while the cover groups were composed of newer types such as the MiG-3 and Yak-1, whose task was to engage enemy fighter escorts. These operations were undertaken by the 7th Fighter Corps, together with units of the Baltic Fleet Air Force.

**19–25 July** Following the capture of Smolensk by the Germans on 19 July, the Soviet Air Force launched a maximum effort in support of ground forces, trying to break through the encircling enemy. Regiments of the 47th (Composite) and 43rd Fighter Air Divisions were divided into elements of one or two squadrons which operated from unprepared strips 7–12.5 miles (11–20 km) behind the front line in order to increase the sortie rate.

**21/22 July** Moscow was attacked for the first time by Ju 88s of KG 3 and 54 and He 111s of KG 28, 53 and 55, with *Kampfgruppe* 100 and III/KG 26 forming a pathfinder force. The 127 bombers, flying over distances of up to 380 miles (610 km) to the Russian capital, attacked through very heavy AA and searchlight defences, dropping 104 tons of HE and 46 000 incendiaries. The bombing was haphazard and generally ineffective. On the next night 115 bombers were despatched to Moscow, but after that the numbers declined. Of the 76 raids on Moscow in 1941, 59 were carrried out by groups of between three and ten aircraft. The lack of a long-range strategic bombing force was to be a hindrance to the *Luftwaffe* during the campaign in Russia; the Soviet government quickly set up war production factories that were out of range of existing German bomber aircraft.

**26 July** The *Stavka* formed a new front (the Central Front) from units of the Western Front for continuing operations in the Smolensk area. The new front was supported by the 11th and 28th (Composite) and the 13th Bomber Air Divisions.

**7 August** Five Ilyushin Il-4 bombers of the 1st Bomber Aviation Regiment of the Soviet Baltic Fleet, commanded by Air Force Colonel E.N. Preobrazhenski, took off from the Estonian island of Oesel to raid Berlin. Two of the bombers were shot down during the outward flight, two more failed to find the target, and one bombed the suburbs of Berlin, causing insignificant damage. Four more raids were carried out between 7 August and 4 September, but few of the attacking aircraft found the target and 75 per cent losses were sustained.

**August-September** The Soviet Air Force, although it fought desperately, was deficient in equipment and was tactically no match for the experienced *Luftwaffe* units. In the months that followed the German invasion, it was powerless to prevent one catastrophe after another overwhelming the Soviet armies. Between 3 and 10 August 100 000 Soviet troops were encircled and captured in the Ukraine; further south, the 4th Romanian Army had advanced to Odessa but the garrison, the Independent Coastal Army, held out from 5 August; air cover from then until the Odessa garrison was evacuated to the Crimea early in October was provided by the 69th Fighter Regiment, with as few as 30 aircraft.

In September, 650 000 Russian troops were trapped in the Kiev pocket; only 150 000 escaped. In the north, Leningrad was isolated. The way was open for the seizure by the Germans of the Kharkov industrial region, the Don basin, and the Crimea – and for the massive offensive by Army Group

Centre, supported by *Luftflotte* 2, that was designed to take Moscow itself.

**23 September** Junkers Ju 87 dive-bombers of *Stukageschwader* St.G. 2 *Immelmann* carried out the first of a series of attacks on units of the Soviet Baltic Fleet at Kronshtadt naval base, sinking the 23 600-ton battleship *Marat* and severely damaging the battleship *Oktyabraya Revolutsiya*.

**30 September** The assault on Moscow began with an offensive on the Bryansk Front, the Germans breaking through with the help of massive tactical air support. By 6 October the Germans had seized Bryansk and Orel and were advancing on Tula, but this move was slowed by persistent Soviet Air Force attacks. In an 11-day period, the Russians flew 1700 sorties, over half against the German 2nd *Panzer* Army.

**10 October** A new Soviet defensive line was established at Mozhaisk. Air cover was provided by fighters of the 6th Fighter Air Corps. The main Russian tactical air effort was sustained by units

*In September 1941 the RAF despatched Nos. 81 and 134 Sqns, with Hurricanes, to north Russia to protect the vital Arctic ports. Photograph shows Hurricanes at Vaenga.*

equipped with twin-engined Petlyakov Pe-2 light bombers, which suffered heavy losses. The Ilyushin Il-2 *Shturmovik* assault aircraft, which had entered service in July 1941, was committed to the battle in growing numbers.

**11–31 October** During this period the Soviet Air Force flew 10 200 sorties. These included operations by the 81st Long-Range Air Division (Ilyushin Il-4s) which attacked German communications and airfields. Between 30 September and 14 October the Russians claimed to have destroyed 1020 German aircraft, 54 per cent on the ground, 40 per cent in air combat and 16 per cent shot down by AA.

**15 November** The Germans, having taken 700 000 Russian prisoners in the preceding three weeks,

**Above:**
*During the Soviet winter offensive in the Moscow
sector, paratroop forces were dropped behind
German lines by Tupolev TB-3 aircraft.*

**Below:**
*When Nos. 81 and 134 Sqns left Russia, their
Hurricanes were turned over to the Soviet Naval Air
Arm's 72nd Air Regiment. One of them is seen here
in Russian markings.*

launched the second phase of their offensive. This was an attempt to encircle Moscow from the Tula and Kalinin areas, but very slow progress was made. The Russian winter was now in its early stages, hampering operations in the air and on the ground. By the end of the month the German offensive had come to a standstill.

**6 December** For outstanding operations in the defence of Moscow, the 29th and 129th Fighter Regiments and the 215th Ground Attack Regiment were designated as Guard Regiments, the first units to be so honoured. During these defensive operations, all units were integrated for the first time under the command of the Red Army Air Force, rather than being responsible to the commanders of the various Army Fronts. Centralized control of this kind was to remain a key feature of Soviet Air Force operations.

On 6 December 1941, the Red Army went over to the offensive in the Moscow sector. Before the counter-attack was launched, advanced airstrips were laid down between 9½ and 19 miles (15–30 km) behind the front. Units assigned to these bases were supported by teams sent from airfield service battalions and sufficient supplies were stockpiled for two or three sorties by a complete air regiment. Other supplies, spares etc. were stockpiled at depots set up between 155–220 miles

(250–400 km) behind the front, and these held sufficient stocks for 15 to 20 days of operations.

The Russian counter-offensive was supported principally by the Moscow Military District Air Force, a composite air group under the command of General I.F. Petrov, and the 6th Fighter Air Corps, which now assumed the ground attack role. Much of the air effort was devoted to the direct support of the Russian spearhead, the 1st and 30th Shock Armies. By 9 December, air reconnaissance established that the Germans were in retreat. On the night of 15/16 December, in order to cut the main enemy line of retreat along the Klin-Teryayeva Slboda road, 415 paratroops were dropped from TB-3 aircraft; they carried out harassing attacks on the enemy until 31 December, when the survivors joined the 30th Army. Further paratroop drops were made between 18 and 31 January 1942, some 3600 men being involved, and in February the entire 4th Parachute Corps of around 10 000 men was dropped behind enemy lines, together with a large quantity of supplies and arms. Both civil and military aircraft were involved in these operations, which contributed in no small measure to the removal of the German threat to Moscow. But there was no major Russian breakthrough; both sides, by the beginning of 1942, had fought themselves to a standstill.

# The Air War Against Japan, 1941–42

## 1941

**7 December** Japanese carrier aircraft launched a devastating attack on ships of the United States Pacific Fleet at Pearl Harbor, Hawaii. The attack involved a force of six aircraft carriers, the *Hiryu*, *Akagi*, *Kaga*, *Soruo*, *Shokaku* and *Zuikaku* and 465 aircraft under the command of Admiral Nagumo. The first strike, launched at dawn from a point 230 miles (370 km) north of Oahu, was made by 40 Nakajima B5N *Kate* torpedo-bombers, 49 *Kates* carrying armour-piercing bombs, 51 Aichi D3A1 *Val* dive-bombers and 43 Mitsubishi A6M2 *Zero* fighters. The attack lasted 30 minutes and struck

the anchorage and outlying air bases. The second strike, just over an hour later, was made by 54 *Kate* bombers, 78 *Val* dive-bombers and 35 fighters; this lasted 65 minutes but was hampered by dense smoke from the burning anchorage and by heavy anti-aircraft fire, as well as by small numbers of US fighters. Of the 94 US warships in the harbour, 18 were sunk or suffered major damage; eight were battleships. Of the 384 US aircraft on the island, 188 were destroyed and another 159 damaged. The cost to the Japanese was five *Kates*, nine *Zeros* and fifteen *Vals*.

The three aircraft carriers of the US Pacific Fleet were not present at the time of the attack. The USS *Saratoga* (CV-3) was just out of overhaul and was moored at San Diego; the USS *Lexington* (CV-2)

was at sea about 425 miles (680 km) southeast of Midway, towards which she was heading to deliver a Marine Scout Bombing Squadron; the USS *Enterprise* (CV-6) was also at sea about 200 miles (320 km) west of Pearl Harbor, returning from Wake Island after delivering a Marine Fighter

**Left:**
*As well as inflicting enormous damage on the US Pacific Fleet, the Japanese attack on Pearl Harbor devastated neighbouring air bases.*

*Pearl Harbor, 7 December 1941: firefighting and rescue operations under way around the stricken battleship* West Virginia.

Squadron. Her Scouting Sqn 6 (VF-6, Grumman F4F Wildcats), launched early in the morning to land at Ewa airfield on Oahu, arrived during the second strike and joined Curtiss P-40s of the 47th Pursuit Sqn in engaging the enemy.

Also on 7 December, a Lockheed Hudson patrol aircraft of No. 1 Sqn RAAF, flying from Kota Bharu in Malaya, sighted a Japanese battleship, 5 cruisers, 7 destroyers and 22 freighters 265 miles east of the Malay Peninsula in the Gulf of Siam. Two Catalina flying boats of No. 205 Sqn RAF (Seletar, Singapore) were despatched to shadow the convoy; one was shot down by Japanese fighters.

**8 December** Japanese forces invaded Siam (Thailand) and made amphibious landings on the east coast of Malaya. The landings in the Kota Bharu area were opposed by Hudsons of No. 1 Sqn RAAF, which attacked singly. Their bombs hit the freighter *Awagisan Maru*, which exploded with heavy loss of life. As a result of the determined Australian bombing attacks, it was later revealed that 15000 enemy troops had been killed at the beachhead. No. 1 Sqn RAAF lost eight aircraft; the remaining five were evacuated to Kauntan, 150 miles (240 km) to the south.

The Japanese landings in Malaya were accompanied by bombing attacks on the airfields of Sungei Patani, Penang, Alor Star and Butterworth, the aircraft dropping fragmentation bombs. Singapore was also bombed for the first time. The airfield attacks were mainly carried out by Mitsubishi Ki 21 *Sally* bombers of the 3rd *Hikoshidan* (Air Division) operating from French Indo-China under naval fighter escort.

At the time of the Japanese invasion the fighter defence of Malaya and Singapore was the responsibility of No. 243 Sqn RAF, No. 488 Sqn RNZAF and Nos. 21 and 453 Sqns RAAF, all equipped with Brewster Buffalo Mk Is, and No. 27 Sqn RAF with Blenheim IFs. The bomber force comprised Nos. 34, 60 and 62 Sqns with Blenheim Mk Is, and Nos. 1 and 8 Sqns RAAF with Lockheed Hudsons. There were two torpedo-bomber squadrons, Nos. 36 and 100, with obsolete Vickers Vildebeests. By nightfall on 8 December, only 50 of the original 110 Commonwealth aircraft in northern Malaya remained airworthy, and the key airfields of Singora and Patani in Siam were in enemy hands.

**9 December** Blenheims of Nos. 34 and 62 Sqns carried out a successful attack on Singora and Patani, losing five aircraft. Shortly after their return, their base was heavily attacked by enemy aircraft, which destroyed all but one of the re-

maining Blenheims. The survivor carried out a lone attack on Singora through strong fighter opposition; its pilot, Flight Lieutenant A.S.K. Scarf of No. 62 Sqn, regained his airfield at Alor Star but later died of wounds. Five years later, when the full facts of his heroism was established, he was awarded a posthumous VC.

**10 December** Following heavy air attacks by Mitsubishi G3M *Nell* and G4M *Betty* bombers of the Imperial Japanese Navy, Japanese amphibious forces began landing at strategic points in the Philippine Islands. The initial air attacks destroyed 103 American aircraft on the ground. At the time of the Japanese invasion, the US air defences on the islands comprised the 24th Pursuit Group (3rd, 17th, 20th and 21st Pursuit Sqns with Curtiss P-40s) and the 34th Pursuit Sqn with Seversky P-35As. The Filipino Army also had a small number of ex-USAAF Boeing P-26s. Also included in the inventory were a number of Boeing B-17C Flying Fortresses and Douglas B-18s. By the end of December, only ten of the original 90 fighters were still operational.

In the afternoon of 10 December, 60 G3M2 *Nells* of the Genzan and Mihoro *Kokutais* (Air Corps) joined with 26 G4M1 *Bettys* of the Kanoya *Kokutai* in sinking the British battleship HMS *Prince of Wales* and the battle cruiser HMS *Repulse* off Malaya with bombs and torpedoes. Eleven Brewster Buffaloes of No. 453 Sqn RAAF arrived in the area too late to intervene.

Aircraft from the USS *Enterprise* attacked and sank the Japanese submarine I-70 north of the Hawaiian Islands. The I-70, which had been used to reconnoitre Pearl Harbor, was the first enemy warship sunk by US aircraft in World War II.

**11 December** An attempted Japanese landing on Wake Island was frustrated by four Grumman F4F-3 Wildcats of Marine Fighter Squadron 211 (VMF-211), which attacked with 100 lb (45 kg) bombs and machine-gun fire. The Japanese destroyer *Kisaragi* was sunk and several other ships damaged. Seven of the Squadron's original 12 Wildcats had been destroyed in an air attack on 8 December.

**21 December** The final Japanese assault on Wake Island began with an attack by 29 *Kate* and 99 *Val* bombers, escorted by 18 Zeros, from the carriers *Soryu* and *Hiryu*. A second attack the next day, by 33 *Vals* escorted by six *Zeros*, was opposed by VMF-211's two surviving Wildcats, which destroyed two *Zeros* before being overwhelmed. Wake Island fell to the Japanese on 23 December.

**23 December** 60 Japanese bombers escorted by 20 Nakajima Ki 27 *Nate* fighters, carrying out the first air raid on the Burmese capital, Rangoon, were intercepted by Curtiss P-40s of the 3rd Pursuit Sqn, American Volunteer Group, and Buffaloes of No. 67 Sqn RAF. The defenders destroyed six bombers and four fighters, but the RAF lost five Buffaloes and the AVG four P-40s.

**25 December** In a second air attack on Rangoon, again by 60 bombers and 20 fighters, the AVG and RAF dispersed the attacking force, destroying 18 bombers and six fighters before they reached the capital. Pilots of No. 67 Sqn claimed to have destroyed a further 12 over Rangoon itself.

**28 December** Japanese bombers, this time escorted by *Zeros*, carried out heavy attacks on the docks area of Rangoon and the AVG/RAF airfield at Mingaladon, using feint tactics to break through the fighter defences.

# 1942

**3 January** 51 Hawker Hurricane fighters (20 fitted with long-range tanks and flown off the carrier

*The brunt of the early air war against Japan was borne by the Curtiss P-40 Tomahawk, which was outclassed by the Mitsubishi Zero fighter. These aircraft of the USAAF 49th Fighter Group are seen at Darwin early in 1942.*

HMS *Indomitable*, the remainder offloaded in crates from merchant ships) arrived in Singapore with the advance parties of Nos. 17, 135, 136 and 232 Sqns, intended to reinforce the island. The Hurricanes fought against mounting odds and scored some notable successes, as on 20 January, when they shot down eight of a formation of 27 unescorted Japanese bombers over Singapore.

**26 January** At 1 p.m., nine Vickers Vildebeests of No. 100 Sqn and three of No. 36, escorted by a small number of Hurricanes and Buffaloes, attempted to make a torpedo attack on transport ships supporting a Japanese landing at Endau in southern Malaya. Five Vildebeests were shot down, mostly by Japanese fighters. At 3 p.m., nine Vildebeests of No. 36 Sqn made a second attack, again with a small fighter escort; all the torpedo-bombers were destroyed.

Reinforcements for Sumatra: on 26 January, 48 Hawker Hurricane Mk IIA fighters were flown off HMS *Indomitable* by pilots of Nos. 242, 258 and 605

Sqns RAF and dispersed on two airstrips in the Palembang area. These aircraft operated under the control of the newly-formed No. 226 Group (Air Commodore S.F. Vincent).

The remnants of the RAF bomber force on Singapore were also evacuated to Sumatra; these were accompanied by the survivors of three squadrons of Martin 139 bombers and one squadron of Buffaloes which had been sent to Malaya by the Dutch East Indies Air Force immediately on the outbreak of war. The Dutch operated a miscellany of aircraft, including Martin bombers, Buffaloes, Curtiss Hawk 75As, Curtiss-Wright CW-22 Falcons, Curtiss-Wright CW 21B interceptors and Koolhoven FK.51 observation aircraft. Most of the Dutch aircraft were withdrawn to Java by 1 February, the Martin 139s in particular having suffered very heavy losses. In all, about 80 Dutch bombers and 83 fighters saw action against the Japanese.

Reinforcements for Burma: at the end of January, 30 Hurricane Mk Is (later formed into No. 135 Sqn) and the Blenheims of No. 113 Sqn arrived in Burma from the Middle East. The Hurricanes were assigned to the defence of Rangoon, leaving the AVG and the Blenheims to attack the enemy's bases in Thailand. Later, the Hurricanes also joined in attacks on enemy airfields, using long-range fuel tanks.

**1 February** The Mingaladon Wing was formed under the command of Wing Commander Frank Carey for the defence of Rangoon. By mid-February this comprised three Hurricane squadrons, Nos. 17, 135 and 136, and the 3rd Pursuit Sqn of the AVG.

**3 February** First Japanese air attacks (by 165 aircraft) on Java. The raids were opposed by Dutch aircraft and by the P-40s of the 17th (Provisional) Pursuit Sqn, USAAF, newly arrived from Australia. The defenders claimed 22 Japanese fighters and several bombers destroyed; Allied losses were 14 Dutch fighters and three P-40s, with four B-17s destroyed on the ground. Later in February the 20th and 3rd Pursuit Sqns were also deployed to Java; the 20th PS lost eight out of 18 P-40s in clashes with the enemy during the ferry flight, and the 3rd PS lost nine out of 18 P-40s which crashed into high ground in fog.

**6–14 February** The Japanese mounted a series of heavy air attacks on the Palembang area. The Allied loss of 60 aircraft included 39 RAF Hurricanes, mostly destroyed on the ground on the 7th. On 14 February, the Japanese captured Palembang airfield with the use of airborne forces. A large

enemy convoy en route with forces for the occupation of Sumatra was attacked by Hudsons of Nos. 1 and 8 Sqns RAAF and Blenheims of Nos. 27, 62, 84 and 211 Sqns RAF, escorted by Hurricanes. Six enemy transports were sunk for the loss of seven aircraft.

**15–16 February** British, Dutch and American aircraft launched a maximum-effort operation against Japanese invasion forces off Sumatra, inflicting heavy destruction on landing ships in the Banka Strait and the mouth of the Palembang River. The enemy landing plan was completely disrupted, and thousands of troops killed. However, no Allied forces were available to exploit this success, and the position in Sumatra quickly became untenable, the remaining air units being evacuated to Java.

**18 February** The evacuation to Java was completed. At this point the RAF had 25 Hurricanes left, of which 18 were serviceable; these were divided between Nos. 232 and 605 Sqns and assigned to the defence of Batavia. The bomber force was reduced to 12 Hudsons and six Blenheims. On this day Japanese forces landed on the island of Bali, cutting off Java from the east.

**19 February** About 150 Japanese bombers and torpedo-bombers made a heavy attack on shipping in Port Darwin, northern Australia, sinking 11 transports and supply vessels. As Port Darwin was the only base in northern Australia from which Java could be supplied, this devastating attack virtually sealed the fate of the defenders there.

**20 February** USAAF B-17s and other Allied bombers attacked the Japanese invasion fleet off Bali, sinking one transport and damaging four warships. Six B-17s were lost, four after returning to base. Japanese aircraft carried out heavy attacks on Allied airfields.

**27 February** The seaplane tender USS *Langley*, the US Navy's first aircraft carrier, was sunk by enemy air attack 74 miles (119 km) from her destination while ferrying 32 USAAF P-40s to Tjilatjap, Java. This day saw the Battle of the Java Sea, in which four Japanese cruisers and 14 destroyers that were escorting their invasion force inflicted crippling losses on an Allied naval squadron.

**28 February** All available Allied bomber aircraft were despatched to attack enemy naval forces off Java. US bombers sank a transport and damaged a cruiser; Dutch Martin 139s hit a cruiser and a destroyer. RAF Blenheims and four Vildebeest torpedo aircraft destroyed a warship and hit several other vessels. Japanese occupation forces landed on Java.

*1 March* Martin 139s, Buffaloes, Hudsons and Blenheims attacked Japanese ships landing troops on Java. One Martin and one Buffalo were lost. In a second attack by all available aircraft, two troop-ships were sunk and heavy losses were inflicted on enemy forces. Allied losses included three CW-22 Falcons. The Japanese occupied Kalidjati, capturing a number of British aircraft; many Dutch and American fighters were destroyed in air attacks on Malang and Ngoro airfields.

*2 March* Martin 139s attacked Japanese shipping, sinking two large transports and damaging three others. Other Martins attacked Kalidjati, destroying many Japanese fighters on the ground. Two Martins were shot down. Thirteen British and Dutch fighters repeated the attack at dusk, also strafing Japanese troops.

*3 March* Allied aircraft began evacuating from Java. Small numbers of RAF and Dutch fighters continued to cover Allied ground forces until 7 March. Allied forces on Java capitulated the next day.

*8 March* Japanese forces entered Rangoon. The remnants of No. 221 Group RAF were moved north to Magwe and Akyab Island, where they were formed into Burwing (Nos. 17 and 45 Sqns) and Akwing (Nos. 67 and 139 Sqns).

*20 March* Ten Hurricanes and nine Blenheims from Magwe attacked Mingaladon, destroying 16 Japanese aircraft on the ground and 11 in the air. In the following 24 hours, 230 enemy aircraft attacked Magwe, destroying 11 Hurricanes and all but six Blenheims. The survivors were evacuated to Akyab.

*27 March* The Japanese launched a three-day assault on Akyab, destroying a further seven Hurricanes. The surviving Allied aircraft were evacuated to India. During these final days over 8600 civilians were airlifted to safety by Douglas Dakota transport aircraft of No. 31 Sqn RAF and the 2nd Troop Carrier Sqn, USAAF.

During the campaign in Burma, the Allied fighters had claimed the destruction of 233 enemy aircraft in the air and 58 on the ground, with a further 76 probably destroyed and 116 damaged, for the loss in air combat of 38 of their own number, including 22 Hurricanes.

*April* During the month, the 49th Fighter Group, USAAF (7th, 8th and 9th Fighter Sqns) was deployed to northern Australia for the air defence of Darwin, equipped with Curtiss P-40s. The Group was to be in action continually from this time until the end of the war.

*4–9 April* Action off Ceylon. On 4 April, a Catalina patrol aircraft of No. 205 Sqn RAF reported that a Japanese carrier task force was approaching Ceylon. At dawn the next day, a strong force of 150 Japanese aircraft attacked Colombo harbour in the hope of surprising the Royal Navy's Eastern Fleet at anchor. In fact, the Fleet was at sea. Thirty-six Hurricanes of Nos. 30 and 258 Sqns, together with six Fulmars of Nos. 803 and 806 Sqns, Fleet Air Arm, took off to intercept the enemy over the sea, having been alerted by radar. Fifteen Hurricanes and four Fulmars, outclassed by the *Zeros*, were shot down. At that time it was estimated that the Japanese had lost 18 aircraft in combat and five more to anti-aircraft fire, but these claims were never substantiated. A more accurate assessment is that the enemy lost seven aircraft, mostly to AA fire. The following morning, 12 Hurricanes of No. 261 Sqn and six RN Fulmars being operated by No. 273 Sqn RAF were scrambled to intercept an enemy raid on China Bay airfield and the neighbouring dockyards. Fifteen enemy aircraft were claimed destroyed for the loss of eight Hurricanes and three Fulmars. The surviving Hurricanes and Fulmars suffered further losses in subsequent attacks, particularly in the defence of Trincomalee. On 9 April, the surviving fighters were despatched to provide air cover for the carrier HMS *Hermes* and other warships which were being attacked by Japanese torpedo-bombers and dive-bombers. By the time the fighters arrived the *Hermes* was already on fire and sinking, as were the Australian destroyer *Vampire*, the corvette HMS *Hollyhock* and two Fleet Auxiliaries. Earlier, Japanese carrier aircraft had also sunk the cruisers HMS *Dorsetshire* and HMS *Cornwall*. In these attacks the enemy dive-bombing – by Aichi D3A1 *Vals* – was devastatingly effective, the aircraft achieving an accuracy of up to 87 per cent.

*18 April* From a position at sea 668 miles (1075 km) from Tokyo, the aircraft carrier USS *Hornet* launched 16 North American B-25 Mitchell bombers of the 17th AAF Air Group, led by Lieutenant Colonel J.H. Doolittle, for the first attack on the Japanese homeland. All the B-25 crews bombed their assigned targets in the Tokyo, Yokosuka and Osaka-Kobe areas and then diverted to China, where they planned to land; this was frustrated by bad weather and most baled out. Of the 80 crew members who took part, ten were killed, either accidentally or as a result of falling into enemy hands in China, and 15 were injured. The Tokyo Raid had far-reaching consequences; as a direct result, Admiral Yamamoto, the Japanese Naval Commander-in-Chief launched an ambitious plan to extend the eastern perimeter of the Japanese conquests in the Pacific and bring the US Pacific Fleet to battle.

**4–8 May** The Battle of the Coral Sea. In the first naval engagement in history fought without opposing ships making contact, United States carrier forces prevented a Japanese attempt to land at Port Moresby, New Guinea, by turning back the enemy's covering carrier force, the latter comprising the aircraft carriers *Zuikaku*, *Shokaku* and *Shoho*. The opening phase of the battle began on **3 May** when Japanese troops landed on the island of Tulagi. Task Force 17 (Rear Admiral F.J. Fletcher) was despatched with the carrier USS *Yorktown* to attack the invasion force. On **4 May**, the *Yorktown* launched a strike force comprising Douglas SBD Dauntless dive-bombers of Squadron VS-5, Douglas TBD Devastator torpedo-bombers of VT-5, and Grumman F4F Wildcats of VF-5. One destroyer, a minelayer, a transport and a number of seaplanes were destroyed and the Japanese evacuated the landing force. On **5 May**, the *Yorktown* joined other Allied naval units, including Task Force 11 (Rear Admiral A.W. Fitch) with the carrier USS *Lexington* south of the Louisiades, and after stationing an attack group in the probable track of the enemy transports, moved northward in search of the enemy covering force. On **7 May** the light carrier *Shoho* was attacked and sunk by TBDs and SBDs of the *Lexington*'s air group, together with TBDs of VT-5; meanwhile, Japanese aircraft attacked the separately operating attack group, sinking the destroyer USS *Sims* and the fleet oiler USS *Neosho*. On **8 May**, the fleet carrier *Shokaku* was attacked and heavily damaged by aircraft from both US carriers, but Japanese carrier aircraft, in a parallel attack, hit the *Lexington* with two torpedoes and damaged the *Yorktown* with a bomb hit below decks, although she remained operational. Later, fuel vapour in the *Lexington* exploded, causing uncontrollable fires; the carrier was abandoned and sunk by a US destroyer. Although a tactical victory for the Japanese, the battle forced the Port Moresby invasion to be called off, resulting in a clear strategic victory for the Allies.

**3–6 June** The Battle of Midway. A strong Japanese thrust in the central Pacific, with the intention of occupying Midway Island, was led by a four-carrier Mobile Force comprising the *Akagi*, *Kaga*, *Hiryu* and *Soryu*, supported by heavy units of the Main Body (First Fleet) and covered by a diversionary attack by carrier aircraft on Dutch Harbor in the Aleutians. The thrust towards Midway was met by a greatly outnumbered US carrier force composed of Task Force 17 (Rear Admiral F.J. Fletcher) with the USS *Yorktown* and Task Force 16

(Rear Admiral R.A. Spruance) with the USS *Hornet* and USS *Enterprise*, and also by Navy, Marine Corps and Army air units based on Midway. The opening action of the battle took place on **3 June** when the Japanese fleet was sighted by a PBY Catalina; six TBF Avengers of VT-8's shore-based detachment were launched to attack the Japanese together with Army B-17s and Marine SB2U Vindicators. None of the Avengers scored a hit and only one returned to Midway. At 7 a.m. on **4 June**, the *Enterprise* and *Hornet* launched their strike groups, 14 TBDs of VT-6 and 15 of VT-8, with F4Fs of VF-6 flying top cover. VT-8 attacked first and all 15 aircraft were shot down by *Zeros*; only one crew member survived. VT-6, attacking the *Kaga* in turn, lost ten aircraft before they reached their dropping points. The *Enterprise*'s air group, attacking the *Soryu* with 12 TBDs of VT-3 and 17 SBDs of VB-3, escorted by six F4Fs of VF-3, fared no better. Only five TBDs survived to make their torpedo attacks, and three of these were shot down on the way out. Of the 41 TBDs launched, only six returned to the Task Force, and one of these ran out of fuel and ditched.

The sacrifice of the three VT squadrons was not in vain; they had absorbed the bulk of the enemy fighter attacks, and the *Zeros* were still scattered when 37 Dauntless dive-bombers from the *Enterprise*'s VB-5 and the 17 from *Yorktown*'s VB-3 made their attack, sinking the *Akagi*, *Kaga* and *Soryu*. The cost to the dive-bombers was 16 aircraft from the *Enterprise* air group. A Japanese counter-attack from the *Hiryu* damaged the *Yorktown*, but she returned to full operation after a short time. Then a second attack was made by six *Kate* torpedo-bombers; two were shot down, but the other four launched their torpedoes and two hit the carrier, which had to be abandoned. She was later sunk by a submarine. At 5 p.m., the *Hiryu* was crippled in an attack by 24 SBDs from the *Enterprise*; her burned-out hulk was sunk by a Japanese destroyer the next day. For the cost of 92 aircraft and the *Yorktown*, the US Navy had destroyed four fleet carriers, three-quarters of the Japanese Navy's carrier striking force. With control of the air irretrievably lost, the Japanese withdrew under attack by Midway-based aircraft (5 June) and carrier air (6 June) in which the heavy cruiser *Mikuma* was sunk and the *Mogami* severely damaged in an air strike from USS *Enterprise*.

Other US losses in the Midway battle were 40 shore-based aircraft and the destroyer *Hammann*, sunk by the same submarine that torpedoed the crippled *Yorktown*. In addition to the four carriers, the Japanese lost 258 aircraft and a large percentage of their most experienced carrier pilots. The decisive defeat inflicted on the Japanese put an end to their successful offensive and effectively turned the tide of the Pacific War.

*7 August* The capture of Guadalcanal. Air support for the US Marines' first amphibious landing of World War II was provided by the aircraft carriers USS *Wasp*, USS *Enterprise* and USS *Saratoga* of the Air Support Force (Rear Admiral L. Noyes) and by Navy, Army and Marine units of Aircraft, South Pacific (Rear Admiral J.S. McCain) operating from bases on New Caledonia and in the New Hebrides. Carrier forces withdrew from direct support on *9 August* but remained in the area to give overall support to the campaign, during which they participated in several of the naval engagements fought over the island. Land-based air support, based on the newly-captured Henderson Field, initially comprised the F4F Wildcats of VMF-223 and VMF-224 and the SBD Dauntlesses of VMSB-231 and VMSB-232, the latter delivered by the escort carrier USS *Long Island* on *20 August*.

*23–25 August* The Battle of the Eastern Solomons. On 23 August, land-based bombers from Henderson Field and strike aircraft from the USS *Saratoga* set out in search of Japanese surface units located by US scouting seaplanes, but failed to find the enemy in bad weather. On 24 August, Japanese strike aircraft from the light carrier *Ryujo* were intercepted by Wildcats from Henderson Field and heavily defeated; the *Ryujo* herself was sunk in an attack by 30 SBD dive-bombers and 8 Avengers. Strike aircraft from the main Japanese Striking Force (the carriers *Zuikaku* and *Shokaku*) attacked and damaged the USS *Enterprise*, forcing her to retire, although the attackers suffered heavy losses from American combat air patrols and AAA. The *Shokaku* was slightly damaged by SBDs from the *Enterprise* air group. The Japanese naval commander, Admiral Nagumo, had lost so many aircraft and crews in these encounters that he was forced to withdraw his forces, leaving a troop convoy bound for Guadalcanal without support. Attacked by aircraft from Henderson Field and by AAF bombers, the convoy was also compelled to retire. This action marked the end of the first phase of the battle for Guadalcanal.

*26–27 October* The Battle of Santa Cruz. This action was the climax of a Japanese plan to neutralize and capture Henderson Field as a preliminary to the destruction of the remaining US naval air resources in the Solomons. At this point the US Navy had only two carriers in the area, the USS *Enterprise* and the USS *Hornet*, the latter having replaced the USS *Saratoga*, damaged by a subma-

rine torpedo on 31 August and withdrawn to Pearl Harbor for repair. The Americans had also lost the USS *Wasp*, sunk by a submarine on 15 September while escorting a troop convoy to Guadalcanal.

To activate their plan, the Japanese naval forces put to sea from Truk on *11 October*. They included the Carrier Striking Force with the *Shokaku* and *Zuikaku*, the light carrier *Zuiho* and seven destroyers; the Advance Striking Force with the new carriers *Junyo* and *Hiyo* supported by two battleships, five cruisers and 13 destroyers; and the Battleship Striking Force with two battleships, three cruisers and eight destroyers. The latter subjected Henderson Field to a very heavy bombardment on 13 October and on three successive nights; aircraft losses were partly made good by the deployment of 19 F4Fs of VMF-212 from Espiritu Santo, together with seven SBDs. The total number of aircraft available to defend Henderson Field against attacks by enemy troops (landed on 15 October) was now 60. As well as the USMC Wildcats, these included a small number of AAF Bell P-39 Airacobras.

On *26 October* the opposing carrier task forces located one another almost simultaneously and launched their strike aircraft. The Japanese force, in two waves 45 min apart, comprised 42 Aichi D3A2 *Val* dive-bombers, 36 Mitsubishi B5N2 *Kate* torpedo-bombers and 55 *Zero* fighters from the *Shokaku*, *Zuikaku* and *Zuiho*; the *Hornet* and *Enterprise* launched three waves comprising 30 SBD Dauntlesses, 20 TBM Avengers and 24 F4F Wildcats. While these forces were en route, two SBDs from the *Enterprise*, on an armed reconnaissance, encountered the *Zuiho* and bombed her, damaging her flight deck and rendering it unusable.

At 9.40 a.m., purely by chance, the opposing air groups ran into each other and a brief air battle developed in which the *Zeros* shot down three SBDs and four Wildcats for the loss of five of their own number. At 10.10 a.m., the first Japanese wave located the *Hornet* and subjected her to a bomb and torpedo attack that left her burning and listing in the water. Thirty minutes later, the *Hornet*'s strike aircraft also found the *Shokaku* and scored four hits with 1000 lb (450 kg) bombs, putting the carrier out of the battle. The other US strike aircraft located the enemy cruiser and destroyer forces and attacked with bombs and torpedoes, damaging one cruiser. Meanwhile, the Japanese second wave attacked the *Enterprise*, scoring three bomb hits; torpedo attacks were frustrated by the Wildcat combat air patrols. Further attacks in the afternoon, launched by the *Zuikaku* and *Junyo*, succeeded in sinking the crippled *Hornet*. Fortunately for the Americans, the Japanese were unable to exploit their tactical success. They had exhausted their fuel reserves and were compelled to withdraw to Truk to replenish.

The final stages of the naval battle for Guadalcanal,

in November, were characterized by engagements between battleships, cruisers and destroyers, fought almost entirely at night. The USS *Enterprise* contributed to the sinking of 89 000 tons of enemy shipping, operating from a relatively safe station in the Coral Sea.

# The Air War Over North-West Europe 1941–42

## 1941

**10 January** Six Bristol Blenheim bombers of No. 114 Sqn, escorted by six squadrons of Spitfires and Hurricanes of No. 11 Group, attacked ammunition and supply dumps in the Forêt de Guines, south of Calais, in the first of the RAF's so-called *Circus* operations – co-ordinated bomber and fighter attacks on targets in the area immediately across the Channel.

**10/11 February** First operational mission by Short Stirling heavy bombers; three aircraft of No. 7 Sqn, RAF Oakington, were despatched to attack an oil storage depot at Rotterdam.

**24/25 February** First operational mission by Avro Manchester heavy bombers; six aircraft of No. 207 Sqn, RAF Waddington, attacked warships in Brest harbour. One aircraft crashed on the return flight.

**25/26 February** 80 aircraft of RAF Bomber Command (Wellingtons, Whitleys, Hampdens) were despatched to bomb Düsseldorf, and 64 crews claimed to have bombed the target. Only seven bomb loads actually fell in the city. All aircraft returned safely.

**26/27 February** 126 RAF bombers were despatched to attack Cologne; 106 crews claimed to have bombed the target, but only ten HE and 96 incendiary bombs fell in the city.

**28 February/1 March** 116 Blenheims, Hampdens, Wellingtons and Whitleys made an unsuccessful

attempt to bomb the battleship *Tirpitz* in Wilhelmshaven harbour. One Blenheim FTR.

**1/2 March** 131 Blenheims, Hampdens, Wellingtons and Whitleys were despatched to attack Cologne. The raid caused substantial damage. Six aircraft FTR; 14 more were abandoned over England in dense fog.

**10/11 March** First operational mission by Handley Page Halifax heavy bombers; six aircraft of No. 35 Sqn, RAF Linton-on-Ouse, were despatched to attack Le Havre dockyard. Four bombed the primary, one bombed Dieppe and one aborted. One aircraft (Squadron Leader Gilchrist) was shot down by an RAF night fighter over Surrey while returning to base. The pilot and one crew member survived.

**12/13 March** First raid on Germany by the RAF's new heavy bombers; Halifaxes and Manchesters formed part of a force of 88 aircraft despatched to attack the Blohm & Voss shipyards in Hamburg. The Focke-Wulf aircraft factory at Bremen was also attacked by 54 Wellingtons of No. 3 Group while 33 Blenheims bombed the city centre. Berlin was raided by 72 aircraft, causing damage in the southern suburbs. Seven aircraft FTR from the night's operations.

**13/14 March** 139 bombers were despatched to attack the Blohm & Voss shipyards in Hamburg. The target was hit and the city suffered heavy damage. Six aircraft were lost, including a Manchester shot down by an intruder shortly after take-off.

*The Handley Page Halifax was the second of the RAF's four-engined heavy bombers, the first being the Short Stirling. The example shown is a Mk I of No. 35 Sqn, RAF Leeming.*

**14/15 March** 101 aircraft were despatched to bomb oil plants at Gelsenkirchen; one plant was badly hit and forced to cease production. One Wellington FTR.

**18/19 March** 99 aircraft attacked shipyards in Kiel, causing heavy damage to U-boat production facilities.

**30/31 March** 109 aircraft were despatched to bomb the battlecruisers *Scharnhorst* and *Gneisenau* in Brest harbour, without result. All aircraft returned safely.

**1 April** First operational use of 4000 lb (1812 kg) bombs by RAF Bomber Command; two were dropped on Emden in the early hours of the morning by Wellingtons of Nos. 9 and 149 Sqns.

**6 April** Following further unsuccessful attacks on the German warships in Brest harbour by RAF Bomber Command, six Bristol Beaufort torpedo-bombers of No. 22 Sqn RAF Coastal Command were despatched to attack the *Gneisenau*, which had been moved to a more exposed anchorage while an unexploded bomb was made safe. One of the Beauforts (Flying Officer Kenneth Campbell) made a successful attack on the *Gneisenau* before being shot down, inflicting serious damage that required six months to repair. Campbell was awarded a posthumous VC.

**7/8 April** In the largest raid mounted so far by Bomber Command, 229 aircraft carried out a 5-hr attack on Kiel, causing extensive damage and casualties in the dockyards area. Four bombers FTR. An even more damaging attack on this target was made by 169 aircraft on 8/9 April; 125 people were killed, 300 injured and more than 8000 made homeless.

**14 April** The first Boeing Fortress I destined for Bomber Command arrived in Britain, landing at Prestwick after the fastest Atlantic crossing yet recorded: 8 hr 26 min from Gander, Newfoundland. Fortress Is were allocated to Nos. 90 and 220 Sqns.

**25/26 April** First operational missions by Nos. 304 and 305 (Polish) Sqns; four Wellingtons bombed oil storage tanks at Rotterdam.

**8/9 May** RAF Bomber Command mounted 364 sorties, mainly against Hamburg and Bremen; this was the largest number despatched so far in one night. The attack on Hamburg by 188 aircraft caused severe damage, especially in areas housing oil depot and shipyard workers; 185 people were killed and 518 injured.

**9–18 May** Major Bomber Command operations during this period involved two night attacks on Mannheim and Ludwigshafen, two on Hamburg, two on Cologne, one on Hannover and one on Kiel. Damage in these raids, which involved 100 aircraft on average, was generally scattered and light. Six bombers FTR.

The main effort of Bomber Command was directed against enemy shipping, with particular emphasis on attacks on targets connected with the U-boat threat and on the French Atlantic ports sheltering enemy capital ships. However, the large number of sorties flown by the Command against the French Atlantic ports produced little result, and the AOC Bomber Command, Air Chief Marshal Sir Richard Pierse, felt that the tonnage of bombs would have been used to better effect in attacks on Germany's industrial complexes – so-called 'area' attacks. This type of attack therefore continued, and for the first time Bomber Command began to inflict damage on a large scale. Also during this period, Blenheims of No. 2 Group carried out many sweeps to the enemy coast, attacking shipping and shore installations, while Hampdens of No. 5 Group laid mines in enemy waters.

**12/13 June** First operation by No. 405 (Vancouver) Sqn RCAF; three Wellingtons were despatched to bomb marshalling yards at Schwerte. No. 405 Sqn was the first of many RCAF squadrons to serve in Bomber Command.

**22 June** The first three *Gee* navigational stations were inaugurated in the British Isles. *Gee* was a fixing system that relayed electronic pulses from three ground stations to receiver equipment in aircraft, which measured the difference in time of receipt from each ground station and converted the resulting information into terms of distance. Two sets of readings were plotted on a special chart known as a *Gee* Lattice Chart; the point of intersection was the aircraft's position. This was later developed into *G-H*, a highly accurate blind-bombing system in which an aircraft transmitted pulse signals to two ground stations, which received them and transmitted them back. This enabled the aircraft to measure continuously its distance between two known points, track itself over any target within range of the system and determine its bomb-release point.

**4 July** 15 Blenheims of Nos. 105 and 107 Sqns were despatched to make a low-level attack on Bremen, despite a complete lack of cloud cover en route and in the target area. Three aircraft aborted and four were shot down. The raid leader, Wing Com-

*Power stations in occupied France were high on the list of Bomber Command's priorities in 1941. The photograph shows an attack on a target in Holland.*

mander H.I. Edwards of No. 105 Sqn, was awarded the VC.

**8 July** First operational mission by Fortress Is of No. 90 Sqn; three aircraft made a highly accurate attack on the dock area of Wilhelmshaven, bombing from high level.

**24 July** Daylight attacks were carried out by 79 Wellingtons on the *Gneisenau* and *Prinz Eugen* at Brest. Diversionary attacks were carried out by three Fortresses and 18 Hampdens. The attack encountered strong and prolonged German fighter opposition; two Hampdens and ten Wellingtons were shot down by fighters or flak. Meanwhile, 15 Halifaxes of Nos. 35 and 76 Sqns attacked the *Scharnhorst* at La Pallice; five direct hits were scored, but three bombs passed straight through the ship and the other two failed to explode. Five of the Halifaxes, which were unescorted, were shot down and all the rest damaged, but the damage they had inflicted on the *Scharnhorst* put her out of action for another four months. The attacks on Brest and La Pallice were made in conjunction with a diversionary bombing attack on Cherbourg docks by 36 Blenheims, escorted by Spitfires.

During July, Bomber Command mounted major attacks on 16 German industrial towns and cities. Cologne was attacked five times, over 100 bombers being despatched on each occasion, but the raids inflicted only minor damage. Accurate target location remained a major problem, which would only be resolved with the adoption of new navigational aids and techniques.

**11/12 August** Two Wellingtons of No. 115 Sqn carried out the first operational trial of the new *Gee* navigational device in an attack on Mönchengladbach. The trials continued for two more nights, and were successful. Mass production of the equipment was begun.

**12 August** The Knapsack and Quadrath power stations near Cologne were subjected to a low-level daylight attack by 54 Blenheims of No. 2 Group, each carrying two 500 lb (226 kg) bombs. The bombing was accurate, but ten Blenheims were shot down. The bombers were escorted to the target area by Westland Whirlwinds of No. 263 Sqn; Fighter Command flew a total of 175 sorties in support of the raid, but this was the deepest daylight penetration made so far by Bomber Command and Spitfires did not have sufficient range to escort the Blenheims to the target. Diversionary *Circus* operations were carried out by Blenheims, Hampdens and Fortresses.

**12/13 August** 70 aircraft were despatched to attack Berlin, but only 32 reached the target. Nine bombers (three Manchesters, three Wellingtons, two Halifaxes and a Stirling) FTR.

**29/30 August** Frankfurt was attacked by 143 aircraft, but again the bombing was light and scattered. This was the largest force despatched by Bomber Command in August, raids on other targets usually involving between 50 and 100 aircraft. The attack on Frankfurt saw the first operational mission flown by No. 455 Sqn RAAF, the first Australian bomber squadron to form in Britain. One Hampden (Squadron Leader French) took part.

August saw the first operational use of the *Lichtenstein* B/C airborne interception equipment by the German night-fighter force. The first success was on the night of **9/10 August**, when an unidentified RAF bomber was shot down by a Messerschmitt Bf 110 of *Nachtjagdgeschwader* (NJG) 2 flown by *Oberleutnant* Ludwig Becker and *Feldwebel* Josef Staub.

**7/8 September** Berlin was attacked in good visibility by 197 aircraft, causing considerable damage east and north of the city centre. Fifteen aircraft FTR.

**8 September** Four Fortress Is of No. 90 Sqn, despatched to bomb the *Admiral Scheer* at Oslo, were intercepted by German fighters before reaching the target. Two Fortresses were shot down and a third crashed on landing at RAF Kinloss, Scotland. The Squadron's Fortresses were withdrawn from operations over Europe later in the month.

**10/11 September** 76 aircraft (Wellingtons, Halifaxes and Stirlings) carried out the heaviest attack so far on Turin, Italy, causing damage to the city centre and the Fiat steelworks. Five aircraft FTR.

**12/13 September** An attack on Frankfurt by 130 aircraft once again indicated the problems of target location. Although many crews found the target, many more mistakenly bombed Mainz, 20 miles (32 km) away.

**15/16 September** An attack on Hamburg by 169 aircraft caused heavy damage to various parts of the city, 4000 lb (1812 kg) 'Blockbuster' bombs proving particularly effective. Eight aircraft FTR. One crew member lost on this mission was Sergeant James Ward, a New Zealander of No. 75 Sqn, who had won the VC on 7/8 July 1941 by climbing out on to the wing of his aircraft to extinguish a fire.

**12/13 October** 152 aircraft were despatched to attack Nuremberg for the first time. The raid was characterized by a catalogue of navigational errors, compounded by variable winds; some crews erroneously bombed towns and even villages at up to 95 miles (150 km) from the intended target. Lauingen, on the Danube 65 miles (105 km) from Nuremberg, was subjected to a savage attack that lasted four hours, 200 HE bombs and 700 incendiaries falling on the village. One aircraft making its first operational sortie on this night was Stirling N6086 F-Freddie *MacRobert's Reply* of No. 15 Sqn; the aircraft was donated to the RAF by Lady MacRobert in memory of her three sons, killed flying.

*7/8 November* Despite unfavourable weather reports, Bomber Command mounted a maximum effort, despatching 392 aircraft on operations. A total of 169 aircraft were sent to Berlin in what was to be the last major attack on the German capital until January 1943; bombing was scattered and mostly on the outskirts. Twenty-one aircraft were lost, many when they ran out of fuel after encountering unexpected headwinds during the return flight. Mannheim was also attacked by 55 aircraft, seven Wellingtons being lost, while Cologne was raided by 61 Hampdens and 14 Manchesters of No. 5 Group for no loss. Most of the crews in these two attacks appear to have missed the target. Elsewhere, 30 aircraft carried out minelaying and minor bombing operations; six FTR, including three Halifaxes out of 13 minelaying off Oslo. The total effort for the night was 392 sorties for the loss of 37 aircraft.

*15 November* The de Havilland Mosquito light bomber entered service with No. 105 Sqn (No. 2 Group) at RAF Swanton Morley.

In November 1941 the RAF suspended *Circus* operations, which had been generally unsuccessful. Handling the large fighter formations that were being sent across the Channel presented enormous problems, and it was soon apparent that the Spitfire was quite unsuited to escort duties. It was only when they were escorting bombers attacking targets near the coast that the Spitfire pilots enjoyed some freedom of action in seeking out enemy fighters; when escorting raids that penetrated deeper inland they were forced to stay close to the bombers in order to conserve fuel, and there was very little margin left for combat. The German tactics were to stay high above the RAF formations until the latter turned for home, short of fuel, when the Bf 109s would dive down on selected victims and then climb hard for altitude again. A classic case was *Circus* 62, one of the biggest mounted in 1941; on 7 August 18 squadrons of Spitfires and two of Hurricanes accom-

panied six Blenheims in an attack on a power station near Lille, and at the end of the day the RAF had lost six fighters against a claim of only three Bf 109s destroyed. Matters became even worse in September, when pilots reported encountering a new radial-engined enemy fighter. It was the Focke-Wulf Fw 190, and within weeks it had established air superiority for the Germans.

*December* Following the losses sustained in November, much of Bomber Command's effort in this month was devoted to renewed attacks on German naval facilities in the Atlantic and North German ports. Brest, for example, was attacked 16 times in the course of the month.

*7 December* Stirlings of Nos. 7 and 15 Sqns made the first of a series of attacks on the *Scharnhorst* and *Gneisenau* at Brest using an early type of blind-bombing device known as *Trinity*. This was in effect the protoype of *Oboe*, a radio aid to bombing in which two ground stations transmitted pulses to an aircraft, which then received and retransmitted them. By measuring the time taken for each pulse to go out and return, the distance of the aircraft from the ground stations could be accurately measured. If the distance of the target from Station A was known, the aircraft could be guided along the arc of a circle whose radius equalled this distance. The bomb-release point was calculated and determined by Station B, which 'instructed' the aircraft to release its bomb-load when the target was reached.

*24 December* The Lancaster Mk I entered service with No. 44 Sqn at RAF Waddington.

*27 December* In the first Combined Operations raid of the war against German-held territory, 19 Blenheims and ten Hampdens of Bomber Command flew in support of a landing operation by Commandos on the Norwegian island of Vaagso. The Blenheims attacked enemy airfields, while the Hampdens bombed gun positions and laid a smoke-screen. Eight bombers out of 29 despatched FTR.

# 1942

During the early weeks of 1942, RAF operations over NW Europe were again mainly concerned with attacks on German warships and naval facilities in the Atlantic and North German ports. Other operations involved intruder missions by Blenheims of No. 2 Group to enemy airfields in France, Holland and Belgium

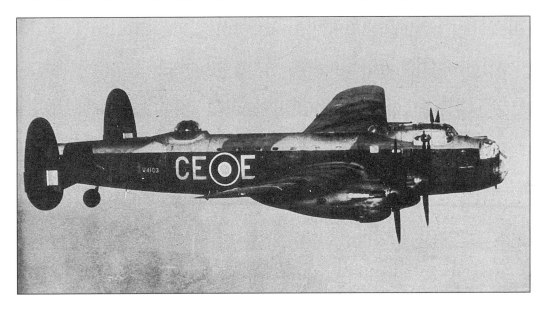

*The famous Avro Lancaster, which with the Halifax devastated Germany's cities in area bombing attacks. The aircraft shown belongs to an Operational Training Unit.*

**12 February** The Channel Dash. The news that the battlecruisers *Scharnhorst* and *Gneisenau* and the light cruiser *Prinz Eugen* had left their Atlantic harbours and were proceeding at speed through the English Channel was broken by a Spitfire pilot of Fighter Command, who located the warships off Le Touquet. On 4 February, every available aircraft of Bomber Command had been armed and placed on two hours' readiness in anticipation of the breakout, while Nos. 10, 11 and 12 Groups of Fighter Command stood ready to provide air cover. After a week, however, the state of readiness had been downgraded and squadrons released for other operations, with the result that on 12 February only the Hampdens of No. 5 Group were on four-hour readiness. The three Coastal Command squadrons of Beaufort torpedo-bombers were widely dispersed around the UK (one was in Scotland, waiting to attack the *Tirptiz* if she emerged from her Norwegian anchorage); between them they could muster only 35 aircraft, to which were added six Swordfish of the Fleet Air Arm. The main hope of inflicting damage on the warships therefore rested with Bomber Command, but when the vessels broke out it was in bad weather, with a cloud base of only 600 ft (180 m). This meant that the armour-piercing bombs with which many of the aircraft were loaded were useless, as they had to be dropped from at least 6000 ft (1830 m) for maximum effect. By the time the bomb loads were changed and the bombers got airborne, the warships had already been subjected to a gallant attack by six Swordfish of No. 825 Sqn, Fleet Air Arm (which earned a posthumous VC for their leader, Lieutenant Commander Eugene Esmonde) and a torpedo strike by a handful of Coastal Command Beauforts. All six Swordfish and three Beauforts were shot down.

A total of 242 Bomber Command sorties went out in three waves but, although most aircraft reached the target area, only one in six managed to attack the warships. Most failed to sight the enemy vessels at all; others were unable to bomb because of the low cloud base. Fifteen bombers were lost, in addition to six Swordfish and three Beauforts. Overhead, RAF fighters fought savage battles with the *Luftwaffe*, which was up in strength to provide cover for the vessels.

The passage of the warships (two of which were subsequently damaged by mines before reaching port in Germany) through the English Channel in broad daylight revealed the seriously depleted state of Coastal Command's torpedo strike capability. Soon afterwards, No. 144 Sqn was transferred from Coastal to Bomber Command and its Hampdens converted to carry torpedoes; three other squadrons, Nos. 51, 58 and 77, were also withdrawn from the Bomber Command Order of Battle and assigned to maritime patrol duties with their Whitley aircraft.

**27/28 February** Whitley aircraft of No. 51 Sqn dropped 119 British paratroops at Bruneval, north of Le Havre, to capture parts of a German *Würzburg* radar installation. The raiding force was evacuated by sea.

*3/4 March* 235 aircraft of Bomber Command were despatched to attack the Renault Factory at Billancourt, Paris, which was producing war material for the Germans; 223 aircraft bombed the target with excellent results, halting production for four weeks. A feature of the raid was the use of experienced crews to mark the target with flares, foreshadowing the 'pathfinder' technique that would be developed later. One unfortunate aspect was that 367 French people were killed and hundreds more injured – a higher casualty toll than had so far been sustained by any German city.

*8 March* First attack on a land target by Douglas Boston bombers of No. 2 Group: a daylight raid on the Matford works at Poissy under cover of diversionary *Circus* operations, the latter newly resumed after a five-month break. The Bostons, which were operated by Nos. 88 and 226 Sqns, had played a limited part in the warship attacks of 12 February.

*8/9 March* First large-scale use of *Gee* by Bomber Command: 74 Wellingtons equipped with the device formed the leading wave of a force of 211 aircraft despatched to attack the Krupps factories at Essen. Although *Gee* assisted the main force in navigating to the target area, the raid was disappointing because Essen was shrouded in industrial haze and the main target was not hit at all.

Eight aircraft FTR. A second raid on the next night was also a disappointment, bombs falling over a wide area of the Ruhr.

*10/11 March* Avro Lancasters carried out their first bombing attack on a German target: two aircraft of No. 44 Sqn formed part of a force of 126 aircraft despatched to attack Essen. Once again results were disappointing, only two bombs falling near the Krupps factory.

*13/14 March* The first successful *Gee* attack: 50 aircraft equipped with the device led a 135-strong force to Cologne, where industrial establishments suffered heavy damage. It was later estimated that this raid was five times more effective than the average of previous attacks on this target. Only one aircraft – a Manchester – was lost.

*28/29 March* 191 aircraft of Bomber Command (out of 234 despatched) made a devastating incendiary attack on Lübeck, destroying 200 acres of the Old Town and destroying or damaging 62 per cent of the town's buildings; 320 people were killed and several hundred injured. Twelve aircraft FTR. This raid was the first major success for Bomber Command against a German target and was achieved in excellent visibility without the aid of *Gee*, the town being out of range. This was the only time Lübeck was heavily bombed by the RAF, the port being used for the shipment of Red Cross supplies.

*10/11 April* During an attack on Essen by 254 aircraft, a Halifax of No. 76 Sqn (Pilot Officer M.

# THE BAEDECKER RAIDS

THE so-called *Baedecker* raids of 1942, directed against British towns and cities which had little strategic value but which were of great historic and cultural importance, were launched on the orders of Adolf Hitler as a reprisal for the attack on the ancient Hanseatic city of Lübeck by 234 aircraft of RAF Bomber Command on Palm Sunday night (28/29 March) 1942. The first raid was carried out on 23/24 April 1942 against Exeter by 45 aircraft, mostly Dornier Do 217Es of KG 2; this proved abortive and was followed by two more against Bath on 25 and 26 April. The city suffered heavily, and in three more successive raids Norwich was attacked twice and York once, the latter city

suffering heavy damage from incendiary bombs. The most successful attack was on 3/4 May, when 131 tons of bombs were dropped on Exeter, severely damaging the city centre. During the remainder of the month Cowes, Norwich, Hull, Poole, Canterbury and Grimsby were all raided, but then the emphasis switched to more important strategic targets such as Birmingham, Southampton and Middlesbrough. Between 23 April and 31 July 1942 the *Baedecker* raids cost the *Luftwaffe* 67 aircraft, mostly Do 217Es of KG 2. About 20 enemy aircraft were destroyed during this period by Mosquito night-fighters, the aircraft which, at last, was beginning to tip the scales against the German night bombers.

Renaut) dropped Bomber Command's first 8000 lb (3630 kg) bomb. Bombing in this raid was poor and fourteen aircraft FTR. Essen was attacked again by 251 aircraft on 12/13 April, with equally poor results. There were no further major raids on this target – which so far had cost Bomber Command 69 aircraft – until September 1942.

*17 April* 12 Lancasters of Nos. 44 and 97 Sqns flew at low level across occupied Europe to make a daylight attack on the M.A.N. factory at Augsburg, which manufactured diesel engines for U-boats. Four Lancasters were shot down by fighters en route. Eight crews succeeded in attacking the target, but three more aircraft were lost subsequently. The raid leader, Squadron Leader J.D. Nettleton of No. 44 Sqn, who returned in a badly damaged aircraft, was awarded the VC. Severe damage was inflicted on the target, but because of the losses suffered by the attacking force this type of operation was not repeated.

*19 April* The *Luftwaffe* initiated a series of attacks on British coastal targets using bomb-carrying Messerschmitt Bf 109F-4B aircraft of 10 (*Jabo*) JG 2 and 10 (*Jabo*) JG 26. These two units had been established late in 1941 and had specialized in hit-and-run attacks on targets such as ports and gasholders. The new wave of attacks were better co-ordinated; while JG 2 concentrated on shipping targets, JG 26 attacked coastal towns. Between 19 April and 19 June, 10 (*Jabo*) JG 26 made 32 sorties, eight against railway installations, eight against barracks, six against ships, five against factories, two against gasholders and two against dock installations, plus one armed reconnaissance. 10 (*Jabo*) JG 2 claimed the destruction of 20 ships totalling 63 000 tons during this period. As a result of these incursions, Fighter Command's first three Hawker Typhoon squadrons – Nos. 56, 266 (Rhodesia) and 609 – were brought to operational readiness to counter the low-flying fighter-bombers.

*23/24 April* 161 aircraft of Bomber Command made the first of four raids on the Baltic port town of Rostock and the adjacent Heinkel factory. Despite clear weather, the results were disappointing. The most effective raid was the fourth and last of the series on *26/27 April*, the town and the factory being heavily damaged. In reporting these raids, the expression *Terrorangriff* (terror attack) was used for the first time by German radio announcers. Bomber Command's loss in the four attacks was eight aircraft. The raid of 26/27 April was the last operation flown against a German land target by Whitley aircraft (of No. 58 Sqn).

*4/5 May* 121 aircraft of Bomber Command made the first of three consecutive nightly raids on

Stuttgart. The raids produced poor results, mainly because the Germans had set up a clever decoy, complete with searchlights and AA batteries, near the town of Lauffen 15 miles (24 km) to the north. Because of this decoy, the unfortunate people of Lauffen were bombed 37 times in the course of the war.

*30/31 May* The first thousand-bomber raid: on this night, 1047 aircraft were despatched to Cologne, a proportion of the force being drawn from Operational Training Units. A total of 868 aircraft bombed the main target, dropping 1455 tons of bombs, two-thirds of which were incendiaries. The city suffered very severe damage and the death toll was 469, a new record for a Bomber Command raid. Over 600 acres of Cologne's built-up area had been destroyed. About 250 factories, including metal works, rubber works, blast furnaces, chemical works, an oil storage plant and other establishments manufacturing many different types of component were destroyed or badly damaged. The toll of property included 18 432 houses, flats, workshops and public buildings destroyed and 40 586 damaged. Fifty per cent of the city's power supply was put out of action, and the gas and water supplies were also disrupted. The railway repair shops, employing 2500 people, were totally destroyed and 12 000 fires were started, some of which burned for days. Bomber Command sustained a record loss of 41 aircraft, of which 29 were Wellingtons; these had formed the bulk of the attacking force. Flying Officer L.T. Manser of No. 50 Sqn was awarded a posthumous VC for remaining at the controls of his Manchester to allow his crew to bale out after his aircraft suffered severe damage on the run-up to the target, which he bombed. By the time the last crew member left, Manser was unable to save himself as the aircraft was too low.

*31 May* First operational mission by de Havilland Mosquitoes of Bomber Command; four aircraft of No. 105 Sqn carried out a dawn bombing and reconnaissance sortie over Cologne.

*1/2 June* The second thousand-bomber raid: 956 bombers were despatched to Essen; 767 crews claimed to have attacked the target, but subsequent reconnaissance revealed little damage. Many crews bombed Oberhausen, Mülheim and Duisburg by mistake; 31 aircraft FTR.

*25/26 June* The third thousand-bomber raid: as had been the case in the attack on Essen, the force assembled for this mission by Bomber Command fell short of the 1000 aircraft mark, only 960 bombers of all types being available, including some Bostons and Mosquitoes of No. 2 Group. To strengthen the force, a further 102 Wellingtons and Hudsons were provided by Coastal Command. The target was Bremen, and despite heavy cloud, the bombers caused considerable damage, particularly to the Focke-Wulf aircraft factory, which was hit by a 4000 lb (1800 kg) bomb; 44 aircraft of Bomber Command and five of Coastal Command FTR. This raid marked the last operational use of the Avro Manchester (by Nos. 49, 50, 61 and 106 Sqns). The Manchester had been plagued by technical problems, particularly involving its Rolls-Royce Vulture engines, since the start of its career, and many had been lost accidentally.

*29 June* A crew of the 8th United States Army Air Force (Captain Kegelman) flew in a Douglas Boston of No. 226 Sqn in a daylight attack on Hazebrouck marshalling yards. This was the first operational action by the 8th AAF , which was then being established in Britain.

*4 July* 12 Douglas Bostons of No. 2 Group were despatched to make low-level attacks on four airfields in Holland. Six of the Bostons were flown by crews of the 8th AAF; three were shot down by intense coastal flak, including the aircraft flown by Captain Kegelman.

*11 July* 44 Lancasters of No. 5 Group were despatched to make a dusk attack on the submarine

yards at Danzig, the most distant target so far attacked by Bomber Command. The raid involved a round trip of 1500 miles (2415 km), the aircraft flying in formation at low level over the North Sea before splitting up to cross Denmark in cloud. About one-third of the attacking force failed to locate the target and bombed the town instead, but the plan generally worked well. Two aircraft FTR.

*21–30 July* During this ten-day period, Bomber Command mounted three heavy night attacks on Duisburg, two on Hamburg and one on Saarbrücken. The three raids on Duisburg produced indifferent results, although a good deal of property was damaged, and cost the Command 27 aircraft. Hamburg was extensively damaged, but aircraft losses were heavy; of the 659 bombers that attacked this target on two nights (26/27 and 28/29 July), 59 FTR.

*31 July/1 August* Bomber Command despatched 630 aircraft to attack Düsseldorf. 484 crews claimed to have made a successful attack, dropping 900 tons of bombs. Bombing was spread over the city

*In 1942, the Bristol Blenheims of No. 2 Group were being replaced by more modern types, such as the American-built Douglas Boston. The aircraft shown belongs to No. 88 Sqn.*

and heavy damage was caused, but 29 bombers FTR – 11 from No. 92 (OTU) Group, which contributed 105 aircraft.

**15 August** An important step forward was taken in the efficiency of RAF Bomber Command when orders were issued for the creation of a Pathfinder Force to be responsible for target marking ahead of the main bomber stream. With its HQ at RAF Wyton, Huntingdonshire, the new force, commanded by Group Captain D.C.T. Bennett, consisted originally of five squadrons, one drawn from each operational Group. The PFF flew its first operational mission on **18/19 August**, when it was despatched to Flensburg. This mission was frustrated by unexpected winds, many bombs falling on Danish territory.

**17 August** First mission by the USAAF VIIIth Bomber Command. Twelve B-17 Flying Fortresses of the 97th Bomb Group (340th, 342nd and 414th Sqns), escorted by ten squadrons of RAF Spitfires, bombed Rouen's Sotteville railway complex. All the bombers returned safely to their base at Grafton Underwood, Northamptonshire. The raid was supported by a diversionary feint over the North Sea by six 97th Group B-17s from Polebrook, also covered by ten Spitfire squadrons; a flight of Boulton Paul Defiants from RAF Northolt, fitted with *Moonshine* radar jamming equipment, also took part.

**19 August** The Dieppe operation. On this day squadrons of RAF Fighter Command, Army Co-operation Command and No. 2 Group Bomber Command flew intensively in support of Operation *Jubilee*, the Anglo-Canadian 'reconnaissance in strength' involving a large-scale amphibious landing at Dieppe. One of the primary objectives was to bring to battle the whole forces of the *Luftwaffe* in France and the Low Countries, and for this purpose 60 squadrons of Spitfires, Hurricanes, Typhoons and Mustangs, as well as five Boston squadrons of No. 2 Group, were placed under the operational control of Air Vice-Marshal Trafford Leigh-Mallory, the Air Officer Commanding No. 11 Group. No. 2 Group flew 62 smoke-laying sorties in support of the landing, losing three Bostons. While the Spitfire, Typhoon and Hurricane squadrons maintained constant air cover over the landing area and the invasion fleet, the four squadrons of North American Mustangs (Nos. 26, 239, 400 RCAF and 414 RCAF) monitored enemy troop movements in the areas to the rear of Dieppe, the aircraft operating in pairs. Of the 106 RAF aircraft of all types which failed to return from the day's operations, ten were Mustangs. The *Luftwaffe* was slow to react at first, but

in the afternoon the Focke-Wulf Fw 190s of JG 26 came up to challenge the RAF in strength, while the Fw 190 fighter-bombers of JG 2 and JG 26 attacked the invasion force. The Dornier Do 217E-2s of KG 2 were also active in the area, but suffered heavy losses. The total *Luftwaffe* loss during the day was 48 aircraft. The operation showed that the RAF was deficient in ground support techniques for handling a commitment of this size, and this resulted in a recommendation for the establishment of a fully integrated Tactical Air Force to support major ground operations.

**29 August** First operation by aircraft of the USAAF VIIIth Fighter Command: Lockheed P-38F Lightnings of the 1st Fighter Group, Ibsley, Hampshire, were scrambled to intercept an enemy bomber, but did not make contact.

**10/11 September** Operating in support of an attack on Düsseldorf by 479 aircraft, the RAF Pathfinder Force made the first operational use of *Pink Pansies*, incendiaries in a 4000 lb (1800 kg) bomb casing.

**14/15 September** Last operational mission by Hampden aircraft of Bomber Command: four aircraft of No. 408 Sqn, RCAF, carried out an attack on Wilhelmshaven.

**19 September** Six Mosquitoes of No. 105 Sqn attempted to make the first daylight bombing raid on Berlin. One aircraft bombed the target, two bombed Hamburg, two aborted with technical trouble, and one FTR.

**25 September** Four Mosquitoes of No. 105 Sqn were despatched to make a low-level attack on the Gestapo HQ at Oslo, Norway. One Mosquito was shot down by Fw 190s during the attack; three bombs hit the target but all failed to explode.

**29 September** On this day the three American-manned fighter squadrons in the RAF – Nos. 71, 121 and 133 (Eagle) Squadrons – were assigned to the USAAF VIIIth Fighter Command, becoming the 334th, 335th and 336th Sqns of the 4th Fighter Group at Debden, Essex. All three units were equipped with Spitfire Vs. At this time there were two other Spitfire-equipped USAAF fighter groups in Britain. The first to arrive, in June, was the 31st Fighter Group, which equipped with Spitfires at Atcham in Shropshire; it was followed by the 52nd Fighter Group, which was based at Goxhill in Lincolnshire.

**30 September** First day combat by a Mosquito fighter: Wing Commander R.F.H. Clerke of No. 157 Sqn shot down a Ju 88 of I/KG 26 30 miles off the Dutch coast.

**17 October** 94 Lancasters drawn from nine sqadrons of No. 5 Group, RAF Bomber Command, were despatched to make a dusk attack on the Schneider Armament Factory at Le Creusot and the power station at Montchanin; 86 aircraft bombed the factory and six the power station. One Lancaster of No. 61 Sqn failed to return, having crashed into a building during its low-level bombing run.

**24 October** 74 Lancasters of No. 5 Group (out of 88 despatched) made a daylight attack on Milan after flying across France in cloud cover. The same target was attacked by Halifaxes, Stirlings and Wellingtons on the following night. Seven aircraft FTR from these two attacks.

**3 November** First operational mission by Lockheed Venturas of RAF Bomber Command: three aircraft of No. 21 Sqn (No. 2 Group) were despatched to bomb a diesel plant at Hengelo, in Holland. The crews were unable to find the primary and railways were attacked instead.

**28/29 November** During an attack on Turin by 228 aircraft of Bomber Command, two Lancasters of No. 106 Sqn – R5551 (Wing Commander G.P. Gibson) and R5573 (Flight Lieutenant W.N. Whamond) – dropped 8000 lb (3630 kg) bombs, the first time this weapon had been used against an Italian target.

**6 December** 93 Bostons, Venturas and Mosquitoes of No. 2 Group were despatched to make a daylight attack on the Philips radio and valve factories at Eindhoven, Holland. Fourteen aircraft (including nine Venturas) FTR and 53 more suffered damage, but the factories did not resume full production until six months later. This was the first operational mission by No. 464 Sqn RAAF (14 Venturas despatched, three FTR) and No. 487 Sqn RNZAF (16 Venturas despatched, three FTR). A total of 84 USAAF B-17s escorted by RAF Spitfires flew a diversionary mission to Lille.

**20/21 December** First operational use of *Oboe* blind-bombing aid: six Mosquitoes of No. 109 Sqn were despatched to bomb a power station at Lutterade, Holland. Three aircraft bombed the primary, but the remainder developed faults in their *Oboe* equipment and bombed alternates.

# The Battle of the Atlantic, 1941–44

By the end of 1940, the war at sea had cost 1281 British, Allied and neutral ships, of which 585 were sunk by U-boats. German submarine losses during this period amounted to only 32 craft, none of which had fallen victim to aircraft alone. Technical improvements were beginning to help in the fight against the submarine, at the beginning of 1941 about a sixth of RAF Coastal Command's maritime patrol aircraft were equipped with ASV radar, although this was still in a primitive stage of development and as yet was only effective against U-boats that were fully surfaced and within three miles of the search aircraft.

Until the acquisition of long-range patrol aircraft such as the Consolidated Catalina and the B-24 Liberator, on order from the USA, there was little Coastal Command could do to provide effective cover for convoys sailing through the dangerous gap between the Shetland Islands and the Arctic Circle. On the Western Approaches, however, a firm step was taken to promote close cooperation between Coastal Command and the Royal Navy with the creation, in February 1941, of a new No. 19 Group to keep watch on the Bay of Biscay. In times to come, operating with the Navy's hunter-killer groups, No. 19 Group would tip the scales in the Battle of the Atlantic. Meanwhile, the uphill struggle was long and hard.

# 1941

**8–12 February** The submarine U-37 directed five Focke-Wulf Fw 200 *Kondor* aircraft of I/KG 40 (Bordeaux–Mérignac) and the cruiser *Admiral Hipper* in an attack on convoys HG53 and SLS64, sinking 16 out of 25 ships.

**26 February** Operating in conjunction with U-47,

six *Kondors* of KG 40 sank seven ships of convoy OB290 and damaged four more.

**March** No. 252 Sqn (RAF Chivenor, Devon) became operational with Bristol Beaufighter Mk I aircraft. In the following month the squadron moved to Aldergrove, Northern Ireland, for operations against Fw 200s which, in their maritime reconnaissance/attack role, were flying from Bordeaux to Stavanger, Norway, and returning via the Atlantic route west of Ireland. When No. 252 Sqn left for Egypt in May, its task was taken over by No. 143 Sqn, also flying Beaufighters from the same location.

**20–26 May** The hunt for the *Bismarck*. On 20 May, the battlecruiser *Bismarck* and the light cruiser *Prinz Eugen* passed through the Kattegat en route for the North Atlantic convoy routes. On **21 May** they were sighted by a Spitfire of the RAF Photographic Reconnaissance Unit near Bergen,

*The Focke-Wulf Fw 200 Kondor long-range maritime patrol aircraft was developed from the pre-war civil airliner, pictured here.*

Norway. On **22 May** a Martin Maryland reconnaissance aircraft of No. 771 Sqn, Fleet Air Arm, confirmed that the warships had departed Bergen. On **24 May** the German warships were engaged by units of the British Home Fleet in the Denmark Strait, between Iceland and the Faeroe Islands; the *Bismarck* sank the battlecruiser HMS *Hood* and damaged the *Prince of Wales* but also sustained damage herself, making her Atlantic foray impracticable. The *Prinz Eugen* was detached and both warships set course independently for Brest on the French Atlantic coast. Later in the day the *Bismarck* was attacked by nine Fairey Swordfish torpedo-bombers of No. 825 Sqn, HMS *Victorious*; one torpedo hit the cruiser but did little damage. on **26 May** the *Bismarck* was sighted by a Catalina of No. 209 Sqn, RAF Coastal Command; contact was retained by another Catalina of No. 240 Sqn. Later, the *Bismarck*'s steering gear was crippled in a torpedo attack by Swordfish from HMS *Ark Royal* and she was subsequently destroyed by surface forces.

**30 May** US Navy Sqn VP-52 began operational patrols with PBY-5 Catalinas over the North Atlantic convoy routes, the first US squadron to do so. The unit was based at Argentia, Newfoundland, and supported by the seaplane tender *Albemarle*.

**1 June** No. 120 Sqn, RAF Coastal Command, formed at Nutts Corner, Northern Ireland, with Consolidated Liberator Mk I aircraft for long-range maritime patrol. The squadron began operational patrols in September.

**12 June** Nine Bristol Beaufort torpedo-bombers of No. 42 Sqn and five of No. 22 Sqn set out from Leuchars and Wick, Scotland, to search for the German battleship *Lützow*, which had been sighted off Stavanger by a Blenheim of No. 114 Sqn. The warship was located by Beaufort 'W' of No. 42 Sqn (Flight Sergeant R.H. Loveitt) and torpedoed in moonlight conditions. The damaged vessel recovered to Kiel for repair; Loveitt was awarded the DFM.

**4 July** PBY-5 Catalinas of US Navy Sqn VP-72, supported by the seaplane tender USS *Goldsborough*, flew protective patrols from Reykjavik, Iceland, until the 17th, to cover the arrival of Marine Corps garrison units from the USA.

**18 July** Installation of British ASV radar was completed in one PBY-5 each of Patrol Sqns VP-71, VP-72 and VP-73, and in two Martin PBM-1 Marlins of VP-74. ASV equipment in all aircraft of Patrol Wing 7 was completed in September, this unit becoming the first to operate with radar-equipped aircraft in the US Navy. Its squadrons operated from Norfolk (Virginia), Quonset Point and advanced bases on Greenland, Iceland and Newfoundland.

**25 July** The aircraft carrier USS *Wasp* left Norfolk with 30 P-40 fighters of the 33rd Pursuit Sqn, USAAF, for Reykjavik, in support of the US garrison there.

**1 August** The US Navy began trials with an AI-10 microwave radar developed by the Radiation Laboratory and installed in a Lockheed Model 14 aircraft. During the trials, which lasted until October, surface vessels were detected at ranges of up to 40 miles. Operational radars developed from this equipment included the ASG for K-type airships and the AN/APS-2 for patrol aircraft.

**2 August** A Hawker Hurricane of the Merchant Ship Fighter Unit, flown by Lieutenant R.W.H. Everett RNVR, was catapulted from the naval auxiliary vessel *Maplin* to intercept and destroy a Focke-Wulf Fw 200 that was shadowing a convoy bound for the UK from Sierra Leone. Everett ditched his Hurricane after the combat, was picked up safely and was later awarded a DSC. At this time 16 CAM (Catapult Aircraft Merchantman) vessels were assigned to convoy protection in addition to four naval auxiliaries; three of the latter carried Fairey Fulmar fighters, the remainder Hurricanes.

**6 August** US Navy Patrol Sqns VP-73 and VP-74 began routine convoy protection patrols from Reykjavik, Iceland.

**27 August** The German submarine U-570 was attacked and damaged by a Lockheed Hudson of No. 269 Sqn (Squadron Leader J. Thompson) off Iceland. The Hudson circled the U-boat, which was unable to dive, until its crew indicated that they wished to surrender. The Hudson was relieved by a Catalina and the submarine towed to Iceland by an armed trawler.

**September** The escort carrier HMS *Audacity*, with a complement of six Grumman Martlet fighters, began operations on the UK–Gibraltar route. *Audacity* made two round trips, escorting four convoys; three of them came under air and U-boat attack, and in the course of these operations her Martlets (of No. 802 Sqn) shot down five Fw 200 *Kondors*, damaged three more and drove off another. Nine U-boats were spotted by the aircraft, one of them – the U-131 – being sunk by an escorting destroyer. HMS *Audacity* was torpedoed and sunk by U-741 on 21 December 1941.

**29 October** US Navy Patrol Sqn VP-82 received its first PBO-1 (Lockheed Hudson) aircraft at NAS Norfolk. The squadron's aircraft had originally been destined for the RAF and were painted in British camouflage and markings.

**17 November** The escort carrier BAVG-1 was transferred to the Royal Navy as HMS *Archer* – the first of 38 such vessels transferred to Britain from the USA during the war.

**29 November** An Armstrong Whitworth Whitley of No. 502 Sqn, Limavady, Northern Ireland, made the first successful attack on a U-boat by a Coastal Command aircraft using ASV radar and unassisted by any other force, sinking U-206 in the Bay of Biscay.

# THE ANTI-SUBMARINE WEAPONS

IN EARLY encounters between RAF aircraft and enemy submarines, it was the standard 250 lb (113 kg) bomb that was used to attack the U-boats. It was not until 1940 that the depth charge was acknowledged as the really effective anti-submarine weapon, and even then the early depth bombs, filled with Amatol, were notoriously unreliable and prone to disintegrate on hitting the surface of the sea. Matters improved with the introduction of modifications in 1941, and in particular with the use of a new explosive called Torpex, which was 30 per cent more effective than Amatol. The 250 lb charge was set to explode at a depth of between 25 and 50 ft (7–15 m), and the weapons were dropped in sticks, usually of six, with 100 ft (30 m) between them (earlier spacings of 36 and 60 ft/ 11–18 m had proved unsuccessful). Release height was very low, between 50 and 75 ft (15–23 m).

In May 1943, British and American patrol aircraft received a new weapon. Known for security reasons as the Mk 24 mine, it was in fact an air-launched torpedo with an acoustic homing head, developed in the USA. The first squadrons to equip with it were Nos. 86 and 120, whose Liberators carried two torpedoes in addition to their usual load of depth charges. Rocket projectiles were also used in attacks on surfaced U-boats. Finally, there was the Intelligence weapon: the *Ultra* decrypts at Bletchley Park, which – albeit with gaps caused by enemy code changes and other factors – were able to determine where the U-boat wolf packs would assemble, and consequently the routes that convoys might take to avoid them.

# 1942

**1 March** A Lockheed PBO-1 Hudson of VP-82 (Ensign William Tepuni, USNR) attacked and sank the submarine U-656 south-west of Newfoundland; this was the first German submarine sunk by US forces in World War II.

**7 March** The practicability of using a radio sonobuoy in aerial anti-submarine warfare was demonstrated in a US Navy exercise conducted off New London by the non-rigid airship K-5 and the S-20 submarine. The buoy could detect the sound of the submerged submarine's propellers at up to 3 miles (4.8 km), and reception aboard the airship was satisfactory at up to 5 miles (8 km).

**9 March** Fairey Albacore torpedo-bombers from HMS *Victorious* made an unsuccessful attack on the German pocket battleship *Tirpitz* off northern Norway. Two of the attacking aircraft were shot down.

**27–31 March** The Russian-bound convoy PQ 13, dispersed in bad weather, was attacked by Junkers Ju 88s of KG 30, which sank two freighters. Three more were sunk by U-boats and destroyers.

**16 May** 27 Beauforts, eight Beaufighters, 13 Hudsons and six Blenheims of RAF Coastal Command were despatched to attack the light cruiser *Prinz Eugen*, heading for Germany after receiving temporary repairs at Trondheim to torpedo damage sustained following the 'Channel Dash' of February. The cruiser was sailing under strong fighter cover and the attack was unsuccessful.

**3/4 June** A Wellington of No. 172 Sqn, Chivenor, Devon, carried out the first sortie and night attack on a U-boat using the 'Leigh Light', a 24-in (61 cm) Naval carbon searchlight developed by Squadron Leader Humphrey Leigh and modified to fit into the Wellington's retractable belly gun turret. The device was intended to illuminate the target following the initial ASV radar approach. On this occasion the U-boat escaped.

**13 June** The US Navy carried out the first airborne trial of LORAN (Long Range Air Navigation Equipment) using a K-2 airship from NAS Lakehurst. The success of this and subsequent trials led to a crash programme to install LORAN equipment in maritime patrol aircraft.

**30 June** US patrol aircraft combined with naval convoy escorts to attack and destroy the U-158 off Bermuda.

**5 July** Junkers Ju 88s of KG 30 began a five-day series of attacks on Russia-bound convoy PQ 17, which had been ordered to scatter in the belief that major German naval units were in the vicinity. Twenty-four out of the convoy's 36 ships were sunk, 8 by air

*The Vickers Wellington was used by several Coastal Command squadrons. This aircraft is being fitted with an air-sea rescue lifeboat.*

attack, although the *Luftwaffe* damaged several more which were later sunk by U-boats.

*5/6 July* A Wellington of No. 172 Sqn carried out the first successful Leigh Light attack on an enemy submarine, sinking the U-502 in the Bay of Biscay.

*6 July* A US Navy PBM-1 patrol aircraft sank the submarine U-153 in the Caribbean.

*7 July* A Lockheed PBO-1 Hudson of VP-82 sank the submarine U-701 off the eastern coast of the United States.

*15 July* US patrol aircraft combined with naval convoy escorts to sink the U-576 off the eastern coast of the United States.

*17 July* The submarine U-751 was sunk in the Bay of Biscay by a Whitley of No. 502 Sqn, assisted by a Lancaster of No. 61 Sqn (temporarily assigned to maritime operations).

*31 July* The submarine U-754 was sunk by a Catalina of the Royal Canadian Air Force off Nova Scotia: the RCAF's first U-boat 'kill'.

*1 August* A Grumman J4F Widgeon (Ensign Henry C. White) of US Coast Guard Sqn 212, sank the submarine U-166 off the passes of the Mississippi; this was the USCG's first U-boat 'kill'.

*10 August* The submarine U-578 was sunk in the Bay of Biscay by a Wellington of No. 311 (Czech) Sqn, Talbenny, Wales.

*20 August* Catalina aircraft of USN Patrol Wing 7 joined with convoy escort vessels in the sinking of U-464 off Iceland.

*22 August* The submarine U-654 was sunk in the Caribbean by a US maritime patrol aircraft (type unknown).

*28 August* The submarine U-94 was sunk off the West Indies in a joint operation by Catalina aircraft of Patrol Wing 11 (Puerto Rico) and warships of the US and Royal Canadian Navies.

*1 September* A Catalina of Navy Patrol Wing 7 located the submarine U-756 in the North Atlantic; the U-boat was sunk by convoy escorts.

*3 September* An Armstrong Whitworth Whitley of No. 77 Sqn (RAF Chivenor, Devon) attacked and sank the U-705 in the Bay of Biscay.

*12–14 September* The Russia-bound convoy PQ

18, escorted by the carrier HMS *Avenger* with Nos. 802 and 883 Sqns FAA (total of 12 Hawker Sea Hurricanes), came under heavy air attack on 12 September off North Cape by six Ju 88s of KG 30 and 40 He 111s of KG 26 while the escort carrier's Fighter Battle Flight was absent chasing a Blohm und Voss Bv 138 reconnaissance aircraft. The torpedo attack by KG 26 sank eight freighters. Five Heinkels were shot down. The convoy was again attacked on 13 and 14 September; these attacks were broken up by the Sea Hurricanes. In all, the fighters and the convoy's AA (mainly the latter) accounted for 41 enemy aircraft during the three days. Four Sea Hurricanes were shot down, three of them by the convoy's own defences.

*15 September* Fairey Swordfish aircraft of No. 825 Sqn, HMS *Avenger*, located the submarine U-589 in the vicinity of convoy PQ 18. The U-boat was sunk by escort vessels. Also on 15 September, the U-261 was attacked and sunk by a Whitley of No. 58 Sqn off the Faeroe Islands.

*17 September* Bristol Beaufighters of No. 235 Sqn, on interceptor patrol over the Bay of Biscay, shot down a Focke-Wulf Fw 200 *Kondor* and two Junkers Ju 88C-6 aircraft of KG 40. One Beaufighter was shot down by an armed trawler.

*23 September* The submarine U-253 was attacked and sunk in the Arctic by a Catalina of No. 210 Sqn, Coastal Command, from Sullom Voe, Shetland Islands.

*1 October* No. 206 Sqn, Coastal Command, began full anti-submarine operations with Boeing Fortress IIAs from Benbecula, Outer Hebrides. This was the Command's second Fortress squadron, No. 220 Sqn (Ballykelly, N. Ireland) having equipped with the type earlier in the year.

*2 October* The submarine U-512 was sunk off French Guiana by a US maritime patrol aircraft.

*5 October* A Lockheed Hudson of No. 269 Sqn attacked the U-582 off Iceland; the U-boat was sunk by convoy escort vessels.

*12 October* A Liberator of No. 120 Sqn, Ballykelly, attacked and sank the U-597 in the North Atlantic. The pilot of this aircraft was Squadron Leader Terence Bulloch, who was to become the most decorated pilot in Coastal Command. In the course of operations he accounted for four U-boats destroyed, three damaged and many others attacked.

*15 October* A Liberator of No. 120 Sqn attacked and sank the U-661 in the North Atlantic. The aircraft captain was Pilot Officer Esler.

*20 October* A Liberator of No. 224 Sqn on convoy escort attacked and sank the U-216 in the Bay of Biscay.

*22 October* The U-412 was attacked and sunk off the Faeroe Islands by a Wellington of No. 179 Sqn from Skitten, Caithness.

*24 October* A Liberator of No. 224 Sqn attacked and sank the U-599 in the North Atlantic during a convoy escort mission.

*27 October* A Fortress of No. 206 Sqn, escorting a convoy, attacked and sank the U-627 in the North Atlantic.

*30 October* Sunderlands of the Royal Canadian Air Force on convoy escort duty attacked and sank the U-520 and U-658 in the North Atlantic.

During October, the Ju 88C-6 long-range fighters of KG 40 destroyed 16 RAF maritime patrol aircraft over the Bay of Biscay. KG 40 now had two *Staffeln* of these aircraft, reinforced by two more in November. Combats between the Ju 88s and the Beaufighters of Nos. 235 and 248 Sqns became more frequent.

*5 November* A Liberator of No. 120 Sqn on convoy escort in the North Atlantic attacked and sank the U-132. (Note: from September 1942 to April 1943 No. 120 Sqn sent detachments to Reykjavik, Iceland, to increase the coverage of its aircraft.) Also on 5 November, the U-408 was sunk by a PBY-5 of Patrol Wing 7 off Iceland. (During November, the US Navy's Patrol Air Wings were redesignated Fleet Air Wings.)

*13 November* US Navy Patrol Sqn VP-73 (Catalinas) deployed to Port Lyautey from Iceland to begin anti-submarine operations from French Morocco over the Western Mediterranean, the Strait of Gibraltar, and its approaches.

*21 November* Swordfish aircraft of the Fleet Air Arm attacked and sank the U-517 in the North Atlantic.

*8 December* A Liberator of No. 120 Sqn, operating from Iceland, attacked and sank the U-254 in the North Atlantic.

*10 December* The U-611 was attacked and sunk by a Catalina of Fleet Air Wing 7, USN.

*27 December* The USS *Santee* (ACV-29), the first of 11 US escort carriers assigned to hunter-killer duty, left Norfolk with Air Group 29 for freelance anti-submarine and anti-surface raider operations in the South Atlantic.

*The Junkers Ju 86C long-range fighter presented serious problems for Allied maritime aircraft operating in the Bay of Biscay area. The Ju 88C-6 seen here is a captured night fighter version; note the radar antennae on the nose.*

# 1943

**6 January** The U-164 was sunk by a B-24 Liberator of the USAAF escorting a convoy off the Brazilian coast.

**13 January** The U-507 was sunk off the Brazilian coast by a US patrol aircraft (type not known).

**16 January** The U-337 was attacked and sunk by a Fortress of No. 206 Sqn on convoy escort in the North Atlantic.

**3 February** The U-265 was sunk by a Fortress of No. 206 Sqn on convoy escort in the North Atlantic.

**7 February** The U-624 was attacked and sunk by a Fortress of No. 220 Sqn, Ballykelly, on convoy escort in the North Atlantic.

**10 February** The U-519 was sunk in the Bay of Biscay by a USN Catalina.

**12 February** The U-442 was attacked and sunk by a Lockheed Hudson of No. 48 Sqn, operating from Gibraltar.

**14 February** A Catalina of No. 202 Sqn, Gibraltar, attacked and sank the U-620 off the coast of Portugal.

**15 February** The U-529 was attacked and sunk in the North Atlantic by a Liberator of No. 120 Sqn on convoy escort.

**19/20 February** The U-268 was sunk in the Bay of Biscay by a 'Leigh Light' Wellington of No. 172 Sqn, Chivenor.

**21 February** The U-623 was attacked and sunk in the North Atlantic by a Liberator of No. 120 Sqn.

**1 March** The US Navy's Fleet Airship Group 2 was commissioned at Richmond, Florida, with Goodyear K-type non-rigids for inshore convoy patrol operations. Fleet Airship Group One was already operational at Lakehurst, New Jersey.

**5 March** The escort carrier USS *Bogue* (ACV-9), with the Grumman Avengers of VC-9 on board, began convoy escort duty in the eastern to mid-Atlantic. The *Bogue* formed the nucleus of Task Group 24.4.

**7 March** A Fortress of No. 220 Sqn attacked and sank the U-633 off Iceland.

**8 March** The U-156 was attacked and sunk off the West Indies by a USAAF Liberator.

**20 March** A Short Sunderland of No. 201 Sqn, Castle Archdale, N. Ireland, attacked and sank the U-384 in the North Atlantic during a convoy escort sortie.

**22/23 March** The U-665 was attacked and sunk by a Wellington of No. 172 Sqn in the Bay of Biscay.

**22 March** The U-524 was attacked and sunk by a Catalina of VP-73, operating off the Canary Islands.

**25 March** A Fortress of No. 206 Sqn attacked and sank the U-169 during a patrol off Iceland.

**27 March** A Fortress of No. 206 Sqn attacked and sank the U-169 during a North Atlantic patrol.

**5 April** A Lockheed Hudson of No. 233 Sqn, Gibraltar, attacked and sank the U-167 during a patrol off the Canary Islands.

**6 April** The U-632 was attacked and sunk by a Liberator of No. 86 Sqn, Aldergrove, N. Ireland, during a convoy escort sortie.

**10 April** A Wellington of No. 172 Sqn attacked and sank the U-376 in the Bay of Biscay.

**14 April** The USN's Fleet Air Wing 16 was transferred from Norfolk to Natal, Brazil, for anti-submarine operations in the South Atlantic.

**23 April** A Liberator of No. 120 Sqn attacked and sank the U-189 during a convoy escort sortie in the North Atlantic.

**24 April** The U-710 was attacked and sunk by a Fortress of No. 206 Sqn on convoy escort duty in the North Atlantic.

**25 April** The U-203 was sunk in the North Atlantic by a Swordfish of No. 811 Sqn, Fleet Air Arm, from the escort carrier HMS *Biter*.

**27 April** The U-174 was sunk by a Catalina patrol aircraft of the US Navy off Nova Scotia.

**30 April** The U-227 was sunk off the Faeroe Islands by a Hampden of No. 455 Sqn, Royal Australian Air Force.

**2 May** The U-332 was sunk in the Bay of Biscay by a Sunderland of No. 461 Sqn, RAAF.

**4 May** A Liberator of No. 86 Sqn attacked and sank the U-465 during a North Atlantic convoy escort.

**4 May** The U-630 was sunk by a Sunderland of the RCAF on a convoy escort sortie in the North Atlantic.

**7 May** Three U-boats fell victim to RAF patrol aircraft on this day. The U-447 was sunk off Gibraltar by a Hudson of No. 233 Sqn, while the U-109 and the U-663 were respectively sunk in the Bay of Biscay by a Sunderland of No. 10 Sqn RAAF and a Halifax of No. 58 Sqn RAF.

**11 May** Royal Navy warships and a Halifax of No. 58 Sqn combined in the sinking of the U-528 in the North Atlantic.

**12 May** Swordfish aircraft of No. 811 Sqn, FAA (HMS *Biter*) combined with destroyers of the 5th Escort Group, RN, to sink the U-89 in the North Atlantic.

**13 May** A Liberator of No. 86 Sqn combined with a Sunderland of No. 423 Sqn RCAF and warships of the RCN to sink the U-456 in the North Atlantic.

**14 May** The U-266 was attacked and sunk by a Liberator of No. 86 Sqn. On the same day, a Catalina of VP-84 sank the U-657. Both sinkings were in the North Atlantic.

**15 May** A Halifax of No. 58 Sqn RAF attacked and sank the U-463 during a Bay of Biscay patrol; the U-176 was also sunk by a US Navy Catalina on convoy escort off the east coast of the United States.

**17 May** The U-128 was attacked and sunk by warships of the US Navy and a USAAF B-24 Liberator off the Brazilian coast. In the North Atlantic, the U-646 was sunk off Iceland by a Hudson of No. 269 Sqn RAF.

**19 May** The U-273 was sunk by a Hudson of No. 269 Sqn escorting a convoy off Iceland. In the North Atlantic, the U-954 was sunk by a Liberator of No. 120 Sqn. (Among the crew of this submarine was *Leutnant-zur-See* Peter Dönitz, whose father was Admiral Karl Dönitz, the Commander U-boats.)

**20 May** The U-258 was attacked and sunk by a Liberator of No. 120 Sqn in the North Atlantic.

**22 May** Grumman Avengers of VC-9, based on the USS *Bogue*, attacked and sank the U-569 in the North Atlantic; this was the first U-boat sinking registered by an escort carrier on a hunter-killer patrol (as opposed to convoy escort).

**23 May** A Swordfish of No. 819 Sqn, FAA (HMS *Archer*) attacked and sank the U-752 with rocket projectiles in the North Atlantic.

**24 May** The U-441 was attacked and damaged in the Bay of Biscay by a Sunderland of No. 228 Sqn, which was itself shot down by Ju 88s. The significance of this engagement was that the U-441 was the first heavily-armed flak submarine; following the heavy losses sustained by the U-boats in May, they were now ordered to remain on the surface and fight it out with attacking aircraft.

**25 May** The U-467 was attacked and sunk by a USAAF B-24 Liberator on convoy escort in the North Atlantic.

**28 May** A Liberator of No. 120 Sqn attacked and sank the U-304 while escorting a North Atlantic convoy.

**31 May** A Halifax of No. 58 Sqn joined with Sunderlands of Nos. 228 and 10 (RAAF) Sqns in the sinking of the U-563 in the Bay of Biscay. On the same day, the U-440 was also sunk in the Bay of Biscay by a Sunderland of No. 201 Sqn.

The air-sea war of May 1943 cost the Germans no fewer than 41 U-boats, of which 38 were lost in the Atlantic and the Bay of Biscay. The total number of submarines lost in the period January to May 1943 was 96, of which 52 were sunk by aircraft. It was an insupportable loss rate, and it compelled Admiral Dönitz to curtail his all-out assault on the Atlantic convoys by U-boat 'wolf packs'. The focus of operations now switched to the Bay of Biscay.

**1 June** The U-418 was sunk in the Bay of Biscay by rocket projectiles fired by a Bristol Beaufighter of No. 236 Sqn, Predannack, Cornwall.

**2 June** A Sunderland of No. 461 Sqn RAAF (Flight Lieutenant C.B. Walker) was intercepted over the Bay of Biscay by eight Ju 88s. In a 45-minute battle the Sunderland's crew fought off successive attacks, shooting down at least three Ju 88s. Flight Lieutenant Walker, who was later awarded the DSO, brought his damaged aircraft back for a landing near Marazion, Cornwall, with one crew member dead and four others wounded. This action was indicative of the severe air fighting that often took place over the Bay, the Ju 88s of KG 40 now having been joined by Focke-Wulf 190s. To combat this threat, Coastal Command instituted *Instep* patrols, with detachments of Fighter Command Mosquito squadrons operating from Predannack.

**14 June** The U-564 was attacked and sunk in the Bay of Biscay by a Whitley of No. 10 Operational Training Unit. The Whitley, badly hit by defensive gunfire, was forced to ditch; the crew were picked up and became PoWs.

The RAF lost 15 aircraft in operations over the Bay of Biscay during June 1943. Four Ju 88s were claimed as destroyed by *Instep* fighters.

**11 June** The U-417 was attacked and sunk to the east of Iceland by a Fortress of No. 206 Sqn.

*As the war progressed, RAF Coastal Command developed the Strike Wing concept, with rocket-armed Beaufighters and Mosquitoes seeking out enemy shipping. These photographs show an attack on German minesweepers.*

**12 June** The U-118 tanker submarine was attacked and sunk by Grumman Avengers of VC-9, USS *Bogue*, off the Azores.

**2/3 July** The U-126 was attacked and sunk by a 'Leigh Light' Wellington of No. 172 Sqn in the Bay of Biscay.

**3 July** The U-628 was sunk in the Bay of Biscay by a Liberator of No. 224 Sqn, St Eval, Cornwall.

**5 July** A Liberator of No. 53 Sqn attacked and sank the U-535 in the Bay of Biscay.

**7 July** The U-951 was attacked and sunk off Finisterre by a B-24 Liberator of the 1st Bombardment Sqn, USAAF, operating from Gibraltar.

**8 July** The U-514 was sunk in the Bay of Biscay by three salvoes of 24 lb (10.9 kg) solid-shot rocket projectiles fired by a Liberator of No. 224 Sqn RAF. On the same day the U-232 was sunk off Finisterre by a B-24 Liberator of the 2nd Bombardment Sqn, USAAF.

**9 July** The U-435 was attacked and sunk in the Bay of Biscay by a Wellington of No. 179 Sqn.

**13 July** The 479th Anti-Submarine Group USAAF (4th and 19th Sqns) began operations over the Bay of Biscay from St Eval, Cornwall, with B-24 Liberators.

**13 July** The U-607 was sunk in the Bay of Biscay in a joint attack by a Halifax of No. 58 Sqn and a Sunderland of No. 228 Sqn.

**13 July** Grumman Avengers of VC-13 from the escort carrier USS *Core* attacked and destroyed the tanker submarine U-487 south of the Azores. The U-487 was to have refuelled a group of ten U-boats bound for the Indian Ocean. There were now four hunter-killer groups, each with an escort carrier and three destroyers, operating in the central Atlantic with the US Tenth Fleet; the carriers were the USS *Bogue, Card, Core* and *Santee*. The US Groups sank seven U-boats before the end of July.

**18 July** The Goodyear airship K-74, on night patrol off the Florida coast, attacked a surfaced U-boat and in the gun duel that followed was shot down with the loss of one crew member (who was killed by a shark). This was the only airship lost to enemy action in World War II. The submarine, the U-134, was damaged in the attack and forced to return to base.

**19 July** The U-558 was sunk in a joint attack by a B-24 of the 19th Sqn USAAF and a Halifax of No. 58 Sqn RAF in the Bay of Biscay.

**23 July** Patrol Sqn VP-63 arrived at Pembroke Dock, Wales, to take part in anti-submarine operations with its Catalinas. This was the first US Navy squadron to operate from Great Britain in World War II.

**24 July** The tanker submarine U-459 was attacked and sunk by a Wellington of No. 172 Sqn 200 miles (320 km) NW of Cape Ortegal, Spain.

**28 July** The U-404 was sunk by a Liberator of No. 224 Sqn RAF after being damaged in previous attacks by B-24s of the 4th Sqn, USAAF.

**29 July** The U-614 was attacked and sunk 275 miles (443 km) NW of Cape Ortegal by a Wellington of No. 172 Sqn.

**30 July** The U-461 was attacked and sunk off Portugal by a Sunderland of No. 461 Sqn RAAF. In the same area the U-462 was also destroyed by a B-24 of the 19th Sqn USAAF. Several aircraft – Liberators, Sunderlands, Halifaxes and a Catalina – had earlier been involved in attacks on these two U-boats. The action of 30 July completed the destruction of an entire U-boat group by aircraft and naval forces.

**1 August** The U-454 was attacked and sunk in the Bay of Biscay by a Sunderland of No. 10 RAAF Sqn. The Sunderland was shot down in the engagement; six of the crew survived. Later on 1 August, the U-383 was also attacked and sunk by a Sunderland of No. 228 Sqn.

**2 August** The U-706 was attacked and sunk in the Bay of Biscay by a B-24 Liberator of the 4th Sqn USAAF. Also on 2 August, the U-106 was attacked and sunk by a Sunderland of No. 228 Sqn.

**24 August** The U-134 was attacked and sunk southwest of Cape Ortegal by a 'Leigh Light' Wellington of No. 179 Sqn, Gibraltar.

During August, while U-boat sightings were few, there were many air combats between fighters of KG 40, maritime patrol aircraft and *Instep* fighters. Aircrews of No. 19 Group reported seeing 232 Ju 88s, 20 Fw 200s and 14 Fw 190s during the month. The RAF lost 17 maritime aircraft and six fighters; German losses were five Ju 88s and one Fw 190. In addition, the Americans lost six patrol aircraft. One of the blackest days was 25 August, when No. 143 Sqn – newly arrived at St Eval to take part in *Instep* patrols – lost four Beaufighters to Fw 190s.

The Battle of the Atlantic was by no means over, but by the end of August 1943 the back of the U-boat offensive had been broken. It was a victory in which air power had played a decisive part.

# The Middle East and Mediterranean
# June 1941–May 1943

## The Syrian Campaign, June–July 1941

On 8 June 1941, an expeditionary force of British Empire and Free French troops invaded the Vichy French territories of Syria and the Lebanon to secure them against Axis intervention and the threat this would present to the Canal Zone. The invasion was supported by Hurricanes of Nos. 80 and 208 Sqns RAF and No. 806 Sqn Fleet Air Arm (flying ex-RAF fighters), reinforced later by the P-40 Tomahawks of No. 3 Sqn RAAF and the Hurricanes of No. 260 Sqn RAF. Bombing operations were undertaken by Blenheims of Nos. 11 and 203 Sqns and Wellingtons of No. 70 Sqn. In opposition, the Vichy forces had about 100 aircraft, many of them modern types such as the Martin 167s of GB I/39, the Dewoitine D.520s of GC III/6 and the LeO 451s of GB I/12 and I/31. The invasion was resisted fiercely, the Vichy aircraft making determined efforts to attack Royal Navy warships off the Lebanese coast and troop columns advancing into Syria. On 15 June, the 15th Cruiser Squadron off the Lebanon was also attacked by Ju 88s of II/LG 1 from Greece. The campaign was concluded on 14 July, by which time the Vichy air force had lost 179 aircraft, mostly on the ground.

*A Potez 63 reconnaissance aircraft of the Vichy French Air Force. These aircraft were badly mauled by the RAF's Hurricanes in the Syrian campaign.*

## Malta, June–December 1941

Following the departure of *Luftwaffe* units from Sicily to take part in the Balkan and Russian campaigns, attacks on the island of Malta and its supply convoys became the exclusive task of the *Regia Aeronautica*. The air defence of Malta was now undertaken by Nos. 126, 185 and 249 Sqns, all equipped with Hawker Hurricane IIB fighters, and the Bristol Beaufighters of No. 252 Sqn. Offensive bombing operations from the island were carried out by detachments of Wellingtons and Blenheims from squadrons in the Canal Zone, while Swordfish and Albacores of the Fleet Air Arm flew torpedo attack missions against Axis convoys. Malta, in fact, was the key factor in the battle of the Mediterranean convoys.

*15 June* The aircraft carriers HMS *Victorious* and HMS *Ark Royal* flew off 47 reinforcement Hurricanes for Malta, the aircraft having been ferried to Gibraltar in the carrier HMS *Furious*. All but four arrived safely. A further 64 Hurricanes were flown into Malta before the end of June.

*23 July* Aircraft of the *Regia Aeronautica* launched a co-ordinated attack on a convoy of six fast merchant ships bound from Gibraltar to Malta under heavy escort. First to attack were ten S.79 bombers of the 32° *Stormo*, one of which was shot down by Fulmars from HMS *Ark Royal*. While the fighters were drawn off, the S.79 torpedo-bomb-

ers of the 283ᵃ *Squadriglia* made their attack, one of them damaging the cruiser *Manchester* so badly that she had to be sent back to Malta (she was out of action for nine months). The destroyer HMS *Fearless* was also hit and set on fire; she was later abandoned and sunk. In a second attack an S.79 of the 32° *Gruppo* hit the destroyer HMS *Firedrake* with a 550 lb (250 kg) bomb. All the merchantmen reached Malta unharmed.

**11 August** An S.79 of the 281ᵃ *Squadriglia Aerosiluranti* torpedoed the netlayer HMS *Protector* off the Nile Delta, putting her out of action for the rest of the war.

**20 August** The 4727-ton tanker *Turbo* was torpedoed and sunk between Alexandria and Port Said by two S.79s of the 281ᵃ *Squadriglia*.

**29 August** Two S.79s of the 279ᵃ *Squadriglia* attacked the cruiser HMS *Phoebe* 30 miles (48 km) north of Bardia. Hit by one torpedo, she was put out of action for eight months.

**24 September** Nine large merchant vessels loaded with Malta's most urgent requirements sailed from Gibraltar, heavily escorted by warships of Force H. At noon the next day, the convoy was attacked by five S.84s of the 108° *Gruppo*, approaching from two different directions at sea level. Three aircraft were shot down but one torpedo hit the battleship HMS *Nelson*, causing damage that took eight months to repair. Later, in an attack by S.79s of the 278ᵃ *Squadriglia* from Pantelleria, the 12 427-ton merchant ship *Imperial Star* was so badly damaged that she had to be abandoned and sunk; the remaining ships reached

Malta safely. Other attempted attacks on the convoy by the S.79s of the 130° *Gruppo* and the 109° *Gruppo* (S.84s) were broken up by Fulmars from the *Ark Royal*. Total Italian losses were six S.84s, one S.79, two CANT Z.506s and two Fiat CR.42 fighters which were escorting the bombers.

**16/17 October** 16 Wellingtons of No. 38 Sqn operating from Luqa, Malta, carried out a heavy raid on Naples, hitting docks, factory buildings, the Arsenal and a torpedo factory. The aircraft dropped a number of 4000 lb (1800 kg) bombs, the first time that weapons of this calibre had been used in the Mediterranean Theatre.

**13 November** 37 replacement Hurricanes for Malta were flown off the carriers HMS *Argus* and HMS *Ark Royal*. (The latter was torpedoed and sunk by the U-81 as she turned back towards Gibraltar.) The fighter reinforcements were badly needed, because some *Regia Aeronautica* units operating over Malta were now equipped with a new fighter, the Macchi C.202, which had arrived in Sicily with the 9° *Gruppo* of the 4° *Stormo* at the end of September 1941. In their first action, the C.202s engaged Hurricanes of No. 185 Sqn over Malta and shot down three for no loss.

**Note:** between 1 June and 31 October 1941, no less than 220 000 tons of Axis shipping was sunk on the convoy routes to Libya; of this total, the RAF and the Fleet Air Arm accounted for 115 000 tons, the Malta-based squadrons accounting for at least

*The wreckage of a Dornier Do 17 reconnaissance aircraft lies burning on Malta*

three-quarters of it. The main target of Malta-based Wellingtons was Tripoli, attacked 72 times between mid-June and mid-October; the Egypt-based squadrons concentrated on Benghazi, which they attacked 102 times.

*December* As a preliminary to neutralizing Malta as a strategic base, the *Luftwaffe* deployed II *Fliegerkorps* to Sicily. This comprised I/KG 54, II and III/KG 77, KGr 606 and KGr 806, all with Junkers Ju 88A-4s; I and II/StG 3 with Ju 87s; I/NJG 2 with Ju 88Cs (for night intruder operations); III/ZG 26 with Messerschmitt Bf 110s; and JG 53 with Bf 109Fs. Initially, the bombers carried out dispersed dive-bombing attacks in small groups and suffered substantial losses, but by the end of the year *Fliegerkorps* II had worked out a revised bombing policy. The aim, which the Germans would attempt to implement early in 1942, was threefold. First, to destroy the RAF fighter defences on Malta by means of heavy and repeated air attacks; second, to neutralize the bomber and torpedo-bomber bases on the island; and third, to attack the docks and harbour installations around Valletta. When these objectives were achieved, the island would be open to invasion.

## North Africa, June–December 1941

In June 1941, the *Regia Aeronautica*'s strength in North Africa stood at 70 fighters and 25 bombers:

*The air war situation in North Africa became worse for the Allies with the arrival of* Jagdgeschwader *27, whose Messerschmitt Bf 109Fs outclassed both the Hurricane and the P-40.*

the fighter *gruppi* were the 2° and 155° with Fiat G.50s and the 18° and 151° with Fiat CR.42s, while two *gruppi* of the 43° *Stormo* had Fiat BR.20s for night bombing. There were also three reconnaissance units. In July this force was joined by the 153° and 157° *Gruppi* with Macchi MC.200s, and the 209ª *Squadriglia* with Junkers Ju 87Bs. The *Luftwaffe* forces in North Africa were still relatively small, the principal bomber force comprising the Ju 87s of II/StG 2 and I/StG 3; detachments of Bf 110s were rotated from Greece, and it was not until the late summer of 1941 that the *Afrika Korps* received adequate fighter protection in the form of the first echelons of JG 27, with Bf 109Fs.

*14 June* British and Empire forces launched Operation *Battleaxe*, an attempt by armour and infantry to break Rommel's hold on Cyrenaica and relieve Tobruk. The offensive was supported by every available Allied aircraft, amounting to 105 bombers and 98 fighters. Offensive air operations were carried out mainly by No. 253 Wing, comprising Nos. 113 and 229 Sqns RAF (Blenheims and Hurricanes) and Nos. 450 and 451 Sqns RAAF (Tomahawks and Hurricanes). In addition, No. 1 Sqn SAAF (Hurricanes) and No. 24 Sqn SAAF (Marylands) were also committed. Squadron strengths were increased by the allocation of aircraft from units which were just arriving in Egypt. *Battleaxe* was a costly failure, the RAF losing 33 aircraft in the air. The operation underlined the need for effective air/ground communication.

*18 November* British and Empire forces launched Operation *Crusader*, with the aims of destroying the bulk of Rommel's armour, relieving Tobruk and retaking Cyrenaica as a preliminary to invading Tripolitania. The offensive was supported by 14 squadrons of short-range fighters (Hurricane Is and Tomahawks), two of long-range fighters (Beaufighters and Hurricane IIs), eight squadrons of medium bombers (Blenheims and Marylands) and three tactical reconnaissance squadrons (two Hurricanes, one Boston). Strong fighter sweeps by Hurricane and Tomahawk squadrons quickly established air superiority deep inside Libya, while bombing attacks were made on enemy shipping, oil and supply storage facilities and the ports used by Rommel's forces in North Africa and Italy. The offensive enjoyed initial success, although an attempted breakout by the Tobruk garrison was forestalled by the rapid redeployment of Rommel's armour. The German defensive line at Gazala was breached in December and British forces pushed on towards Benghazi, but were halted at El Agheila in December.

*Desert Air Force pilots donning their kit prior to an offensive sweep over the Western Desert, 1941.*

## Malta, 1942

**January/February** The *Luftwaffe*, implementing the first phase of the plan to subjugate Malta, continued its attacks on the island's airfields, although these were hampered by bad weather. An attempt to supply Malta from Alexandria with the aid of three fast merchantmen on 12 February failed, two being sunk and one disabled.

**7 March** The first 15 Spitfires reached Malta, flown in at enormous risk from the carrier HMS *Eagle*.

**20 March** The *Luftwaffe* began a massive onslaught aimed at the destruction of Malta's dwindling fighter force, 60 Ju 88s attacking Takali airfield. The airfield was again heavily bombed on the following day.

**22 March** Four supply ships, escorted by four light cruisers and 16 destroyers, attempted to reach Malta from Alexandria. An attempt to intercept the convoy by Italian warships was beaten off in the Gulf of Sirte, but the ships were later subjected to heavy air attack. The transport *Clan Campbell* was sunk 20 miles (32 km) short of the island and the naval supply ship *Breconshire* was so badly damaged that she had to be beached. The other two transports reached Valletta harbour, but both were sunk by air attack two days later. Only one-fifth of the convoy's supplies reached Malta's storehouses.

**25 March** 12 Hurricane Mk IICs of No. 229 Sqn, fitted with long-range fuel tanks, arrived at Takali from Gambut, Egypt. The next day they were deployed to Hal Far airfield, where most were quickly destroyed in bombing raids.

**20 April** The American carrier USS *Wasp*, having sailed from the Clyde via Gibraltar, flew off 54 Spitfires for Malta, of which 47 reached the island. By the end of the next day, under repeated air attack, only 18 remained airworthy.

**9 May** The USS *Wasp* and HMS *Eagle* flew off 64 Spitfires for Malta, 60 reaching the island safely.

**11 May** Royal Navy warships from Alexandria, attempting to intercept an Axis convoy, were attacked by Ju 88s of I and II/LG 1 from Crete and Greece. Three out of four British destroyers involved were sunk.

**10 June** Bristol Beaufort torpedo-bombers of No. 217 Sqn arrived at Luqa, Malta, from the United Kingdom.

**14–15 June** Convoy *Harpoon*, consisting of six large merchant ships and an escort that included the carriers HMS *Eagle* and HMS *Argus*, came under heavy air attack by German and Italian aircraft. The convoy's fighter cover consisted of 16 Sea Hurricanes of No. 801 Sqn on the *Eagle* and a small number of Fulmars on the *Argus*. Six enemy aircraft were shot down by the defending fighters, but three Hurricanes were lost. Eleven enemy aircraft were claimed destroyed by the Hurricanes and Fulmars by the end of the day, with many others damaged and driven off. On 15 June the carrier support force turned back for Gibraltar, the convoy relying on Malta-based fighter cover. Only two of the merchant vessels reached the island. A second convoy from Alexandria, menaced by the Italian Fleet, was forced to turn back.

*11–13 August* Operation *Pedestal*. Thirteen freighters and the tanker *Ohio* passed through the western Mediterranean en route for Malta with an escort that included the carriers *Victorious* (No. 809 Sqn with Fulmars and No. 885 Sqn with Sea Hurricanes), *Indomitable* (Nos. 800 and 880 Sqns with Sea Hurricanes), *Formidable* (No. 806 Sqn with Sea Hurricanes and No. 884 Sqn with Martlets) and *Eagle* (No. 801 Sqn with Sea Hurricanes and No. 804 Sqn with Fulmars). The convoy also included HMS *Furious*, with 38 Spitfires for Malta. The convoy was shadowed by Ju 88 reconnaissance aircraft as it passed south of Majorca on 11 August, and that afternoon HMS *Eagle* was torpedoed and sunk by the U-73, taking most of her aircraft down with her. Later, after the *Furious* had flown off her Spitfires, the convoy was attacked by 35 Ju 88s, three of which were shot down by AA fire. The next day the convoy, now well within range of enemy airfields, was subjected to a series of very heavy air attacks in which *Indomitable*'s two Sea Hurricane squadrons gave a particularly good account of themselves, claiming 18 enemy aircraft destroyed. Fourteen more were claimed by the other FAA squadrons. Total enemy losses in the air fighting around the convoy were 38 aircraft, of which 24 belonged to the *Regia Aeronautica*. The Fleet Air Arm's loss, not counting the aircraft that went down with the *Eagle*, was 13. Only five ships of the convoy, three of them damaged – including the vital tanker *Ohio* – reached Malta. The arrival of the *Ohio* allowed Malta's strike squadrons, which had been grounded since 28 July through shortage of fuel, to resume operations. No. 39 Sqn was now the RAF's resident torpedo attack squadron on Malta, and was allotted a Beaufighter squadron to work with it during shipping strikes.

The arrival of the remnants of the *Pedestal* convoy ensured Malta's salvation. The island once again went over to the offensive, the Beauforts of No. 39 Sqn being joined by torpedo-carrying Wellingtons of Nos. 38 and 221 Sqns, detached from their main bases in Egypt. Also operating in the anti-shipping role from Malta were the Fairey Albacores of Nos. 828 and 830 Sqns, Fleet Air Arm, which between them sank 30 ships and damaged 50 more. In October, the *Luftwaffe* subjected Malta to a nine-day series of heavy raids, but the attacks were broken up by the RAF, which could now put up around 100 fighters, and the AA defences, which were no longer short of ammunition. Moreover, events in North Africa were turning the war irrevocably against the Axis powers.

## North Africa, 1942–3

# 1942

*January* Fortified by two supply convoys that reached Tripoli, General Rommel's forces launched a counter-attack in Cyrenaica. On 22 January, they almost succeeded in destroying the fighters of No. 258 Wing – comprising Nos. 1 (SAAF), 94, 238 and 274 (RAF) Sqns with Hurricanes and No. 2 (SAAF) and 3 (RAAF) with Tomahawks – when their armour surrounded the Wing's forward airfield at Antelat. Most of them escaped just before the airfield was overrun by enemy tanks. By the end of January the British forces in Cyrenaica were once more in retreat. Only intense air attack by the Desert Air Force stopped Rommel's armour breaking through into Egypt, and in February the *Afrika Korps* was halted on a line stretching from Gazala to Bir Hakim.

**March–May** This period witnessed a developing struggle for air superiority in North Africa as a preliminary to Rommel's planned summer offensive. The *Luftwaffe*'s forces were strengthened by the arrival of units of II *Fliegerkorps* from Sicily. More units were also assigned to the Desert Air Force's three fighter/fighter-bomber wings; these included Nos. 7 and 40 Sqns SAAF, with Hurricanes. By the beginning of May, the ageing Bristol Blenheims had virtually disappeared from the Desert Air Force's light bomber units; No. 3 (SAAF) Wing now had three squadrons of Douglas Boston IIIs (Nos. 12 and 24 Sqns SAAF) and one of Martin Baltimores (No. 223 Sqn RAF). It was during this period that No. 3 Wing developed new bombing techniques involving mass take-offs by boxes of 18 aircraft followed by bombing in tight formation under strong fighter escort. This enabled the Wing to maintain shuttle-bombing operations against enemy forces during daylight.

**26 May** The *Afrika Korps* launched a fierce assault on the Gazala Line. At the start of the battle the Desert Air Force had 290 serviceable combat aircraft, the Germans and Italians 497. By 31 May the British fighter squadrons had flown 1500 sorties in the Army co-operation task and lost 50 aircraft, around 20 per cent of the fighter force. Sixteen British aircraft were lost on 31 May alone; the Germans lost three fighters and two dive-bombers.

**1 June** The first Spitfires became operational with the Desert Air Force with No. 145 Sqn. They were later joined by Nos. 92 and 601 Sqns.

**7–10 June** All squadrons of the Desert Air Force were committed to the support of Free French forces holding the fort of Bir Hakim, at the southern end of the Gazala Line, which was under heavy and continual attack by the *Stukas* of StG 3 escorted by the Bf 109Fs of JG 27. 7 June saw the first operational mission by the Hurricane IIDs of No. 6 Sqn RAF; these were fitted with two wing-mounted 40 mm Vickers Type 'S' cannon for the anti-tank role. The Desert Air Force flew 1500 sorties in support of Bir Hakim, 950 by fighters,

*Armed with 40 mm cannon, the Hawker Hurricane became a formidable ground attack aircraft in North Africa.*

and lost 20 aircraft; the *Luftwaffe* flew 1400 sorties and lost 15, while the Italians lost at least five. Bir Hakim was evacuated on the night of 10/11 June, the Free French Brigade having suffered very heavy casualties in its gallant nine-day stand. Its resistance prevented three German divisions from turning the Allied flank and encircling the Gazala Line, enabling the British Eighth Army to regroup and withdraw into Egypt.

**20 June** The *Luftwaffe* and *Regia Aeronautica* launched a massive air assault on the defences of Tobruk, the Germans flying 580 sorties and the Italians 177 on this one day. As a result of this effort, and the earlier one at Bir Hakim, Axis aircraft serviceability dropped greatly. Tobruk fell, but Rommel pushed on towards Egypt with severely depleted air cover.

**1–22 July** The first Battle of El Alamein. During the first week of the month the Desert Air Force flew 5458 sorties; these included 60–70 sorties each night by the Wellingtons of No. 205 Group, the Fairey Albacores of Nos. 821 and 826 Sqns FAA acting as flare-droppers. During the July fighting, Middle East Command lost 113 aircraft compared to the Germans' 80 and the Italians' 18, but continual air attack delayed the enemy advance and enabled the Eighth Army to take up its positions at El Alamein.

**21 August** The Desert Air Force began a nine-day series of strikes on Rommel's forces, dropping more than 450 tons of bombs. At the same time, anti-shipping operations deprived Rommel of 25 per cent of general military cargo and 41 per cent of the fuel despatched to North Africa.

**30 August–6 September** The Battle of Alam Halfa. During this battle – Rommel's last attempt to regain the offensive initiative – practically the whole burden of offensive operations against the Germans devolved on the Desert Air Force, the Army now committed to a defensive role while marshalling its forces. Twenty-two squadrons of fighters, including three of Spitfires, cleared the way for day bombers (Bostons, Baltimores and one squadron of USAAF B-25 Mitchells), while No. 205 Group Wellingtons and FAA Albacores maintained the pressure at night. On the night of 31 August/1 September the Wellingtons dropped 90 tons of bombs, attacking transport and tank leaguers; the 112 tons dropped on the following night included some 4000 lb (1800 kg) bombs, their first use in North Africa.

**October** Build-up of the United States Army Middle East Air Force (designated US Ninth Air Force from 12 November). The IX Bomber Command comprised two Heavy Bombardment Groups of six squadrons (one B-17, five B-24), a Medium Bombardment Group (four squadrons of B-25s) and a Fighter Group (three squadrons of P-40s) under Major-General Lewis H. Brereton. The medium bombers and fighters were under the operational control of the Desert Air Force commander, Air Vice-Marshal Arthur Coningham. The American contribution brought the total of squadrons available to the Allied Air Forces in the Middle East in October 1942 to 96.

**23 October** The second Battle of El Alamein. This was preceded by a four-day heavy bombing programme against enemy airfields. When the battle opened, Desert Air Force fighters were able to maintain a continuous patrol over the Axis forward airfields.

**3 November** This was the busiest day of air operations in the Battle of El Alamein. In the space of 24 hours the RAF flew 1208 sorties and dropped 396 tons of bombs; 53 more sorties were flown by USAAF medium bombers. British fighter losses were 16 aircraft, with 11 more damaged. During the whole battle 23 October–4 November, the RAF flew 10 405 sorties and the Americans 1181; the British lost 77 aircraft and the Americans 20. On the Axis side, the Germans flew 1550 sorties and lost 64 aircraft, and the Italians lost about 20 in an estimated 1570 sorties.

**8 November** Operation Torch: the Allied landings in North Africa. This involved three amphibious assaults at Casablanca, Oran and Algiers by British and American task forces. The British landings were supported by the Fleet carriers *Formidable*, *Victorious*, *Furious* and *Argus* and the escort carriers *Biter*, *Avenger* and *Dasher*, while the American landings were covered by the *Ranger*, *Sangamon*, *Suwannee* and *Santee*. The operation saw the operational debut of the Supermarine Seafire, the naval version of the Spitfire; these equipped Nos. 801 and 807 Sqns FAA. Air cover during the preliminary phase of the landings and the subsequent consolidation was undertaken by naval fighters, with the exception of the Hurricanes of No. 43 Sqn RAF which were flown into Maison Blanche, Algeria, after the airfield was captured by a US combat team. They were quickly followed into Algerian airfields by the Hurricanes of No. 225 Sqn, the Spitfires of Nos. 72, 81, 93, 111, 152 and 242 Sqns and the Beaufighters of No. 255 Sqn. An RAF bomber wing was established as well, comprising the Bisleys (Canadian-built Blenheim Mk Vs) of Nos. 13, 18, 114 and 614 Sqns. The P-38 Lightnings of the 1st, 14th and 82nd Fighter Groups USAAF were also deployed to North Africa from the United Kingdom to form part of the new Twelfth Air Force. By the end of November, *Luftwaffe* units in North Africa were beginning to receive the Focke-Wulf Fw 190, mostly the G-1 ground-attack version. The first unit to equip was II/SchG 2 at Zarzun, Tunisia. November also saw the North African debut of the Henschel Hs 129 ground-attack aircraft with IV/SchG 2, transferred from Poland.

As the Allied advance rolled across North Africa from east to west, the Desert Air Force, supporting the Eighth Army, maintained the air superiority it had won before Alamein, mounting continual attacks on the enemy convoys that jammed the coast road that led through Cyrenaica. In north-west Africa, however, the situation in the air was different. Here, handicapped by the lack of suitable airfields that forced their aircraft to operate at ever-growing distances from the front line, the Allied air forces suffered heavily; the *Luftwaffe* had mastery in the battlefield area. A particularly black day was 4 December, when ten Bisleys of No. 18 Sqn RAF set out to bomb the airstrip at Chouigui; the bombers were unescorted and all ten were shot down by enemy fighters. For his determination in pressing home the attack, and in trying to shepherd his aircraft to safety afterwards, the raid leader, Wing Commander H.G. Malcolm, was awarded a posthumous Victoria Cross. Also lost on this day were six Spitfires of No. 93 Sqn, destroyed on the ground, and five P-38s of the 14th FG. The latter suffered particularly heavily on operations, losing 20 aircraft and 13 pilots between 18 November and 23 January 1943, when it was withdrawn from operations.

# 1943

*7 April* On this day, after weeks of bitter fighting, the US II Corps linked up with the Eighth Army, isolating the Axis forces in Tunisia. At the same time, the Allied air forces began an all-out campaign to destroy the remnants of the *Luftwaffe* in North Africa. The Desert Air Force now had crushing air superiority: 535 fighters, fighter-bombers and tank-destroyers, 140 medium bombers and 80 heavy bombers, against 80 serviceable German and 40 Italian aircraft. The RAF and the USAAF

IX Bomber Command also launched a series of heavy attacks on enemy airfields in Sicily and southern Italy, where the enemy had assembled fleets of transport aircraft – Junkers Ju 52s and Messerschmitt Me 323s – in an attempt to fly supplies and troops into Tunisia. The losses suffered by these transport aircraft were appalling. The first major encounter occurred on 5 April, when P-38s of the 1st and 82nd FG attacked 65 Ju 52s off Cape Bone and destroyed 11, together with several escorting fighters. The biggest battle was on *18 April*, when 47 P-40s of the IX Air Force's 57th and 324th FG, with 12 Spitfires of No. 92 Sqn RAF providing top cover, encountered 90 Ju 52s escorted by 50 German and Italian fighters off Cape Bone and destroyed 77 enemy aircraft for the loss of six P-40s and a Spitfire. On *22 April*, RAF Spitfires and SAAF Kittyhawks followed up this success by shooting down 21 Me 323s, all laden with fuel, and seven of their escorting fighters. Of the 140 aircrew of *Transportgeschwader* 5 who took part in this operation, only 19 survived. The fighting in North Africa ceased on *7 May 1943* with the capture of 275 000 Axis prisoners – three times the number taken at Stalingrad.

*The* Luftwaffe *suffered terrible transport aircraft losses in its attempts to ferry men and supplies to Tunisia. Here, a Messerschmitt Me 323 comes under attack by a Martin Marauder of No. 14 Sqn RAF.*

# Air War Over Russia, 1942–43

## 1942

**20 February** Junkers Ju 52 transports began a major airlift operation to an airstrip at Demyansk, North Russia, to supply 100 000 troops of the German X and XI Army Corps, encircled by the Red Army's January offensive. Eight transport *Gruppen* were eventually involved. At first the Ju 52s flew in singly at low level, but as losses increased due to Soviet air action, the transports adopted tight formations, with strong fighter escort provided by the Bf 109s of III/JG 3 and I/JG 51. The airlift was successful; up to 20 May 1942 the Ju 52s flew in 24 303 tons of supplies – a daily average of 276 tons – to the Demyansk pocket. In addition, five million gallons of petrol and 15 446 replacements were flown in, and 22 093 wounded evacuated. Aircraft losses were 262 Ju 52s, many resulting from accidents in the winter conditions. In May, a land corridor was opened up to Demyansk, and the number of Ju 52 *Gruppen* supporting the operation was reduced to three.

**March** The Air Force for Long-Range Operations (ALFRO) was formed from heavy bomber units of the Soviet Air Force. Commanded by General A. Ye. Golovanov, this was under the operational control of the *Stavka*.

**May** The Soviet Air Force underwent considerable reorganization with the formation of new frontal air armies consisting of air divisions equipped with one type of aircraft. Separate training air regiments were also established.

**July** The Germans launched major offensives into the Caucasus and to the Volga. During the preliminary battles, a thrust by the German Army Group B towards Voronezh, on the River Don, was halted short of its objective by rocket-firing Il-2 *Shturmoviks* of the 16th Air Army.

**17 July** Air operations began on the distant approaches to Stalingrad, units of the Soviet 8th Air Army and AFLRO supporting the 62nd and 64th Armies fighting on the Chir and Tsimlya rivers. The strength of the 8th Air Army at this time was 300 aircraft; in addition, AFLRO provided 150 long-range bombers and the 102nd Fighter Air Division, responsible for the defence of Stalingrad, about 60 fighters. Ther *Luftwaffe* had some 1200 aircraft of all types in the Stalingrad sector.

**23 July** All available ground-attack and bomber aircraft of the 8th Air Army operated in support of part of the 62nd Army, trapped by a German breakthrough to the Don in the Kalach area. The main Soviet air effort involved direct support of the 1st and 4th Tank Armies, which were counter-attacking. During these operations, the Russians set up a primitive forward air control system; this mainly involved the direction, by radio, of groups of Soviet fighters towards German ground-attack formations observed over the front line. During the first 18 days of the battle, pilots of the 434th Fighter Regiment claimed 36 enemy aircraft destroyed.

**31 July** A new German offensive developed from the south-west towards the Caucasus, led by the 4th Tank Army. The 8th Air Army flew up to 600 sorties a day in support of Soviet ground forces; crews of the 150th Bomber Regiment (Lieutenant Colonel I.S. Polbin) were especially active, developing dive-bombing tactics with their Pe-2 bombers against supply dumps and communications. LaGG-3 fighters of the 268th Fighter Air Division, fitted with a nose-mounted 37-mm cannon in place of the more usual 20-mm, operated in the anti-tank role with limited success, while Il-2s of the 228th Ground-Attack Division carried out a number of successful airfield attacks. Russian top cover over the battlefield was provided by Yak-1 fighters of the 183rd Fighter Air Regiment.

**17 August** The 8th and 16th Air Armies began a seven-day series of attacks on river crossings on the approaches to Stalingrad, flying over 1000 sorties. The bombers suffered heavy losses, as the *Luftwaffe* still had air superiority.

**20 August** The 287th Fighter Air Division (Colonel S.P. Danilin) arrived to reinforce the 8th Air Army with new Lavochkin La-5 fighters. In a 27-day period of operations, the 287th claimed the destruction of 97 enemy aircraft.

**23 August** 200 bombers of *Luftflotte* 4, escorted by 50 Messerschmitt Bf 109s, carried out the first large-scale air attack on Stalingrad. The raids continued at intervals all day, the *Luftwaffe* flying about 2000 sorties. Soviet fighters and AA claimed the destruction of 90 German aircraft over the city and its approaches for the loss of 30 of their own number.

**September** In the early part of the month the German Sixth Army penetrated the outer defences of Stalingrad and the battle began for pos-

*The Ilyushin Il-2* Shturmovik *assault aircraft was one of the Soviet Air Force's most effective weapons in the air war against Germany.*

session of the city. This period saw a major revision of Soviet fighter tactics and air control. The complement of fighter regiments was increased from 22 to 32 aircraft; the basic battle unit became the flight, consisting of two pairs of aircraft. A target control network was set up within the 16th Air Army's area of operations; this consisted of a central radio station located near the 16th Air Army HQ, radio stations in divisions and regiments located on airfields, and also forward air control radio posts located along the line of the front, these having direct communication with fighter pilots in the air.

**24 *September*** Lieutenant Valeria Khomyakova became the first woman fighter pilot to destroy an enemy aircraft at night, shooting down a Ju 88 over Stalingrad. Her unit was the 586th Fighter Air Regiment, which formed part of the all-female 122nd Air Group together with the 587th Bomber

Air Regiment and the 588th Night Bomber Air Regiment. The 586th was equipped with Yakovlev Yak-7b fighters.

**19 *October*** Pe-2 aircraft of the 272nd Night Bomber Air Division, operating in support of the first Soviet counterattack to the north of Stalingrad, flew 375 sorties against targets in the city itself. Each attack was preceded by Po-2 biplanes acting as flare-dropping pathfinders. Po-2s were also used to fly in supplies to the defenders of Stalingrad; during the September–December period they made 1008 flights in support of the 62nd Army on the right wing of the front, delivering about 200 tons of cargo.

**1–19 *November*** The 17th, 16th and 8th Air Armies were respectively assigned to the Southwestern, Don and Stalingrad Fronts in readiness for the coming counter-offensive. Two composite air corps and seven air divisions were held in reserve, while the 2nd Air Army was reassigned from the Voronezh Front to the Southwestern Front. Including reserve aircraft, the Soviet air strength available for the counter-offensive stood at 1414 aircraft, of which 426 (Po-2s, R-5s and SB-2s) were used only at night. In opposition, the *Luftwaffe* had 1216 aircraft. This total included units of the Hungarian, Romanian and Italian Air Forces; the latter had been operating an expeditionary force comprising the 21°, 22° and 61° *Gruppi* in support of the Italian Eighth Army in Russia since the early months of the war.

**19 *November*** The start of the Soviet counter-offensive. Air operations, which were preceded by Po-2 attacks during the night on staff headquarters and communications, were initially hampered by bad weather. During the first four days of the assault, the four armies involved flew only about 1000 sorties, but after 24 November the sortie rate averaged 800 a day. By this time the German Sixth Army was already virtually surrounded. *Luftwaffe* operations during this initial phase were restricted to a few offensive sorties by the He 111s of KG 55 and the Ju 87s of StG 2.

**25 *November*** The *Luftwaffe* began a maximum-effort operation in an attempt to supply the Sixth Army by air. The transport aircraft fleet initially comprised eleven *Gruppen* of Ju 52s and two of Ju 86s, amounting to 320 machines, but only about one-third were serviceable. Consequently, during the first two days of the airlift, Stalingrad received only 65 tons of fuel and ammunition instead of the required 300. The operation was further complicated by renewed bad weather.

**30 *November*** Heinkel He 111s of KG 27, KG 55

and KG 100 joined the airlift into Stalingrad, with the Bf 109s of JG 3 assigned as fighter escort. On this day the quota of supplies delivered rose to 100 tons – still barely one-sixth of the amount required by the Sixth Army.

*December* Operations were again hampered by bad weather during the early part of the month. By 16 December supplies in Stalingrad were exhausted, and – in direct contravention of Hitler's order to fight to the last man – a breakout was planned. In response to this, between *19 and 21 December* the transport units flew 450 sorties and landed 700 tons of supplies at Pitomnik airfield near Stalingrad. On 22 December, freezing fog brought a halt to the airlift operation.

*24 December* Two Soviet Guards Armies, having destroyed the Italian Eighth Army on the Don, threatened the two main *Luftwaffe* airlift bases at Tazinskaya and Morosovskaya. At Tazinskaya, 125 out of 180 transport aircraft, mostly Ju 52s and Ju 86s, managed to escape to various other airfields. The two airstrips at Morosovskaya were overrun on 1 January 1943.

# 1943

*9 January* 18 Focke-Wulf Fw 200 Kondor maritime patrol aircraft of I and III/KG 40 were assigned to the Stalingrad airlift, operating from Stalino. These aircraft initially landed at Pitomnik, but when this airfield was overrun they dropped supply containers by parachute. Two Junkers Ju 290 transports and seven Heinkel He 177 bombers were also assigned to the airlift; the He 177s proved useless in the transport role and were used on bombing operations. A total of 40 He 177s were eventually committed to operations in the Stalingrad sector.

*9 January* Seven Ilyushin Il-2s, with strong fighter escort, made a low-level attack on the airfield at Salsk, where about 150 German transport aircraft were based. Twelve Ju 52s were destroyed and 40 badly damaged.

*10 January* MiG-3 fighters of the 235th Fighter Air Division (Colonel I.D. Podgorny) intercepted a formation of 16 Ju 52 transports heading for Pitomnik and shot down 15 of them.

*16 January* Soviet forces overran the airfield at Pitomnik. This left only the airstrip at Gumrak within the Stalingrad perimeter. This airstrip was virtually unusable due to bomb damage and

wrecked aircraft; nevertheless, transport aircraft continued to land there whenever possible. The last mission to Gumrak was on the night of 21/22 January, when 21 He 111s and four Ju 52s landed. The airstrip was overrun soon afterwards.

*2/3 February* The *Luftwaffe* flew its last supply-dropping mission over Stalingrad, crews reporting no sign of friendly recognition signals from the ground. As far as may be ascertained, the final mission was flown by *Leutnant* Kuntz of I/KG 100.

Total *Luftwaffe* transport aircraft losses in the Battle of Stalingrad were 266 Ju 52s, 165 He 111s, 42 Ju 86s, 9 Fw 200s, 7 He 177s and 1 Ju 290 – 490 machines, the equivalent of five *Geschwader*. Apart from flying in supplies, the transport aircraft had evacuated 42 000 wounded in the course of the battle. Aircraft of all types lost totalled 1249, of which over 900 were claimed by fighters and flak. A further 542 aircraft, mostly badly damaged, were captured by Soviet forces when they overran enemy airfields. The Red Army Air Force flew 45 325 sorties during the siege and dropped 15 000 tons of bombs; Soviet air losses were never publicly revealed. The 220th and 268th Fighter Divisions, the 228th and 26th Ground-Attack Divisions, the 263rd Bomber Division, the 272nd Night Bomber Division, the 3rd, 17th and 24th Air Divisions of the AFLRO, and the 102nd Fighter Air Division were designated Guards Divisions for their part in the battle.

## The Battle for the Kuban Bridgehead, March–April 1943

By the end of March 1943 the southern front, with the exception of the Kuban region, had stabilized. After their defeat at Stalingrad, the Germans hoped to salvage something by launching a new offensive towards the Caucasus, and to this end they poured troops and equipment into the Kuban valley area of the Northern Caucasus. To support the ground operations, the *Luftwaffe* could call on the support of about 820 aircraft of *Luftflotte* 4. In opposition, the Russians initially had 200 aircraft of the 5th Air Army, 70 aircraft of the Black Sea Fleet and 60 aircraft of the AFLRO; by mid-April, thanks to a rapid injection of reserves, this figure had been boosted to 900, of which 370 were fighters, 170 ground-attack aircraft, 165 day bombers, and 195 night bombers.

The Kuban battle, which lasted seven weeks, was characterized by clashes between large air formations. The Soviet fighters often operated at full regiment strength, flying in stepped-up battle formation. As usual, the fighters were employed mainly in escorting assault and light bomber air-craft – Il-2s and Pe-2s – and the ratio of fighters to bombers on these missions depended on the number of bombers engaged. For example, four bombers would be escorted by ten fighters, 16–24 bombers by 20 fighters. Offensive fighter sweeps usually involved one *Gruppa* (three or four pairs, six to eight fighters) patrolling within a defined sector, with a second *Gruppa* at readiness. In this way a fighter regiment with four *Gruppi* could maintain a constant patrol over the combat area. In addition, ranger patrols (*Svobodnaya Okhota*) were frequently carried out by fighters operating in pairs. Fighter units were now mainly equipped with Yak-1, Yak-7B and La-5 aircraft, although they also used some numbers of P-39 Airacobras supplied under lend-lease to the USSR.

When escorting ground-attack aircraft, the fighter cover was usually split into two parts: the imme-diate escort and the assault group. The immediate escort remained constantly near the ground-at-tack aircraft and flew between 300 and 1000 ft (90–305 m) higher. These fighters had the task of engaging any enemy fighters that managed to break through the forward assault group to present a direct threat to the ground-attack formation. They normally broke away over the target and circled out of range of the enemy anti-aircraft defences, ready to take up their original position for the withdrawal flight. Often, if no enemy fighters showed up, the immediate escort would themselves dive down to strafe targets on the ground.

The fighters of the assault group flew between 1500 and 3000 ft (460–915 m) higher than the immediate escort, and either directly above or half a mile ahead of the assault formation. One pair was usually sent out in advance to scout for enemy fighters, while a second pair cruised at high altitude, up-sun of the assault formation, ready to dive out of the sun to surprise attacking enemy fighters.

Over the target, the assault group normally went up to 10 000 ft (3000 m) or so – clear of most of the light flak – and patrolled over a fixed area until they were required to cover the withdrawal of the ground-attack aircraft. Changes in the strength of the escort – which was dependent on such factors as the distance to the target, weather and expected enemy fighter opposition as well as the size of the bomber formation – did not influence these tac-tics. When a reduction in size had to be made, an equal number of fighters was withdrawn from both the immediate escort and assault groups. If it was felt necessary to increase the size of the escort,

this was done by slotting in additional formations of fighters ahead of, behind or below the ground-attack aircraft.

That these tactics were developed at all was thanks to a handful of men, all of them rising stars in the Red Army Air Force. Notable among them were Lieutenant Aleksandr I. Pokryshkin of the 16th Guards Fighter Air Regiment, then equipped with P-39 Airacobras, and Major-General Ivan S. Polbin of the 301st Bomber Aviation Division, who dur-ing the past two years had virtually written the standard manual of bombing tactics. The revised tactical methods did not bring the Red Army Air Force overall superiority during the Kuban offen-sive, which in the event failed to dislodge the Germans (they were forced to withdraw in Sep-tember, when their position became untenable). What they did was to lay a sound foundation for future operations in which, for the first time, the Russians would have numerical superiority – and aircraft that matched the *Luftwaffe*'s equipment from the technical standpoint.

With the coming of the spring thaw, large-scale operations along the whole front came to a stand-still. As they had done a year earlier, both sides took the opportunity to strengthen their forces in preparation for a summer offensive. The Ger-mans knew that everything depended on the outcome of this summer of 1943. If they regained the initiative they might have a second chance to take Moscow; but if they lost it, the way would be open for a Russian advance into central Europe.

The spring lull in the fighting had left the Soviet Central and Voronezh Fronts in a potentially dan-gerous situation, with two German salients at Orel and Kursk flanking a deep bulge to the west of Kursk. In this bulge the Russians had concen-trated twelve armies, including two crack Guards and two tank armies. If the Germans could smash their way through the Russian defences to the north and south of Kursk, they would split the Soviet front in two, cutting off all the Russian forces within the Kursk salient and destroying them. If the German plan succeeded, the Red Army would have little hope of recovering from such a shattering defeat.

On paper, the German chances of success were good. For the Kursk offensive they had assembled 70 divisions and nearly a million men, and several of the *Panzer* divisions had re-equipped with the new Tiger and Panther tanks and with Ferdinand self-propelled guns. To support the land offen-sive, the *Luftwaffe* had about 2000 aircraft. Many ground-attack units were now equipped with the Henschel Hs 129A anti-tank aircraft, which had made its operational debut in the Crimea in the previous autumn, and the fighter *Geschwader* had begun to receive the Focke-Wulf Fw 190A-4. One thousand of the German aircraft were earmarked to support the southern arm of the projected pincer movement, which was to be led by the 4th Panzer Army; the rest were detailed to support the northern thrust by the 9th Army.

Six of the Soviet armies in the Kursk salient were assigned to the northern sector, supported by the 16th Air Army, while the other six – supported by the 2nd Air Army – were responsible for the defence of the southern part. In addition, there were five more Soviet armies in reserve, together with the 5th and 17th Air Armies. The 1st and 15th Air Armies were assigned to the armies in the Orel sector. With 2800 aircraft of all types, the Russians had numerical air superiority. This, then, was the line-up prior to what was to be the decisive battle of the Eastern Front; a battle that would be decided by armour and air power. It began in May 1943, with a struggle for control of the air that lasted for two months.

## Operation Citadel

*6 May* 17 German airfields were attacked by 112 bombers, 156 ground-attack aircraft and 166 fighters along a front stretching 745 miles (1200 km). The Russians claimed 194 enemy aircraft destroyed on the ground and 21 in air combat for the loss of 21 of their own. Airfield attacks in this phase continued until 9 May; during this period the Russians claimed 506 enemy aircraft destroyed or damaged, admitting the loss of 122 Soviet aircraft.

*2 June* The *Luftwaffe* launched a heavy attack on Kursk with 287 bombers under strong fighter escort, the main target being the railroad junction. The raid was intercepted by 280 fighters of the 2nd and 16th Air Armies and 106 fighters of the 101st Fighter Air Division, Air Defence Forces. The Russians claimed to have destroyed 145 German aircraft, a figure that should be treated with caution.

*8–10 June* 28 German airfields were attacked by bombers of the 1st, 2nd and 15th Air Armies, supported by the AFLRO. The purpose of these attacks was to destroy *Luftwaffe* bomber forces that were making strategic attacks at night on the tank factories at Gorki, oil refineries at Saratov and the rubber works at Yaroslavl.

*5 July* Following intensive operations by both air forces against troop concentrations and communications, the German offensive at Kursk began. The German ground forces were supported by powerful groups of up to 150 bombers and ground-attack aircraft, each group escorted by up to 60 fighters, concentrating their attacks in an area 15–18 miles (25–30 km) long and 6–9 miles (10–15 km) deep.

Soviet air defence sorties over this sector were flown by the 6th Fighter Air Corps and the 1st Guards Fighter Air Division; there were 76 major air battles in which the Germans lost 106 aircraft, the Russians 98. Offensive Soviet air operations were flown by the 3rd Bomber Air Corps, the 6th Composite Air Corps, the 2nd Guards Air Division and the 299th Ground-Attack Air Division, operating in groups of six to eight aircraft with strong fighter escort.

*6 July* 140 Russian bombers and fighter-bombers, escorted by the 127th Fighter Air Regiment, carried out heavy attacks on German armoured and mechanized infantry columns using PTAB hollow-charge anti-tank bombs, fragmentation and delayed-action bombs. These attacks slowed down the German advance, but did not halt it.

*8 July* Strong Soviet armoured forces, attempting to make a flank attack on the 4th *Panzer* Army, were subjected to concentrated attacks by Henschel Hs 129s of *Schlachtgeschwader* 9. The Hs 129s attacked with 30 mm cannon fire, directed at the Russian tanks' thinly-armoured sides and rear. Many tanks were knocked out and the remainder withdrew in confusion. Accompanying infantry forces were disrupted by Fw 190s dropping fragmentation bombs.

By 10 July, the German offensive in the northern part of the Kursk salient, starved of reserves, had virtually spent itself. By this time, early deficiencies in the Soviet air control system had been remedied and the Russians had gained command of the air. On 11 July, the Russians counter-attacked north and east of Orel, forcing the *Luftwaffe* and the *Wehrmacht* on to the defensive and threatening the 2nd and 9th Panzer Armies with encirclement. The situation was saved by 1 *Fliegerdivision*, which on 19 July threw every available aircraft against a Russian armoured brigade that was blocking the Germans' escape route and averted a catastrophe on a scale even more terrible than Stalingrad.

The Russians were not slow in exploiting their success. At the end of August 1943, supported by 100 air divisions totalling 10 000 aircraft, the whole Soviet battlefront began to roll westwards. Kharkov was recaptured on 23 August, and the

*The Yakovlev Yak-3 was one of the best Soviet fighters to see service in World War II. These examples belong to the French* Normandie-Niemen *Regiment, which flew with the Russians.*

German armies, their reserves exhausted, fell back towards the River Dnieper. By mid-September the Soviet southern and southwestern fronts had driven the enemy from the Donets basin, and on the 22nd of that month the Dnieper was reached by the 3rd Guards Tank Army. On 6 November the Russians recaptured Kiev after bitter fighting, and Soviet forces crossed the Dnieper at a number of other points. Further north, the Central Front under General Rokossovsky breached the river and reached the Pripet marshes, while the Western Front recaptured Smolensk and drove on towards Vitebsk.

The Red Army Air Force was now master of the sky. Kursk had been the *Luftwaffe's* last major operation in the east; from now on its units were dispersed over the vast area of the Russian front or withdrawn for the defence of Germany.

# The Air War against Japan, 1943

**New Guinea, Australia and the Solomons**
During 1942, following their initial landings in eastern New Guinea, the main Japanese effort had been devoted to attempts to capture the vital harbour of Port Moresby, stepping-stone for an invasion of Australia. The air defence of this objective was the responsibility of No. 75 Sqn RAAF, with P-40E Kittyhawks, while the USAAF's 49th Fighter Group, also with P-40s, undertook the air defence of Darwin, which had previously been subjected to air attacks by Japanese bombers.

On 28 April 1942 No. 75 Sqn RAAF, badly depleted, was withdrawn from Port Moresby and replaced by the 8th FG USAAF, with P-39 Airacobras. As the year progressed, the Allied Air Forces in the South-West Pacific Theatre were substantially reorganized under the leadership of General George C. Kenney, commanding the US Fifth Air Force. The USAAF forces at his disposal in August 1942 were the 8th and 35th FG, with P-39s; the 49th FG with P-40s; the 3rd Attack Group with a mixture of A-20 Bostons, A-24 Dauntlesses and B-25 Mitchells; the 19th BG with B-17s; the 22nd Bomb Group with B-26 Marauders; and the 38th BG with B-25s. A second B-17 Group, the 43rd, was re-equipping. There were two Troop Carrier Groups, the 21st and 22nd, with C-47s. RAAF forces in the theatre comprised

Nos. 2 and 13 Sqns with Hudsons, Nos. 75, 76 and 77 Sqns with Kittyhawks, No. 31 Sqn with Beaufighters and No. 100 Sqn with Beauforts. No. 18 (Netherlands East Indies) Sqn was re-equipping with B-25s. In August, these forces were heavily committed to the support of ground troops in the battle at Milne Bay, which thwarted a Japanese pincer movement towards Port Moresby.

During September and October 1942 the USAAF troop carrier groups, assisted by B-17s, flew thousands of American and Australian troops into New Guinea, while other troops were landed by sea. The Allies now had control of the air, and their ability to move forces by sea and air ensured the eventual defeat of the Japanese in the theatre. In October, the 19th Bomb Group was relieved and replaced by the 90th BG, with B-24 Liberators, although in the event the 19th BG remained in action for some time after this while the 90th's crews received additional training.

*Japanese fighter pilots being briefed by their squadron commander before a mission, 1943. Note the parachute harnesses. Earlier in the war, before combat losses became unacceptably high, many Japanese aviators scorned the wearing of parachutes, not wishing to be taken prisoner.*

# 1943

*January* No. 1 Fighter Wing, comprising No. 54 Sqn RAF and Nos. 452 and 457 Sqns RAAF, all with Spitfire VCs, was established for the air defence of Darwin, the 49th FG USAAF having deployed to New Guinea.

*6–8 January* A Japanese convoy carrying reinforcements from Rabaul to Lae, New Guinea, was heavily attacked by RAAF and USAAF aircraft. Two transports and a light cruiser were sunk, although the enemy succeeded in landing 4000 troops. In supporting air operations, 69 enemy aircraft were destroyed.

*28 January* 57 C-47 transports airlifted 814 troops, together with ammunition and medical supplies, to the airstrip at Wau, in the Lae area, in support of Australian forces carrying out guerrilla operations. On 30 January, Beaufighters of No. 30 Sqn RAAF helped to repel an enemy attack on the airstrip. The airlift continued on 1 February. Most of the transport missions were flown by the 374th Troop Carrier Group, USAAF, supported by No. 30 Sqn and No. 22 Sqn RAAF, the latter being equipped with Douglas Bostons. Commonwealth Wirraway aircraft of No. 4 Sqn RAAF acted in the reconnaissance and target-marking roles.

*6 February* Nine Japanese bombers escorted by 30 *Zeros* attacked the airstrip at Wau. They were intercepted by four P-38 Lightning squadrons of the 35th and 49th Fighter Groups, both of which had recently re-equipped with this type. Two bombers and 25 *Zeros* were destroyed.

*11 February* The Chance-Vought F4U Corsair flew its first combat mission when 12 aircraft of VMF-124 based on Guadalcanal escorted a PB2Y rescue aircraft to Vella Lavella. The flight was uneventful. On 14 February, during an escort mission to Kahili Airfield, Bougainville, with US Navy Liberators and USAAF P-38s and P-40s, VMF-124 encountered 50 *Zeros*. Four P-38s, two Liberators, two P-40s and two Corsairs were shot down; the Japanese lost four *Zeros*.

*21 February* In the first of a series of amphibious operations directly and indirectly supported by USMC, USN and USAAF aircraft, Central Pacific Forces landed unopposed in the Russell Islands from Guadalcanal. The intention was to move gradually up the Solomon Islands chain towards the Japanese naval base at Rabaul.

*1–5 March* The Battle of the Bismarck Sea. 14 enemy ships were sighted on a westerly course 40 miles (65 km) north-west of Ubili, heading for Lae. Seven B-17s were sent out to attack the convoy, but failed to locate it. Meanwhile, six Bostons of No. 22 Sqn RAAF bombed the Japanese airfield at Lae to try to make it unusable. On 2 March, the convoy was attacked by 39 B-17s. The next day, the convoy was again attacked by 13 Beaufighters, 13 B-17s and 25 B-25s, escorted by P-38s; they were intercepted by *Zeros*, 20 of which were destroyed for the loss of three P-38s and a B-17. Twenty-three B-25 Mitchells fitted with four-gun 'nose packages' for the strafing role attacked the convoy in the afternoon, followed by another 15 and then five Bostons of No. 22 Sqn RAAF. Early on 4 March, the sole surviving ship of the convoy, a badly damaged *Asashio*-class destroyer, was sunk by a B-17. Later that morning 11 Beaufighters of No. 30 Sqn raided Malahang airfield near Lae, destroying six aircraft on the ground for the loss of one Beaufighter. The Japanese lost 3664 men in their abortive attempt to reinforce Lae; 2427 survivors were taken to Rabaul. For three days after this action, Allied aircraft swept the waters of Huon Gulf, strafing barges and rafts crowded with survivors from the sunken ships. Only about 800 got ashore.

*2–15 March* Air defence of N.W. Australia. On 2 March, a raid by 16 bombers on Coomalie airfield was intercepted by Spitfires of No. 54 Sqn; two *Zeros* and one *Kate* were destroyed for no loss. On 15 March, during the 53rd enemy raid on Darwin, 21 bombers and 24 fighters were intercepted by the Spitfire Wing. Four *Bettys* and three *Zeros* were shot down for the loss of three Spitfires.

*20 March* 42 US Navy and Marine Corps Grumman Avengers, on a night flight from Henderson Field, Guadalcanal, mined Kahili Harbour, Bougainville. A co-ordinated attack by AAF bombers on Kahili airfield contributed to the success of this, the first aerial mining mission in the South Pacific.

*12 April* Japanese aircraft made their 106th and last raid on Port Moresby, destroying three B-25 Mitchells and one Beaufighter on the ground. 24 enemy aircraft were shot down.

*18 April* 16 Lockheed P-38 Lightnings of the 339th Fighter Sqn, Thirteenth Air Force, were despatched from Henderson Field on a 435-mile (700 km) overwater flight to intercept a Mitsubishi G4M *Betty* carrying Admiral Isoroku Yamamoto on a tour of Japanese bases in the Bougainville area. The *Betty* was shot down by Captain Thomas Lanphier Jr and all on board were killed. Two

more *Bettys* and three *Zeros* were also destroyed for the loss of one P-38. The death of Yamamoto was to have a profound effect on the conduct of the Japanese naval war in the Pacific.

**Note:** By the end of April 1943 the Commander, South-West Pacific Area had 69 operational squadrons at his disposal, divided more or less equally between the USAAF and RAAF. Opposing these, with a total strength of about 400 aircraft, was the Japanese 4th Air Army, comprising the 6th and 7th Air Divisions, and the Navy's XI Air Fleet, comprising the 25th and 26th Air Flotillas. Most of the Japanese aircraft were based on Rabaul, and in the northern Solomons and northern New Guinea area.

**2 May** 18 *Bettys*, escorted by 27 *Zeros*, attacked Darwin. They were intercepted by the three squadrons of the Spitfire Wing, which destroyed five fighters and one bomber. Five Spitfires were shot down, five more had to make forced landings due to fuel shortage, and three more suffered engine failures.

During May and June 1943, the Allied air units in the South-West Pacific were occupied mainly with airfield attacks, anti-shipping operations and support of ground forces in contact with the enemy in New Guinea. Construction of forward airstrips received high priority as part of the overall plan

*Long after the war's end, the wreckage of the* Betty *bomber in which Admiral Yamamoto was killed was discovered in the jungle of Rabaul.*

aimed at the reduction of Rabaul. Dual offensives in New Guinea and the Solomons would begin with a landing on Rendova Island near New Georgia by South Pacific forces; at the same time Woodlark and Kiriwina islands, at the south-east tip of New Guinea, and Nassau Bay, about 50 miles (80 km) up the New Guinea coast from Morobe, would be seized as a preliminary to a drive on Lae. The key to the success of these operations was air superiority, which the Japanese had achieved by mid-June 1943.

**18 June** First operation by Vultee Vengeance dive-bombers in the SW Pacific area: 11 aircraft of No. 12 Sqn RAAF, escorted by Beaufighters of No. 31 Sqn, carried out airfield attacks.

**30 June** Allied forces landed on Woodlark, Kiriwina and Rendova islands. Among air units supporting the latter operation was No. 14 Sqn Royal New Zealand Air Force, with P-40E Kittyhawks; this had replaced No. 15 Sqn, also with P-40s, two weeks earlier. Nos. 14, 15, 16 and 17 Sqns RNZAF, equipped initially with P-40s and later with F4U Corsairs, were to play a significant part in fighter-bomber operations in the Solomons.

**30 June** 27 *Bettys*, escorted by 23 *Zeros*, attacked Fenton (Northern Territory). This was the base of the 380th BG, whose B-24s had been carrying out heavy attacks on enemy airstrips. The Japanese force was intercepted by the Spitfire Wing, which destroyed six *Bettys* and three *Zeros* for the loss of four Spitfires (three due to engine failure).

**July** The 348th Fighter Group, USAAF, began operations from Port Moresby with Republic P-47 Thunderbolts. This was the first P-47 unit to serve in the SW Pacific area. In the first three months of combat, the 348th FG destroyed 51 Japanese aircraft for two losses.

**26 July** 26 *Bettys*, escorted by 21 *Zeros*, attacked the Liberator bases in the Darwin area. The raid was intercepted by 36 Spitfires, which destroyed seven *Bettys* and two *Zeros* for the loss of eight of their own (two due to engine failure). This was the last major daylight raid mounted by the Japanese in the Darwin area.

**August** In a move involving 480 aircraft and 10 000 personnel, the Japanese Fourth Air Army redeployed to the northern coast of New Guinea, leaving the Naval Air Forces to defend Rabaul.

*The Lockheed P-38 Lightning entered service in the Pacific Theatre in the summer of 1943. Photograph shows the P-38L bomber version.*

**13 August** Twelve B-24s of the 380th BG flew a 14-hour, 2400-mile (3860-km) mission from northern Australia to Balikpapan, Borneo, causing severe damage to the oil refineries and harbour. This was the first of a series of attacks on this target.

**15 August** 35 P-39 Airacobras of the 35th FG, covering the landing of C-47 transports at the newly established airfield of Tsili Tsili, New Guinea, intercepted 12 *Sally* bombers and 12 *Zeros*. Eleven *Sallys* and three *Zeros* were shot down for the loss of four P-39s.

**16 August** The 475th FG flew its first combat mission in New Guinea with P-38 Lightnings. Two P-38 Groups were now operational with the Fifth Air Force.

**17 August** Enemy airstrips at Wewak, home to the newly arrived Japanese Fourth Air Army, were attacked by 47 B-24s and B-17s, followed by low-level strafing attacks by B-25s. The USAAF claimed 100 enemy aircraft destroyed for the loss of three of their own.

The offensive against the Wewak airstrips continued throughout August, and by the end of the month Japanese air power in the area had been decimated, with 175 aircraft destroyed on the ground for the loss of two B-25s, three B-24s and six P-38s.

**31 August** US Navy Task Force 15, built around the carriers *Essex*, the new *Yorktown* (CV-10) and *Independence*, launched nine strike groups in a day-long attack on Japanese installations on Marcus Island. This operation marked the first combat use of the Grumman F6F Hellcat fighter (Navy Sqns VF-5, VF-6 and VF-9).

**1 September** Two light carriers of Task Group 11.2 (the USS *Princeton* and *Belleau Wood*, with the Hellcats of VF-23 and VF-22 embarked) provided day and night air cover for naval units landing occupation forces on Baker Island, east of the Gilberts.

**5 September** Following heavy air attacks by 48 Mitchells, 24 Liberators and 17 B-17s, 96 C-47 transports escorted by 146 fighters dropped 1700 US and Australian paratroops at Nadzab in an operation designed to cut off the Japanese in the area and give the Allies control of the Markham River Valley, New Guinea. The airdrop took only 70 seconds and was completely successful, the paratroops linking up with Australian forces which had earlier been landed by sea.

**16 September** Allied forces captured Lae. The fall of this key town (and of Salamaua, taken four days earlier) followed the neutralization of Japanese strongpoints by ground-attack aircraft – notably the Vengeances of No. 24 Sqn RAAF from Tsili Tsili, which carried out dive-bombing attacks on pinpoint targets.

**18 September** Strike aircraft from the carriers USS *Lexington*, *Princeton* and *Belleau Wood* carried out a two-day series of strikes on Tarawa, Makin and Abemama Atolls in the Gilbert Islands. These targets were also attacked by B-24s of the Seventh Air Force, operating from forward airfields on Canton and Funafuti Islands. The Seventh AF was responsible for the Central Pacific west of Hawaii.

**October** Allied air forces began the neutralization of Rabaul, the main Japanese fortress in the SW Pacific area. On five airfields there, the enemy had some 329 aircraft protected by 367 AA guns.

**5–6 October** US Navy Task Force 14, comprising the carriers USS *Essex*, *Yorktown*, *Lexington*, *Cowpens*, *Independence* and *Belleau Wood*, with seven cruisers and 24 destroyers – the largest carrier task force yet assembled – bombed and shelled Japanese installations on Wake Island. This operation provided the basis for many tactics used in later task force operations.

**15 October** In retaliation for the heavy air attacks on Rabaul, 27 Aichi D3A *Vals* escorted by 20 *Zeros* attempted to attack the New Guinea ports. All were shot down. A second raid, on 18 October, also incurred heavy losses.

**31 October** Lieutenant H.D. O'Neil USN, flying a Vought F4U-2 Corsair of VFN-75 from Munda, New Georgia, destroyed a *Betty* during a night attack off Vella Lavella, the first kill by a radar-equipped night fighter of the Pacific Fleet. VFN-101 also operated radar-equipped Corsairs from the USS *Essex*.

**2 November** In support of Allied landings at Bougainville, B-25s of the 3rd Attack Group, 38th and 345th Groups, escorted by P-38s of the 475th Group, attacked enemy shipping at Rabaul. The US aircraft encountered strong enemy fighter and AA opposition; eight B-25s and nine P-38s were lost. The P-38 pilots claimed to have destroyed 42 enemy fighters, the B-25s 16 in air combat with 16 more on the ground.

**5 November** The carriers USS *Saratoga* and *Princeton* launched 45 SBD Dauntlesses and TBF Avengers, covered by Hellcats, in the first naval air strike on Rabaul, damaging several warships of the Japanese Second Fleet. Ten US aircraft were lost. Rabaul was also attacked by 27 B-24s of the 43rd BG, escorted by 58 P-38s.

**11 November** Two carrier task forces comprising the USS *Saratoga*, *Princeton*, *Essex*, *Bunker Hill* and *Independence* launched a second heavy air attack on Rabaul, sinking one Japanese destroyer and damaging several other vessels, including a cruiser. This attack saw the first use of the Curtiss SB2C Helldiver in action. *Val* and *Kate* bombers, escorted by *Zeros*, attempted to attack the carrier force but were dispersed by Hellcats and Corsairs. Total Japanese losses for 11 November were around 50 aircraft; the Americans lost 18. The Rabaul raids crippled Japanese warships that might have threatened operations in the Solomons, and also destroyed most of the enemy bomber force on Rabaul.

**18–26 November** Occupation of the Gilbert Islands. Six heavy and five light carriers of Task Force 50 opened the campaign to capture the Gilbert Islands with a two-day series of air attacks on airfields and defensive installations, and also covered the landings of Marines and Army troops on Tarawa and Makin Atolls (20 November). Eight escort carriers, operating with the Attack Forces, covered the approach of assault shipping on 18–20 November, flew anti-submarine and combat air patrols in the area, and close support missions as required. After the islands were secure (24 November), one carrier group remained in the area for a further week as a protective measure. The first unit of the garrison air force (VF-1, F6F Hellcats) deployed to the Tarawa airstrip from the escort carriers *Barnes* and *Nassau* on 25 November. One escort carrier, the USS *Liscome Bay*, was lost to submarine attack on 24 November and the light carrier USS *Independence* damaged by a torpedo launched by a G4M *Betty* on 20 November. The first attempts at night interception from carriers was made during the campaign by a team of two Hellcats and one radar-equipped Avenger operating from the *Enterprise* and led by Air Group Six's commander, Lieutenant Commander E.H. 'Butch' O'Hare. In operation the fighters formated on the Avenger and after being vectored to the vicinity of the enemy aircraft by the ship's fighter director relied on the Avenger's radar to get within visual range. No intercepts were made on the first trial, but on the second (26 November) the improvised night-fighter flight disrupted an enemy formation. O'Hare was lost in unknown circumstances during this action.

*17 December* Following an Allied landing at Arawe on the south-west coast of New Britain, South Pacific Command carried out the first major fighter sweep over Rabaul. Eighty aircraft were involved, including 24 P-40s of the RNZAF. Day fighter sweeps of this kind were henceforth mounted at regular intervals.

By the end of 1943, the air attacks on Rabaul had effectively neutralized the base, which was now by-passed. At the same time, Allied control of the Gilbert Islands group provided a springboard from which operations against the Marshall Islands could be launched in what was to be the decisive year of 1944.

# The China–Burma–India Theatre, 1943

## China

On 4 July 1942, the China Air Task Force was activated in India as a unit of the Tenth Air Force. Command of the CATF devolved upon Brigadier-General Claire Chennault, who for several months had led the American Volunteer Group in action against the Japanese. With the activation of the CATF the AVG ceased to exist as an independent fighting unit, and few of its pilots, who had held the line for so long in the face of impossible odds in Burma alongside the dwindling squadrons of the RAF, elected to remain in the theatre. Those who did, provided a nucleus of experienced pilots for the newly-activated 23rd Fighter Group, which absorbed the resources of the AVG. These amounted to 57 aircraft (54 P-40s and three P-43s) of which 40 were airworthy, together with seven B-25s of the Tenth Air Force, which at this stage was little more than a paper command. With its 47 operational aircraft, the CATF faced a formidable enemy along a 2000-mile (320-km) front stretching from Honkew to Hong Kong and Burma to Indo-China. In terms of air strength, the CATF was outnumbered by eight to one. Despite its shortcomings the CATF carried out a number of very successful offensive operations during the latter months of 1942, the B-25s being supplemented by B-24s on temporary deployment from India, but early in 1943 shortages of fuel and spare parts forced the curtailment of all CATF activites.

## Burma

In central Burma, following the Allied retreats of 1942, the front had stabilized and become fairly static along the Chindwin River that ran roughly north-south along the India–Burma border. In the south, a poorly-defined front lay in the Arakan, east of the Bay of Bengal, running north-east from Akyab then veering inland to Kalewa, Myitkyina and Fort Hertz. At the end of 1942 there were 12 squadrons of Hawker Hurricanes in the theatre, although three of these were retained for the defence of Ceylon and two for the defence of Calcutta.

In addition, two squadrons (Nos. 5 and 155) were equipped with Curtiss Mohawks (Hawk 75As) and four (Nos. 45, 82, 84 and 110) with Vultee Vengeance dive-bombers, which had replaced the Bristol Blenheim in these units. The RAF front-line squadrons were committed to the support of a limited offensive in the Arakan early in 1943, the main effort being aimed at the disruption of enemy supply routes. During this period, both sides

despatched small escorted bomber raids in support of forward troops, and there were numerous air battles as the RAF and the Japanese strove to establish air superiority. In these, the principal Japanese fighter type engaged – the Nakajima Ki 43 *Hayabusa*, known by the Allied code-name *Oscar* – was superior to the Hurricane on most counts, although the greater skill of the RAF pilots redressed the balance somewhat and losses were about even.

In both China and Burma, the year of 1943 was one of consolidation and planning. There were, however, a number of significant events involving air operations, and these are detailed below.

**14 February** Douglas Dakotas of No. 31 Sqn RAF and Lockheed Hudsons of No. 194 Sqn began air supply missions in support of *Chindit* forces working behind enemy lines in northern Burma. During these operations, which lasted until early May, the two squadrons flew 178 sorties and dropped 303 tons of supplies. Daylight supply sorties were usually escorted by the Mohawks of Nos. 5 and 155 Sqns.

**1 March** The US Fourteenth Air Force (Major-

*As in North Africa, the Hawker Hurricane gave invaluable service in Burma. This tactical reconnaissance Hurricane has had a landing mishap.*

General Chennault) was activated in China to replace the China Air Task Force. Its primary objectives were first of all to establish air superiority over the Japanese, and then to launch a sustained offensive against enemy shipping along the China coast.

**April–May** The first reinforcements arrived for the Fourteenth AF: P-40s, followed by 35 B-24 Liberators of the 308th Bombardment Group. The B-24s gave the Fourteenth AF the capability to strike against all Japanese installations in China, Indo-China, Burma and Thailand.

**August** The first two de Havilland Mosquito Mk II reconnaissance aircraft assigned to the CBI theatre began operations with No. 681 (PR) Sqn at Dum Dum. No. 681 Sqn also used B-25s and Hurricane IIBs in the PR role.

**14 August** 14 B-24s of the 308th BG attacked Haiphong without fighter escort; two were shot down and ten badly damaged. A week later, five more B-24s were shot down in an unescorted raid on Hankow. These losses prompted an urgent demand from Fourteenth AF for long-range fighter escort.

*September* The first Spitfire fighters (Mk Vs) arrived in India, initially replacing the Hurricanes of Nos. 607 and 615 Sqns. This month also saw the first deliveries of North American P-51A Mustangs and Lockheed P-38 Lightnings to the Fourteenth AF. The P-51s were assigned to the 23rd Fighter Group (74th, 75th and 76th FS) while the P-38s were operated by the 449th FS. The Tenth Air Force, operating against the Japanese in Assam, also received Mustangs and P-38s in the late summer of 1943. The Mustangs, a mixture of P-51As and A-36s, were assigned to the 311th Fighter-Bomber Group (528th, 529th and 530th Sqns) which, together with the 80th FG (P-40s) provided support for deep-penetration ground forces such as Merrill's Marauders. The P-38s were assigned to the 80th FG's 459th FS.

*1 October* No. 684 (PR) Sqn was formed at Dum Dum equipped with four B-25 Mitchells, two Mosquito IIs and three Mosquito VIs for reconnaissance and tactical support operations. On the same day, the USAAF 8th Photo Reconnaissance Group was activated in Tenth AF with F-5, F-6 and F-7 aircraft (PR versions of the Lightning, Mustang and Liberator). These units provided the Allies with full PR coverage of the Burma operational area.

*25 November* 14 B-25s, escorted by eight P-51s and eight P-38s, made a spectacularly successful attack on Shinchiku airfield, Formosa, where Four-teenth AF reconnaissance aircraft had detected 75 Japanese fighters and bombers the day before. Flying at low altitude across the Formosa Strait to avoid detection, the Americans, joined by Chinese-manned B-25s of the Chinese-American Composite Wing, achieved complete surprise and destroyed 42 enemy aircraft on the ground for no loss.

*5 December* The Japanese attacked Calcutta by daylight, the force comprising 18 Mitsubishi Ki-21 *Sally* bombers of the Army's 12th and 98th Air Regiments, escorted by 100 Nakajima Ki-43 *Oscars* of the 33rd, 50th 64th, 77th and 204th Air Regiments, and 9 Mitsubishi G4M *Bettys* of the Navy's 28th Air Regiment (705th *Kokutai*) escorted by 27 Mitsubishi A6M *Zeros* of the 331st *Kokutai*. The raid was intercepted by Spitfires and Hurricanes and the outcome was decidely in favour of the Japanese. Nine Hurricanes and a Spitfire were lost, against a claim of only one enemy bomber and one fighter destroyed.

*15 December* The Troop Carrier Command, comprising the 443rd Group USAAF (1st and 2nd Troop Carrier Sqns, C-46s and C-47s) and No. 177 Wing RAF (Nos. 62 and 194 Sqns with Dakotas, and No. 177 Sqn with Beaufighters for escort) was formed for operation in north-west Burma.

*18 December* The RAF 3rd Tactical Air Force was formed for offensive support operations on the Arakan and Imphal fronts, Burma.

*The Douglas C-47 transport, known as the Dakota in RAF service, was widely used to parachute supplies to forward bases in Burma.*

# Sicily, Italy and the Balkans, 1943–45

## 1943

**1–8 July** As a preliminary to the invasion of Sicily, Allied bombers mounted heavy attacks on enemy airfields and gun emplacements on the island, forcing the remaining units of *Luftflotte* 2 to redeploy to bases on the Italian mainland. The *Regia Aeronautica*, however, retained about 160 aircraft on the island.

**9/10 July** Operation *Husky*: the invasion of Sicily. The assault on Sicily began with glider landings by the 1st Air Landing Brigade of the 1st Airborne Division and a parachute drop by the US 82nd Airborne Division to seize key objectives in the sectors assigned to the British Eighth Army and the US Seventh Army. For the glider assault, the US Troop Carrier Command provided C-47 tugs, while No. 38 Wing RAF provided Albemarles and Halifaxes (Nos. 296 and 297 Sqns). Ahead of the glider force, Hurricanes of No. 73 Sqn patrolled the drop zones, ready to attack searchlights, while Wellingtons of No. 205 Group made diversionary attacks and dropped dummy paratroops to confuse the defences. The airborne operation was a disaster. Unexpected strong winds and insufficient night-flying training for the C-47 crews wrecked the 1st Airborne Division's assault; out of 137 gliders released, 69 came down in rough seas with heavy loss of life, 56 were scattered along the south-eastern coast of Sicily, and only 12, all towed by the RAF, reached the landing zone. In the 82nd Airborne Division's drop, only 250 paratroops out of 3000 came down in the right place, the remainder being scattered as much as 50 miles (80 km) apart.

In contrast, the seaborne landings were an outstanding success. These took place under an umbrella of fighters and fighter-bombers provided by the Desert Air Force and the 1st Tactical Air Force (Spitfires, Mustangs, P-40s and P-38s) which flew 1092 sorties on 11 July. The Axis air forces made no attempt to oppose the landings, but

*A Martin Baltimore of the South African Air Force bombing a target in Italy. Two bombs, just released, can be seen below the aircraft.*

made sporadic attacks on the invasion fleet later in the day, sinking 12 ships. First into action were the Reggiane Re.2002 fighter-bombers of the 5° Stormo Assalto, which sank the transport *Talambra* but lost four of their number to the Allied fighters. After dark, the beaches were patrolled by the Beaufighters of No. 108 Sqn and the Mosquitoes of No. 23 Sqn, operating out of Malta.

**13 July** No. 244 Wing of the Desert Air Force (Nos. 92 and 145 Sqns RAF and No. 1 Sqn SAAF with Spitfire IXs) deployed to Sicily from Malta, the first Allied aircraft to do so. USAAF units which followed were the 27th and 86th Fighter-Bomber Groups (A-36A Mustangs), the 31st and 52nd Fighter Groups (Spitfire IXs) and the 33rd, 324th and 325th Fighter Groups (P-40s). These units inflicted very heavy losses on the *Regia Aeronautica* units still operating in Sicily; the remnants of these were withdrawn on 27 July.

**25 July** A formation of Ju 52 transports, attempting to land reinforcements on a coastal strip near Milazzo, northern Sicily, was intercepted by Spitfires of No. 322 Wing RAF. Twenty-one Ju 52s and four escorting Bf 109s were shot down.

**4 August** The town of Troina, scene of some of the most bitter fighting of the Sicilian campaign, was attacked by 72 A-36A Mustangs of the 27th and 86th FBG, which dropped 500 lb (227 kg) bombs on the defences. US forces broke into the town the next day, leaving the A-36As free to support an assault by the US 7th Infantry on Monte Fratello. For 13½ hours the Mustangs, operating in relays, attacked enemy positions on the high ground and also laid smoke to conceal the movements of the attacking troops, which took the objective on 8 August. The Sicilian campaign was completed nine days later with the capture of Messina. Axis aircraft losses during the campaign amounted to 1000 destroyed or damaged on the ground and 740 in air combat; Allied losses were 385, of which at least 25 were shot down by 'friendly' fire during the seaborne landing phase.

**9 September** Following a diversionary landing by British forces at Reggio, Calabria, on 3 September, an Allied invasion force went ashore at Salerno in south-west Italy. The Italian Government had surrendered on the previous day. Because of the distance of Salerno from Sicilian airfields, which restricted fighter patrol times, much of the air cover was provided by USAAF Mustangs and Lightnings and by Seafires of the Fleet Air Arm, operating from escort carriers. In the afternoon of 9 September, six Dornier Do 217K-2s of III/KG 100, operating from Marseille, attacked units of the Italian Fleet – which was sailing for Malta to surrender to the Allies – with PC 1400X (Fritz-X) guided missiles. The battleship *Roma*, hit by two missiles, sank with the loss of 1255 lives; the battleship *Italia* was also hit, but reached Malta under her own steam. After this success III/KG 100 operated against ships of the invasion support fleet off Salerno, damaging the cruiser USS *Savannah* and (on 16 September) the battleship HMS *Warspite*, which had to be towed to Malta for repairs. The cruiser HMS *Uganda* was also damaged.

**14 September** Land-based fighter cover at Salerno was now provided by three squadrons of Spitfires (No. 324 Wing), USAAF Lightnings and FAA Seafires, deployed ashore from their carriers. This day marked the crisis of the battle, with 700 sorties flown by the 1st Tactical Air Force while heavy and medium bombers of the USAAF and No. 205 Group RAF attacked road and rail targets. By 16 September the Salerno beachhead was secure, and on 1 October Allied forces entered Naples. The battle of Salerno had cost the *Luftwaffe* 221 aircraft for an Allied loss of 89.

Despite enjoying overwhelming air superiority, the Allies had advanced only 70 miles (113 km) beyond Salerno by the end of 1943. There, 80 miles (129 km) from Rome, they were confronted by the enemy's Gustav Line, a formidable obstacle running along the courses of the Garigliano and Rapido Rivers. Its central strongpoint was Cassino, overlooked by the 1700-ft (518-m) hill on which stood the ancient abbey of St Benedict.

**10 December** HQ Mediterranean Allied Air Forces was formed, amalgamating the Mediterranean Air Command and North-West African Air Force and comprising all operational Allied air units in the Mediterranean Theatre, excluding the Middle East.

# 1944

**22 January** In support of Allied landings at Anzio and Nettuno on the west coast of Italy, a move designed to outflank the Gustav Line, Allied air forces carried out heavy attacks on airfields in central Italy. In the first days of the operation at Anzio, Fritz-X attacks were made on Allied vessels, the cruiser HMS *Spartan* and the destroyer HMS *Janus* being sunk. Between 22 January and 15 February 1944 the Allied air forces dropped 12 500 tons of bombs on enemy airfields and communications, but this did not prevent the

*A Spitfire Mk Vc over Italy. Note the tropical filter under the nose.*

Germans from counter-attacking in strength in February. The counter-offensive was supported by the Focke-Wulf Fw 190G-1s of I and II/SG 4. It was contained with the help of strong Allied air support, including the dropping of more than 10000 fragmentation bombs on enemy troop concentrations, but the invasion force at Anzio was unable to break out.

*15 February* Beginning at 8.30 a.m., 142 B-17s of the US Fifteenth Air Force and 112 B-25s and B-26s of the Twelfth Air Force dropped 576 tons of bombs on the abbey at Monte Cassino, reducing its interior to rubble. The bombing attacks created exactly the opposite effect to that required, the tumbled blocks of masonry and piles of rubble forming excellent defensive positions where none had previously existed. Not until two months later, after one of the most bitter and prolonged close-quarter battles of the war, did Cassino fall.

*March* During this month, the Mediterranean Allied Air Forces made a determined attempt to paralyse the enemy communications network in Italy by mounting Operation *Strangle*, in which 19460 tons of bombs were dropped on the road and railway system. A further 51500 tons were dropped in a subsequent operation, code-named *Diadem*, but although severe damage was inflicted on the Italian railway system the attacks lacked concentration and repairs were quickly effected. With hindsight, it would have been better to select a limited number of very important targets, such as repair and maintenance facilities, and subject them to continual heavy attacks.

*21 April* The USAAF's 31st Fighter Group carried out its first major operation with P-51D Mustangs: an escort mission for Fifteenth AF B-24s raiding the oil refineries at Pliesti, Romania. The 31st FG's task was to meet the bombers after they had left the target area and escort them home. Near Bucharest the Mustang pilots sighted a formation of B-24s being attacked by at least 60 enemy fighters. Attacking out of the sun, the Americans took the enemy by surprise and in the ensuing battle, the 31st FG's pilots claimed 17 enemy aircraft destroyed, seven probably destroyed and ten damaged for the loss of two of their own. The 31st FG (which, together with the 52nd FG, was the first to re-equip with P-51Ds in Italy) was awarded a Distinguished Unit Citation for this action.

The first RAF unit to equip with Mustangs in Italy, also in April 1944, was No. 260 Sqn, which replaced its Kittyhawks with Mustang IIIs (P-51Bs). In May, No. 213 Sqn also deployed to Italy from Egypt with Mustang IIIs for operations with the Balkan Air Force. By the end of the year most RAF, RAAF and SAAF fighter-bomber squadrons had re-equipped with Mustangs, which were capable of flying long-range fighter sweeps over Yugoslavia and Albania. In the USAAF, two more fighter groups, the 325th and 332nd FG, also used P-51Ds, which replaced P-47 Thunderbolts. P-47s continued to be used in the theatre by the 57th, 27th, 79th, 86th, 324th and 350th FG, while P-38 Lightnings were operated by the 1st, 14th and 82nd FG.

*June* Following the Allied landings in Normandy on 6 June 1944, many *Luftwaffe* units in Italy were transferred to north-west Europe, leaving *Luftflotte* 2 with only three *Staffeln* of Bf 109s (about 30 aircraft) for tactical reconnaissance, about 100 fighters of all types (including aircraft of the Italian fascist *Aeronautica Nazionale Repubblicana* (FNR), a long-range reconnaissance *Gruppe* with Ju 88s and three *Staffeln* of night bombers, also with Ju 88s.

From June 1944 the RAF's long-range Mustang III squadrons in Italy were assigned to support the Balkan Air Force (formed 1 June 1944). Its operations mainly involved attacks on road and rail traffic in Yugoslavia in support of Marshal Tito's partisan forces. In the first month of operations the Mustangs, together with Balkan Air Force Spitfires, claimed 262 locomotives destroyed or damaged, of which about a third were pulling troop trains.

*July* In July 1944 the fighter-bomber groups of the USAAF XII Tactical Air Command in Italy moved to Corsica in readiness to support the forthcoming Allied invasion of southern France (Operation *Dragoon*). Consequently, the RAF Desert Air Force was left to provide close air support along the whole Italian front. With the invasion successfully concluded, the Tactical Air Command returned to Italy to assume, under the name of XII Fighter Command, control of operations in support of the US Fifth Army, releasing the Desert Air Force to support the British Eighth Army and the eastern sector of the front.

**12 July** German forces in Yugoslavia launched a determined attack against the Partisan II Corps in Montenegro, converging movements from the east and north being supported by a force of 20–30 Junkers Ju 87s and Fieseler Fi 156 *Storchs*. The Partisans counter-attacked vigorously with the support of Spitfires and Mustangs of the Balkan Air Force, and the enemy offensive was halted within a few days.

**22 July** The P-51Ds of the 31st FG landed at Piryatin, Russia, with P-38s of the 82nd FG after a bombing and strafing attack on airfields and oil refineries at Ploesti. On 25 July, flying from Piryatin, the 35 Mustangs escorted the P-38s on a ground-attack mission to the German airfield at Mielec in Poland. During the return flight they encountered a formation of 36 Ju 87 *Stukas*, heading for the Russian lines, and destroyed 27 of them. This action earned the 31st FG its second Distinguished Unit Citation. The Mustangs and Lightnings returned to their Italian bases on 26 July.

**23 August** Mustangs of No. 213 Sqn RAF provided fighter escort for Dakota aircraft of the 60th Troop Carrier Group, USAAF, and No. 267 Sqn RAF, which flew to a landing strip near Brezna, Yugoslavia, and evacuated 1078 wounded Partisans.

During August 1944, No. 6 Sqn RAF, equipped with rocket-firing Hurricane IVs and operating in the anti-shipping role with No. 281 Wing of the Balkan Air Force, sank 43 enemy vessels and damaged 26 more. The squadron had carried out its first RP sortie in Italy on 29 March, and on 6 July two of its aircraft had sunk the 5000-ton freighter *Italia* with 16 rockets. In August, the Balkan Air Force flew 2822 sorties and lost 54 aircraft.

**September** The situation in the Balkans underwent a complete change when two of Germany's allies, Bulgaria and Romania – threatened with massive destruction by the advancing Soviet armies – changed sides and declared war on their former partner. Immediately, the pressure on the partisans in Montenegro was lifted. Another consequence was that the continued occupation of

Greece and the Aegean Islands became impossible for the Germans, and their evacuation a difficult and hazardous undertaking. BAF Intelligence had estimated that the Germans, who were operating supply and evacuation missions at night, had call on a transport force of about 100 Ju 52/3ms, plus 30 Ju 52/3w floatplanes and Dornier Do 24 flying boats. To counter their activities B-24 Liberators of the Fifteenth Air Force raided their bases, destroying 50 transport aircraft. In addition, BAF intruder sorties destroyed ten Ju 52/3ms, seven floatplanes and two of the 20 Heinkel He 111s that the Germans had been forced to use as transports. The Balkan Air Force flew 3533 strike sorties in September, sinking 25 ships; these included the 51 000-ton Italian liner *Rex*, which was sunk in an RP attack – the largest merchant ship attacked and sunk during World War II.

**12 October** Beginning of the Allied invasion and occupation of southern Greece (Operation *Manna*). Fourteen Dakotas with paratroops and Halifaxes with supply containers made an air drop on Megara airfield on the Greek mainland. The operation was badly affected by a strong wind and a second air drop planned for the next day had to be cancelled, although nine gliders carrying machinery were landed so that runway repairs could be undertaken. On 14 October, 68 Dakotas made further supply drops, but heavy rain brought a halt to further operations and also caused the main runway to subside. However, the airfield at Kalamaki, only 5 miles (8 km) from Athens, was cleared on 17 October and was used for bringing in further supplies. During the Greek operation, Allied aircraft dropped or landed 2700 tons of supplies, the RAF delivering about two-thirds of the total.

**November** With the last German *Jagdgeschwader* withdrawn for the defence of the homeland, the air defence of northern Italy was now the responsibility of the II° *Gruppo Caccia* of the ANR, which was equipped with Messerschmitt Bf 109Gs. After conversion for type, this unit resumed operations on 19 October, when the Italian pilots shot down eight B-26s of the 319th BG for the loss of one of their own number. In five engagements between 4 and 16 November, the II° *Gruppo*, operating from Aviano, destroyed seven B-17s, five B-26s, two P-47s and two P-51s for the loss of four Bf 109Gs. Seven more Bf 109Gs were subsequently destroyed on the ground in Allied bombing attacks. Two more ANR *Gruppi*, the I° and III°, were meantime converting to Bf 109Gs in Germany, where some pilots also received limited training on the Messerschmitt Me 163 *Komet* rocket fighter.

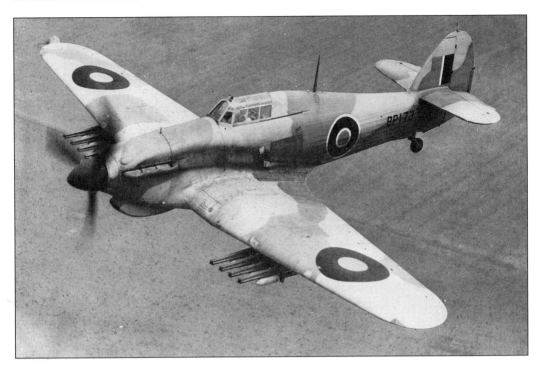

**22 December** The 31st Fighter Group scored the Fifteenth Air Force's first jet fighter 'kill' when a Messerschmitt Me 262 was shot down by Lieutenants Eugene P. McGlauflin and Roy L. Scales during a photo-reconnaissance mission.

# 1945

**January** The I° *Gruppo Caccia* of the ANR redeployed to Italy with 52 Bf 109G-10s, beginning operations late in the month alongside the II° *Gruppo*. The latter had suffered considerable attrition during previous weeks, but replacement aircraft were still readily available from German stocks in southern Germany and Austria. In February, the II° *Gruppo* claimed ten B-25s that were attacking the Brenner Pass lines of communication, but lost six Bf 109s.

**3 March** 22 Bf 109Gs of the II° *Gruppo Caccia* intercepted a B-26 Marauder formation of No. 3 Wing SAAF, claiming eight bombers destroyed against the loss of two Messerschmitts.

**4 March** The *Sonderkommando* Sommer began operations from Udine, near Trieste, with three Arado Ar 234B-1 jet reconnaissance aircraft. This

unit was established in Italy following complaints from German forces of inadequate surveillance of Allied troop movements in the vicinity of the Gothic Line, the last defensive bastion in northern Italy. The Ar 234s were able to make uninterrupted sorties over the Ancona and Leghorn sectors at altitudes of up to 39 400 ft (12 000 m).

**14 March** In its first engagement since returning to Italy, the I° *Gruppo Caccia* lost three Bf 109s in combat and three in forced landings, claiming only one 350th FG P-47.

**19 March** In support of the newly-formed Yugoslav Fourth Army's assault on Bihac, the main enemy stronghold in West Bosnia, 24 Marauders and 18 Baltimores of the BAF bombed strongpoints in the town, while Hurricanes of No. 6 RAF Sqn and No. 351 (Yugoslav) Sqn attacked headquarters buildings and barracks at Gospic, destroying an ammunition dump. Attacks continued at high intensity until 25 March, when Yugoslav forces penetrated Bihac. Close support operations were now being flown from the Yugoslav mainland by No. 281 Wing at Zara (No. 6 Sqn with Hurricane IVs, No. 213 Sqn with Mustang IIIs and IVs, Nos. 73, 249 and 253 Sqns with Spitfire IXs, and Nos. 351 and 352 [Yugoslav] Sqns with Hurricane IVs and Spitfire VCs). No. 281 Wing continued to support operations in Yugoslavia until the end of hostilities.

**Left:**
*Armed with eight rocket projectiles, the Hurricane
Mk IVs of No. 6 Sqn RAF wrought great execution
among enemy shipping in the Adriatic.*

**Right:**
*A Beaufighter launching a salvo of rockets at a
German headquarters building in Yugoslavia, 1944.*

**2 April** 21 Bf 109Gs of the II° *Gruppo*, scrambled to
intercept a B-25 formation heading for the Brenner Pass, were 'bounced' by P-47s flying top cover.
Fourteen Messerschmitts were shot down against
a claim of one B-25 and four P-47s. At this time
there were plans to re-equip one *Squadriglia* of this
unit with Me 262 jet fighters, and modifications
were under way to Ghedi and Villafranca airfields, but the Italian front collapsed before this
could be implemented.

**19 April** The two ANR fighter *Gruppi* flew their
last operations, shooting down a B-24. In this
sortie the I° *Gruppo* lost two aircraft and the II°
*Gruppo* five, shot down by Mustangs of the 325th
FG. Hostilities in Italy ceased on 2 May.

# Air Operations over North-West Europe
# January 1943–June 1944

# 1943

**1 January** No. 6 (Royal Canadian Air Force)
Bomber Group assumed operational status with
eight squadrons based on airfields in Yorkshire.

**8 January** RAF Bomber Command's Pathfinder
Force was redesignated No. 8 Group (PFF).

**16 January** Lancasters of No. 5 Group, RAF Bomber
Command, made the first use of 250 lb (113 kg)
target indicator bombs during an attack on Berlin.

**20 January** 28 Fw 190 and Bf 109G fighter-bombers carried out a daylight attack on London while
others flew diversionary sweeps, inflicting heavy
damage and severe casualties in the docks area.

The attacking force was intercepted by Typhoons
of No. 609 Sqn, RAF Manston, which claimed
three Fw 190s and three Bf 109Gs. Other defending units shot down three more Fw 190s.

**21 January** The Casablanca Directive, defining
Allied bombing policy, was issued by the Combined Chiefs of Staff. The principal aim of the
Directive was to weld the strategic bombing forces
of the RAF and USAAF into a single mighty
weapon whose task would be to achieve 'the
progressive destruction and dislocation of the
German military, industrial and economic system, and the undermining of the German people
to a point where their capacity for armed resistance is fatally weakened'.

**27 January** In the first raid on Germany by the
US VIIIth Bomber Command, 64 B-17s led by

the 306th BG were despatched to attack Wilhelmshaven. Fifty-eight aricraft bombed the target; three FTR. Two of these were B-24 Liberators which made an unsuccessful attempt to attack the same objective. The *Luftwaffe* lost 7 fighters, although the American gunners claimed 22. This was a foretaste of the exaggerated claims which, made in the heat of combat, were to be a constant feature of the daylight strategic bombing offensive.

*30 January* Six Mosquitoes of Nos. 105 and 139 Sqns, No. 2 Group, made the first daylight attack on Berlin in an operation designed to disrupt large rallies being addressed by Nazi leaders. The attack was successful, but one Mosquito of No. 139 Sqn FTR.

*30/31 January* Stirlings and Halifaxes of Nos. 7 and 35 Sqns, No. 8 (PFF) Group, made the first operational use of H2S bombing radar in a main force attack on Hamburg.

During January, the 4th Fighter Group, USAAF, which had been flying Spitfires from Debden in Essex, received its first P-47 Thunderbolts. The 56th and 78th FG also re-equipped with P-47s soon afterwards.

*4 February* US VIIIth Bomber Command B-17s attacked Emden; six aircraft FTR.

*A de Havilland Mosquito runs up its engines before taxying out at the start of a night bombing mission.*

*16 February* Eight B-17s of the US VIIIth Bomber Command FTR from a raid on St Nazaire. By the end of February, the Command had lost 22 out of an effective strength of 84 aircraft.

*22 February* First operational use of North American B-25 Mitchells by RAF Bomber Command: Nos. 98 and 180 Sqns attacked oil installations at Terneuzen, Holland.

*25 February* The beginning of the Allied 'round-the-clock' strategic bombing offensive. During the next 48 hours, the Allied Strategic Air Forces flew more than 2000 day and night sorties against enemy targets.

*5/6 March* Bomber Command's 'Battle of the Ruhr' began with an attack by 345 aircraft on Essen. The raid saw the first large-scale use of the *Oboe* blind-bombing device. Fourteen bombers FTR and 32 were damaged.

*8 March* Fifty B-17s of VIIIth Bomber Command attacked the marshalling yards at Rennes as part of a bombing campaign against enemy rail targets.

*18 March* VIIIth Bomber Command despatched

73 B-17s and 24 B-24s to attack the Vulcan ship-building yards at Vegesack, on the Weser south of Bremen, in the biggest mission carried out by the Command to date. Subsequent missions were despatched to Wilhelmshaven, Rouen and Rotterdam on 9 and 10 March. Eight bombers FTR from these missions, the last two of which were heavily escorted by P-47s and Spitfires.

*25 March* Royal Air Force Transport Command was formed from the former Ferry Command.

*4 April* 85 B-17s dropped 251 tons of high explosive on the Renault factory in the suburbs of Paris while aircraft of No. 2 Group RAF carried out diversionary attacks elsewhere. This target, rebuilt after the devastating RAF attack on 3/4 March 1942, was once again heavily damaged. Four bombers FTR.

*17 April* 117 B-17s were despatched to attack the Focke-Wulf aircraft factory at Bremen. As they began their bombing run, they were attacked by two *Gruppen* of JG 1, which destroyed 15 aircraft. A 16th was shot down by AA. All the losses were sustained by the 306th Bomb Group (ten aircraft) and the 401st Sqn of the 91st BG (six aircraft). Another 48 B-17s were damaged.

**Above:**
*The Consolidated B-24 Liberator was more vulnerable to fighter attack than the B-17, and burned more readily.*

**Below:**
*High over Bremen, a formation of B-17s releases its load of high explosive.*

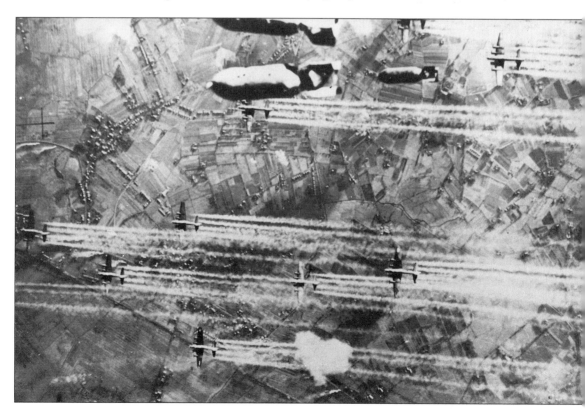

**18 April** Nine Torbeaus (torpedo Beaufighters) of No. 254 Sqn, together with six Beaufighters each from Nos. 143 and 236 Sqns, escorted by Spitfires and Mustangs, destroyed an enemy convoy in Dutch coastal waters. This action vindicated the concept of the Coastal Command Strike Wing, and in the summer of 1943 a second such unit was formed, comprising No. 455 Sqn RAAF and No. 489 Sqn RNZAF, operating Torbeaus from Leuchars, Scotland.

**3 May** 11 Lockheed Venturas of No. 487 (RNZAF) Sqn were despatched to attack the main power station in Amsterdam. Their Spitfire escort was engaged by large numbers of enemy fighters short of the target and the Venturas continued unescorted. All 11 were shot down.

**14 May** The VIIIth Bomber Command carried out large-scale attacks on several different targets simultaneously, with 200 B-17s and B-24s despatched to attack Ijmuiden, Courtrai, Antwerp and Kiel. The power station at Ijmuiden was unsuccessfully attacked by the B-26 Marauders of the 322nd Bombardment Group, carrying out its first operational mission. Eleven aircraft, mostly B-24s, FTR from the day's operations.

**16/17 May** The Möhne and Eder Dams, in the Ruhr, were attacked and breached by specially-modified Lancasters of No. 617 Sqn RAF carrying 9250 lb (4195 kg) mines. The attack was led by Wing Commander G.P. Gibson, who was subsequently awarded the VC. A third dam, the Sorpe,

*The Möhne Dam pictured before and after the famous attack by No. 617 Sqn RAF on the night of 16/17 May, 1943.*

was also damaged in this raid. An estimated 1294 people were killed by the released floodwaters, easily a new record for a raid on Germany. Eight Lancasters of 19 despatched FTR and 53 aircrew were killed, three survivors being taken prisoner.

**17 May** 12 B-26 Marauders of the 322nd BG were despatched, without fighter cover, to make a second attack on the Ijmuiden power station. One aircraft aborted; the other 11 were shot down by AA and fighters. All B-26 units in the European Theatre were subsequently assigned to the medium-level bombing role, the aircraft being assessed as unsuitable for low-level attacks against strongly defended targets.

**1 June** The RAF Army Co-operation Command was dissolved and the Tactical Air Force formed in its place. This followed an assessment of Exercise *Spartan*, a tactical air exercise which, held in March 1943, was designed to assess the operational efficiency of Army co-operation squadrons under mobile conditions. It was, in reality, a preliminary rehearsal for the invasion and ultimate liberation of North-West Europe.

**11/12 June** Major Werner Streib of I/NJG 1, flying a pre-production Heinkel He 219A-0 night fighter from Venlo, Holland, destroyed five RAF Lancasters in a single sortie. The He 219 was equipped with *Lichtenstein* SN-2 AI radar and armed with six 20 mm cannon.

*20/21 June* RAF Bomber Command carried out its first 'shuttle-bombing' operation; 60 Lancasters of No. 5 Group attacked the Zeppelin works at Friedrichshafen, which were producing radar equipment, and then flew on to Algiers. Three nights later, the same force bombed La Spezia on the return flight to the UK. No aircraft were lost.

*30 June* Beaufighters of No. 141 Sqn, Fighter Command, began operations against enemy night-fighters with the help of *Serrate*, a radar countermeasures device enabling the Beaufighters to home on to *Lichtenstein* AI transmissions. In its first three months of *Serrate* operations, No. 141 Sqn scored 23 kills.

June 1943 marked the end of an intense phase of enemy fighter-bomber activity over south-east England. The transfer of II and IV/SKG 10 to Sicily during the month left only the Fw 190s of I/SKG 10 operational on the Channel coast.

*24 July* The US Eighth Air Force began its so-called 'Blitz Week' of bombing operations with an attack on the German U-boat base at Trondheim, Norway, involving a round trip of 1900 miles (3650 km).

*24/25 July* 728 aircraft of RAF Bomber Command carried out the first of four large-scale attacks on Hamburg (Operation *Gomorrah*), dropping 2284 tons of bombs in 50 minutes and killing 1500 people. Twelve aircraft FTR. The attack saw the first use of *Window* countermeasures (strips of tinfoil, cut to the wavelength of enemy warning radar and dropped in bundles from attacking aircraft to confuse the defences).

*25 July* VIII Bomber Command attacked the Blohm und Voss shipyards at Hamburg as a follow-on to the previous night's raid by the RAF. Other US formations attacked the shipyards at Kiel and the *Luftwaffe* training school and airfield at Wustrow. Nineteen B-17s FTR.

*27/28 July* 729 aircraft of RAF Bomber Command dropped 2326 tons of bombs on the working class districts of Hamburg, causing an intense firestorm. About 40 000 people were killed in the attack, and 1 200 000 more subsequently fled the city. Seventeen aircraft FTR. The third attack on Hamburg was carried out by 707 aircraft on the night of 29/30 July (28 aircraft FTR). The fourth attack, on 2/3 August, was a failure because of thunderstorm conditions.

*28 July* P-47 Thunderbolts of the 4th FG, carrying out their first mission with long-range fuel tanks,

escorted 77 B-17s as far as the German border before turning back. En route to their targets (the Fieseler works at Kassel-Bettenhausen and the AGO factories at Aschersleben, near Magdeburg) the bombers were subjected to furious fighter attacks, one unit – II/JG 2 – using 500 lb (227 kg) bombs, dropped from 3000 ft (915 m) above the B-17s, to break up the American formations. The Bf 109s of II/JG 2 alone destroyed 11 bombers out of a total of 22 lost.

*1 August* 179 B-24 Liberators of the US Ninth Air Force (44th, 93rd, 98th, 376th and 389th Bomb Groups) were despatched from North African bases to make a low-level attack on oil refineries at Ploesti, Romania. One aircraft crashed on take-off, 11 more aborted and the B-24 carrying the lead navigator was lost in the Mediterranean. As a consequence, the remaining Liberators began to straggle and the raid lost its cohesion, with aircraft attacking the target at different altitudes and from different directions. The bombers were heavily engaged by AA batteries over the target and subjected to severe fighter attacks. The target was left in flames but the damage to Germany's fuel supplies was not as great as had been hoped. The cost to the Ninth Air Force was 53 Liberators and 440 aircrew killed or missing, with 200 more taken prisoner after baling out. This disaster brought an effective halt to deep-penetration daylight missions over southern Europe by the USAAF until long-range escort fighters became available early in 1944.

*17 August* VIIIth Bomber Command despatched 376 B-17s of the 1st and 4th Wings to attack ball-bearing factories at Schweinfurt and the Messerschmitt assembly plant at Regensburg on the deepest penetration mission so far mounted by the USAAF. The Regensburg force was to fly on to North Africa. Both targets were hit, but 60 bombers were shot down and many more were badly damaged. During this operation the B-17s were subjected to attacks by Bf 109Gs of JG 1, JG 3, JG 26 and JG 27 fitted with underwing 210 mm air-to-air rockets.

*17/18 August* RAF Bomber Command despatched 597 heavy bombers in the first attack on the German rocket research centre at Peenemünde, on the Baltic coast (Operation *Hydra*). The establishment was heavily damaged and the V-2 rocket programme set back at least two months. Forty aircraft FTR.

*18 August* Junkers Ju 188 bombers operated over the British Isles for the first time, three aircraft of I/KG 66, Chartres, bombing a factory in Lincoln.

**25 August** A Dornier Do 217E-5 of II/KG 100, Cognac, attacked a British submarine in the Bay of Biscay with a Henschel Hs 293A guided missile – the first operational use of this weapon. The attack was unsuccessful, but a second operation on 27 August sank the corvette HMS *Egret*.

The month of August 1943 saw the first large-scale use of *Wilde Sau* (Wild Boar) tactics by JG 300. Equipped with single-engined fighter aircraft, its task was to patrol directly over German cities, the pilots endeavouring to pick out bombers in the glare of fires and searchlights. On 17/18 August, 148 fighters of JG 300 were airborne but failed to intercept the Peenemünde force, having been drawn off by Mosquitoes making a diversionary attack on Berlin, but three major night raids on Berlin – on 23/24 August, 1/2 September and 4/5 September – cost Bomber Command 123 aircraft destroyed, with a further 114 damaged.

**15/16 September** First operational use of the 12 000 lb (5443 kg) *Tallboy* deep-penetration bomb: eight Lancasters of No. 617 Sqn were despatched to make a low-level attack on the Dortmund-Ems Canal. Five aircraft were shot down by flak, one failed to find the target and aborted, and two bombed the target with inconclusive results.

**22/23 September** RAF Bomber Command employed 'Spoof' tactics for the first time, with main

*Thumbs-up for the crew of a Halifax of No. 6 Royal Canadian Air Force Group as it taxies out at Croft, Yorkshire, for a mission over Germany.*

force aircraft attacking Hannover while electronic countermeasures aircraft of No. 8 Group simulated a raid against Oldenburg.

**7/8 October** First operational use of G-H blind bombing equipment by a Mosquito of No. 139 Sqn in a raid on Aachen. The device was first used on a large scale by Lancasters of Nos. 5 and 6 Groups during an attack on Düsseldorf on 3/4 November, and later in the war was widely employed on formation daylight bombing operations.

**10 October** No. 38 (Airborne Forces) Group RAF was formed at Netheravon, Wiltshire.

**14 October** VIIIth Bomber Command despatched 291 B-17s on a second attack on the Schweinfurt ball-bearing factories; 77 bombers FTR and 133 more were damaged. This day, known as 'Black Thursday', was the climax of a week's operations that cost the Command 148 heavy bombers and nearly 1500 aircrew.

**8 November** No. 100 (Bomber Support) Group was formed at RAF West Raynham for the purpose of operating airborne and ground radio countermeasures and carrying out a long-range fighter offensive against the German air defences.

**15 November** The Allied Expeditionary Air Force was formed in the UK, comprising the RAF 2nd Tactical Air Force and the USAAF IX Tactical Air Command.

**18/19 November** RAF Bomber Command struck the opening blow in the Battle of Berlin, despatching 764 aircraft to the German capital. Twenty-six bombers FTR. This was the last occasion on which Short Stirling bombers were sent to a German target. The onslaught on Berlin lasted until 24/25 March 1944, during which Bomber Command carried out 16 major attacks involving the despatch of 9111 sorties and 16 minor attacks involving 208 sorties, the latter by Mosquitoes. During this period 492 aircraft FTR and 954 were damaged, of which 95 were destroyed on returning to base.

**1 December** First operational mission by P-51B Mustang fighters with the USAAF in Britain: a familiarization flight by aircraft of the 354th Fighter Group from Boxted, Essex, along the Belgian coast. The 354th flew its first escort mission (B-17s to the Amiens area) on 5 December, and on 13 December, operating in concert with P-38s of the 55th FG, the Group flew a round trip of 1000 miles (1609 km), escorting B-17s to Kiel.

# 1944

**January** Despite increasingly effective long-range fighter escort, VIIIth Bomber Command once again suffered heavy losses during the month as it continued its attacks on Germany's aircraft industry. On 11 January, out of 238 bombers despatched to attack the fighter production factories at Aschersleben, 60 FTR.

**21 January** The *Luftwaffe* began Operation *Steinbock*, a series of heavy attacks on British targets, including London, by all available bombers on the Western Front. The night raids were under the control of the *Angriffsführer* England (Attack-Leader England), *Generalmajor* Dietrich Pelz, who had under his command seven *Gruppen* of Junkers Ju 88A-4s, one (I/KG 51 *Edelweiss*) with Messerschmitt 410s, and two *Staffeln* of Heinkel He 177s. The first attack, on the night of 21/22 January, involved 447 bombers; of the 500 tons of bombs dropped only 30 tons fell in the London area. The raid was led by 'pathfinder' Do 217s of I/KG 66 and *Duppel* – the German version of *Window* – was used. Nine bombers were shot down by Mosquito night-fighters. The so-called

*With the advent of the P-51 Mustang long-range escort fighter, the American daylight bombers had a far higher chance of survival. The aircraft in the photograph are P-51Ds, which replaced the earlier P-51B.*

'Little Blitz' of 1944 cost the *Luftwaffe* dearly; 57 bombers were claimed by fighters and AA in the two raids that took place in January, 72 in February, 75 in March, 75 in April and 50 in May. Mosquitoes equipped with Mk VIII AI accounted for 129 of this total.

**18 February** Mosquitoes of No. 464 Sqn RAAF and 487 Sqn RNZAF carried out a low-level attack with delayed-action bombs on the walls of Amiens prison in order to release imprisoned French patriots; 258 prisoners escaped, but many of these were common criminals who had nothing to do with the Resistance. Most were later recaptured. During the attack 102 inmates were killed, and there were civilian casualties outside the prison. Two Mosquitoes were shot down, including the aircraft flown by the raid leader, Group Captain P.C. Pickard, as well as a Typhoon of No. 198 Sqn, part of the escort force.

**20 February** The US Strategic Air Forces launched Operation *Argument*, a week-long onslaught by the Eighth and Fifteenth Air Forces against key aircraft factories between Leipzig and Braunschweig. In the course of this offensive, 3800 sorties by B-17s and B-24s dropped 10000 tons of bombs for the loss of 226 bombers and 28 fighter escorts. Combined with night attacks by Bomber Command, Operation *Argument* destroyed or damaged 68 per cent of the factory buildings associated with the German aircraft industry. Many of the bomber losses during the daylight missions were caused by Bf 110s firing 210 mm rockets into the bomber formations to break them up, making the B-17s and B-24s easier prey for the single-engined Fw 190s and Bf 109s.

*6 March* First USAAF raid on Berlin. VIIIth Bomber Command despatched 502 bombers, escorted by 770 P-38s and P-51s of the VIIIth and IXth Fighter Commands, to make the first successful attack on Berlin. The raid was costly, 46 bombers and 23 fighters being shot down, but the Americans claimed 80 enemy fighters destroyed. An earlier attempt to raid Berlin, on 3 March, had been aborted through bad weather, but some P-38 pilots of the 55th FG failed to hear the recall order and became the first American fighter pilots to fly over the German capital. Berlin was again attacked by 580 bombers escorted by 800 fighters on 8 March, the Americans losing 54 aircraft. By this time the *Luftwaffe* fighter force was also suffering severe attrition, losing an average of 50 aircraft every time the USAAF mounted a major attack.

*6/7 March* Lancasters and Halifaxes of Nos. 5 and 6 Groups, RAF Bomber Command, opened the Allied air offensive against the enemy's transportation system in occupied Europe with an attack on marshalling yards at Trappes, France. In all, 80 targets such as locomotive sheds and repair depots were designated for attack, 37 being allocated to RAF Bomber Command and the remaining 43 to the Eighth Air Force and the Allied Expeditionary Air Force.

*16 March* Mustangs of VIIIth Fighter Command, escorting B-17s in a raid on Augsburg, destroyed 26 out of 43 Bf 110s of ZG76 which attempted to intercept the bombers. After this action, the Bf 110 was withdrawn from the daylight air defence role and replaced by the Messerschmitt 410 *Hornisse* (Hornet).

From late March 1944, Ninth Air Force P-51 Mustang units were authorized to attack ground targets. This work was pioneered by the 354th FG, which on 26 March attacked the marshalling yards and adjacent airfield at Creil with 500 lb (227 kg) bombs.

*30/31 March* RAF Bomber Command despatched 795 heavy bombers to attack Nuremberg. The bomber stream was heavily engaged by German night-fighters to and from the target; 95 bombers were destroyed and 71 were damaged. This loss – 11.8 per cent of the attacking force – was the highest ever sustained by the Command, and represented the greatest German night-fighter success of the war.

*11 April* In a brilliant low-level precision attack, six Mosquitoes of No. 613 Sqn RAF destroyed the Dutch Central Population Registry in den Haag, Holland, with 500 lb (227 kg) bombs. The building housed Gestapo files. Only one aircraft was slightly damaged.

*14 April* Strategic bombing operations in the European Theatre were placed under the control of the Supreme Commander Allied Expeditionary Force, General Dwight D. Eisenhower, in preparation for the Allied invasion.

*20 April* New precision target marking techniques were used for the first time in an attack by 269 bombers on marshalling yards at La Chapelle, France. First of all the target was indicated by 'proximity marking' – markers released blindly by Mosquitoes equipped with *Oboe* – and then flares were dropped, enabling the target to be marked with great accuracy from low level.

*22 April* 13 B-24s which were returning after dark from a raid on the Hamm marshalling yards were shot down as they approached their bases by intruding Ju 88s and Me 410s. The Germans lost one Me 410.

*12 May* The Allied strategic bombing emphasis switched from attacks on the enemy aircraft industry to oil installations. By day, 935 USAAF heavy bombers escorted by 1000 fighters attacked the synthetic oil plants at Brüx, Böhlen, Leuna, Zwickau and Lützendorf. The plant at Brüx was completely destroyed, and production at the others was cut back by as much as 60 per cent. From the day's operations, 46 aircraft FTR.

During the last two weeks of May 1944 the Allied Strategic and Tactical Air Forces carried out heavy attacks on enemy coastal batteries and radar installations. Since Allied air superioty had virtually eliminated *Luftwaffe* reconnaissance flights over the Channel area, the Germans depended almost entirely on their coastal radar to give warning of the approach of an invasion fleet. By the first week of June 1944, air attack had destroyed about 80 per cent of the enemy's coastal radar capability.

*5/6 June* RAF Bomber Command carried out extensive tactical operations in support of the Allied landings in Normandy. Operations included attacks on heavy coastal gun batteries, radio countermeasures and the simulation of airborne landings by dropping dummy paratroops. Lancasters of No. 617 Sqn and Stirlings of No. 218 Sqn carried out Operation *Taxable*, dropping *Window* at fixed intervals over the Channel between Le Havre and Boulogne to simulate the approach of an invasion fleet. During the night, aircraft of

Nos. 38 and 46 (Transport) Groups RAF dropped airborne forces of the 6th Airborne Division in the Caen area, while the USAAF IX Troop Carrier Command dropped the 82nd and 101st Airborne Divisions at the base of the Cotentin peninsula.

*6 June*D-Day: Operation *Overlord*. During the 24 hours of D-Day, the Allied air forces flew 14674 sorties for the loss of 113 aircraft, some of which were shot down by 'friendly' fire. Combat Air Patrol sorties immediately over the invasion fleet were flown by VIIIth Fighter Command's P-38 groups, the twin-tailed Lightnings being easily identifiable to naval gunners. Top cover over the invasion beaches was provided by nine squadrons of Spitfires, while Typhoons and Mustangs of the 2nd Tactical Air Force, together with Mus-

*A Mustang Mk I of No. 26 Sqn RAF. Mustangs carried out valuable tactical reconnaissance work during the D-Day landings.*

tangs, Thunderbolts and Lightnings of IX Tactical Air Command flew armed reconnaissance missions inland. Communications throughout the day were heavily attacked by medium bombers of the Allied Tactical Air Forces. *Luftwaffe* reaction on the first day of the invasion was sporadic, involving attempted attacks by small numbers of fighter-bombers, although on one occasion the 4th FG, patrolling the Rouen sector, lost seven P-51s in an engagement with Fw 190s. So complete was Allied air supremacy, in fact, that the *Luftwaffe* flew only 319 sorties on 6 June.

# Air Operations in North-West Europe
# D-Day plus One to VE Day

## 1944

*7 June* Typhoon and Mustang squadrons of Nos. 83 and 84 Groups, RAF, attacked the German *Panzer Lehr* armoured division, which was moving towards the invasion area from Alençon, with

rockets, bombs, cannon and MG. The aircraft destroyed 90 lorries, 40 fuel tankers, five tanks and 84 self-propelled guns, half-tracks and other vehicles, effectively crippling the German Seventh Army's only fighting-efficient, full-strength armoured division in Normandy.

*8 June* First air combat by Hawker Tempest Mk V fighters of No. 150 Wing, No. 85 Group 2nd TAF

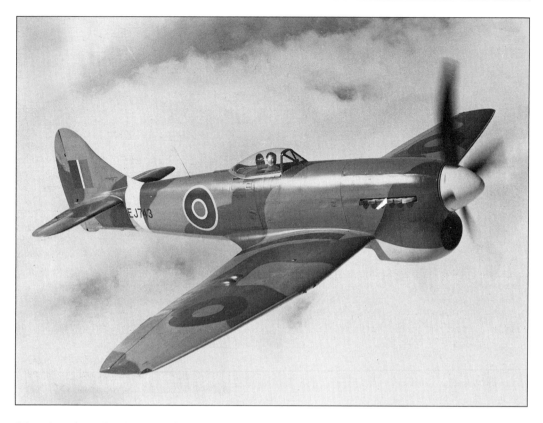

(Nos. 3 and 486 Sqns); nine Bf 109Gs were engaged between Le Havre and Cherbourg. Four enemy aircraft were destroyed and two damaged for no loss. (The Tempest had been operational since 15 May, attacking transport and airfields in France.)

*The formidable Hawker Tempest Mk V, the fastest piston-engined fighter to see service in World War II, was rushed into action to counter the V-1 flying bomb threat.*

**8/9 June** First operational use of a strengthened deep-penetration version of the 12000 lb (5443 kg) *Tallboy* bomb: 19 were dropped by Lancasters of No. 617 Sqn in a successful raid on the Saumur railway tunnel in southern France. The tunnel, a vital point on the main line running from the south-west to the Normandy front, was effectively blocked.

**10 June** First deployment of Allied fighter aircraft to temporary airstrips in Normandy: Spitfires of No. 144 (RCAF) Wing deployed to Ste Croix-sur-Mer. Eventually, 31 similar strips were set up in the British zone of operations and 50 in the American, enabling fighter-bombers to take off and attack targets on demand.

**12/13 June** The first Fieseler Fi 103 pilotless bomb (V-1) was launched against London from a site in the Pas de Calais by *Luftwaffe Flak Regiment 155*, the unit manning the weapon's ground launch-

ers. The presence of the V-1 launching sites had been known for some time and they had been under attack by Allied aircraft since December 1943. Eleven squadrons of the Air Defence of Great Britain (ADGB) were assigned to anti-V-1 *Diver* patrols; the most successful type used in this role was the Hawker Tempest. Between 13 June and 5 September 1944, when the V-1 sites were overrun, Tempests of No. 150 Wing (Nos. 3, 56, and 486 RNZAF Sqns) destroyed 638 V-1s out of the RAF's total of 1771. In June 1944, RAF Bomber Command dropped 16 000 tons of bombs on the V-1 sites for the loss of 38 aircraft; a further 44 335 tons of bombs were dropped between the end of June and 5 September. Following the loss of the launching sites in France, V-1s were air-launched against England by Heinkel He 111s of KG 53; these operations continued until 14 January 1945, by which time KG 53 had lost 77 aircraft, mostly to RAF Mosquito night-fighters.

**14/15 June** A Mosquito night-fighter of No. 410

Sqn destroyed a *Mistel* (Mistletoe) composite aircraft off Normandy. The *Mistel* combination consisted of an unmanned Ju 88, fitted with an explosive warhead, with a control aircraft – either a Bf 109 or Fw 190 – mounted on top. After locking-on to a target in a shallow dive, the control aircraft released the bomber component. In Normandy, *Mistel* combinations were operated by II/KG 101, St Dizier.

**24/25 June** Five *Mistel* combinations of II/KG 101 were despatched to attack Allied shipping in the Seine Bay. The mission was escorted by Bf 109G-6s of I/JG 301. Four *Mistel*s hit their targets; the fifth malfunctioned and was jettisoned.

**21 June** 1234 heavy bombers of VIIIth Bomber Command were despatched to attack Berlin, Potsdam, Stendal and other targets. Of this total, 163 B-17s were to attack oil installations at Ruhland and then fly to Russian bases at Poltava and Mirgorod in the Kiev area. This arrangement came under the terms of Operation *Frantic*, an agreement which permitted the USAAF to use Soviet airfields for shuttle-bombing operations. At Poltava, 75 B-17s were subjected to a surprise night attack by He 111s and Ju 88s of KG 4, 27, 53 and 55, which destroyed 47 American bombers and damaged 26 more.

*The cumbersome* Mistel *composite aircraft. This particular combination comprises a Junkers Ju 88 and a Focke-Wulf Fw 190.*

**3 July** Northrop P-61 Black Widow night fighters of the 422nd and 425th Sqns began operations over Normandy. At the end of July, the 422nd Sqn was deployed to Maupertus, near Cherbourg, as part of IX Tactical Air Command.

**7 July** 457 aircraft of RAF Bomber Command dropped 2363 tons of bombs on targets north of the city of Caen in support of the Anglo-Canadian drive to capture that objective. The Allied advance became bogged down – partly because of the bombing, which had filled the area with craters and rubble – and on 18 July, 1570 heavy and 349 medium bombers of Bomber Command, VIIIth Bomber Command and the Tactical Air Forces dropped 7700 tons on Caen itself. Four more major bombing attacks took place up to mid-August, but not all were successful; in some cases bombs fell wide of the mark and caused heavy casualties among Allied troops.

**18 July** VHF R/T equipment fitted in Sherman tanks was first used operationally to provide a direct ground-air link between British armour and rocket-firing Typhoons of 2nd TAF in the Caen sector.

**20 July** Arado Ar 234 jet reconnaissance-bombers of I/*Versuchsverband, Oberkommando der Luftwaffe*, carried out their first operational sorties from Jouvincourt, near Reims.

**25 July** A Mosquito of No. 544 Sqn, on a photo-reconnaissance mission at 30 000 ft (9150 m) over Munich, was subjected to a series of cannon at-

*The Messerschmitt Me 262 jet fighter came as a nasty surprise to the Allies, and might have altered the course of the war but for Hitler's insistence on turning it into a fast bomber.*

tacks by an enemy aircraft before escaping into cloud; this was the first confirmed engagement with a Messerschmitt Me 262 jet fighter.

*28 July* P-51 Mustangs of the 359th Fighter Group, escorting B-17s over Merseburg, were attacked by Messerschmitt Me 163 rocket-propelled fighters, the first encounter with this type. The appearance of German jet and rocket fighters led to a revision of the Eighth Air Force's fighter escort tactics; instead of sweeping ahead of the bombers, escort fighter groups were now required to operate astern of, and in closer proximity to, the bomber formations. The neutralization of the enemy's relatively few jet fighter airfields became a matter of high priority.

*4 August* A Gloster Meteor Mk I jet fighter of No. 616 Sqn, RAF Manston, Kent, engaged a V-1 flying bomb and the pilot, Flying Officer Dean, positioned his fighter's wing under that of the missile, using the turbulent airflow to topple the V-1, which crashed and exploded in open country. Shortly afterwards, Flying Officer J.K. Roger, also in a 616 Sqn Meteor, became the first RAF pilot to destroy an enemy aircraft by gunfire while flying a jet fighter when he shot down a V-1 with his cannon. The Meteor had become operational with No. 616 Sqn late in July and had at once been assigned to *Diver* patrols.

*7 August* A German armoured counter-attack in the Mortain sector was smashed by Allied fighter-bombers, notably Typhoons of 2nd TAF.

*17 August* The remnants of 16 German divisions, including nine *Panzer* divisions, were trapped in a 25-mile- (40-km) wide corridor between Mortain

and Falaise and systematically destroyed by concentrated air attack. In three days, continual operations by the Allied Tactical Air Forces resulted in the destruction of all the heavy equipment of the Fifth and Seventh *Panzer* Armies. Of the 2300 German tanks and assault guns committed in Normandy, only about 120 were brought back across the Seine. German casualties in the Falaise pocket were 10 000 killed, with 50 000 more taken prisoner. *Luftwaffe* fighters which tried to interfere with Allied air operations were decimated; by mid-August 1944 the fighter component of *Luftflotte* 3 in the west had been reduced to 75 serviceable aircraft.

*27 August* For the first time since August 1941, RAF Bomber Command mounted a major daylight raid on Germany, despatching 216 Halifaxes of No. 4 Group and 14 Mosquitoes and 13 Lancasters of No. 8 (PFF) Group to Homberg. The raid was escorted by nine squadrons of Spitfires outbound and seven squadrons on the homeward flight. Only one enemy fighter, a Bf 110, was sighted. All aircraft returned safely.

*September* The Messerschmitt Me 262A-2 became operational early in the month with KG 51 *Edelweiss* in the bomber-reconnaissance role. Other bomber units which subsequently equipped with the Me 262 were KG 6, KG 27 and KG 54, although only small numbers of the jet aircraft were used.

*8 September* The last operational mission by Stirling aircraft of RAF Bomber Command: an attack on Le Havre by aircraft of No. 149 Sqn. This attack was part of a series of operations against the Channel ports, where strong German garrisons continued to hold out.

*17 September* The airborne invasion of Holland: Operation *Market Garden*. As part of an overall plan to position the British Second Army across the rivers Maas–Waal and Nederijn in the area Grave–Nijmegen–Arnhem, and to control the country as far as the Zuider Zee in order to cut German communications to the Low Countries, the First Allied Airborne Army was allotted the task of laying an 'airborne carpet' ahead of XXX Corps to capture and control the main river and canal crossings. *Market* was the airborne operation; *Garden* the advance on the ground. To achieve this objective, the 1st British Airborne Division, with the 1st Polish Brigade Group, was to capture the bridges at Arnhem and establish a bridgehead around them, enabling land forces to move northwards; the US 82nd Airborne Division was to capture crossings at Nijmegen and Grave and to hold the high ground between Nijmegen and Groesbeck; and the US 101st Airborne Division

**Above:**
*Ground crew preparing a Spitfire for another sortie from an airstrip in Normandy, August 1944.*

**Below:**
*Conditions in Normandy were hot and dusty. Here, a Tempest taxies past a group of seemingly unconcerned French peasants.*

was to seize the bridges and defiles between Eindhoven and Grave. Air transport forces available for the operation were the US IX Troop Carrier Command, with 14 groups (42 squadrons) of C-47s, plus Waco Hadrian gliders; No. 38 Group RAF, with six Stirling, two Halifax and two Albemarle squadrons, plus Horsa and Hamilcar gliders; and No. 46 Group RAF, with six squadrons of Dakotas plus Horsa gliders. During the first lift to the dropping/landing zones, on the morning of 17 September, no fewer than 3887 aircraft and 500 gliders were airborne; in addition to the 1534 Allied transport and tug aircraft, 1240 fighters and 1113 bombers were used in support. All objectives were reached, but the Arnhem force met with unexpectedly strong enemy resistance. The initial operation cost 26 aircraft destroyed and 222 damaged; no transports were lost during the Arnhem landings.

**18 September** The second lift. Because of bad weather, all missions were ordered to fly along the northern route. *Luftwaffe* attempts to interfere with the transport serials were kept at bay by strong fighter escort. Eight resupply aircraft were shot down and 45 damaged. By 1 p.m. on 18 September, the 101st Airborne Division had captured Eindhoven and was in contact with the Guards Armoured Division at Grave, which had been captured by the 82nd Airborne.

**19 September** The third lift. The situation at Arnhem on the third day was very serious and it was decided to postpone the dropping of the Polish Parachute Brigade. During resupply operations at Eindhoven, 17 aircraft were shot down and five more wrecked, with 170 more damaged. Resupply missions to Nijmegen were frustrated by bad weather; two aircraft were lost and 15 damaged. At Arnhem, 13 aircraft were shot down and 97 damaged. For gallantry on this day, Flight Lieutenant D.S. Lord of No. 271 Sqn RAF was awarded a posthumous Victoria Cross, the only one to be awarded to a Transport Command pilot.

**20 September** The fourth lift. Little progress was made in the American sectors, but the bridge at Nijmegen was captured before nightfall. At Arnhem the situation was becoming increasingly desperate. The weather was again poor, hampering both resupply and ground attack operations. The Polish paratroop mission was again postponed. Nine aircraft were lost and 62 damaged over Arnhem, where most dropping zones were now in enemy hands.

**21 September** The fifth lift. Stirling resupply aircraft in the Arnhem area were heavily engaged by Fw 190s, which shot down most of the 13 aircraft

that failed to return. Ten Dakotas of No. 46 Group were also shot down; 38 aircraft were damaged. The Polish Parachute Brigade was dropped into the Arnhem sector by the 52nd Troop Carrier Wing, USAAF.

**23 September** The sixth lift. After a day of very bad weather, conditions were now favourable and Allied air operations resumed at high intensity. Transport resupply missions were resumed under strong fighter escort; the RAF provided 14 Spitfire and three Mustang squadrons, while VIIIth Fighter Command provided 13 groups of P-51s, P-47s and P-38s. In all, 854 fighters were airborne. Flak was very heavy; the RAF lost six aircraft, with 63 damaged. The loss would probably have been higher had it not been for the flak suppression activities of the 78th Fighter Group's P-51s. USAAF transport losses were nine aircraft, with 96 damaged; VIIIth Fighter Command lost 16, mostly to ground fire, but claimed 46 enemy fighters.

**24 September** The seventh lift. No resupply missions were flown from England, but 21 Dakotas of No. 46 Group, operating from Brussels, made drops to the British forces at Arnhem and to the US 82nd Airborne Division. The Dakotas were escorted by 36 Spitfires and none was lost, although the four assigned to Arnhem were all damaged by flak.

**25 September** The eighth lift. The last resupply mission to Arnhem was undertaken by seven Dakotas of No. 575 Sqn, operating from Brussels. One was shot down and three damaged by flak. On this day the remnants of the British 1st Airborne Division were evacuated from Arnhem at the end of their heroic nine-day stand. Equally as heroic were the attempts by the RAF and USAAF transport crews to supply the airborne forces; their combined loss during the battle was 238 aircraft and 139 gliders.

**3 October** Following operational trials by *Erprobungskommando* 262, the first German jet fighter unit, *Kommando* Nowotny, became operational with Me 262A-1a aircraft at Achmer and Hesepe.

**7 October** 13 Lancasters of No. 617 Sqn, armed with *Tallboy* bombs, breached the Kembs Dam on the upper Rhine north of Basle to prevent the Germans from releasing flood waters to impede the Allied advance.

**10–17 October** As part of the Allied response to the Me 262 threat, four Gloster Meteors of No. 616 Sqn carried out a week-long programme of fighter affiliation exercises with the US Eighth AF to give

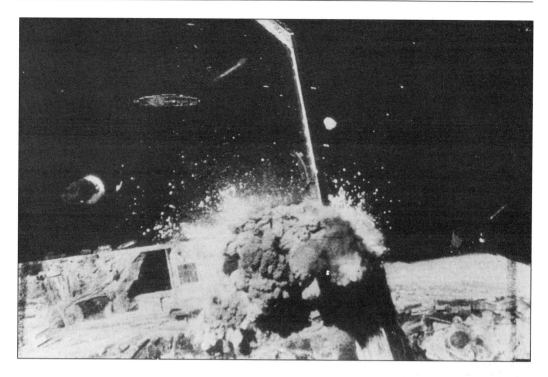

*The* Tallboy *bomb was a devastating weapon. This one is exploding on U-Boat pens.*

bomber crews experience of high-speed jet fighter attacks.

*14 October* RAF Bomber Command and US VIIIth Bomber Command mounted Operation *Hurricane*, a maximum effort with all available bombers. The RAF despatched 1013 aircraft to Duisburg, while the USAAF sent 1251 heavy bombers escorted by 749 fighters to targets in the Cologne area. RAF casualties were 14 bombers, the Americans losing five bombers and one fighter. During the night Duisburg was again attacked by 1005 aircraft, seven of which FTR; 9000 tons of bombs fell on this target in the two attacks. Brunswick was also attacked by 240 RAF bombers that night, so that the total Bomber Command effort was 1572 sorties – a record never exceeded.

*29 October* RAF Bomber Command despatched 36 Lancasters – 18 from No. 9 Sqn and 18 from No. 617 Sqn – from Lossiemouth, Scotland, to attack the German battleship *Tirpitz*, moored near the Norwegian port of Tromsö. The *Tirpitz* had been damaged in April 1944 in an attack by four squadrons of Fairey Barracuda dive-bombers of the Fleet Air Arm (Operation *Tungsten*); four more FAA attacks in July and August had been unsuccessful, but the battleship had sustained further damage in an attack by Nos. 9 and 617 Sqns on 15 September, the Lancasters flying from a Russian base on that occasion. For the 29 October mission

the Lancasters had their mid-upper gun turrets and other equipment removed to allow the installation of extra fuel tanks. Unfortunately, the target became obscured by cloud as the aircraft began their bombing run and no direct hits were scored, although 32 *Tallboys* were released.

*31 October* 25 Mosquitoes of Nos. 21, 464 and 487 Sqns carried out a low-level attack with 500 lb (227 kg) bombs on the Gestapo HQ at Aarhus, Denmark. The building was destroyed, 200 Gestapo officials were killed and all the files on the Danish resistance movement burned.

*4/5 November* The Dortmund-Ems Canal was attacked and breached by 174 Lancasters of No. 5 Group. This target had been breached in September but repaired since. The damage to this, one of Germany's remaining transport arteries, caused severe setbacks to war production.

*12 November* 30 Lancasters of Nos. 9 and 617 Sqns flew from Lossiemouth to attack the *Tirpitz*, still moored at Tromsö. The warship was hit by at least two *Tallboys* and suffered a violent internal explosion, subsequently capsizing with the loss of 1000 crew. One No. 9 Sqn Lancaster was damaged by flak and made an emergency landing in Sweden.

**16 November** RAF Bomber Command and VIIIth Bomber Command despatched 1188 and 1239 daylight sorties to targets in the area between Aachen and the Rhine in support of an offensive by the US First and Ninth Armies. More than 9400 tons of bombs were dropped by the Anglo-American force.

**21 November** VIIIth Bomber Command despatched 1291 B-17s to targets in Germany, principally Merseburg, with an escort of 954 fighters. The attacks were bitterly contested by 300 enemy fighters, mainly Fw 190s. The escorting P-51 groups scored heavily, the 352nd FG claiming 19 victories, the 364th 18 and the 359th 17. Of the German units engaged, III/JG 54 and I/JG 26 were now equipped with the 'long-nose' Fw 190D-9.

**26 November** VIIIth Bomber Command, attacking oil targets in the Hannover area, was heavily engaged by the *Luftwaffe*. The enemy suffered substantial losses, escorting Mustangs claiming 114. Top-scoring group was the 339th, with 26.

**16 December** German forces launched a surprise attack through the Ardennes, achieving complete surprise and initial success. A contributory factor was extensive pre-offensive reconnaissance by Me 262s and Ar 234s. The attack took place under

*Towards the end of 1944, RAF Bomber Command carried out many daylight attacks. Photograph shows a Lancaster over the Rhine.*

cover of snow and fog, so that it was several days before the Allied air forces were able to react.

**24 December** In clearing weather, the US Eighth AF despatched 2046 heavy bombers, escorted by 853 fighters, in support of Allied forces in the Ardennes. Together with substantial contributions from the Ninth AF and the RAF 2nd TAF, this was the largest air strike of World War II. During the following week air operations were once again hampered by bad weather, but in clear spells RAF and USAAF tactical aircraft scored heavily against enemy transport. On 29 December, Typhoons and Tempests claimed to have destroyed or damaged 47 locomotives and 222 goods wagons, including two ammunition trains. The Spitfire squadrons of 2nd TAF, on armed reconnaissance sorties, had frequent encounters with the *Luftwaffe* and claimed 32 aircraft destroyed. RAF losses were 16.

**31 December** Mosquitoes of No. 627 Sqn carried out a low-level attack on the Gestapo HQ at Oslo with inconclusive results.

# 1945

**1 January** At dawn on New Year's Day, the *Luftwaffe* launched Operation *Bodenplatte*, a massive attack on Allied airfields in Belgium, Holland and northern France by about 800 fighter-bombers, led by Ju 88 night-fighters and bombers. One group came in over the Zuider Zee to strike at Brussels-Evère, another attacked Eindhoven and the third flew down past Venlo to hit the American airfields. The surprise was complete, and almost 300 Allied aircraft were destroyed – but this success was wiped out by a comparable German loss, made even more tragic for the *Luftwaffe* by the fact that about 200 aircraft were shot down by their own flak when they passed through an area that was thick with V-2 rocket launch batteries and consequently heavily defended. The flak batteries had been given no prior warning of the operation. Among the dead German pilots were 59 experienced fighter leaders. What was conceived as a brilliant operation therefore turned into a disaster from which the *Luftwaffe* never recovered. Nevertheless, the operation badly disrupted the Allied air effort; during much of January, this was sustained by the Hawker Tempests of No. 122 Wing from Volkel in Holland, which had escaped the attack. The Tempests scored some spectacular successes against German rolling stock during the month, and also destroyed 45 enemy aircraft for the loss of 9 of their own.

**4 February** The first Gloster Meteor F.Mk.3 jet fighters of No. 616 Sqn were deployed to Melsbroeck, Belgium, for operations with 2nd TAF. The Meteors flew a number of ground-attack operations before the end of hostilities, but never met the *Luftwaffe* in combat.

**13/14 February** 796 Lancasters and nine Mosquitoes dropped 1478 tons of high explosive and 1182 tons of incendiary bombs on Dresden. The attack created a firestorm and large areas of the city were wiped out. A further 311 tons of bombs were dropped by USAAF B-17s on the following day. Dresden was crammed with refugees fleeing from the east, and the casualty figure resulting from these controversial attacks has never been fully established. It ranges from 50 000 to 135 000 dead.

**14 February** Allied tactical aircraft made 81 cuts in railway lines serving German forces south and west of Wesel. About 55 Me 262s and Ar 234s of KG 51 and KG 76 attacked Allied forces in the Kleve sector. During the afternoon, Spitfires, Typhoons and Tempests attacked the Münster–

*Bremen*

*Cologne*

Rheine group of airfields, where about 86 Fw 190s had been assembled to provide cover for the jets as they came in to land.

**22 *February*** The Allied air forces launched Operation *Clarion*, a concerted effort to wipe out all means of transport still available to the enemy in the space of 24 hours. Nearly 9000 aircraft, operating from bases in England, France, Holland, Belgium and Italy, delivered attacks over a quarter of a million square miles of German territory. Railway targets, from signal boxes to marshalling yards, were attacked, as well as bridges and canal locks, level crossings and transport of all kinds.

During the last week of February, Me 262s of III/ JG 7, armed with 5 cm R4M air-to-air rockets as well as their 30 mm cannon, destroyed 45 American four-engined bombers and 15 escorting fighters for the loss of four 262s. In addition to JG 7, *Jagdverband* JV 44, manned by the most experienced pilots under the command of General Adolf Galland, was also operating Me 262 fighters.

**3/4 *March*** The *Luftwaffe* despatched 140 intruder aircraft to attack airfields in eastern England. The intruders, mainly Ju 88G-6s and Ju 188s, bombed 14 airfields and destroyed 19 bombers; six enemy aircraft were shot down by the defences.

**14 *March*** First operational use of the 22 000 lb (9980 kg) *Grand Slam* bomb by the RAF; dropped on the Bielefeld Viaduct by Lancaster I PD112 of No. 617 Sqn, flown by Squadron Leader C.C. Calder. Forty more *Grand Slams* were dropped on enemy targets before the end of hostilities.

**18 *March*** 1250 American heavy bombers, heading for Berlin to deliver the heaviest attack of the war on the German capital, were attacked by 37 Me 262s of JG 7, armed with R4M rockets. The jets shot down 19 bombers for the loss of two of their own number.

**21 *March*** Mosquitoes of Nos. 21, 464 and 487 Sqns carried out a successful low-level attack on the Gestapo HQ at Copenhagen.

**24 *March*** Operation *Varsity*: the Rhine Crossing. This was preceded by heavy USAAF attacks on enemy airfields, attacks on communications by RAF Bomber Command and the Tactical Air Forces, and diversionary missions by RAF Coastal Command along the Dutch coast. The plan for the crossing of the Rhine involved large-scale paratroop and glider landings in the Wesel-Emmerich area; the northern and southern parts of the assault area were to be seized respectively by the British 6th Airborne Division and the US XVII Airborne Division. The latter was based on

the Continent and was to be airlifted by the US XI Troop Carrier Command; the 6th Airborne Division was to be lifted from the UK by Nos. 38 and 46 Groups RAF and the 52nd Wing of the US IX Troop Carrier Command. The US VIIIth Fighter Command was to provide a fighter screen east of the landing area during the period of the landings; RAF squadrons were to provide air escort for the transports from the UK, while IX Tactical Air Command was responsible for escorting the transport aircraft from France. Both were to be relieved by 2nd TAF, which was to cover the final stages of the fly-in.

The operation, involving 1500 aircraft and 1300 gliders. was successful. Immediately after the landings, resupply operations were carried out by 239 B-24s of the 2nd Bomb Division, VIIIth Bomber Command, directed by three RAF Halifaxes in contact with Forward Visual Control Posts and acting as Master Supply Aircraft. Throughout the operation, responsibility for preventing interference from enemy aircraft was undertaken by 2nd TAF; less than 20 enemy aircraft were sighted, but heavy flak was encountered. IX Troop Carrier Command lost 46 aircraft shot down by ground fire and 348 damaged; the RAF lost 4 aircraft and 32 suffered damage.

**29 *March*** Lancasters of Nos. 9 and 617 Sqns destroyed U-boat pens at Farge, north of Bremen, with *Tallboy* and *Grand Slam* bombs.

**30/31 *March*** *Oberleutnant* Welter, commanding 10/NJG 11, flying a Messerschmitt Me 262B-1aU1 night-fighter, shot down four Mosquitoes in one sortie on the approach to Berlin.

**31 *March*** Halifaxes of No. 6 (RCAF) Group, operating over Hamburg without fighter cover, were attacked by 30 Me 262s and eight bombers were shot down.

**4 *April*** 49 Me 262s attacked 150 B-17s over Nordhausen, destroying 15.

**7 *April*** Me 262s of JG 7, engaging US fighters escorting B-17s, shot down 28 P-51s and P-47s. Elsewhere, 183 piston-engined German fighters were destroyed in a series of air combats.

**9/10 *April*** The German pocket battleship *Admiral Scheer* was hit and capsized, and the cruisers *Emden* and *Hipper* badly damaged, in an attack on Kiel by 591 Lancasters.

**10 *April*** Over 1000 US bombers carried out massive attacks on the jet fighter bases of Oranienburg, Brandenburg-Briest, Parchim and Rechlin, forcing the remaining Me262s to scatter to locations as far afield as Prague. Sporadic jet fighter operations continued until the aircraft were grounded through lack of fuel.

**10 April** An Arado Ar 234 of I (*Fernaufklärungs-gruppe*) 33 from Stavanger-Sola, Norway, made a reconnaissance flight from Scapa Flow in the Orkneys to the Firth of Tay. This was the last recorded mission by a *Luftwaffe* aircraft over the British Isles.

**17 April** The Allied Command announced that the objectives of Operation *Pointblank* had been achieved.

**25 April** 318 Lancasters of Nos. 1, 5 and 8 Groups attacked Hitler's mountain chalet and the SS barracks at Berchtesgaden in support of an offensive by the US Seventh Army, while 468 Lancasters, Halifaxes and Mosquitoes of Nos. 4, 6, 8 and 100 Groups attacked coastal gun batteries on the island of Wangerooge. The bombers assigned to the Berchtesgaden attack were escorted by Mustangs of the 78th Fighter Group, USAAF. The US Eighth Air Force also flew its final combat missions on this day.

**25/26 April** 107 Lancasters and 12 Mosquitoes attacked an oil refinery at Tonsberg, Norway – the last raid by main force heavy bombers of the RAF in World War II. A Lancaster of No. 463 Sqn came down in Sweden, the last of more than 3300 Lancasters lost in the war. All the crew survived. Fourteen Lancasters of No. 5 Group also carried

out the RAF's last minelaying mission, in Oslo Fjord.

**29 April** Tempests of No. 122 Wing, supporting Operation *Enterprise* – the crossing of the Elbe – destroyed 14 enemy aircraft and destroyed or damaged 110 road vehicles.

**2/3 May** Last offensive action by RAF Bomber Command in World War II: 303 sorties flown by Mosquitoes of No. 8 Group against enemy airfields.

**3 May** Typhoons and Tempests of 2nd TAF, together with aircraft of Coastal Command and IX Tactical Air Command, carried out devastating attacks on enemy shipping in the Baltic. Large numbers of transport aircraft and flying boats, all taking part in a planned evacuation to Norway, were also destroyed.

**4 May** This was the last day of air operations in north-west Europe. During the period 1–4 May, 2nd TAF claimed the destruction of 141 enemy aircraft for the loss of 29, mostly shot down on anti-shipping operations in the Baltic.

**7 May** The last U-boat to be sunk in the European war was destroyed by a Catalina of No. 210 Sqn. This was the 196th U-boat destroyed unaided in an aircraft of RAF Coastal Command.

**8 May** Unconditional surrender of Germany.

# The Eastern Front, 1944–45

# 1944

**January** 2360 Soviet aircraft of the 2nd, 5th, 8th and 17th Air Armies were assigned to support a major offensive in the Ukraine, designed to liberate the right bank of the river Dnieper. In support of the 1st Ukrainian Front, Russian aircraft flew 4200 sorties, of which 2500 were against tanks, before the offensive was halted by a German counter-attack. On the 2nd Ukrainian Front, the 5th Air Army lent support to Russian forces liberating Kirovgrad; the 1st Guards Bomber Division

(Pe-2s), the 205th and 302nd Fighter Air Divisions and the 1st Ground-Attack Air Corps (Il-2s) flew 1100 sorties in support of this operation.

**14 January** A major Soviet offensive in the Leningrad sector began in the morning. During the preliminary artillery barrage, 30 Il-2s of the 277th Ground-Attack Air Division attacked enemy artillery in bad weather. Il-2s of this unit, and of the 9th Air Division, were assigned to direct battlefield support. Fighter cover was provided by the 275th Fighter Air Division. Il-2s of the 281st Ground-Attack Air Division flew in support of a parallel offensive at Novgorod, north of Lake Ilmen; other units involved here were the 269th

Fighter Air Division, the 4th Guards Bomber and the 386th Night Bomber Air Regiments. Many sorties were also flown by units of the Baltic Fleet Air Force, including the 73rd Bomber Air Regiment. By the end of January 1944, the German blockade of Leningrad had been broken.

*February* In the south, offensive operations by the 3rd and 4th Ukrainian Fronts were supported by the 8th and 17th Air Armies. During the initial phase of these operations, Il-2s and Pe-2s of the 9th Composite Air Corps were particularly active in attacking enemy rail communications. Operations continued throughout March and culminated in an advance on Odessa early in April.

*10 April* Soviet forces, directly supported by the 9th Composite Air Corps and the 288th Fighter Air Division, liberated Odessa. Meanwhile, transport groups equipped with Li-2s (licence-built C-47s) flew 4817 sorties, transporting 670 tons of fuel and supplies and over 5000 personnel (reinforcements and wounded). The transport aircraft were escorted by Yak-9s of the 866th Fighter Air Regiment, whose Commanding Officer, Captain A.I. Koldunov, was to end the war with a score of 46 enemy aircraft destroyed.

*12–18 April* The Soviet Air Force flew 4666 sorties

*The Yak-3 was a basic and extremely rugged aircraft, capable of operating from primitive airstrips.*

in support of troops of the 4th Ukrainian Front, completing the liberation of the Crimea. On two nights, 15 and 16 April, 233 aircraft bombed ships and transports in the bays at Sevastopol, sinking several vessels (mostly barges).

*1–5 May* In support of an offensive towards Sevastopol by the 2nd Guards Army, aircraft of AFLRO and the 8th Air Army dropped more than 2000 tons of bombs and 24 000 anti-tank bombs on enemy positions. On 6 May, prior to the assault on Sevastopol itself, Il-2s of the 136th and 307th Air Regiments carried out heavy attacks on the enemy's perimeter defences. Sevastopol was liberated by 9 May, the remnants of the enemy forces withdrawing to the Khersonesky Cape for evacuation. On 11 May, evacuation vessels came under heavy attack by Soviet aircraft and warships of the Black Sea Fleet; 13 ships were sunk and 8000 troops drowned. During eight days of operations in the Sevastopol Fortified Region Soviet aircraft flew more than 13 000 sorties; the *Luftwaffe* flew only about 700 sorties during this period.

*June* Operations in Karelia. On 1 June, the Germans and their Finnish allies had six divisions in the Karelian Isthmus area, supported by *Luftflotte* 1 and units of the Finnish Air Force. Russian air support for the offensive on this front was provided by the 13th Air Army, the 2nd Guards Fighter Air Corps of the ADF, and aircraft of the Red Banner Baltic Fleet.

*9 June* On the day before the offensive in Karelia began, 215 Soviet bombers and 155 ground-attack aircraft with fighter escort carried out very accurate and effective attacks on enemy strongpoints in the first line of defence. Other attacks were made on railroad communications to the rear, and on known artillery positions. Air operations continued at maximum effort up to 19 June, by which time Soviet troops had broken through the enemy's third line of defence. In the air, resistance stiffened as the *Luftwaffe* moved the Fw 190s of JG 54 and the Ju 87s of StG 1 to the Vyborg sector; because of the distance from their bases created by the rapid Soviet advance, the fighters of the 275th Air Division were no longer able to provide continuous cover. The Soviet advance in Karelia continued, but at a slower rate.

With the German Army Groups North and South practically driven from Russia and the Ukraine, the stage was set for a mighty onslaught against Army Group Centre, holding an exposed salient from Minsk to the Pripet Marshes. German forces on this front were supported by 1342 aircraft of *Luftflotte* 6, their numbers having been reduced by transfers to Germany. The Russians had about 6000, including 1100 bombers and 2000 fighters. Appropriately, the offensive against Army Group Centre in White Russia was timed to begin on 22 June 1944 – the third anniversary of Germany's invasion of the Soviet Union. However, fog hampered air operations on the first two days, and it was not until 25 June that the Soviet Air Force could give effective air support.

*25 June* In addition to providing direct support for ground forces, Soviet aircraft carried out heavy attacks on enemy airfields, especially those occupied by the Fw 190s of JG 51. The latter's HQ airfield at Orsha was badly hit and the command post burned down, with the result that ground control over the fighter units was lost for some crucial hours.

*27 June* 526 bombers of the 16th Air Army dropped 159 tons of bombs on German troops and armour surrounded near Bobruisk, killing about 1000. The remainder were liquidated, together with four divisions of the 53rd Corps at Vitebsk.

*28 June* Soviet aircraft flew some 2000 sorties up to 4 July against German columns of the Fourth Army, retreating on the 2nd White Russian Front. The air attacks destroyed more than 3000 vehicles on the road between Mogilev and Minsk. By this time, Soviet units were moving up to occupy airfields vacated by the enemy.

*5–11 July* German assault groups, with air support, attempted to recapture airfields occupied by the Russians but were beaten off by support units of the 4th Air Army. During the same period, a concentration of 11 000 enemy troops, encircled near Minsk, was smashed and demoralized by continual Il-2 attacks mounted by the 1st Guards Ground-Attack Air Division. The pocket was subsequently liquidated.

*7–13 July* 103 Pe-2s and 51 Il-2s of the 1st Air Army carried out heavy attacks on the Lithuanian capital of Vilnius, where enemy forces were surrounded. One of the units that took part in these operations, and in subsequent air activities over the river Niemen, was the 1st French Fighter Air Regiment (*Normandie-Niemen*), which was part of the 303rd Fighter Air Division, and was equipped with Yakovlev Yak-9 aircraft. (It later re-equipped with Yak-3s.)

During operations in White Russia, transport aircraft were widely used to deliver supplies to air units, armoured formations and mechanized cavalry units. *Aeroflot* transport regiments flew about 35 000 sorties and transported more than 43 000 men, and Li-2s of the AFLRO transported 11 000 men and about 3500 tons of cargo.

*13 July* The Russians launched a major offensive against Army Group North Ukraine, where 31 German and 12 Hungarian divisions occupied the Lvov area. This was supported by five air corps with 1500 aircraft, opposing about 750 aircraft of *Luftflotte* 4. In addition, the German command could call upon 300–400 aircraft of *Luftflotte* 6.

*14 July* In support of the Lvov offensive, 252 aircraft of the 2nd Guards Air Corps and 4th Bomber Air Corps attacked enemy troop concentrations. Ninety minutes later, a second attack was made by 366 Il-2s, opening gaps for the attacking forces. In parallel, another mass attack by 1400 aircraft was made on the enemy rear areas, causing significant tank losses.

*15 July* 135 Pe-2s of the 4th Bomber Air Corps attacked enemy tank concentrations near Plugow; the attack was led by General I.S. Polbin, commanding the 2nd Guards Air Corps, the leading Soviet dive-bomber exponent. The bombers were escorted by P-39 Airacobras of the 9th Guards Fighter Division, whose commander, Colonel A.I.

Pokryshkin, was to end the war with a score of 59 enemy aircraft destroyed. In all, the Russians flew 3288 sorties on 15 July, completely disrupting a planned counter-attack by the 8th *Panzer* Division. Lvov was liberated on 27 July.

*1 August* With Russian advance units attempting to cross the river Vistula, the Polish Home Army in Warsaw rose in an attempt to seize the city from the occupying German forces. The Russians have long been criticized for not driving on across the Vistula to the relief of Warsaw and the insurgents, but in fairness it should be stated that their footholds on the river were under heavy attack by the *Luftwaffe*, operating in groups of 30 to 40 aircraft. The early days of August saw intense air battles over the Vistula between the Germans and the 6th and 12th Guards Fighter Air Divisions and the 304th Fighter Air Division. The Allies attempted to supply the Polish Home Army by air from Italy, starting on 4/5 August with a mission by seven Halifaxes of No. 148 (Special Duties) Sqn and seven from No. 1586 (Polish) Flight from Brindisi. Only three aircraft succeeded in dropping their supplies and four of the No. 148 Sqn aircraft FTR, a fifth being destroyed in a landing accident. In addition to the special duties units, supplies were also dropped by the Liberators of Nos. 31 and 34 Sqns, SAAF, from Foggia, and of No. 178 Sqn RAF from Amendola. In four nights, between 13 and 16 August, 17 Polish and 62 British and South African Halifaxes and Liberators attempted to reach Warsaw. Thirty-four succeeded, but of this total only 20 were able to make drops, 15 of which reached the Home Army. These four nights cost the Poles three aircraft, the South Africans seven and the British five – almost 50 per cent of those which got through to the Polish capital. Another three were lost in landing accidents, and almost all the others had battle damage. Fourteen more aircraft were lost during the last two weeks of August and, with the prospect of further serious losses during the September moon period, operations to Warsaw were halted.

*20 August* The forces of the 2nd and 3rd Ukrainian Fronts began a major offensive at Iasi (Jassy) on the border of eastern Romania with the support of 398 aircraft of the 5th and 17th Air Armies. On 24 August, Romania unilaterally ceased hostilities against the Soviet Union, causing the Germans to withdraw into the west of the country or into Hungary and Bulgaria. The Romanian forces changed sides, the 1st Romanian Air Corps being subordinated to the 5th Air Army from 6 September. It had seven groups with a total of 113 aircraft, including IAR.80s, Bf 109Gs, Fw 190s and Henschel Hs 129As.

By the end of August 1944, Polish and Czech air units were also operating with the Soviet air armies. The Polish element was the 1st Polish Composite Air Division, comprising the 1st *Warsaw* Fighter Regiment with Yak-3s, the 2nd *Krakow* Night Bomber Regiment with Pe-2s, and the 3rd Ground Attack Regiment with Il-2s. The Czech element was the 1st Czechoslavak Fighter Regiment, which was equipped with Lavochkin La-5s.

*9 September* The Bulgarian Air Force, with eight air regiments equipped with a miscellany of German types, was assigned to the Soviet 17th Air Army following a Bulgarian–Soviet armistice. Its first offensive operations alongside its new ally were in support of Bulgarian troops engaging the *Prinz Eugen* 7th SS Division near the city of Prokuplje.

*18 September* 110 B-17s of the Eighth Air Force, carrying 1320 containers and escorted by 70 P-51s, dropped supplies to the Polish Home Army in Warsaw. Most fell into German hands. The B-17s flew on to Russian bases. By this time the Soviet Air Force had also begun to drop supplies to the insurgents, but the Home Army's gallant 63-day battle was now over.

*21 September* The 1st Czechoslovak Fighter Regiment flew 21 La-5FN fighters over the German lines and the Carpathian Mountains and began operations from Tri Duba airfield near Zvolen in support of a Slovakian national uprising. Its first task was to escort Soviet Li-2 transports flying in supplies; it then carried out successful strafing attacks on German-occupied airfields.

With German forces cleared from Soviet territory, the last three months of 1944 were spent in making preparations for the assault on Germany itself. By the end of the year, all Germany's allies were gone except Hungary; she had 1960 aircraft left in the east to face 15 540 Soviet. Of her five remaining army groups, Army Group North (renamed Kurland) was trapped in Latvia; Army Group Centre (renamed North) was in East Prussia and northern Poland; Army Group A (renamed Centre) held a line in Poland from Warsaw to the Carpathians; Army Group South was in Hungary, and Army Group F in Yugoslavia.

# 1945

*13 January* The 3rd White Russian Front, supported by the 1st and 3rd Air Armies, began its offensive into East Prussia. On the following day

the 2nd White Russian Front also attacked, supported by the 4th Air Army.

**17 January** Warsaw was liberated by Soviet and Polish forces, supported by the 16th Air Army. In the week that followed, Soviet forces had reached the river Oder. As the rapid advance was once again causing problems for the air support units, 32 airfields were built and 15 restored to operational condition between 26 January and 7 February. In addition, aircraft of the 15th Fighter Air Regiment and 9th Guards Fighter Air Division began operations from stretches of *Autobahn*. In the 20 days of the Vistula–Oder campaign, the 2nd and 16th Air Armies flew more than 54 000 sorties, claiming the destruction of 908 enemy aircraft in the course of 1150 air battles. *Luftwaffe* resistance in East Prussia was weaker; the focus here was on ground-attack operations as Soviet forces systematically overcame heavily-fortified German towns and other strongpoints.

**February** German forces now began consolidating behind two major defensive systems: the Oder–Neisse defence line and the Berlin fortified region. The *Luftwaffe* had about 2000 aircraft in the Berlin area, of which 70 per cent were fighters; the total included about 120 Me 262 jets. A well-prepared air base system ensured that the *Luftwaffe* was able to concentrate its aircraft in the most important sectors. For the assault on Berlin the Russians had assembled 7500 aircraft of the 2nd, 4th and 16th Air Armies; 297 of these belonged to the 1st and

*Yakovlev Yak-3 fighters of a Soviet Guards Fighter Regiment, early 1945.*

4th Polish Composite Air Divisions. Much of the *Luftwaffe*'s effort during this period was devoted to the attempted destruction of road and rail traffic bridges on the Oder and Neisse rivers, about 120 of which had fallen intact into enemy hands.

*6 March* A Heinkel He 111 H of II/KG 200 achieved a direct hit on the Oder bridge at Görlitz with a Henschel Hs 293 guided bomb.

*8 March* Four *Mistels* (Ju 88/Bf 109 combinations) of II/KG 200 attacked the Oder bridges at Görlitz. Two bridges were hit and one *Mistel* was shot down. A Ju 188, one of five attacking anti-aircraft sites in the target area, was also lost.

*25/26 March* Four *Mistels* attacked the Oder bridges with unknown results; other *Mistels* were despatched to attack bridges over the Vistula. It was planned to launch a major attack (Operation *Eisenhammer*) on Soviet power stations with 56 *Mistels* on the night of 28/29 March, but this was called off because bridge targets were given higher priority.

*31 March* Six *Mistels* of II/KG 200 set out to attack the railway bridge at Steinau, escorted by 24 Bf 109s of JG 52. Two Ju 88s and two Ju 188s were to make a diversionary attack on Steinau railway station. Three *Mistels* aborted with technical trouble; one achieved a hit on the bridge and the other a near miss. The bridge was out of action for several days.

**8/9 April** Five *Mistels* (Ju 88/Fw 190) of KG 30 were despatched to attack the Vistula bridges at Warsaw. All the Fw 190 pilots returned safely, but four of the Ju 88 components were destroyed by AA fire after release. The next day, the principal *Mistel* base at Rechlin-Lärz was destroyed by USAAF bombers, although operations continued from other bases.

**10 April** The German fortress of Königsberg, East Prussia, capitulated after four days of air attack in which the Soviet Air Force flew 14090 sorties and dropped 4440 tons of bombs.

**16 April** At dawn, Soviet forces launched their offensive towards Berlin across the Oder, Neisse and Spree rivers. The assault was preceded by night bombing attacks in enemy rear areas and supported by ground-attack aircraft of the 16th Air Army, but operations were initially hampered by patches of fog. As the weather cleared, about 75 per cent of air operations were flown in support of the attacking Soviet tank armies. The day saw the last *Mistel* attacks, when the composite aircraft were used together with Hs 293s to attack enemy bridgeheads.

During the Russian advance on Berlin, the *Luftwaffe* managed to mount about 1000 sorties a day during April; the Russian average was 15000. Among the latest German types encountered by the Russians during the Berlin campaign was the Focke-Wulf Ta 152 (the 'Ta' being an abbreviation of the name of the designer, Kurt Tank). A few of these aircraft served with JG 301, which was charged with the protection of jet fighter bases, but they also undertook escort duties in the last month of the war. On 19 April, one was shot down over Berlin by the leading Soviet fighter pilot, Guards Major Ivan Kozhedub, who also had a Me 262 to his credit. He ended the war with 62 enemy aircraft destroyed.

**21 April** Soviet forces broke through the Oder defensive line and began the encirclement of Berlin.

**29 April** Units of the German Twelfth Army launched a strong counter-attack in an attempt to relieve Berlin. Their effort was frustrated by 400 Russian bombing and ground-attack sorties. By this time German troops were fighting in Berlin, which had been subjected to a series of massive Russian bombing attacks, and Soviet fighter units were operating from captured airfields in the city: the 515th Fighter Air Regiment from Tempelhof and the 347th and 518th Fighter Air Regiments from Schönefeld.

**2 May** The Berlin garrison surrendered. During the campaign, the Soviet Air Force had flown 92000 sorties, destroying 1132 enemy aircraft for the loss of 527.

**9 May** The German garrison in Prague, the last pocket of resistance, surrendered. On this day, Guards Major Victor Golubev destroyed a Bf 109 over the city. As far as may be ascertained, this was the last aircraft destroyed in combat during the European war.

# The Air War Against Japan, 1944–45
# The Pacific

# 1944

**29 January** Six heavy and six light aircraft carriers, operating in four groups of Task Force 58, opened the campaign to capture the Marshall Islands with heavy air attacks on Maloelap, Kwajalein and Wotje. By the end of the first day the Japanese air forces in the area had been eliminated. Eight escort carriers also arrived in the area early in the morning of D-Day, their aircraft flying top cover and anti-submarine patrols for the invasion fleet and providing air support for the landings.

**30 January** To neutralize Wake Island during the Marshalls operation, two squadrons of Consolidated PB2Y Coronados from Midway made the first of four night bombing attacks on that objective. The missions involved a round trip of 2000 miles.

**17 February** The first strike on Truk was carried out by the Truk Striking Force built around three fast carrier groups. In two days, the carriers launched 1250 combat sorties against this key naval base, sinking 37 war and merchant ships and inflicting heavy damage to base installations. In this action the first night bombing attack in the history of US carrier aviation was carried out by 12 radar-equipped TBF-1C Avengers of VT-10 (USS *Enterprise*). Japanese aircraft made several night attacks on the task force and the USS *Intrepid* was hit by a torpedo. Night-fighter detachments of VF(N)-76 and VF(N)-101, equipped with F6F-3s and F4U-2s, operated from five carriers but achieved little success.

**23 February** Two carrier groups of Task Force 58 attacked targets on Saipan, Tinian, Rota and Guam for the dual purpose of reducing enemy air strength in the Marianas and gathering photo intelligence for the impending invasion. Japanese aircraft attacked the carriers as they approached their flying-off positions; 67 were shot down and 101 more destroyed on the ground.

**15 March** North American Mitchells (PBJ-1s) carried out their first combat mission in US Navy service: an attack on Rabaul by Marine Bombing Squadron VMB-413.

**26 March** Corsairs of VMF-113, carrying out their first escort mission (AAF B-25s against Ponape, Caroline Islands), proved so effective at neutralizing Japanese fighters that later missions over the island were unmolested.

**30 March** In an operation designed to eliminate opposition to Allied landings at Hollandia and to gather photo intelligence, eleven carriers of Task Force 58 launched a series of attacks on Palau, Yap, Ulithi and Woleai atolls in the Western Carolines. Palau Harbour was mined by Torpedo Squadrons 2, 8 and 16, the first such mission by carrier aircraft and the first large-scale daylight mining operation of the Pacific war. The attacks accounted for 157 enemy aircraft destroyed, 28 ships of 108 000 tons sunk, and the denial of Palau Harbour for an estimated six weeks.

**16 April** After successfully attacking targets at Hollandia, Fifth Air Force B-24s, B-25s, A-20s and P-38s encountered unexpected bad weather as they returned to their New Guinea bases. Thirty-one aircraft were lost, the worst blow suffered by the Fifth AF in the whole war.

**18 April** In preparation for the campaign to occupy the Marianas, Liberators of photo-mapping squadron VD-3 obtained complete coverage of Saipan, Tinian and Aguijan Islands. The photo aircraft were escorted by AAF B-24s, which carried out diversionary bombing attacks. This was the first mission by land-based aircraft over the Marianas.

**19 April** The aircraft carriers HMS *Illustrious* and USS *Saratoga*, operating with the British Eastern Fleet, launched 83 aircraft (Barracudas, Corsairs, Hellcats, Dauntlesses and Avengers) in an attack on Sabang Harbour and neighbouring airfields in the Netherlands East Indies. Two Japanese freighters were sunk and severe damage caused to the harbour installations; 25 aircraft were destroyed on the ground and three out of four G4M *Bettys* shot down by Hellcats. One Hellcat was lost, its pilot being rescued by a British submarine.

**21–24 April** Aircraft from five heavy and seven light carriers of Task Force 58 attacked airfields in the Hollandia area of New Guinea, covering the Allied landings there. Thirty enemy aircraft were destroyed in the air and 103 on the ground. Allied forces later found 340 enemy aircraft wrecked on the Hollandia airfields.

**29 April** In two further days of air strikes on Truk, carrier aircraft destroyed 145 enemy aircraft and sank three small ships.

**17 May** The carriers HMS *Illustrious* and USS *Saratoga* launched 45 Avengers and Dauntlesses, escorted by 40 Corsairs and Hellcats, in an attack on the Japanese aviation fuel dump at Soerabaja, Java. The results were disappointing and one Avenger was lost.

**19–20 May** Aircraft from three carriers began a two-day series of air strikes on Marcus Island. On 23 May, the same force (Task Group 58.6) made five bombing, strafing and rocket strikes on Wake Island.

**11 June** Seven heavy and eight light carriers of Task Force 58 began the campaign to occupy the Marianas with a late afternoon fighter sweep that destroyed one-third of the defending air force. During the next three days the carrier aircraft carried out intensive bombing and strafing attacks on shore installations and shipping, preparing the way for the amphibious assault on Saipan that took place on 15 June.

**15 June** The Far East Air Forces was formed under the command of General George C. Kenney. It combined the Fifth and Thirteenth Air Forces, the latter playing a supporting role.

**15 June** First air attack on the Japanese mainland by shore-based aircraft: B-29 Superfortresses of the newly-activated XX Bomber Command, Twentieth AF, operating from bases in SW China, attacked steel works on Kyushu.

**19–20 June** Battle of the Philippine Sea. Japanese carrier forces from the *Taiho*, *Zuikaku* and *Shokaku* (601st Air Group), *Hiyo*, *Junyo* and *Ryuho* (62nd Air Group) and *Chitose*, *Chiyoda* and *Zuiho* (653rd Air Group) launched a day-long attack on Task Force 58 along with shore-based aircraft. In a battle that became known as the Marianas Turkey Shoot, American combat air patrols and AA fire destroyed 325 enemy aircraft, including 220 of the 328 launched by the carriers. American losses were 16 Hellcats in combat, and seven other aircraft destroyed by Japanese fighters or ground fire. On 20 June, US strike aircraft, attacking the retreating Japanese fleet, sank the carrier *Hiyo* and two fleet oilers.

**6/7 July** A Northrop P-61 Black Widow of the 6th Night Fighter Squadron – the USAAF's first specialized night-fighter unit in the Pacific – scored the first P-61 kill in the theatre, shooting down a G4M *Betty* over New Guinea. On the following night, a Mitsubishi Ki-46 *Dinah* was destroyed by a P-61 of the 421st NFS.

**14 July** PB4Y Liberators of VB-109 operating from Saipan, which was occupied on 9 July, made the first attack on Iwo Jima by land-based aircraft.

**25–28 July** Following successful Allied landings on Guam and Tinian, carriers of Task Force 58 carried out further strikes on the Western Carolines and aircraft obtained photo intelligence of enemy defences for future operations.

**10 August** The end of organized enemy resistance on Guam on this date brought the Marianas Campaign to an end. During the campaign, US carrier aircraft had accounted for 110 000 tons of shipping sunk and 1223 aircraft destroyed.

**September** The month saw intensive operations by the US Fast Carrier Task Force in support of landings by the Central and Southwest Pacific forces on Palau, Morotai, Peleliu, Angaur and Ulithi; many air attacks were directed against airfields, military installations and shipping in the central Philippines. During a month of continual action, carrier aircraft destroyed 893 enemy aircraft and sank 67 vessels totalling 224 000 tons.

**10 October** Occupation of Leyte. As a preliminary to this campaign, 17 carriers of Task Force 38 attacked airfields on Okinawa and the Ryukyus. This action was followed later in the month by heavy attacks on airfields on northern Luzon, Formosa and in the Manila area, the Americans claiming 438 enemy aircraft destroyed in air combat and 366 on the ground.

**23–26 October** The Battle of Leyte Gulf. The Japanese Fleet, converging on Leyte Gulf in three elements (Southern, Central and Northern Forces) attempted to disrupt Allied operations in the Philippines. On 24 October, Fast Carrier Force aircraft attacked the enemy's Southern and Central Forces, sinking the 64 000-ton battleship *Musashi* and a destroyer; Japanese air attacks resulted in the loss of the USS *Princeton* (CVL-23). Units of the US Seventh Fleet turned back the Southern Force, sinking two battleships and three destroyers. Meanwhile, the Japanese Central Force made a night passage through the San Bernardino Strait and, at dawn on 25 October, engaged US escort carriers and their screening warships. The USS *Gambier Bay* (CVE-73) and one destroyer were sunk by enemy gunfire, but the Japanese lost three cruisers to carrier strikes. At the same time, the Fast Carrier Force met the enemy's Northern Force off Cape Engano, carrier aircraft sinking the heavy carrier *Zuikaku* and the light carriers *Chiyoda*, *Zuiho* and *Chitose*. Surviving Japanese warships were attacked by 47 USAAF B-24s without result.

The battle of Leyte saw the first planned attacks by Japanese *Kamikaze* (Divine Wind) suicide pilots. In October 1944, 14 *Kamikaze* units were operational in the Philippines, each equipped with 12 *Zeros* armed with a pair of 500 lb (227 kg) bombs. The suicide pilots' primary targets were the aircraft carriers, and off Leyte they sank the *St Lo* (CVE-63) and damaged the *Sangamon*, *Suwannee*, *Santee*, *White Plains*, *Kalinin Bay* and *Kitkun Bay*. Further *Kamikaze* attacks on 29 and 30 October damaged the carriers *Intrepid*, *Franklin* and *Belleau Wood*; the *Intrepid* was hit again in November, and the *Lexington*, *Essex* and *Cabot* were also damaged.

**1 November** A USAAF B-29 made a photographic reconnaissance of the Tokyo area after flying from Saipan, 1500 miles (2414 km) away. On the same day, the Japanese released the first of 9000 balloons which, carrying an explosive charge, were intended to drift on the prevailing winds 6000 miles (9656 km) to the North American continent. Most landed harmlessly, but some casualties were caused.

During November 1944, the 82nd Tactical Reconnaissance Sqn at Morotai began to replace its P-40s with the F-6D; this was the first Mustang variant to see service in the Pacific Operational Area. Plans were also made to allocate Mustangs

*Although the atomic bombs brought a swift end to the war, it was conventional bombing by the B-29 Superfortress that brought Japan to her knees.*

# 1945

to the 110th TRS, but because this squadron's TacR P-40s were heavily involved in support of the fighting at Leyte and Mindoro conversion was delayed until February 1945.

**24 November** 111 B-29s were despatched from Saipan to attack the Nakajima Aircraft Company's works on the outskirts of Tokyo. Cloud obscured the target and the B-29s bombed at random. One aircraft FTR, rammed by a Japanese fighter. In 11 raids on the factory, only two per cent of the bombs dropped hit the target; the attacks cost the Americans 40 bombers and 440 aircrew. The Saipan-based B-29s were assigned to XXI Bomber Command.

**14–16 December** In support of landings on Mindoro, seven heavy and six light carriers of Task Force 58 flew continuous fighter sweeps over the Luzon airfields, while six escort carriers of Task Unit 77.12.1 and Marine Corps shore-based aircraft supported the landings themselves. Japanese losses in the short campaign were 341 aircraft, in the air and on the ground.

**3–22 January** The invasion of Luzon. During the invasion and occupation of Luzon by Southwest Pacific Forces, which were supported by seven heavy and four light carriers of Task Force 38 and 17 escort carriers of Task Group 77.4, *Kamikaze* aircraft again provided serious opposition, sinking the *Ommaney Bay* (CVE-79) and damaging the *Manila Bay*, *Savo Island*, *Kadashan Bay* and *Salamaua*. Task Force 38, operating in bad weather, carried out attacks on Luzon, Formosa and the Ryukyus, destroying over 100 enemy aircraft and sinking 40000 tons of shipping in the first week of operations. The Task Force then made a high-speed run through Luzon Strait for operations in the South China Sea, where strike aircraft sank a further 149000 tons of shipping before moving north to the Hong Kong area and concluding with operations against Formosa and Okinawa. In three weeks of action, the Task Force claimed 600 enemy aircraft destroyed and sank 325000 tons of shipping. Two carriers, the *Ticonderoga* and *Langley*, were damaged by enemy air attack.

**24 January** British strike aircraft from the carriers HMS *Illustrious*, HMS *Victorious*, HMS *Indomitable* and HMS *Indefatigable* carried out a heavy attack on Japanese oil refineries at Palembang, Sumatra, while en route from Ceylon to the Pacific. A second strike was made five days later. During the two attacks Fleet Air Arm Corsairs and Hellcats destroyed 30 enemy aircraft in air combat; many more were destroyed on the ground.

**3 February** B-29s of the 73rd and 313th Bombardment Wings dropped 160 tons of incendiaries on Kobe, hitting fabric and synthetic rubber plants and halving the capacity of the shipyard. Japanese targets were especially vulnerable to this type of attack, and incendiary raids became an established practice for XXI Bomber Command. The most effective incendiary device was the 500 lb (227 kg) M76 pyrotechnic gel bomb which contained a mixture of jellied oil, heavy oil, petrol, magnesium powder and sodium nitrate.

**16–17 February** 11 heavy and five light carriers of Task Force 58 launched heavy attacks on airfields in the Tokyo area in a covering operation for the US landings on Iwo Jima, which took place on 19 February. The Task Force then moved south to support the landings before returning for a second strike on Tokyo on 25 February. After attacking Okinawa and the Ryukyus on 1 March, the Task Force returned to Ulithi Atoll, by which time

it had destroyed 648 enemy aircraft and sunk 30 000 tons of merchant shipping. *Kamikazes* were again in evidence during the Iwo Jima operations, sinking the escort carrier *Bismarck Sea* and seriously damaging the *Saratoga* in a dusk attack on 21 February.

**25 February** 172 B-29s dropped 450 tons of incendiaries in the first 'fire raid' on Tokyo. 30 000 buildings were gutted.

**6 March** P-51D Mustangs of the 15th Fighter Group, VII Fighter Command, began operations from Iwo Jima while fighting for possession of the island was still in progress. The Mustangs maintained constant air patrols between dawn and dusk and also strafed ground targets. At night, two P-51s of the 548th NFS took over. Other fighter units subsequently deployed to Iwo Jima were the 549th NFS (P-61s), the 21st and 506th Fighter Groups (P-51Ds).

**9/10 March** 279 B-29s of XXI Bomber Command carried out a devastating fire raid on Tokyo, dropping 1667 tons of incendiaries and killing more than 83 000 people. 267 000 buildings were destroyed and over a million people made homeless.

**12/13 March** 285 B-29s dropped 1790 tons of in-

*B-29s of the Twentieth US Air Force in formation.*

cendiaries on Nagoya, but the bombing was scattered and generally ineffective.

**14/15 March** 274 B-29s carried out an attack on Osaka, Japan's second city, with 1732 tons of incendiaries; 135000 houses were destroyed and 3988 people killed. Japanese fighters made 40 unsuccessful interception attempts.

**17 March** 307 B-29s of XXI Bomber Command made a radar-directed daylight attack on the port of Kobe, dropping 2355 tons of incendiaries; 66 000 buildings were destroyed and 2669 people killed. The Kawasaki shipyards were heavily damaged. Japanese fighters made 93 attacks, without success.

**18–22 March** Ten heavy and six light carriers launched heavy neutralization air strikes on Kyushu, Japan, prior to the US landings on Okinawa. Air attacks accounted for 482 enemy aircraft and another 46 were destroyed by ships' gunfire.

**19/20 March** 290 B-29s dropped 1858 tons of incendiaries on Nagoya, destroying 3 miles² (7.8 km²) of the city.

*Personnel from the USS* Santa Fe *assist in damage control operations aboard the carrier USS* Franklin, *damaged in a* Kamikaze *attack off Okinawa, 19 March 1945.*

**21 March** 16 G4M2 parent aircraft of the 721st *Kokutai*, carrying Yokosuka *Okha* Model 11 rocket-powered piloted bombs on a mission against TF 58, were intercepted and forced to release their weapons short of the target. This was the *Okha*'s first operation.

**26 March** The four aircraft carriers and escorting warships of the British Pacific Fleet, designated Task Force 57, began operations south of Okinawa, their aircraft neutralizing airfields on Sakishima Gunto and Formosa and intercepting air raids heading for the Okinawa assault area. All four carriers were hit in *Kamikaze* attacks, but – thanks mainly to their armoured flight decks, which significantly reduced damage – all remained operational. During operations in March, *Kamikaze* attacks also damaged the US carriers *Enterprise*, *Intrepid*, *Yorktown*, *Franklin* and *Wasp*.

**1 April** The battleship *West Virginia* was damaged

by an *Okha* piloted bomb, the first success registered by this weapon.

**6 April** The Battle of the East China Sea. The Japanese Navy made its last sortie of World War II in opposition to the Okinawa landings with a task force of one light cruiser, eight destroyers and the world's largest battleship, the 72 809-ton *Yamato*. The task force was attacked by US carrier aircraft, and only four destroyers survived.

**7 April** 108 Mustangs of VII Fighter Command escorted B-29s of the 73rd Bombardment Wing in an attack on the Nakajima-Musashi factory, the first time that US land-based fighters had flown over the Japanese home islands. On this and subsequent missions to Japan each P-51D carried two 165 US-gallon drop tanks. From April, B-29 escort missions were also flown by P-47N Thunderbolts of the 318th Fighter Group, based on the island of Ie Shima. In May, the 413th and 507th Fighter Groups were also operating P-47Ns from the island.

**12 April** The first Allied ship to be sunk by an *Okha* piloted bomb, the destroyer *Mannert L. Abele*, was lost off Okinawa.

**13/14 April** In their second largest incendiary attack on Tokyo, 327 B-29s dropped 2139 tons on the city. This, and a second incendiary raid on 15/16 April, destroyed 249 000 buildings in Tokyo, Kawasaki and Yokohama.

**17 April** B-29s of XXI Bomber Command began attacks on *Kamikaze* bases on Kyushu and Shikoku in support of operations on Okinawa. Up to 11 May the B-29s flew 2104 sorties against 17 airfields; Japanese fighters and flak destroyed 24 aircraft and damaged 233. The enemy airfields were also strafed by Mustangs using high-velocity aircraft rockets (HVAR). These attacks restricted *Kamikaze* operations, but the suicide aircraft continued to present a serious threat. During operations in April, *Kamikazes* damaged the carriers *San Jacinto, Hancock, Enterprise, Essex* and *Intrepid*.

**14 May** Returning to strategic operations, XXI Bomber Command despatched 472 B-29s on a daylight incendiary attack on Nagoya. The bombers dropped 2515 tons, destroying over 3 miles$^2$ (7.8 km$^2$) of the town. Ten B-29s were destroyed and 64 damaged by determined fighter attacks; the B-29 gunners and escorting fighters claimed 18 Japanese aircraft.

**16/17 May** 475 B-29s dropped 3609 tons of incendiaries on the harbour area of Nagoya, devastating 3.8 miles$^2$ (9.8 km$^2$). No aircraft was lost. XXI

Bomber Command was now strengthened by the redeployment of XX Bomber Command B-29s from China, operations by strategic aircraft having ceased there.

**23 May** XXI Bomber Command launched its biggest raid so far on Japan: 562 B-29s dropped 3600 tons of incendiaries on Tokyo, destroying 5.3 miles$^2$ (13.7 km$^2$). Four B-29s FTR and 69 were damaged, all by AA fire.

**25 May** The Japanese launched heavy *Kamikaze* attacks on Allied naval forces operating off Okinawa. Thunderbolts of the 318th FG alone shot down 34 enemy aircraft in four hours of combat air patrols.

**25/26 May** XXI Bomber Command carried out the heaviest Tokyo raid so far; 502 B-29s dropped 3262 tons of incendiaries, destroying 16.8 miles$^2$ (43.5 km$^2$) of the city. 26 B-29s FTR.

**29 May** XXI Bomber Command launched a final series of daylight incendiary raids, the first target being Yokohama; 150 enemy fighters were engaged by 101 Mustangs of VII Fighter Command, which shot down 26 enemy aircraft for the loss of three of their own number.

**1 June** VII Fighter Command despatched 149 Mustangs on an escort mission to Kobe. Severe thunderstorms were encountered en route and 27 Mustangs were lost, mostly in mid-air collisions.

**5 June** 473 B-29s bombing Kobe without fighter escort were subjected to 647 individual attacks by Japanese fighters; two B-29s were lost and 176 damaged.

**15 June** On this date, an attack on Osaka brought the urban incendiary campaign to an end. XXI Bomber Command now turned its attention to a new series of daylight precision attacks on the Japanese aircraft industry, and in parallel with this Mustang and Thunderbolt groups joined carrier-based aircraft in intensive strikes on enemy airfields, the aim still being to reduce the *Kamikaze* threat to negligible proportions. The *Kamikaze* operations dictated the course of Allied air tactics in the Pacific at this stage in the same way that the Me 262 threat had influenced the latter stages of the air war over Europe, although the destructive potential of the suicide aircraft was far greater. During the Okinawa campaign, March–June 1945, 1465 *Kamikaze* aircraft took part in day and night attacks, claiming 26 Allied ships sunk and 164 damaged.

**17/18 June** Part of XXI Bomber Command's offensive switched to Japan's smaller industrial towns. Up to the end of the war the Command flew 8014

**Above:**
P-51D Mustangs en route to Japan. Mustang escorts enabled B-29 bombers to mount attacks in daylight.

**Below:**
Volcanic dust on Iwo Jima caused many engine failures. This Mustang suffered one and came to grief, but the pilot escaped.

sorties against these targets and dropped 54 184 tons of bombs in attacks on 57 towns.

**10 July** 14 carriers of Task Force 38, joined on 16 July by four carriers of the British Task Force 37, began heavy attacks on airfields, war and merchant shipping, naval bases and military installations on the Japanese home islands, from Kyushu in the south to Hokkaido in the north.

**21 July** A B-29 of the 393rd Sqn, 509th Bomb Group, released a 10 000 lb (4536 kg) special store known as a *Pumpkin* over the marshalling yards at Kobe. Several similar missions had been flown by lone B-29s of the 509th since the Group arrived at Tinian some weeks earlier. They were, in fact, training sorties leading up to the dropping of the first atomic bomb.

**24 July** 625 B-29s carried out a series of precision attacks on industrial targets in the Nagoya and Osaka areas, dropping 3529 tons of bombs.

**6 August** B-29 44-86292 *Enola Gay* of the 509th Bomb Group dropped the world's first operational atomic bomb, a uranium device nicknamed *Little Boy*, on the city of Hiroshima, southern Honshu, killing 75 000 people and injuring 70 000 more, many of whom would subsequently die.

Initial reports indicated that the bomb produced a yield of over 20 kilotons (equivalent to 20 000 tons of TNT), but the actual yield was nearer 15 kt.

**7 August** 131 B-29s attacked the naval base at Tokokawa.

**8 August** 221 B-29s escorted by Thunderbolts hit enemy steelworks at Yawata, followed by an incendiary attack on Fukuyama.

**9 August** B-29 44-27297 of the 509th Bomb Group (*Bock's Car*) dropped the second operational atomic bomb on Nagasaki, Kyushu. This weapon, nicknamed *Fat Man*, was a plutonium device producing a yield of about 18 kt. The explosion killed 35 000 people.

**14 August** 449 B-29s, escorted by 186 P-51s and P-47s, attacked the naval arsenal at Hikari, the Osaka Army Arsenal, the Marifu marshalling yards near Hiroshima and the Nippon Oil Company plant at Atika.

**14/15 August** 372 B-29s were despatched to attack Kumagaya and Isezaki – the last strategic mission undertaken by XXI Bomber Command in World War II.

**15 August** Unconditional surrender of Japan.

# The China–Burma–India Theatre, 1944–45

# 1944

**5 March** Chindit operations, Burma. Eighty Hadrian gliders carrying Chindit forces were towed by Dakotas from Lalaghat, Assam, to two jungle clearings named *Piccadilly* and *Broadway*. Two nights later, resupply missions were flown by 62 Dakotas, and on 23 March another Chindit brigade was flown to a third strip code-named *Aberdeen*.

**16 March** The Japanese 33rd Division advanced across the Manipur plain and isolated the garrison at Imphal, beginning a three-month siege. During that time the garrison of 150 000 men had to rely entirely on air supply for their survival; more than 400 tons of stores had to be flown every

day into a valley surrounded by enemy guns. Air operations in the Imphal sector were controlled by No. 221 Group RAF, which had three squadrons of Spitfires for air defence and six squadrons of Hurricane fighter-bombers for offensive operations.

**4 April** Japanese forces launched an offensive against Kohima, which was also isolated. In 16 days, four Hurricane fighter-bomber squadrons flew 2200 sorties against the Japanese 31st Division, while four squadrons of Vultee Vengeance dive-bombers struck at the enemy's supply dumps and base camps. As was the case at Imphal, the Kohima garrison was supplied entirely by air until it was relieved in mid-May.

**May** The siege of Myitkyina, a strategic town and airstrip in northern Burma by Chinese and US forces following an advance from Assam along

*A Douglas Dakota, flying at low level over the Burmese jungle, prepares to drop supplies to the Imphal garrison.*

the Hukawng Valley, was supported by P-51 and A-36 Mustangs of the 311th Fighter-Bomber Group and P-40s of the 80th Fighter Group, which had earlier provided support for US Ranger forces (Merrill's Marauders) during deep-penetration jungle operations. During these operations, US ground-attack pilots achieved excellent results with the combined use of grid coordinates superimposed on reconnaissance photographs and forward air control by radio link. In all, the fighter-bombers flew 2515 sorties between 17 May 1944, when the siege began, and 3 August, when Myitkyina was captured.

*June* After the lifting of the sieges of Imphal and Kohima, the British Fourteenth Army in Burma went over to the offensive, pursuing the Japanese Fifteenth Army through the monsoon season in a retreat that was to end virtually in Rangoon. The offensive was sustained by 23 RAF and USAAF transport squadrons; this would not have been possible without complete air superiority, established over the battle zone by the RAF's Spitfires and at longer ranges by the Mustangs of the USAAF, which on one occasion destroyed 31

Japanese aircraft on the ground at Don Muang, near Bangkok, after a flight of 780 miles (1255 km) to the target. Enemy airfields were also attacked frequently by RAF Liberators of Nos. 159, 160 and 356 Sqns, although their main task was to sever rail links throughout the theatre.

*14 September* No. 261 Sqn RAF (221 Wing) carried out its first operational sortie with P-47 Thunderbolts, an armed reconnaissance over the Chindwin River. Eight more RAF squadrons in Burma had exchanged their Hurricanes for Thunderbolts by the end of 1944.

*November* Operations in China. Following a major Japanese offensive in the summer of 1944, the strength of the Fourteenth Air Force in China was increased to 36 combat squadrons, grouped under the 68th and 69th Composite Wings, the Chinese–American Composite Wing, and the 312th Fighter Wing. Most fighter units were equipped with P-51s and P-47s, although Chinese-manned squadrons still used P-40s. Bomber units operated B-25s and B-24s. The principal Japanese Army Air Force fighter encountered by the Allies in the CBI Theatre was the Nakajima Ki-43 *Oscar*, but as the war progressed numbers of Nakajima Ki-44 *Tojo* fighters began to appear. Japanese Navy units were better equipped with the Mitsubishi A6M5 *Zero* and the J2M3 *Jack*.

# 1945

*January* Operations in the Arakan. Following the capture of Akyab Island in the Bay of Bengal, the British 3rd Commando Brigade landed on the Burmese mainland at Myebon, to the south-east, under cover of a smokescreen laid by Hurricanes, which then provided close support in conjunction with USAAF B-25s. In all, Allied bombers and fighter-bombers flew 1150 sorties in support of the landing, dropping 750 tons of bombs. On 21 January, Ramree Island was also captured, the landing being covered by RAF Spitfires and Thunderbolts, USAAF P-38s and Fleet Air Arm Hellcats, the latter operating from the carrier HMS *Ameer*.

*1 February* Allied forces crossed the Irrawaddy River and pushed on to take the crucial junction and airfield at Meiktila in central Burma. The airfield was defended against strong Japanese counter-attacks by men of the RAF Regiment, enabling supplies and reinforcements to be flown in.

*20 March* Mandalay was captured after its strongest position, Fort Dufferin, was reduced by heavy air attacks. The fighter-bombers of No. 221 Group now carried out devastating attacks on Japanese forces on the Mandalay plain, inflicting terrible casualties. By the second week in April, organized resistance in central Burma had been effectively smashed.

*12 April* The Fourteenth Army began its march on Rangoon. In support of this, supply dumps were heavily attacked by all available strategic bombers. Rangoon fell on 3 May.

*21 July* 18 000 Japanese troops, attempting to escape across the Sittang River, were attacked by every available squadron of No. 221 Group. In nine days the RAF flew 3000 sorties and killed 10 000 enemy soldiers.

In China, the Fourteenth Air Force had finally established overall air superiority following heavy attacks on enemy airfields early in 1945. The emphasis was now on interdiction, aimed at destroying Japanese communications. Operations extended into Indo-China where, by June 1945, the Japanese were forced to abandon rail transportation and rely solely on motor vehicles.

The last Japanese offensive in China, by 60 000 men supported by a small number of air squadrons, began on 10 April 1945. For two months, in one of the first truly coordinated air-ground actions of the war in China, the Chinese and Americans held the enemy in check. While the Chinese held the Japanese on the ground, Fourteenth Air Force Thunderbolts, P-40s, Mustangs and medium bombers attacked them with napalm and anti-personnel bombs and fired millions of rounds of ammunition, inflicting very heavy casualties and forcing the enemy into a general retreat.

*8 August* 76 Il-4 bombers of the Soviet 19th Bomber Corps attacked Japanese targets in Manchuria at the start of a Soviet offensive against the Japanese Kwantung Army. During this short campaign, which ended on 29 August, Russian paratroops were used to capture key enemy airfields. Most of the air support was provided by Il-2s of the 253rd Ground-Attack Air Division and Pe-2s of the 34th Bomber Air Division.

*It took the Americans a long time to establish air superiority in China. This photograph shows the remains of a P-51 Mustang, destroyed during their retreat from Nanking.*

# 5
# THE YEARS OF THE COLD WAR 1946–90

## 1946

*1 March* The US Navy conducted Operation *Frost-bite*, cold weather trials inside the Arctic Circle. The trials were centred on the USS *Midway* and her Air Group 74, comprising F-8F Bearcats, FR-1 Fireballs and HNS-1 helicopters. The Ryan Fireball, of which only 66 were built, was the first aircraft combining a piston engine and a turbojet to enter service.

*3 March* The de Havilland Vampire F.Mk. 1, the RAF's second operational jet fighter, entered service with No. 247 Sqn at RAF Odiham, Hampshire.

*21 March* The Strategic Air Command (SAC) was established as one of the three major combat commands of the USAAF, the others being Tactical Air Command and Air Defense Command.

*1 May* The de Havilland Hornet F.Mk 1 entered service with No. 64 Sqn at RAF Horsham St Faith, Norfolk. Developed from the Mosquito, the Hornet was the fastest twin piston-engined fighter to see service anywhere.

*22 May* The US Navy completed an initial series of trials with an XCF dunking sonar, carried by an HO2S helicopter, off Key West.

*1 July Dave's Dream*, a B-29 of the 509th Composite Group temporarily based at Kwajalein, dropped a Nagasaki-type (i.e. plutonium) atomic bomb on 73 ships laying off Bikini. Five ships were sunk and nine badly damaged. The trials, part of Operation *Crossroads*, also involved an underwater burst. At this time, the 509th Group was the only unit in SAC capable of dropping atomic weapons.

*30 July* The 412th Fighter Group USAAF, the first to equip with the Lockheed P-80 Shooting Star jet

fighter, was redesignated the 1st Fighter Group. It comprised the 27th, 71st and 94th Fighter Squadrons.

*August* During the month, the Lavochkin La-11 fighter became operational with the 9th Guards Fighter Air Division of the Soviet Air Force. The La-11 was Russia's last piston-engined fighter.

*October* B-29s of the 28th Bomb Group, USAAF, deployed to Elmendorf, Alaska, for a six-month period of temporary duty (TDY) training in Arctic conditions. This was the first time an entire SAC bomb group deployed outside the continental limits of the United States.

*November* Six B-29s of the 43rd Bomb Group, deployed to Rhein-Main in Germany, made a series of 'showing the flag' flights along the borders of Soviet-occupied Europe and also surveyed airfields for possible future use by SAC's bombers.

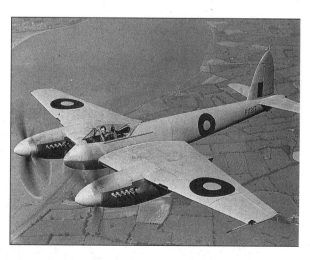

*The de Havilland Hornet F.Mk 1, the fastest twin piston-engined fighter to see service anywhere.*

**December** The MiG-9, the first jet aircraft to see service with the Soviet Air Force, became operational during the month.

**16 December** The first 20 Douglas AD-1 Skyraider carrier-borne attack aircraft were allocated to Attack Squadron VA-19 for trials, the aircraft having undergone a number of modifications since its first flight in March 1945.

# 1947

**March** The Lockheed P2V-1 Neptune maritime patrol aircraft became operational with US Navy Patrol Squadron VP-ML-2.

**June** The de Havilland Sea Hornet, the naval version of the Hornet, was first delivered to No. 801 Sqn, Fleet Air Arm. The squadron's Sea Hornets went to sea on HMS *Implacable* in 1949.

**June** The Republic F-84B Thunderjet became operational with the 14th Fighter Group, USAAF. Thunderjets were subsequently widely used by NATO air forces.

**July** The Hawker Sea Fury X, the Royal Navy's

*The Republic F-84 Thunderjet, which entered service with the USAF in 1947, was widely used by NATO air forces.*

last piston-engined fighter, entered service with No. 807 Sqn FAA. The Mk X was later modified to become a widely-used Sea Fury FB.11 fighter-bomber.

**26 July** The USAAF became the United States Air Force, no longer subordinated to the Army.

**August** The Fairey Firefly Mk 4 fighter-bomber entered service with No. 825 Sqn, Fleet Air Arm. Earlier versions of the Firefly had equipped 11 FAA squadrons at the end of 1945.

**December** The North American FJ-1 Fury, the first jet fighter to operate from an aircraft carrier in squadron strength, entered service with VF-51 at San Diego. The FJ-1 began carrier compatibility trials in March 1948 with Fighter Squadron 5A.

**December** The Yakovlev Yak-15, Russia's first mass-produced jet fighter, began to enter service. Most of the 280 built were assigned to training units, forming a nucleus of jet-experienced Soviet pilots. The Yak-17 was a variant with a tricycle undercarriage.

# 1948

**20 February** The first Boeing B-50A (46-017) was delivered to SAC's 43rd Bomb Wing at Davis-Monthan AFB, Arizona. The B-50 was an improved version of the B-29, with more powerful engines and a taller fin and rudder.

**March** The Martin AM-1 Mauler carrier-borne attack aircraft was delivered to US Navy Attack Squadron VA-17A. Some AM-1s were later converted to the electronic surveillance role as AM-1Qs.

**5 May** Fighter Squadron 17A, equipped with the McDonnell FH-1 Phantom, became the first carrier-qualified jet squadron in the world, operating from the USS *Saipan*. Only 60 FH-1s were built. The type, designed from the outset for carrier operations, first flew on 25 January 1945.

**15 May** Hostilities broke out between the newly-created State of Israel and its Arab neighbours. During Israel's War of Independence, which lasted until January 1949, the Israeli Air Force used a miscellany of combat aircraft acquired from various sources in Europe and the USA. They included Spitfires, Avia C.210s (Czech-built Messerschmitt 109Ks), B-17s, Harvards, C-46s and C-47s. By the end of 1948 the Israelis had achieved air supremacy.

**June** The North American B-45 Tornado, the first American multi-jet bomber to enter production, was first delivered to the 47th Bombardment Wing, replacing the piston-engined B-26.

**26 June** Dakotas of No. 46 Group RAF and C-47s of the 60th and 61st Troop Carrier Groups USAF began flying supplies into Berlin, land access to the city having been cut off by the Russians. These operations marked the start of the Berlin Airlift, the massive air supply operation that was to last a year. When the airlift began, one B-29 squadron of SAC's 301st Bomb Group was on rotational training at Fürstenfeldbruck, Germany. SAC immediately ordered the 301st Group's other two B-29 squadrons to move to Goose Bay, Labrador, in preparation for deployment to Germany; the move was made in July. At the same time, 60 B-29s of the 28th and 307th Bomb Groups deployed to Marham and Waddington in the United Kingdom.

*The McDonnell FH-1 Phantom was the first jet aircraft designed from the outset for carrier operations.*

**Above:**
*The North American B-45 Tornado, seen here using rocket-assisted take-off, was the first American multi-jet bomber to enter production.*

**Below:**
*The Lockheed P-80 Shooting Star, America's first operational jet fighter, gave sterling service for many years.*

**26 June** The first Convair B-36A strategic bomber (44-92004) was delivered to the 7th Bomb Group at Carswell AFB, Texas. The world's largest bomber, the B-36 was powered by six pusher piston engines; four podded J47 turbojets were later added.

**July** The MiG-15 jet fighter began to enter service with the Soviet Air Force. One of the most oustanding combat aircraft of the post-war years, the MiG-15 was produced in great numbers, some 18 000 being built.

**6 July** Two Spitfires of No. 60 Sqn RAF attacked and destroyed a communist terrorist camp in Perak, Malaya, with cannon and rocket projectiles. This was the first offensive mission of Operation *Firedog*, the RAF's contribution to the 12-year Malayan Emergency.

**19 July** SAC's first flight refuelling tanker units, the 43rd and 509th Air Refuelling Sqns, were activated at Davis-Monthan AFB, Arizona, and Roswell AFB, New Mexico. Assigned to the 43rd and 509th Bomb Groups, they were initially equipped with B-29s fitted with the British-designed probe-and-drogue flight refuelling apparatus.

**20 July** 16 Lockheed F-80 Shooting Stars of the 56th Fighter Group left Selfridge AFB, Michigan, and flew to Germany via Goose Bay, Greenland, Iceland and the UK as part of the American response to the Russian stance on Berlin. On 14 August, 75 more F-80s arrived in Britain aboard the carrier USS *Sicily*.

# 1949

*January* The 94th Sqn of the 1st Fighter Wing USAF began equipping with the North American F-86A Sabre, becoming the first unit to achieve operational capability with the type.

*February* The Bristol Brigand B. Mk 1 light bomber entered service with No. 84 Sqn RAF at Habbaniyah, Iraq. The type replaced Tempests and Beaufighters in the RAF's overseas squadrons.

*March* The McDonnell F2H Banshee naval fighter-bomber entered service with VF-51.

*March* The Yakovlev Yak-23 entered limited service with the Soviet Air Force; produced as an insurance against the failure of the MiG-15, it was exported to several Soviet bloc countries.

*May* The Grumman F9F Panther entered service with Navy Squadron VF-51, replacing the unit's F2H-1 Banshees.

*May* The Tupolev Tu-4 strategic bomber became fully operational with the *Dalnaya Aviatsiya*, Russia's long-range aviation. The Tu-4 was a copy of the Boeing B-29 some examples of which had made emergency landings on Russian territory in World War II.

*June* The Berlin Airlift began to run down with the lifting of the Soviet blockade of the city, although it continued to operate at a reduced rate until October. Between June 1948 and September 1949, 2 325 809 tons of supplies were flown into the besieged city, more than half the tonnage consisting of coal. In terms of effort, the USAF contributed 76.7 per cent, the RAF 17.0 per cent and British civil aircraft 6.3 per cent.

*9 August* Lieutenant J.L. Fruin of VF-171 made the first emergency use of an ejection seat in the United States, ejecting from an F2H-1 Banshee over South Carolina.

*September* First deliveries of the North American AJ-1 Savage carrier-borne attack bomber were made to Composite Sqn VC-5. The Savage was the

*The Grumman F9F Panther gradually replaced the Banshee in US Navy service.*

world's first heavy carrier-borne attack aircraft, and the first designed to carry nuclear weapons.

*October* The Lavochkin La-15 jet fighter entered limited service with the Soviet Air Force. The La-15 was designed to the same specification as the MiG-15 but was inferior to the Mikoyan aircraft in the fighter role, equipping only a few units.

*November* The Ilyushin Il-28 twin-jet light bomber began replacing the Tupolev Tu-2 in the Soviet Air Force's tactical aviation units (*Frontovaya Aviatsiya*).

# 1950

*26 March* Eight Avro Lincoln bombers of No. 57 Sqn, deployed from the UK to Tengah, Singapore, attacked a terrorist base in Negri Sembilan, Malaya, with 1000 lb (450 kg) bombs. This was the first of a series of regular three-month detachments to Malaya by Lincolns of RAF Bomber Command for anti-terrorist operations.

*8 April* A US Navy PB4Y Privateer patrol aircraft of VP-26, with ten crew on board, was shot down by Soviet fighters over the Baltic Sea.

*May* The Tupolev Tu-14 jet attack bomber began to enter service with Soviet Naval Aviation Units. The Tu-14 was designed to the same specification as the Il-28, but the latter was better suited to the land tactical role; the Tu-14's longer range made it suitable for development as a naval strike and reconnaissance aircraft.

*25 June* In support of the North Korean invasion of the Republic of Korea (South Korea), NKAF Yak-9 fighters strafed Kimpo and Seoul airfields.

*27 June* F-82 Twin Mustangs of the 68th and 339th Sqns, US Fifth Air Force, covering the evacuation of refugees by air from Kimpo and Seoul, destroyed three NKAF Yak-7 fighters attempting to interfere with the operation. An hour later, four NKAF Il-10s were also shot down by F-80s of the 35th Fighter-Bomber Sqn.

*28 June* Fifth Air Force B-26s and F-80s attacked North Korean troop concentrations and road and rail communications north of Seoul in the first successful strikes of the Korean War.

*28 June* The Martin P4M Mercator long-range maritime patrol aircraft entered service with Patrol Sqn VP-21.

*29 June* First deliveries of the Lockheed F-94A

all-weather jet fighter were made to the 319th All-Weather Fighter Sqn, Air Defense Command.

*30 June* 15 B-29s of the 19th Bomb Group joined B-26s and F-80s in attacks on North Korean forces, dropping 260 lb (118 kg) fragmentation bombs north of the Han River.

*3 July* Carrier aircraft went into action in Korea; the USS *Valley Forge*, with Air Group 5, and HMS *Triumph* (Seafire 47s and Fireflies) launched strikes on airfields, supply lines and transport in and around Pyongyang. This was the first combat test for Air Group 5's F9F Panthers and AD Skyraiders; the F9Fs of VF-51 shot down two Yak-9s.

*7–9 July* B-26s of the 3rd Bombardment Wing destroyed 197 trucks and 44 tanks in three days of operations in the area between Pyongtaek and Seoul.

*13 July* 50 B-29s of the 19th, 22nd and 92nd Bomb Groups attacked the North Korean port of Wonsan.

*3 August* Corsairs of Marine Fighter Sqn 214, operating from the escort carrier USS *Sicily* (CVE-118), carried out a rocket and incendiary bomb attack on Chinju. VMF-323 (USS *Badoeng Strait*) also began operations with the First Marine Aircraft Wing three days later.

*26 August* The first RB-45C jet reconnaissance aircraft was delivered to SAC's 91st Strategic Reconnaissance Wing at Barksdale AFB, Louisiana.

*September* The Northrop F-89 Scorpion all-weather interceptor entered service with Air Defense Command, the first F-89 units being assigned to Arctic defence zones.

*15 September* US carrier aircraft provided support for the landing of the First Marine Division at Inchon. HMS *Triumph*, operating with the Blockade and Covering Force, provided air cover for the assault forces en route.

*September–October* In an operation named *Fox Able Three*, the 27th Fighter-Escort Wing deployed 180 F-84E Thunderjet fighters from the USA to Europe. The operation was completed by 28 October.

*18 October* The first Grumman AF-2 Guardian anti-submarine warfare aircraft was delivered to Navy Sqn VS-25.

*20 October* Paratroops of the 187th Airborne Regimental Combat Team were dropped behind enemy lines north of Pyongyang by 71 C-119 and 40 C-47 transport aircraft. Tactical operations in the dropping zone were carried out by 75 F-51s, 62 F-80s and five B-26s. The US 1st Cavalry Division linked up with the paratroops on 23 October.

*The Lockheed F-94 Starfire was the USAF's first all-weather jet fighter.*

**1 November** United Nations aircrews operating near the Yalu River reported attacks by aircraft bearing Chinese Communist markings. Some of the enemy aircraft were MiG-15s, making their first appearance over Korea.

**7 November** F-80 Shooting Stars of the 51st Fighter Wing, escorting B-29s over North Korea, were engaged by MiG-15s in history's first jet-versus-jet battle. One MiG was shot down by Lieutenant Russell J. Brown.

**9 November** Strikes by US Navy aircraft on bridges crossing the Yalu River at Sinuiju were opposed by MiG-15s, one of which was shot down by Lieutenant Commander W.T. Amen of VF-111 in an F9F Panther. He was the first Navy pilot to destroy a jet aircraft.

**12 November** RAF Vampire FB.5 jet fighter-bombers began deploying to the Far East to re-equip squadrons in Malaya, Singapore and Hong Kong; this was the longest jet delivery flight (8500 miles/ 13 679 km) made by any air force to date.

**6 December** F-84Es of the 27th Fighter-Escort Wing flew their first combat mission from Taegu, Korea. 75 F-84Es had been transported to the theatre by aircraft carrier, the movement beginning on 8 November.

**10 December** The first Marine air squadron to operate jets in combat – VMF-311, F9F Panthers –

arrived at Yonpo and carried out interdiction missions for four days before joining the 35th Fighter-Interceptor Wing at Pusan East.

**17 December** F-86A Sabres of the 4th Fighter-Interceptor Wing, newly arrived in Korea and based at Kimpo, flew their first offensive sweep of the Korean War. They engaged four MiG-15s and one was shot down by Lieutenant Colonel Bruce H. Hinton – the first of 792 MiG-15s which would be claimed by Sabre pilots during the Korean War.

# 1951

**13 January** A B-29 of the 19th Bomb Group destroyed a major railway bridge at Kanggye with a direct hit by a 12 000 lb (5443 kg) radio-guided *Tarzon* bomb. Earlier operations with this weapon, in December 1950, had met with little success.

**23 January** The North Korean airfield of Sinuiju was heavily attacked by 33 F-84E Thunderjets. After the attack the Thunderjets were engaged by MiG-15s; the American pilots claimed four MiGs

destroyed, three probably destroyed and four damaged. The combat took place below 20 000 ft (6096 m), where the F-84 could out-turn the MiG.

*2 April* Two F9F-2B Panthers of VF-191, each carrying four 250 lb (113 kg) and two 100 lb (45 kg) general-purpose bombs, were catapulted from the USS *Princeton* to attack a rail bridge near Songjin. This was the first ground attack sortie flown by US Navy jets in Korea.

*5 April* The Avro Shackleton MR.1 maritime patrol aircraft entered service with No. 120 Sqn at RAF Kinloss, Scotland.

**Opposite:**
*The fighter that trounced Russia's MiGs over Korea: an F-86 Sabre streaks down the runway of a Korean airfield on returning from a mission to the Yalu River.*

**Opposite below:**
*F9F Panthers heading for a target in Korea. Note the rockets under the wing of the nearer aircraft.*

**Below:**
*Sweden's SAAB J-29 was the first swept-wing fighter of European design to enter service after World War II.*

*12 April* B-29s of the 19th, 98th and 307th Groups, attacking bridges at Sinuiju, were engaged by 70 MiG-15s. Three B-29s were destroyed and five badly damaged. B-29 operations in the Sinuiju area were temporarily suspended.

*14 April* By this date, USAF B-29s had destroyed 48 out of 60 bridges and 27 out of 39 marshalling yards assigned to them in North Korea at a cost of eight bombers destroyed.

*1 May* The SAAB J-29 jet fighter entered service with Royal Swedish Air Force Day Fighter Wing F13 at Norrköping. The J-29 was the first swept-wing fighter of European design to enter squadron service after World War II.

*1 May* In the first and only use of aerial torpedoes in the Korean War, eight Skyraiders and 12 Corsairs from the USS *Princeton* attacked and breached the Hwachon Dam, releasing flood waters to hamper the progress of enemy forces.

*25 May* The English Electric Canberra B.2 light jet bomber entered service with No. 101 Sqn at RAF Binbrook, Lincolnshire.

*31 May* United Nations air forces in Korea began Operation *Strangle*, using every means of interdiction in a bid to paralyse the enemy's transpor-

*The English Electric Canberra was Britain's first jet bomber, and remained in service in other roles into the 1990s.*

tation in the zone between the 39th Parallel and the front line. Up to the end of June the UN lost 81 fighter-bombers to ground fire on these operations, including 38 F-51 Mustangs.

**20 June** South Korean forces near Sinuiju were attacked by eight Il-10 fighter-bombers, the first time this type had been committed to action in Korea. Two were shot down and three damaged by Mustangs of the 18th Fighter-Bomber Group, which also destroyed an escorting Yak-9.

**30 June** A Po-2 night intruder biplane was shot down by a Grumman F7F Tigercat of Marine Sqn VMF-513, the type's first victory in Korea.

**6 July** A KB-29M tanker of the USAF Air Materiel Command, operating out of Yokota AB, Japan, conducted the first air refuelling operation over enemy territory under combat conditions, refuelling four RF-80 reconnaissance aircraft over North Korea.

**14 July** The first Boeing KC-97E (51-183) was delivered to the 306th Air Refueling Sqn at MacDill AFB, Florida. Fitted with the flying boom refuelling system, the KC-97 could fly fast enough to match the minimum speed of the B-47 bomber.

**30 July** No. 77 Sqn, RAAF, flew its first operational jet fighter sweep over Korea with 16 Gloster Meteor F.8 fighters. No contact was made with the enemy.

**August** The Supermarine Attacker, the Royal Navy's first operational jet fighter, entered service with No. 800 Sqn Fleet Air Arm at RNAS Ford, Sussex.

**23 August** The USS *Essex* joined Task Force 77 off the east coast of Korea and launched her aircraft in combat. On this strike, McDonnell F2H-2 Banshees of VF-172 went into action for the first time.

**25 August** 35 B-29s, escorted by 23 F9F Panthers and F2H Banshees from the USS *Essex*, dropped 291 tons of bombs on Rashin, close to the Siberian border, obliterating the town's marshalling yards. No aircraft was lost.

**30 August** 15 Sikorsky HRS-1 (S-55) helicopters of Marine Helicopter Transport Sqn 161, based at Pusan, began battlefield support operations in Korea, flying supplies to the 1st Marine Division in mountainous terrain.

**23 October** The first Boeing B-47 Stratojet bomber (50-008) was delivered to the 306th Bomb Wing at MacDill AFB, Florida.

Eight B-29s of the 307th Bomb Group, attacking the airfield at Namsi and escorted by 55

Thunderjets, were engaged by 50 MiG-15s. Three bombers were shot down and the rest were all heavily damaged.

*6 November* The Tupolev Tu-2 light bomber entered combat in Korea with an attack on the island of Taehwa-do in the Yellow Sea.

*30 November* 12 Tu-2s, escorted by 16 La-9s and 16 MiG-15s, were intercepted by 31 Sabres of the 4th Fighter-Interceptor Group. Eight Tu-2s, three La-9s and a MiG-15 were shot down – the biggest air combat success so far for the United Nations.

*1 December* F-86 Sabres of the 51st Fighter-Interceptor Wing began operations in Korea. This brought the total number of Sabres in the theatre to 127, with 40 more in reserve in Japan.

# 1952

*March* The Dassault MD450 *Ouragan*, the first jet fighter of French design to be produced in quantity, entered service with the *Armée de l'Air*.

*23 April* The Martin P5M-1 Marlin long-range maritime patrol aircraft entered service with Patrol Sqn VP-44.

*May* Following service trials, two squadrons of the 374th Wing, USAF, re-equipped with the Douglas C-124A Globemaster II heavy lift transport for operations between the United States, Japan and Korea.

*23 June* Four hydro-electric plants in North Korea were heavily bombed in a coordinated attack by Fifth Air Force and US Navy fighter-bombers. Two more attacks were made on 26 and 27 June. When they ended, nine-tenths of North Korea's hydro-electric system had been laid waste.

*July* The MiG-17 fighter began entering service with units of the Soviet Air Defence Forces (IA-PVO).

*15 July* 58 F-84G Thunderjets of the 31st Fighter-Escort Wing deployed from Turner AFB, Georgia, to Misawa and Chitose Air Bases, Japan, with the

*Bombs dropped by F-84 Thunderjets explode on a hydro-electric plant in North Korea.*

aid of flight refuelling by the KB-29 tankers of the 2nd and 91st Air Refueling Sqns. The F-84s crossed the Pacific from Travis AFB, California, to Hickam Field, Hawaii, and then island-hopped via Midway, Wake, Eniwetok, Guam and Iwo Jima. The operation took ten days to complete.

**25 July** The Lockheed WV-2 early warning and electronic reconnaissance aircraft, based on the Lockheed Constellation airliner, was delivered to USN Early Warning Sqn VW-2. USAF variants were the EC-121C and EC-121D.

**August** The de Havilland Venom FB.1 fighter-bomber began operational service trials with No. 11 Sqn at RAF Wunstorf, Germany.

**9 August** Lieutenant P. Carmichael, RN, flying a Sea Fury of No. 802 Sqn, HMS *Ocean*, became the first piston-engined pilot to destroy an enemy jet in the Korean War, shooting down a MiG-15. No. 802 Sqn claimed two MiG-15s destroyed, with three more damaged.

**November** The Grumman F9F-8 Cougar, a variant of the Panther with swept flying surfaces, entered service with VF-32.

**2 November** Marine Night Fighter Sqn VMF(N)-513 began operations over Korea with 12 Douglas F3D-2 Skynight jet fighters, one of which shot down a Yak-15 jet over Sinuiju on the night of 3/4 November.

# 1953

**January** The Avro Canada CF.100 all-weather fighter began operational trials with No. 445 Sqn, RCAF.

**18 January** A Lockheed P2V Neptune of Navy Sqn VP-22, on patrol over the Formosa Strait, was shot down off Swatow Island by Red Chinese AA fire with the loss of seven crew.

**16 February** No. 848 Sqn, RN, carried out its first operational trooplift operation with S-55 helicopters in Malaya. In the fortnight that followed, the squadron transported 1623 troops and 35 000 lb (15 876 kg) of stores in 415 sorties on anti-terrorist operations.

**10 March** Two Czech AF MiG-15s attacked two USAF F-84G Thunderjets near Regensburg, Bavaria, shooting one American aircraft down. The pilot ejected.

**12 March** Soviet fighter aircraft shot down an

Avro Lincoln bomber of the RAF Central Gunnery School in the Berlin air corridor with the loss of seven lives.

**25 April** The first Boeing RB-47 (51-2194) was delivered to the 91st Strategic Reconnaissance Wing, USAF, at Lockbourne AFB, Ohio.

**May** The Hawker Sea Hawk naval jet fighter-bomber became operational with No. 800 Sqn, Fleet Air Arm.

**13 May** 59 Thunderjets of the 58th Fighter-Bomber Wing carried out the first of a series of attacks on North Korea's irrigation dams, the last target system selected by the UN command before the armistice.

**4–6 June** 45 B-47s of the 306th Bomb Wing, together with KC-97s of the 306th ARS, deployed to the United Kingdom on a 90-day period of rotational training. This followed Exercise *Sky Try*, held earlier in the year, when the 306th BW was subjected to exhaustive tests under simulated combat conditions.

**22 July** Sabres of the 51st Wing met MiG-15s for the last time in the Korean War, shooting one down.

**27 July** An Ilyushin Il-12 transport was destroyed by Captain Ralph S. Parr of the 4th Fighter Wing – the last Communist aircraft to be shot down in the Korean War. The armistice came into effect at 10.01 p.m.

**29 July** A USAF RB-50 reconnaissance aircraft, operating out of Yokota AB, Japan, was shot down by MiG-15s 40 miles (64 km) off Vladivostock. One crew member survived.

**September** The Westland Wyvern turboprop-powered naval strike fighter entered service with No. 813 Sqn FAA, later embarking in HMS *Albion*.

# 1954

**1 January** The North American FJ-2 Fury (a navalized version of the F-86E Sabre) entered service with Marine Fighter Sqn VMF-122.

**13 February** The Supermarine Swift F.1, the first British swept-wing fighter to enter RAF service, was delivered to No. 56 Sqn at RAF Waterbeach, Cambridgeshire.

**March** The 345th Bomb Group (Tactical) began to re-equip with the Martin B-57B Canberra at Langley AFB, Virginia.

*The Hawker Sea Hawk was the Royal Navy's first effective jet fighter-bomber.*

**6 March** Communist Vietminh forces began the siege of the fortress of Dien Bien Phu, Indo-China. By 14 March, artillery fire had closed the principal airstrip; air support could now only come from distant air bases and the carrier *Arromanches* (F6F Hellcats and F8F Bearcats). Intense AA fire forced C-47 supply aircraft to drop their cargoes from 8000 to 10 000 ft (2440–3050 m) altitude, so that up to two-thirds of supplies fell into enemy hands. Enemy gun positions were bombed by Aéronavale PB4Y-2 Privateers, dropping cluster bombs supplied by the USA. The USAF provided C-124 transports to ferry troops from France to Indo-China, but a request for B-29 air strikes was refused. During the Vietminh offensive, which ended with the French surrender on 26 May, the French lost 48 aircraft shot down by AA, 16 destroyed on the ground and 167 damaged.

**April** The Chance-Vought F7U Cutlass naval strike fighter – the first production naval aircraft to achieve supersonic flight – entered service with VF-81.

**April** Marine Attack Sqn VMA-324 landed at Da Nang, Vietnam, and turned over its entire complement of 25 A-1 Skyraider dive-bombers to the French authorities for operations at Dien Bien Phu.

**May** The 407th Strategic Fighter Wing began re-equipping with the Republic F-84F Thunderstreak, the swept-wing version of the Thunderjet. The RF-84F was a tactical reconnaissance variant.

**26 July** Two AD Skyraiders of Air Group 5 from the USS *Philippine Sea*, searching for survivors of a Cathay airliner shot down three days earlier off Hainan Island, were atacked by two Chinese La-7 fighters. The Skyraider pilots returned fire and destroyed both attackers.

**29 July** The first Hawker Hunter F.1 fighter was delivered to No. 43 Sqn at RAF Leuchars, Scotland.

**August** The *Armée de l'Air* took delivery of the first Dassault *Mystère* IIC jet fighters.

**September** The first North American F-100 Super Sabre tactical fighter-bombers were delivered to the 479th Fighter Day Wing at George AFB,

**Left:**
*The Republic F-84F Thunderstreak was a swept-wing version of the Thunderjet. This aircraft is firing a salvo of high-velocity aircraft rockets (HVAR).*

California. The F-100 was the first operational aircraft to reach and sustain supersonic speed in level flight.

**4 September** A P2V Neptune of Patrol Squadron VP-19 was attacked by two MiGs and forced to ditch off the Siberian coast. Nine of the ten crew were rescued.

**October** Avro Lincoln aircraft of RAF Bomber Command carried out effective bombing operations against Mau Mau terrorist camps in Kenya.

**December** The Grumman SF2 Tracker anti-submarine warfare aircraft became fully operational with VS-23 on the USS *Princeton*.

# 1955

**January** The Fairey Gannet anti-submarine warfare aircraft became fully operational with No. 826 Sqn, FAA, at RNAS Lee-on-Solent.

**January** No. 232 Operational Conversion Unit at RAF Gaydon, Warwickshire, formed the nucleus of the first operational Vickers Valiant squadron, No. 138. The Valiant was the first of the RAF's 'V-bombers', and was initially armed with the 10 000 lb (4536 kg) MC Mk 1 *Blue Danube* free-fall nuclear weapon.

**4 April** For the first time, Canberra jet bombers (Mk 6s of No. 101 Sqn, deployed from RAF Binbrook) carried out anti-terrorist strikes in Malaya.

**May** The Dassault *Mystère* IV fighter-bomber entered service with the 12$^e$ *Escadre de Chasse*.

**May** The Myasishchev M-4 *Bison* strategic jet bomber entered service with the Soviet Air Force.

**1 June** The first Convair F-102A Delta Dagger all-weather interceptor was handed over to the USAF. Deliveries to squadrons began a year later.

**22 June** A P2V Neptune of Patrol Sqn VP-9 was attacked in the Aleutians area by two MiG-15s, which set fire to the starboard engine and forced the aircraft to crash-land on St Lawrence Island. There were no fatalities.

*Hawker Hunter F.1 fighters of No. 43 Sqn RAF – the first to equip with the type.*

**29 June** The first Boeing B-52 Stratofortress strategic bomber (52-8711) was delivered to the 93rd Bomb Wing at Castle AFB, California.

**July** The Royal Navy's first jet night-fighter, the de Havilland Sea Venom NF.20, became operational with No. 890 Sqn (HMS *Albion*).

**July** The SAAB A32 *Lansen* fighter/ground-attack aircraft entered service with Attack Wing F17, Royal Swedish Air Force.

**22 August** A US Navy FJ-3 Fury made the first deck landing with the aid of a mirror landing system installed on the USS *Bennington*. The first night landing using this system was made by an F9F-8 Cougar two days later.

**September** The MiG-19 *Farmer*, the first Russian aircraft capable of Mach One in level flight, entered service with the Soviet Air Defence Forces.

# 1956

**3 January** US Navy Airship Early Warning Sqn ZW-1 was commissioned at NAS Lakehurst – the first lighter-than-air unit of its type.

*Striking shot of a formation of SAAB A32 Lansen jet fighter-bombers of the Royal Swedish Air Force.*

**February** The Gloster Javelin FAW.1, the world's first twin-jet delta, entered service with No. 46 Sqn at RAF Odiham, Hampshire.

**7 March** The McDonnell F3H Demon naval interceptor became fully operational with US Navy Fighter Sqn VF-14.

**12 March** US Navy Attack Sqn 83, equipped with F7U-3M Cutlass aircraft armed with Sparrow air-to-air missiles, sailed for the Mediterranean aboard the USS *Intrepid* in the first overseas deployment of a US Navy missile-armed squadron.

**31 March** The Douglas A3D Skywarrior attack bomber became operational with US Navy Heavy Attack Sqn 1 at NAS Jacksonville.

**16 April** The Douglas F4D-1 Skyray naval fighter entered service with the US Navy and Marine Corps, the first unit to equip being VC-3. Because of its excellent rate of climb, the Skyray was also assigned to the North American Air Defense Command.

**31 May** The first RB-57D reconnaissance aircraft with increased wingspan for high-altitude operations was delivered to the 4080th Strategic Reconnaissance Wing at Turner AFB, Georgia.

*July* The Yakovlev Yak-25 *Flashlight*-A all-weather interceptor became operational with the Soviet Air Defence Forces.

*22 August* A Martin P4M Mercator, on night patrol off the Chinese coast, was shot down with the loss of all on board.

*27 September* The Douglas A4D-1 Skyhawk naval attack bomber became operational with Attack Sqn VA-27.

*October* The Tupolev Tu-95 *Bear* strategic turbo-prop-powered bomber became operational with the Soviet Long-Range Aviation.

*11 October* Vickers Valiant WZ366 of No. 49 Sqn made the first live drop of a *Blue Danube* nuclear weapon at Maralinga, South Australia.

*31 October* The Suez Crisis: Operation *Musketeer*. In response to the closure of the Suez Canal by the Egyptian Government, British and French aircraft began attacks on strategic targets in the Canal Zone. At the same time, Israeli forces in Sinai continued operations begun two days earlier, driving towards the Suez Canal with air support by Dassault Ouragans and F-51 Mustangs. Twelve Egyptian airfields in the Canal Zone and the Nile Delta were attacked by RAF Canberra and Valiant bombers.

*1 November* Airfield attacks continued with strikes by RAF Venom FB.4s, Royal Navy Wyverns, Sea Hawks and Sea Venoms, *Armée de l'Air* F-84F Thunderstreaks, and *Aéronavale* Corsairs. The air strikes continued until the morning of 4 November, by which time the Egyptian Air Force had either been eliminated or escaped in part to neighbouring countries, and attacks now concentrated on communications, transportation and strongpoints. On 5 November, key points in the Canal Zone were captured by Anglo-French airborne forces as a preliminary to a major seaborne assault. Offensive operations continued until 7 November, when a ceasefire was arranged. During the crisis, the USAF Strategic Air Command was brought to readiness in case of armed intervention by the Soviet Union.

*December* The Lockheed C-130 tactical transport aircraft entered service with the USAF. The C-130 was to become the most widely-used aircraft of its class in the western world, equipping the transport elements of some 60 air forces. More than 1900 had been built by 1992.

*The McDonnell F3H Demon interceptor became operational with the US Navy in March 1956.*

# 1957

*January* The first Avro Vulcan B.1 delta-wing bomber (XA895) was delivered to No. 230 Operational Conversion Unit, RAF Waddington, Lincolnshire.

*March* Strategic Air Command completed Operation *Try Out*, the first of three exercises to test the ground alert concept, whereby the Command maintained one-third of its effective strength in an armed alert condition at all times. The operation, involving two B-47 wings and two KC-97 air refuelling squadrons, was in response to Soviet ballistic missile developments.

*8 March* The Grumman F-11F Tiger air superiority fighter was delivered to Navy Fighter Sqn VA-156.

*25 March* The Chance-Vought F8U-1 Crusader naval strike fighter was delivered to Fighter Sqn VF-32 at Cecil Field, Florida.

*15 May* Vickers Valiant XD818 of No. 49 Sqn dropped the prototype *Yellow Sun* British thermonuclear weapon over Malden Island in the southwest Pacific in the first of a series of tests known as Operation *Grapple*. Three more tests were carried out in 1957.

*11 June* The first Lockheed U-2 high-altitude strategic reconnaissance aircraft was delivered to the 4080th Strategic Reconnaissance Wing, Laughlin AFB, Texas.

*28 June* The first KC-135 all-jet tanker (55-3127) was delivered to the 93rd Air Refueling Sqn, Castle AFB, California.

*July* Strategic Air Command began its *Reflex Action* alert system, deploying five B-47s from each of four Second Air Force Wings to overseas bases. This system was judged to be more effective than deploying entire wings on 90-day tours of temporary duty.

**Opposite top:**
*The Tupolev Tu-95 Bear, the world's only turboprop-powered strategic bomber. Photographs show the later maritime reconnaissance version.*

**Opposite:**
*The Avro Vulcan, the world's first delta-wing jet bomber and the second of the RAF's V-Bombers. The photograph shows the prototype, VX770, which was later destroyed in a crash at RAF Syerston in September 1958.*

*10 July* The first McDonnell F-101A Voodoo was delivered to the USAF Tactical Air Command.

*1 November* The Dassault *Super Mystère* B2 entered service with the *Armée de l'Air*, equipping the 10ᵉ and 12ᵉ *Escadres de Chasse*.

*28 November* The Handley Page Victor B.1, the third of the RAF's V-bombers, was delivered to No. 232 Operational Conversion Unit at Gaydon, Warwickshire.

*December* The Sud-Aviation S04050 *Vautour* light bomber entered service with the 92ᵉ *Escadre de Bombardement* (1/92 *Bourgogne* and 2/92 *Aquitaine*) at Bordeaux.

# 1958

*January* The Lockheed F-104A Starfighter interceptor entered service with the USAF Air Defense Command.

*May* The Canadair CL-28 Argus long-range maritime patrol aircraft entered service with No. 405 Sqn RCAF.

*June* The Supermarine Scimitar naval strike fighter entered service with No. 803 Sqn, Fleet Air Arm, at RNAS Lossiemouth, Scotland.

*August* The first production Republic F-105B Thunderchief strike fighter was delivered to the 335th Tactical Fighter Squadron, 4th Tactical Fighter Wing, at Eglin AFB, Florida.

*3 November* The first de Havilland Sea Vixen naval strike fighter was delivered to No. 700Y Trials Unit at RNAS Yeovilton; this was recommissioned in July 1959 as No. 892 Sqn.

# 1959

*February* The Fiat G.91 lightweight fighter-bomber began operational trials with the Italian Air Force's 103° *Gruppo*.

*13 February* The first Boeing B-52G, the most widely used variant of the Stratofortress, was delivered to the 5th Bomb Wing at Travis AFB, California. The B-52G was designed to carry two nuclear-armed *Hound Dog* air-to-surface missiles.

*26 March* The Breguet *Alizé* naval anti-submarine warfare aircraft entered service with *Flotille* 6F (operational training unit) at Nîmes–Garons.

June The Convair F-106 Delta Dart all-weather interceptor entered service with the 539th Fighter Interceptor Sqn, USAF Air Defense Command.

16 June A Martin P4M Mercator, on patrol off Korea, was attacked by two MiG-15s. The pilot of the badly damaged aircraft made a successful emergency landing at Miho, Japan, with one crew member wounded.

19 June The ZPG-3W, first of four airships designed for airborne early warning patrol and the largest non-rigid ever built, was delivered to NAS Lakehurst.

August The Sukhoi Su-9 Fishpot all-weather interceptor entered service with the Soviet Air Defence Forces. The Su-11, first seen in 1967, was an improved version.

23 December The first Hound Dog nuclear-armed air-to-surface missile was delivered to the 4135th Strategic Wing, Eglin AFB, Florida.

# 1960

February The SAAB J35A Draken interceptor entered service with the Royal Swedish Air Force.

April The MiG-21F, the first major production version of this interceptor, entered service with the Soviet Air Defence Forces.

The Republic F-105 Thunderchief fighter-bomber was designed to give the USAF Tactical Air Command a formidable nuclear strike capability.

1 May A Lockheed U-2B, under the control of the US Central Intelligence Agency and flown by Captain Francis G. Powers, was shot down near Sverdlovsk in the USSR by an SA-2 Guideline surface-to-air missile battery. U-2s had been carrying out photographic reconnaissance missions over the Soviet Union since 1957.

1 July Strategic Air Command began trials with an Airborne Command Post system at Offutt AFB, Nebraska. Five KC-135s, specially modified as command posts and manned by a team of communications experts under the command of a SAC general officer, were alternately kept on ground alert and ready to take off within 15 minutes of an attack warning being received.

1 July A Boeing RB-47E reconnaissance aircraft was shot down over the Barents Sea by a MiG-19 interceptor. Two of the four crew members were picked up and later repatriated.

30 July The English Electric (BAC) Lightning F.1 interceptor entered service with No. 74(F) Sqn at RAF Coltishall, Norfolk.

1 August The first operational Convair B-58 Hustler medium bomber was delivered to the 43rd Bomb Wing at Carswell AFB, Texas. The B-58 was America's first supersonic bomber.

# 1961

**18 January** HQ SAC announced that the Command had completed a phase of airborne alert training, and that from now on a proportion of the B-52 and tanker force would be on continuous airborne alert as an insurance against missile attack.

**1 February** The Ballistic Missile Early Warning System (BMEWS) site at Thule, Greenland, became operational, providing SAC with sufficient warning time to launch its aircraft before enemy missiles reached US bases.

**3 February** The SAC airborne command post, or *Looking Glass* as it was later called, began continuous operation after an exhaustive test programme.

**9 May** The first Boeing B-52H was delivered to the 379th Bomb Wing at Wurtsmith AFB, Michigan. The B-52H was fitted with a defensive Gatling gun firing 20 mm shells at 4000 rounds per minute.

**16 June** The North American A-5 Vigilante supersonic naval attack bomber was delivered to Heavy Attack Sqn 7 at Sanford, Florida.

**1 July** The Grumman OV-1 Mohawk battlefield surveillance aircraft was deployed with units of the US Seventh Army in Germany.

**September** The Yakovlev Yak-28 *Brewer* light tactical bomber entered service with units of the Soviet Frontal Aviation, replacing the Il-28.

**October** The Dassault *Mirage* IIIC multi-role combat aircraft entered service with *Escadre de Chasse* EC 2 *Cigognes* at Dijon.

**13 November** The US President authorized the deployment of three US Army H-21 helicopter companies (40 aircraft) and a squadron of 16 Fairchild C-123 assault transport aircraft to Vietnam. RF-101 Voodoo detachments had been flying photo-reconnaissance missions over Vietnam and Laos since 20 October.

*When it entered service in 1960, the RAF's Lightning F.Mk 1 was probably the world's best fighter, although it suffered from a limited combat radius – later increased by flight refuelling. Here, four Lightning F.6 aircraft formate on a Vulcan B.2 bomber.*

*A Blackburn (Hawker Siddeley) Buccaneer of the Royal Navy pictured over Trafalgar Square. Many of the Navy's Buccaneers were later modified for RAF use in the low-level strike role.*

# 1962

**January** A detachment of US advisers began training Vietnamese pilots to fly T-28 Trojan ground-attack aircraft supplied by the US to the VNAF 2nd Fighter Sqn. The US training commitment was code-named *Farm Gate*.

**18 January** The Dassault *Etendard* IV naval strike fighter entered service with the *Aéronavale*'s *Flotille* 15F.

**2 February** A USAF C-123 transport crashed during a test defoliation spray flight near Bien Hoa; this was the first USAF aircraft lost in Vietnam. The crew of three were killed.

**22 March** Four Convair F-102 interceptors, deployed to Tan Son Nut from Clark AFB in the Philippines, began operations over South Vietnam following reports that unidentified low-flying aircraft had been sighted over the Central Highlands. No suspect aircraft were encountered.

**April** The Tupolev Tu-22 *Blinder* supersonic bomber entered service with the Soviet Air Forces.

*May* The Tupolev Tu-28 *Fiddler* long-range interceptor, developed as a counter to SAC B-52s armed with the *Hound Dog* missile, entered service with the Soviet Air Defence Forces.

*17 July* The Blackburn (Hawker Siddeley) Buccaneer S.Mk 1 low-level strike aircraft became operational with No. 801 Sqn, HMS *Ark Royal*.

*August* The first Lockheed P-3A Orion long-range maritime patrol aircraft was delivered to US Navy Patrol Sqn VP-8.

*October* The Cuban Missile Crisis. On 14 October, a CIA Lockheed U-2 obtained the first photographic evidence that Soviet SS-4 *Sandal* intermediate-range ballistic missiles were being installed in Cuba. Further intelligence was assembled in the following days by U-2s of the 4080th Strategic Wing. On 22 October, the day that President John F. Kennedy announced an arms quarantine against Russian shipments destined for Cuba and demanded the removal of the missiles already there, SAC battle staffs were placed on 24-hour alert duty, the B-47 force was dispersed, and the B-52 force went on actual airborne alert. All bombers and missiles were armed with nuclear weapons. On 25 October, with the arms quarantine in effect, SAC RB-47s and KC-97s joined other forces in the massive air-sea search for Soviet ships bound for Cuba. On 27 October, an RB-47 of the 55th Strategic Reconnaissance Wing crashed on take-off from Kindley AFB, Bermuda, with the loss of all four crew, and on the same day a U-2 was shot down over Cuba by an SA-2 missile, the pilot being killed. On 28 November, the Soviet Government agreed to remove its offensive missiles from Cuba.

# 1963

*2 January* The entire USAF and VNAF force at Bien Hoa was committed to Operation *Burning Arrow*, an hour-long air strike against Vietcong targets in the Tay Ninh area. The strike was followed by air drops and a trooplift by H-21 helicopters.

*February* The Hawker Siddeley *Blue Steel* stand-off nuclear air-to-surface missile became operational with the Vulcan B.2s of No. 617 Sqn, RAF Scampton. *Blue Steel* had been intended as an interim weapon until the RAF V-Force equipped with the US *Skybolt* intermediate-range air-launched missile, but this was cancelled in December 1962.

*1 February* The Grumman A-6 Intruder naval attack bomber became operational with US Navy Sqn VA-42.

*8 May* The USAF announced that two squadrons of A-1E Skyraiders would be added to the 1st Air Commando Group at Hurlburt AFB, Florida. The intention was that 75 Skyraiders would be sent to Vietnam as replacements for B-26 and T-28 aircraft, which was suffering combat and attrition losses.

*13 June* US Navy F-4A Phantom and F8D Crusader aircraft made the first fully automatic carrier landings with production equipment on board the USS *Midway*.

*The Grumman A-6 Intruder proved a highly effective naval attack aircraft, able to operate at night and in all weather conditions.*

# 1964

*January* The Army of the Republic of Vietnam (ARVN) launched the biggest helicopter operation so far undertaken in South Vietnam, airlifting 1100 troops with 115 helicopters.

*April* The first Northrop F-5 tactical strike fighter was delivered to the USAF Tactical Air Command.

*June* The first Martin RB-57F, final reconnaissance

version of the US-built Canberra, was delivered to the 58th Weather Reconnaissance Squadron.

*9 June* SAC tankers were used to support combat operations in South-East Asia for the first time: four KC-135s, operating out of Clark AFB in the Philippines, refuelled eight F-100s en route to attack Pathet Lao AA emplacements on the Plain of Jars in northern Laos.

*5 August* In response to earlier attacks on US Navy warships by North Vietnamese torpedo boats, 64 A-1, A-4, F-4 and F-8 strike aircraft from the Seventh Fleet carriers *Ticonderoga* and *Constellation* attacked four North Vietnamese torpedo boat bases and oil storage facilities. Ten POL tanks were destroyed, together with eight torpedo boats. An A-1 and an A-4 were shot down by AAA.

*September* The Dassault *Mirage* IVA supersonic tactical and strategic bomber was delivered to 91ᵉ *Escadre de Bombardement*. Sixty *Mirage* IVs were eventually delivered, equipping three *Escadres* to form France's airborne nuclear striking force.

*Northrop F-5 Tigers in formation. The aircraft shown are F-5Es, used by the USAF to simulate Soviet MiG-21s in air combat training. The idea was born in the Vietnam War.*

*1 November* Viet Cong forces shelled Bien Hoa airfield with 81 mm mortars, destroying five B-57s and damaging 15 more.

*9–10 December* VNAF and USAF A-1H and A-1E Skyraiders inflicted more than 400 Viet Cong casualties during air strikes in Quang Tin and Binh Din provinces.

# 1965

*January* The 4252nd Strategic Wing, SAC, was activated at Kadena Air Base, Okinawa, to provide KC-135 air refuelling for Pacific Air Forces'

fighter-bombers engaged in air operations over Vietnam.

**7 February** In response to a Viet Cong attack on US bases in South Vietnam, aircraft of US Navy Task Force 77 (USS *Hancock*, USS *Coral Sea* and USS *Ranger*) launched 83 sorties against North Vietnamese Army barracks and port facilities (Operation *Flaming Dart*). One A-4E was lost and eight damaged.

**11 February** 99 aircraft were launched by the three carriers of TF77 to attack NVA barracks. Three aircraft were lost and several others damaged.

**19 February** First use of USAF jet aircraft in Vietnam: 24 B-57s attacked the Viet Cong 9th Division's base camp near the Cambodian border.

**2 March** 25 F-105s and 20 B-57s attacked an NVA ammunition depot 35 miles (56 km) into North Vietnam, causing heavy damage. Air strikes on the north were now called *Rolling Thunder* operations.

**18 March** Aircraft of Task Force 77 attacked supply depots in North Vietnam.

**26 March** 70 A-4s and F-8s of Task Force 77 attacked four North Vietnamese radar sites, causing heavy damage. One A-4 and one F-8 were lost; the pilots were rescued.

**29 March** 70 aircraft of Task Force 77 attacked radar and communications facilities in North Vietnam. Three aircraft were shot down, two pilots being rescued.

**3 April** Two B-57s, accompanied by a flare-dropping C-130, carried out the first night interdiction mission against enemy forces moving down the Ho Chi Minh Trail towards South Vietnam and Cambodia (Operation *Steel Tiger*).

**5 April** An RF-8 Crusader from the USS *Coral Sea* detected a surface-to-air missile site under construction 15 miles (24 km) south-east of Hanoi. By the end of 1965, air reconnaissance had pinpointed 56 SA-2 missile sites in North Vietnam.

**10 April** Marine Composite Reconnaissance Sqn One (VMCJ-1) deployed to Da Nang with EF-10B Skynight electronic warfare aircraft.

**11 April** Marine Fighter/Attack Sqn VMFA-531 deployed to Da Nang with 15 F-4B Phantoms.

**18 April** For the first time, SAC B-52s operating from Guam attacked a target in Vietnam – a suspected Communist troop base area north of Saigon. The attack was unsuccessful.

**22 May** USAF F-105s attacked an NVA barracks in North Vietnam, the first attack above the 20th Parallel.

**17 June** Two F-4 Phantoms of VF-21, USS *Midway*, destroyed two MiG-17s with Sparrow AAMs, the US Navy's first victories over North Vietnam.

**18 June** 27 B-52F bombers of the 7th and 320th Bomb Wings, Guam, attacked a Viet Cong assembly area with 770 and 1000 lb (450 kg) bombs. The attack was not a success. Missions of this kind were code-named *Arc Light*.

*The McDonnell F-4 Phantom was widely used in Vietnam and was the mainstay of many NATO air forces. This one is shown in* Luftwaffe *markings.*

**20 June** Four A-1 Skyraiders of VA-125, USS *Midway*, were bounced by two MiG-17s while on a rescue combat air patrol mission. The A-1s out-manoeuvred their opponents and shot down one MiG.

**10 July** Two MiG-17s were shot down over North Vietnam by two F-4C Phantoms of the 45th Tactical Fighter Sqn, the USAF's first victories in the war.

**23 July** The first American aircraft, an F-4C Phantom, was shot down by an SA-2 missile over North Vietnam.

**27 July** USAF fighter-bombers (F-105 Thunderchiefs) carried out the first strikes in history against surface-to-air missile sites. The attacks were supported by six EF-10Bs and no aircraft were lost.

**11/12 August** An A-4E of VA-23, USS *Midway*, was destroyed by an SA-2 missile and a second damaged in the explosion during a night sortie. In response, on 12 and 13 August, the USN flew 76 missions to find and destroy the SAM sites. No sites were found; five aircraft were shot down and seven damaged by AAA.

**1 September** Hostilities broke out between India and Pakistan. The conflict, which lasted until 22 September, saw considerable air fighting between Pakistan Air Force F-86F Sabres and Indian Air Force Hunters and Gnats. Ground-attack operations were carried out by IAF *Mystère* IVAs, Vampires, *Ouragans* and Canberras, the latter also attacking strategic targets in Pakistan.

**October** The first of five F-100 fighter-bomber squadrons was deployed to Bien Hoa and Da Nang for tactical support operations.

**November** F-4C Phantoms of the 12th Tactical Fighter Wing were deployed to Cam Ranh Bay, and AC-47 gunships were deployed to Tan Son Nhut on an experimental basis.

**10 December** The first Breguet *Atlantic* long-range maritime patrol aircraft was delivered to the *Aéronavale*. The type equipped *Flottilles* 21F, 22F and 24F.

**22 December** The carriers *Enterprise, Kitty Hawk* and *Ticonderoga* launched over 100 aircraft in a combined strike against the Uong Bi thermal power plant near Haiphong, the first industrial target attacked in North Vietnam. The plant was badly damaged and two A-4s were lost.

During December, modifications to SAC's B-52D fleet to increase the aircraft's capacity from 27 to 84 500 lb (12–38 330 kg) bombs, or from 27 to 42 750

lb (12–19 390 kg) bombs. In addition, the B-52D could carry 24 500 lb (11 113 kg) or 750 lb (340 kg) bombs externally, giving it a maximum bomb load of 30 tons.

# 1966

**January** The Boeing-Vertol CH-47 Chinook helicopter became operational in Vietnam with the 133rd Assault Support Helicopter Company, supporting ground operations by the 1st Cavalry Division.

**7 January** The first Lockheed SR-71 high-altitude reconnaissance aircraft, capable of Mach 3 at altitudes over 80 000 ft (24 380 m), was delivered to the 4200th Strategic Reconnaissance Wing at Beale AFB, California.

**17 January** A SAC B-52 on airborne alert collided with a KC-135 tanker near Palomares, Spain. Two thermonuclear weapons were released and their high-explosive components detonated on impact, releasing radioactive material. A third weapon was recovered under 2500 ft (762 m) of water 5 miles (8 km) offshore after a massive search operation.

**February** During operations in support of the 1st Cavalry Division (Operation *Masher White*) a Sikorsky CH-54 Skycrane heavy lift helicopter made an operational lift of the 155 mm howitzer for the first time.

**11 February** The last two B-47E bombers in service with SAC were retired and placed in storage at Davis-Monthan AFB, Arizona.

**10 March** A-1Es of the 1st Air Commando Sqn carried out 210 air strikes against NVA forces attacking a Special Forces' camp in the A Shau Valley, killing 500 enemy troops. During the day's action Major Bernard C. Fisher became the USAF's first Medal of Honor recipient in SE Asia when he landed under fire to rescue a shot-down pilot.

**11 April** B-52s went into action for the first time over North Vietnam, making a strike against NVA forces near Mu Gia pass.

**18 April** Two A-6A Intruders of VA-85, USS *Kitty Hawk*, carried out a successful night attack with 26 1000 lb (450 kg) bombs on the Uong Bi thermal power plant near Haiphong.

**16 June** A-4 Skyhawks and F-8 Crusaders from the USS *Hancock* carried out the first carrier strikes on North Vietnamese petroleum facilities since 1964

*The Vought (LTV) A-7 Corsair II. These aircraft belong to US Navy Squadron VA-27.*

in the first phase of a renewed campaign against these targets.

**20 July** The USAF and Marines launched a new campaign (*Tally Ho*) against NVA infiltration routes. The offensive reached a peak of 12 000 sorties in September.

**3 September** For the first time, US pilots encountered substantial numbers of MiG-21 fighters over North Vietnam. Operating from five bases in the Hanoi area, which could not be attacked, the MiGs forced the USAF's F-4C Phantoms to divert from their primary strike mission in order to fly counter-air operations. During 1966, US fighters shot down 23 MiGs (17 credited to the USAF) for the loss of nine aircraft.

**October** The LTV (Vought) A-7 Corsair II naval attack aircraft entered service with Attack Sqn VA-174.

**October** During a nine-day battle against regular NVA forces in the Suoi Da area, tactical aircraft flew 2500 sorties, including 487 immediate request for close air support. B-52s also flew 225 sorties. In addition, 3300 tactical airlift sorties delivered 8900 tons of cargo and airlifted 11 400 men.

**November** The EA-6A Prowler tactical electronic warfare aircraft became operational in Vietnam, primarily for countermeasures operations against the growing number of North Vietnamese SAMs.

# 1967

**2 January** MiG-21s came up in strength to intercept what appeared to be a normal *Rolling Thunder* strike by F-105s. It was a trap; the North Vietnamese pilots were engaged by F-4 Phantoms of the 8th Tactical Fighter Wing and, in the biggest air battle over Vietnam to date, seven were destroyed for no loss.

**22 February** The 2nd Battalion, 503rd US Infantry, carried out the first parachute assault in Vietnam (and the first US operation of this kind since the Korean War), jumping from C-130s to attack enemy bases north of Tay Ninh City. This marked the start of an 83-day operation named *Junction City Alternate*, during which tactical aircraft flew 5000 sorties and B-52s 125.

**26 February** Seven A-6A Intruders from the USS *Enterprise* laid mines in the mouths of the Song Ca and South Giang rivers, the first operation of this kind in Vietnam. The mines were dropped at very low altitude.

**10–11 March** F-105s and F-4Cs attacked the Thai Nguyen iron and steel works, about 30 miles (50 km) from Hanoi, disrupting – but not halting – pig iron and steel production. For the first time, USAF aircraft also attacked the *Canal des Rapides* road and rail bridge, 4 miles (6 km) north of Hanoi.

**11 March** A-4 Skyhawks of Attack Sqn VA-212, USS *Bon Homme Richard*, attacked an NVA military barracks at Sam Son with the *Walleye* TV-guided air-to-surface glide bomb, the first use of this weapon in Vietnam.

**April** B-52s began operations from U-Tapao Airfield, Thailand, under the control of the 4258th Strategic Wing. The B-52s could now carry out missions over Vietnam without flight refuelling.

**24 April** Aircraft of Task Force 77 launched their first strikes against fighter bases in North Vietnam with an attack on Kep airfield, 37 miles (60 km) northeast of Hanoi. The attack was delivered by A-6 Intruders and A-4 Skyhawks from the USS *Kitty Hawk* and was followed up by another A-6 attack that night. Two MiG-17s were destroyed by escorting F-4B Phantoms of VF-114.

**May** The Tupolev Tu-126 *Moss* early warning aircraft, developed from the Tu-114 civil airliner, entered service with the Soviet Air Defence Forces.

**19 May** The Hanoi Therman Power Plant was hit by Attack Sqn 212, USS *Bon Homme Richard*, with F-8E Crusaders of VF-24 flying escort and flak suppression. Two F-8s and one MiG-17 were shot down during the attack, and three more MiG-17s were destroyed by F-8s in an air battle south-west of Hanoi.

**1 June** The 522nd Fighter Sqn, Republic of Vietnam AF, began operations with Northrop F-5 jet fighter-bombers.

**5 June** The Arab-Israeli War. In the first of a series of pre-emptive strikes designed to neutralize the air power of Egypt and her allies, Israeli Air Force combat aircraft (*Mirage* IIIs and *Vautours*) carried out heavy dawn attacks on Egyptian airfields in Sinai and the Suez Canal Zone. Airfields in Jordan, Syria and Iraq were also attacked. By the end of the day the IAF had flown about 1000 sorties for

the loss of 20 aircraft, all but one (a *Vautour*) to ground fire. Arab losses totalled 308 aircraft, of which 240 were Egyptian; 30 were destroyed in air combat. Ground operations in Sinai, on the Golan Heights and the West Bank of the Jordan were supported by Fouga *Magisters*, *Ouragans*, *Mystère* IVAs and *Super Mystère* B.2s. By the time a UN ceasefire was imposed on 10 June, the Arab air forces had lost 353 aircraft, about 43 per cent of their effective strength, and the Israeli Air Force 31 aircraft, just over ten per cent of its effective strength. As a demonstration of offensive air power, properly executed, the 'Six-Day War' was unsurpassed.

**21 July** In a fierce air battle between *Bon Homme Richard*'s Carrier Air Wing 21, attacking a petroleum storage area at Ta Xa, and MiG-17s, three MiGs were destroyed and one probably destroyed by escorting F-8s.

**August** The MiG-25 *Foxbat* interceptor, intended to counter a potential threat from a new generation of American supersonic strategic bombers, entered service with the Soviet Air Defence Forces.

**21 August** US pilots attacking targets in North Vietnam counted 80 SA-2 surface-to-air missile launches, a record for a single day in the war. In all, 249 SAMs were counted by pilots during August. 16 US aircraft were lost, ten to enemy fighters and AAA and six to SAMs.

**30 August** 24 strike aircraft from the USS *Oriskany* destroyed the Haiphong highway bridge southeast of the city. In the two weeks that followed, road and rail links to Haiphong were repeatedly cut by air attack.

**1 September** The Bell AH-1G HueyCobra helicopter gunship began operations in Vietnam with the 1st Aviation Brigade, US Army.

**30 October** An A-6A Intruder of VA-196, USS *Constellation* (Lieutenant Commander Charles B. Hunter and Lieutenant Lyle F. Bull) completed one of the most difficult single combat sorties in the history of air warfare, a low-level night attack with 18 500 lb (227 kg) bombs on the Hanoi railroad ferry slip. The crew successfully evaded 16 SAMs and intense AAA fire to hit their target.

**October** The first General Dynamics F-111A variable-geometry tactical strike aircraft were delivered to the 4480th Tactical Fighter Wing at Nellis AFB, Nevada.

**3 December** The USS *Ranger* joined Task Force 77 off Vietnam, bringing two new aircraft types: the A-7A Corsair II (VA-147) and the EKA-3B Tacos, the latter an electronic warfare version of the A-3 Skywarrior.

**18 December** USAF transport aircraft completed the airlift of the 101st Airborne Division to Vietnam. The move had required 369 missions by C-141 Starlifters and 22 by C-133 Cargomasters, ultimately lifting 10 024 troops and 5300 tons of the Division's essential equipment. This was the largest and longest airlift ever attempted into a combat zone.

# 1968

**12 January** The Allied strongpoint Lima Site 85, isolated on a 5200 ft (1585 m) mountain in Laos, 160 miles (258 km) west of Hanoi, was attacked by three Antonov An-2 *Colt* biplanes of the NVAF, their crews firing machine guns from the windows. One An-2 crashed during a strafing attack and a second was shot down by an AH-1G Cobra helicopter, which also drove off the third An-2 and forced it down 18 miles (30 km) from the site. Lima Site 85, which contained an all-weather navigational system, was later captured by NVA forces.

**21 January** NVA forces unleashed heavy attacks on the US Marine base at Ke Sanh. In two and a half months, 24 000 tactical and 2700 B-52 sorties were flown in defence of this strategic position (Operation *Niagara*), and 110 000 tons of ordnance were dropped.

**22 January** A B-52G with four nuclear weapons on board crashed and burned on the ice of North Star Bay while attempting an emergency landing at Thule Air Base, Greenland. The massive operation to clean up radioactive debris lasted until 13 September.

**30 April** Royal Air Force Bomber and Fighter Commands merged to become RAF Strike Command. On 28 November, Coastal Command also merged with Strike Command to become No. 18 (Maritime) Group.

**May** The Hindustan HF-24 *Marut* (Wind Spirit) tactical fighter, India's first indigenous jet combat aircraft, entered service. The type equipped Nos. 10, 31 and 220 Sqns IAF.

**July** The Sukhoi Su-15 all-weather interceptor (*Flagon*) entered service with the Soviet Air Defence Forces.

**31 October** Following talks in Paris, the US Presi-

dent called a halt to the bombing of North Vietnam, bringing to an end three years and nine months of *Rolling Thunder* operations. During that time, US aircraft had flown 304 000 fighter-bomber and 2380 B-52 sorties, dropping 643 000 tons of bombs on North Vietnam's war industry, transportation network and air defence complex. The last attack of *Rolling Thunder* was made against a target near Dong Hoi by an F-4D Phantom of the 8th Tactical Fighter Wing (Major Frank C. Lenahan).

# 1969

**1 April** The Hawker Siddeley Harrier GR.1 short take-off/vertical landing strike aircraft entered service with No. 233 OCU, RAF Wittering. On 1 October, No. 1 Sqn also equipped with this, the world's first operational STOVL aircraft.

**14 April** North Korean aircraft shot down a US Navy EC-121 electronic surveillance aircraft over the Sea of Japan, killing all 31 crew. The US response was to activate Task Force 71, initially with four carriers and cruiser and destroyer screens, to protect such flights over international waters.

**30 June** Vulcan B.2 bombers of the V-Force, which, together with the Victor, had maintained Quick Reaction Alert for 12 years, now relinquished the QRA role. The responsibility for Britain's strategic nuclear deterrent passed to the *Polaris* missile submarines of the Royal Navy.

**2 October** The Hawker Siddeley Nimrod long-range maritime patrol aircraft was delivered to No. 236 Operational Conversion Unit at RAF St Mawgan, Cornwall.

**8 October** The first General Dynamics FB-111A, the strategic bomber variant of the F-111, was delivered to the 340th Bomb Group at Carswell AFB, Texas.

# 1970

**7 January**
In conjunction with commando raids on Egyptian radar installations and SAM sites in the Gulf of Suez, Israeli Air Force Phantoms and *Mirages* carried out a deep-penetration attack on the Egyptian Air Force supply depot at Al Khanka, near

Cairo. Eight more attacks were carried out on targets in the Cairo area during the following month. The IAF lost nine aircraft, bringing its total losses since the Six-Day War to 17. During January, Israeli fighters claimed the destruction of four Egyptian and 17 Syrian aircraft, mostly MiG-21s. During the months that followed, Egyptian aircraft – usually Su-7s – made regular incursions into Sinai, while Israeli aircraft struck at new SAM sites on the west bank of the Suez Canal.

**March** The Sukhoi Su-17 *Fitter-B* variable geometry version of the Su-7 entered service with the Soviet Air Forces. The export version of this type was designated Su-20/22.

**18 March** In conjunction with a US/South Vietnamese thrust into Cambodia to engage North Vietnamese forces there, B-52 bombers began a series of night sorties against Cambodian targets. Between this day and 26 May 1970, the B-52s flew 4308 sorties and dropped 120 578 tons of bombs on enemy base camps. The ground operation ended in June, the Allied forces having killed more than 11 000 enemy and captured massive quantities of arms and ammunition. During the first four days in May, the operation was supported by intensive tactical air strikes by 500 USAF and USN aircraft.

**21 November** Under cover of heavy diversionary air attacks, US Special Forces flew 400 miles (645

*The short take-off, vertical landing (STOVL) Hawker Siddeley Harrier represented one of the most significant advances in the history of military aviation. The aircraft shown are Harrier GR.3s, fitted with laser rangefinding equipment in the nose.*

km) from bases in Thailand to Son Tay, 20 miles (32 km) NW of Hanoi, in HH-53 helicopters in an attempt to rescue American PoWs believed imprisoned in a compound there. The helicopters were supported by A-1E Skyraiders and specially-equipped C-130 Hercules aircraft. In the event, no prisoners were found. The Americans killed 25 Vietnamese and suffered no casualties.

**21/22 November** In response to attacks on US reconnaissance aircraft, 200 US aircraft carried out air strikes against North Vietnamese SAM and AAA sites south of the 19th Parallel.

# 1971

**February** The USAF launched Operation *Slugger* in North Vietnam. In 67 sorties, strike aircraft destroyed five SAM sites, 15 SAM missile transporters, and 15 vehicles in the Ban Karai pass area.

**21–22 March** USAF and USN aircraft flew 234

strike and 20 armed reconnaissance sorties against enemy SAM sites.

**April** The *Mirage* 5 multi-role combat aircraft began to equip squadrons of the Belgian Air Force, replacing F-84F Thunderstreaks. The *Mirage* 5 was intended solely for export and eventually served with the air forces of 20 countries.

**June** The SAAB 37 *Viggen* multi-role combat aircraft entered service with F7 Wing, Royal Swedish Air Force.

**August** In an attempt to restrict enemy road construction across the Demilitarized Zone into South Vietnam, USAF jets flew 473 sorties, seeding the road with munitions and sensors.

**21 September** 196 US tactical aircraft, flying in poor weather, hit three POL storage areas south of Dong Hoi, destroying about 350 000 gallons of fuel. This was the first all-instrument air strike of the Vietnam War, carried out with the aid of the long-range electronic navigation position-fixing bomb system (LORAN).

**7–8 November** USAF and USN aircraft carried out heavy attacks to neutralize the North Vietnamese airfields of Dong Hoi, Vinh and Quan Lang.

**3–15 December** The Indo-Pakistan War. This conflict, which stemmed from the declaration of independence by East Pakistan (Bangladesh), began with attacks on Indian Air Force forward bases by Pakistan Air Force F-86F Sabres. The IAF retaliated with raids on PakAF bases by Hunter F.6s, Canberra B.66s, Sukhoi Su-7s and HF-24s. For air defence, the PakAF had 17 *Mirage* IIIEs, MiG-19s (supplied by China) and Canadair Sabre Mk 6s. On 5 December, the IAF switched its attacks to Pakistani troop concentrations and artillery positions in Kashmir, while on the eastern front MiG-21s, Hunters and Su-7s attacked airfields in the Dacca area. Targets in East Pakistan were also attacked by Seahawks operating from the carrier *Vikrant* in the Bay of Bengal. On 6 December, oil refineries at Karachi and Attock were attacked by rocket-firing Hunters, causing severe damage. By 7 December, the emphasis had switched firmly to ground support operations, with attacks on armour, rolling stock in the rear areas and troop concentrations, and on 9 December, IAF Canberras, *Mystère* IVAs, Su-7s, MiG-21s and

*Sweden's SAAB 37* Viggen *(Thunderbolt) was a very advanced design capable of operating from stretches of motorway.*

Hunters carried out many interdiction sorties. On 15 December, the day of the ceasefire, IAF Canberras launched a heavy night attack against the port of Karachi and associated installations. Losses in the two-week air war are hard to establish, but according to Brigadier-General Charles Yeager, USAF, the American Defence Representative in Pakistan, the PakAF destroyed 102 IAF aircraft for the loss of 34.

**26–30 December** In Vietnam, US aircraft launched the heaviest air strikes since 1968 – 1025 sorties – against a variety of targets south of the 20th Parallel.

# 1972

**30 March** The North Vietnamese Army launched a major three-pronged offensive against South Vietnam, striking at Quang Tri, Kontum and An Loc. Every available US and Vietnamese tactical aircraft was committed to attacks on enemy forces between the 20th Parallel and the battle line inside South Vietnam. Bolstered by B-52 reinforcements from the USA, attack sorties over the extended battlefield averaged 15 000 per month.

**8 May** Following the suspension of peace talks in Paris, President Richard M. Nixon authorized Operation *Linebacker*, the renewed bombing of North Vietnam. For the first time, the United States imposed a naval blockade and mined the waters of Haiphong and other ports. To neutralize North Vietnam's rebuilt air defences, the USAF made full use of new weapons systems, including F-105 *Wild Weasel* defence suppression aircraft and the profusion of laser- and optically-guided bombs developed in the 1960s.

**June** The MiG-23/27 *Flogger* air superiority fighter and ground-attack aircraft entered service with the Soviet Air Force.

**18 December** Following another breakdown in the Paris peace talks, and indications that the North Vietnamese might renew their offensive, President Nixon ordered a resumption of air strikes above the 20th Parallel (*Linebacker* II). This developed into the heaviest bombing offensive of the war, with round-the-clock attacks on targets which had mostly been on the restricted list. Targets included 34 strategic objectives, over 60 per cent of which were within a 25-mile (40-km) radius of Hanoi. The plan called for night attacks by B-52s, with F-111s, F-105s, F-4s and A-6s continuing the

offensive in daylight. The B-52 streams were preceded by F-111 interdictors, attacking fighter bases at low level, and F-4 Phantoms dropping *Window*. The North Vietnamese responded to the 11-day bombing campaign by using up most of their inventory of about 1000 SAMs and opening up a heavy barrage of AAA fire, but electronic countermeasures helped keep losses to a minimum. Of 26 aircraft lost, 15 were B-52s shot down by SAMs, and three others were badly damaged. Deprived of most of their air bases, the NVAF was able to launch only 32 aircraft, of which eight were shot down, two by B-52 tail gunners.

# 1973

**15 January** With Paris talks once again in progress, the United States announced an end to all offensive operations against North Vietnam. A ceasefire came into effect on 28 January, Saigon time.

**May** USAF aircraft, including B-52s, F-111s, A-7s and AC-130s, launched repeated strikes against *Khmer Rouge* insurgents assaulting the Cambodian capital, Phnom Penh.

**June** The first SEPECAT Jaguar tactical strike aircraft was delivered to *Escadrille* 1/7 *Provence*. (The two-seat trainer version, Jaguar E-1, had been in service with this unit since 1972.) The RAF's Jaguar GR.1 also entered service with the OCU at RAF Lossiemouth in June.

**15 August** US aircraft (A-7 Corsairs) carried out the last air strike in Cambodia.

**6 October** The Yom Kippur War. Egypt launched a surprise attack with 70 000 troops, supported by 400 tanks, against Israeli positions across the Suez Canal. At the same time, Syrian forces attacked the Golan Heights. In support of the Egyptian attack, an estimated 250 MiGs and Su-7s struck at Israeli air bases, radar and missile sites in the Sinai. The Israelis counter-attacked strongly on both fronts, using all available air power, initially against enemy airfields and SAMs, of which the Arab forces had considerable numbers. Losses were high; in the first week of the conflict the IDF/AF lost over 80 aircraft, mostly victims of SAMs and AAA, and 38 more were lost in the second week. Having outfought the Syrians, the Israelis turned the full weight of their counter-offensive on the Egyptians, pushing forces across the Suez Canal and encircling the Egyptian Tenth Army before a ceasefire was arranged by the UN on 24 October. In all the IDF/AF lost 118 aircraft, the

Egyptians 113 and the Syrians 149. The Iraqi Air Force, assisting the Syrians, lost 21.

**December** The first Dassault *Mirage* F.1 strike fighters were delivered to the 30ᵉ *Escadre* at Reims.

*The McDonnell Douglas F-15 Eagle, one of the most effective of modern air superiority fighters. In 1991, Eagles scored most of the air combat successes of the Gulf War. These aircraft bear the code markings of the 36th Tactical Fighter Wing, Bitburg, Germany.*

# 1974

**March** The first Lockheed SA-3 Viking anti-submarine warfare aircraft was delivered to the US Navy's VS-41 operational training unit.

The Grumman F-14A Tomcat became operational with US Navy squadrons VF-1 and VF-2, USS *Enterprise*. The Tomcat was designed primarily to establish complete air superiority in the vicinity of a carrier task force.

**August** The Sukhoi Su-24 *Fencer* interdictor/strike aircraft became operational with the Soviet Air Force.

# 1975

**January** The first operationally-configured McDonnell Douglas F-15A Eagle air superiority fighter was delivered to the 57th Tactical Fighter Training Wing, Nellis AFB, Nevada.

**April** The Soviet Union conducted the largest maritime/air exercise ever witnessed, involving over 200 warships and submarines and large numbers of aircraft operating world-wide.

**June** The Israel Aircraft Industries *Kfir* multi-role

combat aircraft became operational with the Israeli Defence Forces/Air Force.

*September* The Tupolev Tu-22M variable-geometry anti-shipping strike aircraft entered service with the Soviet Navy.

*1 November* The Boeing E-4A airborne command post, developed from the Boeing 747 airliner, entered service with the 1st Airborne Command and Control Sqn at Andrews AFB, Maryland.

# 1976

*July* The Yak-38 *Forger*, the USSR's first operational VSTOL aircraft, made its appearance on the aircraft carrier *Kiev* in the Mediterranean. This missile-armed ASW vessel joined the Northern Fleet in August.

# 1977

*March* The Boeing E-3A Sentry Airborne Warning and Control Systems aircraft became operational with the USAF Tactical Air Command.

*April* The Soviet Union carried out a large maritime/air exercise off Norway, with 160 aircraft carrying out a simulated strike against 27 surface vessels.

# 1978

*January* The Fairchild Republic A-10 Thunderbolt II anti-tank aircraft entered service with the 354th Tactical Fighter Wing at Myrtle Beach AFB, Florida.

*April* A Soviet maritime/air exercise south of the Iceland-Faeroes Gap included 250 aircraft sorties, the first reconnaissance flights being made by Tu-95 *Bears* WSW of the British Isles. The exercise was conducted in connection with the transfer of the aircraft carrier *Minsk* from the Mediterranean to the Northern Fleet.

*June* The IAe58 *Pucara* counter-insurgency and attack aircraft entered service with the II *Escuadron de Exploration y Ataque*, Argentine Air Force.

*September* The Mitsubishi F-1 strike fighter, Japan's first indigenous combat aircraft since World War II, was delivered to the Japanese Air Self-Defence Force.

# 1979

*January* The General Dynamics F-16 air superiority fighter entered service with the 388th Tactical Fighter Wing, Hill AFB, Utah.

*18 June* The British Aerospace Sea Harrier FRS.1 was delivered to the Royal Navy's Intensive Flying Trials Unit.

*8–16 July* For the first time, Strategic Air Command exercised every phase of its operational role – short of nuclear warfare – in Exercise Global Shield 79. The exercise was one of the most comprehensive in history, featuring hundreds of bombers, tankers and missiles generated to alert. The aircraft were dispersed to pre-selected bases, from which they flew sorties over radar bomb-scoring sites. The exercise was repeated in 1980.

# 1980

*7 June* Eight Israeli Air Force F-16s, escorted by six F-15s, made a precision bombing attack on Iraq's Osirak nuclear reactor near Baghdad, completely destroying the installation and setting back Iraq's nuclear weapons development programme by several years. All the attacking aircraft returned safely, having covered a distance of over 1000 miles (1600 km), mostly at low level.

*22–25 September* In an exercise called *Busy Prairie*, SAC tested the newly-created Strategic Projection Force concept, the aim of which was to respond immediately with conventional weapons to crisis situations anywhere in the world. Fourteen B-52H bombers of the 5th Bomb Wing, with EC-135, KC-135, U-2 and C-5 support, deployed to Whitman AFB, Missouri, to conduct simulated combat operations over the *Red Flag* training area in central Nevada and demonstrate the B-52's ability to penetrate enemy territory.

*23 September* In support of a three-pronged land offensive on the southern border with Iran, the Iraqi Air Force flew 140 missions against Iranian oil refineries and airfields. Iran claimed 16 aircraft destroyed. In retaliation, Iranian aircraft attacked Habbaniyah air base, Baghdad and Al Kut. After two more raids on Baghdad, the Iraqis claimed the destruction of 67 Iranian aircraft. The Iranians used mainly F-4s and F-5s, the Iraqis MiG-23s, Su-7Bs and Tu-22s. These attacks marked the beginning of a bitter conflict that was to last a decade.

# 1981

**17 March** The first Douglas KC-10A tanker, developed from the DC-10 airliner, was delivered to the USAF. The first six KC-10As were assigned to the 32nd Air Refueling Sqn, 2nd Bomb Wing, in November.

**19 August** Two F-14 Tomcats of US Navy Fighter Sqn CF-41 engaged and destroyed two Libyan Air Force Su-22 fighter-bombers over the Gulf of Sirte. The armed Su-22s were approaching US naval forces with apparently hostile intent.

**15 September** A B-52G of the 416th Bomb Wing made the first training flight with the Boeing AGM-86B Air-Launched Cruise Missile. The entire SAC force of 172 B-52G aircraft was progressively modified to carry the weapon, each B-52 carrying six missiles under each wing on jettisonable pylons and eight on a rotary launcher in the bomb bay.

**15 September** The first Lockheed TR-1A battlefield surveillance aircraft was delivered to the 4029th Strategic Reconnaissance Sqn, 9th Strategic Reconnaissance Wing, at Beale AFB, California.

**23 November** Eight B-52H bombers of SAC's Strategic Projection Force carried out the longest non-stop bombing mission in the Command's history. Four aircraft from the 319th Bomb Wing, Grand Forks AFB, North Dakota, and four from the 5th Bomb Wing, Minot AFB, North Dakota, made a 31-hour, 15 000-mile (24 140 km) round trip with flight refuelling to drop conventional bombs on a simulated runway in Egypt (Exercise *Bright Star*).

**December** The Sukhoi Su-25 *Frogfoot* tactical support aircraft entered service with the Soviet Air Force. The Su-25 underwent evaluation under operational conditions against guerrilla forces in Afghanistan in the following year.

# 1982

**April–June** The Falklands War. Following the Argentine invasion of the Falkland Islands and South Georgia on 2 April, the British Government initiated Operation *Corporate*, the plan to recapture these territories. While a task force was being assembled for this purpose, Hercules aircraft of No. 38 Group RAF flew stores and equipment to Wideawake Air Base on Ascension Island. On 5 April, two Nimrod MR.1s of No. 42 Sqn arrived at this location to begin long-range patrols in support of the Task Force, and on 12 April, they were joined by detachments of Nos. 120, 201 and 206 Sqns, with better-equipped Nimrod MR.2s. On 18 April, the first five Victor K.2 tankers of Nos. 55 and 57 Sqns also arrived; their initial role was maritime radar reconnaissance (MRR).

**20 April** Victor K.2 made a radar search of 150 000 miles$^2$ (388 500 km$^2$) of ocean in the South Georgia area before returning to Ascension Island after a flight lasting 14 hr 45 min. This was the longest operational reconnaissance mission ever carried out, and was an essential preliminary to the re-occupation of South Georgia.

**25 April** As part of the operation to retake South Georgia, the Argentine submarine *Santa Fe* was attacked and disabled by Lynx, Wasp and Wessex helicopters using machine-gun fire and an AS-12 missile launched by a Wasp from HMS *Endurance*. The submarine was beached at Grytviken.

**29 April** The first Vulcan B.2 bombers of the Waddington Wing (Nos. 44, 50 and 101 Sqns) arrived at Ascension Island for operations against the Falklands.

**30 April/1 May** Vulcan XM607, supported by 11 Victor tanker sorties, carried out the first offensive sortie against the Falklands (*Black Buck One*), dropping a stick of 21 1000 lb (450 kg) bombs across the main runway at Port Stanley airfield. The Vulcan recovered safely to Ascension Island after a flight of 15 hr 45 min at the end of the longest-range bombing operation in history under combat conditions.

**1 May** 12 Sea Harriers of No. 800 Sqn, HMS *Hermes*, attacked the airfield at Port Stanley and the airstrip at Goose Green with 1000 lb (450 kg) bombs. One Sea Harrier was damaged. Later in the day the Argentine Air Force launched 40 sorties against the British warships off the Falklands. A *Mirage* III was shot down by a Sea Harrier of No. 801 Sqn (HMS *Invincible*); a second,

damaged, was destroyed by Argentine AAA over the islands. An IAI Dagger (Israeli-built *Mirage* 5) was shot down by a Sea Harrier of No. 800 Sqn, and one of six Canberras of *Grupo* 2 was destroyed by a Sea Harrier of No. 801 Sqn. All Sea Harrier kills were achieved with the AIM-9L Sidewinder AAM.

**3 May** The Argentine patrol craft *Comodoro Somellera* and *Alferez Sobral* were attacked by Lynx helicopters from the destroyers HMS *Coventry* and HMS *Glasgow*. The former was sunk by Sea Skua missiles, the second badly damaged.

**3/4 May** The second *Black Buck* sortie was flown by a Vulcan, 21 1000 lb (450 kg) bombs again being dropped on Port Stanley airfield. No significant damage was caused.

**4 May** Three Sea Harriers of No. 800 Sqn attacked Goose Green; one was shot down by AAA and the pilot killed. Later, the Type 42 destroyer HMS *Sheffield*, on radar picket duty west of the Falklands, was hit and disabled by an *Exocet* ASM launched by a *Super Etendard* of the 2 *Escuadrilla de Caza y Ataque*. The warship was abandoned and later sunk.

*Falklands War, 1982: a British Aerospace Sea Harrier FRS.1 launches from the 'ski-jump' of HMS Hermes for a combat mission over the Argentine-occupied islands.*

**9 May** Following a period of bad weather, air operations resumed on a limited scale. The Argentine trawler *Narwhal* was disabled by a Sea Harrier of No. 800 Sqn; two Skyhawks of the Argentine Air Force's *Grupo* 4, approaching to attack British ships, collided and their pilots were killed. An Argentine Army Puma helicopter was shot down by a Sea Dart SAM launched by HMS *Coventry*.

**12 May** British warships bombarding Port Stanley airfield were attacked by eight Skyhawks of *Grupo* 5. Two were shot down by Sea Wolf SAMs launched by the frigate HMS *Brilliant*, one crashed into the sea and a fourth was destroyed by Argentinian AAA. The destroyer HMS *Glasgow* was damaged and forced to withdraw for repair.

**13–14 May** The airstrip on Pebble Island was attacked by 45 men of D Squadron Special Air Service, flown in by Sea Kings of No. 846 Sqn. Six

*Pucara* and four Turbo-Mentor ground-attack aircraft and a Skyvan transport were put out of action.

**15 May** A new world distance record for an operational reconnaissance mission was created by a Nimrod of No. 201 Sqn, which covered 8300 miles (13 357 km) over the South Atlantic in 19 hr 5 min.

**16 May** Four Sea Harriers attacked two Argentine supply ships in Fox Bay and Falkland Sound with bombs and cannon; both vessels were abandoned.

**18 May** The air component of the Falklands Task Force was reinforced with the arrival, on the MS *Atlantic Conveyer*, of six Harrier GR.3s of No. 1 Sqn RAF and eight Sea Harriers of No. 809 Sqn.

**20 May** Harrier GR.3s of No. 1 Sqn carried out their first attack, against a fuel dump at Fox Bay, West Falkland.

**20–21 May** Ships of the British amphibious landing force entered San Carlos Water under cover of a diversionary SAS attack at Goose Green and began offloading. A *Pucara* on dawn reconnaissance was hit by a Stinger portable missile as it flew over an SAS patrol and was shot down. While Sea Harriers flew combat air patrols, Har-

rier GR.3s carried out attacks in support of the troops ashore; one GR.3 was shot down, the injured pilot being taken prisoner. Argentine attacks on the landing force vessels began with a single run by a Macchi MB.339 of the 1st Naval Attack *Escuadrilla*, which hit HMS *Argonaut* with 30 mm cannon shells and 5-in rockets; this was followed by an attack by six Daggers of *Grupo* 6, one of which was shot down by a Sea Cat SAM. HMS *Antrim* was hit by a bomb which failed to explode, and HMS *Broadsword* was also damaged by 30 mm shells. Two *Pucaras* of *Grupo* 3 were engaged by three Sea Harriers of No. 801 Sqn, and one was shot down. The next force to attack comprised four Skyhawks of *Grupo* 4 and two of *Grupo* 5; one of the former was shot down by a No. 800 Sqn Sea Harrier. Next came four Daggers of *Grupo* 6, one of which was also shot down by a No. 800 Sqn pilot. Meanwhile, Skyhawks attacking ships in Falkland Sound hit HMS *Argonaut* with two 1000 lb (450 kg) bombs, causing severe damage; soon afterwards the surviving Daggers of

*A Sea Harrier lets fly with a salvo of 2.7 in (68 mm) SNEB rockets, widely used by NATO air forces for ground attack work.*

Grupo 6 bombed HMS *Ardent*, which also sustained heavy damage. The frigate was again hit by Skyhawks of *Grupo* 5. Elsewhere, over West Falkland, three Daggers were destroyed by two Sea Harriers of No. 801 Sqn. In the meantime, HMS *Ardent* was attacked yet again, this time by three Skyhawks of the 3rd Naval Fighter and Attack *Escuadrilla*, causing yet more damage with 500 lb (227 kg) Snakeye retarded bombs; these aircraft were engaged by Sea Harriers of No. 800 Sqn, which destroyed one with an AIM-9L and another with 30 mm cannon fire. The third, hit by small-arms fire from *Ardent*, came down off Port Stanley, the pilot ejecting. HMS *Ardent* sank that night, having been hit by seven bombs and an eighth which failed to explode. During the two day's fighting the Argentinians had lost 12 aircraft, nine destroyed by Sea Harriers; British losses were one Harrier GR.3 and two helicopters.

**22 May** Two Sea Harriers of No. 800 Sqn attacked and disabled the Argentine Coast Guard patrol boat *Rio Iguazu* in Choiseul Sound. Four Harrier GR.3s of No. 1 Sqn attacked Goose Green. To the north of the Falklands, a Boeing 707 reconnaissance aircraft of *Grupo* 1 was engaged by Sea Dart SAMs launched by HMS *Bristol* and HMS *Cardiff* at extreme range, but escaped.

**23 May** Sea Harriers destroyed three Puma and one Agusta 109 helicopters on the ground. HMS *Antelope* was attacked in San Carlos water by Skyhawks and was hit by two bombs which failed to explode. One Skyhawk was shot down by a Sea Wolf SAM, another crashed on landing at base. (HMS *Antelope* blew up that night while a bomb disposal team was at work on board.) During the day, Rapier SAM crews claimed the destruction of three Argentine aircraft and a Dagger was destroyed by a Sea Harrier of No. 800 Sqn. One Sea Harrier (No. 800 Sqn) crashed into the sea after take-off from HMS *Hermes*, the pilot being killed.

**24 May** Sea Harriers of No. 800 Sqn and Harrier GR.3s of No. 1 Sqn attacked Port Stanley airfield, but failed to crater the runway. Warships off Pebble Island were attacked by Daggers of *Grupo* 6, one of which was shot down by the Sea Harrier CAP. Vessels at San Carlos were also attacked by Daggers and Skyhawks; one of the latter crashed into the sea. Three ships were hit by bombs, but none exploded.

**25 May** Three Skyhawks were shot down by ground fire during the morning. In the afternoon, six Skyhawks of *Grupo* 5 attacked warships off Pebble Island, sinking HMS *Coventry* with three bomb hits. The container ship *Atlantic Conveyor*,

north-east of the Falklands, was hit by an *Exocet* ASM launched by a *Super Etendard* and had to be abandoned. The ship was lost, together with the stores she carried – including ten helicopters.

**27 May** Harrier GR.3s of No. 1 Sqn attacked Argentine positions in the Goose Green area; one was shot down, the pilot ejecting. Two Skyhawks of *Grupo* 5 successfully bombed a stores dump at Ajax Bay; one aircraft was shot down by 40 mm Bofors fire, the pilot baling out.

**28 May** British paratroops advancing on Goose Green were subjected to attacks by *Pucara* aircraft, which shot down an Army Scout helicopter. One *Pucara* was shot down by a Blowpipe SAM, a second by ground fire, and a third crashed into high ground in cloud. A Macchi 339 was also destroyed by a Blowpipe. Argentine positions at Goose Green were attacked by No. 1 Sqn's Harriers, using cluster bombs and rockets. The Argentine garrison at Goose Green surrendered the next day after fierce fighting.

**29 May** Bad weather hampered air operations. North-east of the Falklands, the tanker *British Wye*, bringing fuel for the Task Force, was attacked by a C-130 Hercules of *Grupo* 1, modified as a bomber. The aircraft released eight bombs, but only one struck the tanker and failed to explode.

**30 May** No. 1 Sqn mounted six Harrier sorties in support of ground forces; one aircraft was shot down, the pilot ejecting. *Super Etendards* made an *Exocet* attack against the main body of the Task Force, but the missiles were deflected by chaff countermeasures. Two Skyhawks of *Grupo* 4 were shot down by Sea Dart SAMs fired by HMS *Exeter*.

**30/31 May** Vulcan XM597 launched two Shrike anti-radar missiles against radar installations in the Port Stanley area without inflicting serious damage. Seven Harrier attack sorties were flown by No. 1 Sqn during the day.

**1 June** Four Canberras of *Grupo* 2 made a high-level bombing attack on Port San Carlos. A C-130 Hercules of *Grupo* 1, carrying out a radar reconnaissance north of San Carlos Water, was intercepted by Sea Harriers of No. 801 Sqn and destroyed by an AIM-9L missile and cannon fire. Two more Harrier GR.3 reinforcements arrived from Ascension Island. In the afternoon, a Sea Harrier of No. 801 Sqn was shot down by a *Roland* missile; the pilot ejected and was picked up by a Sea King after nine hours in his dinghy.

**2 June** Bad weather restricted air operations, but the sole Chinook helicopter operating in the Falklands airlifted paratroops to vital high ground positions overlooking Fitzroy.

**2/3 June** Vulcan XM597 launched two Shrike missiles at radar contacts. The Vulcan's flight refuelling probe fractured during contact with a Victor tanker on the homeward run and the aircraft diverted to Rio de Janeiro, Brazil, where it and its crew were held for a week before being released.

**5 June** Harriers and Sea Harriers were now able to deploy from the carriers to an airstrip at Port San Carlos, enabling them to provide more effective support for the ground forces. Hercules aircraft of No. 38 Group, which now had a flight refuelling capability enabling them to reach the Falklands from Ascension Island, made low-level supply drops to the Task Force at sea.

**7 June** A photo-reconnaissance Learjet of *Escuadron* I was hit and destroyed at 40 000 ft (12 190 m) by a Sea Dart launched by HMS *Exeter*.

**8 June** Skyhawks of *Grupo* 5 and Daggers of *Grupo* 6 launched heavy attacks on vessels at San Carlos and Fitzroy, hitting the logistics ships *Sir Tristram* and *Sir Galahad* and causing heavy loss of life. Another attack just before dusk was intercepted by Sea Harriers of No. 800 Sqn, which shot down three out of four Skyhawks with Sidewinders.

**9 June** No. 1 Sqn, reinforced by two more Harriers from Ascension Island, flew four sorties against enemy gun positions on Sapper Hill and Mount Longdon. The advance on Port Stanley was supported by Sea Kings of Nos. 825 and 846 Sqns, Wessex of Nos. 845, 847 and 848 Sqns, and the lone Chinook of No. 18 Sqn, lifting supplies and ammunition to guns and positions around Mount Kent. Ground attack sorties against targets in the Port Stanley area continued the next day, and some Harriers were damaged by small-arms fire, though none seriously. No. 1 Sqn flew 11 sorties on 11 June, of which ten were against Argentine positions and the other a toss-bombing attack on Port Stanley airfield.

**11/12 June** Vulcan XM607 made a conventional bombing attack on Argentine troop concentrations around Port Stanley, using a mixture of 1000 lb (450 kg) and anti-personnel bombs fuzed to burst in the air. In the course of the day No. 1 Sqn flew six ground-attack sorties against Argentine positions on Sapper Hill.

**13 June** Forward air controllers were now in position on the hills around Port Stanley, enabling No. 1 Sqn to use laser-guided bombs to good effect against the Argentine forward positions. Skyhawks made two unsuccessful attacks on Brit-

ish troops. An Argentine Air Force C-130 made the last of 31 transport flights to Port Stanley since the conflict began, offloading stores and evacuating wounded. A Canberra of *Grupo* 2, bombing Mount Kent from 40 000 ft (12 190 m), was shot down by a Sea Dart SAM launched by HMS *Exeter*.

**14 June** Argentine positions at Port Stanley were attacked by Scout helicopters launching SS11 anti-tank missiles against bunkers. These were the last offensive air operations of the conflict; the Argentine garrison at Port Stanley surrendered later that day.

**9 June** The Israeli Air Force launched the first of a series of attacks designed to destroy Syrian surface-to-air missile systems emplaced in the Lebanon. Remote-controlled pilotless vehicles (RPVs) were used to detect the SAM sites, and strike aircraft operated in conjunction with electronic countermeasures Boeing 707s and EC-2 Hawkeyes. The strike aircraft (A-4 Skyhawks, F-4 Phantoms and *Kfir*s) attacked SAM sites, radar stations and command posts, the Phantoms using Maverick and Shrike missiles while the Skyhawks and *Kfir*s used TV-guided missiles and cluster bombs. The strikes were made in support of the invasion of southern Lebanon by Israeli forces; during this phase the Israelis claimed to have shot down 92 Syrian fighters, about half of them MiG-23 *Flogger*s. F-15 Eagle pilots claimed 40 and F-16 pilots 44, Phantoms and *Kfir*s accounting for the others. The claim was seriously disputed by the Syrians.

**November** The Panavia Tornado IDS (Interdictor/Strike) aircraft, designated GR.1 in the RAF, became fully operational with No. 9 Sqn at RAF Honington and the Federal German Navy's *Marinefliegergeschwader* 1 at Jagel, northern Germany. Both units had taken delivery of their first Tornados in June and July respectively.

# 1983

**January** The McDonnell Douglas F-18 Hornet entered service with Marine Corps Fighter Sqn VFMA-314 at El Toro, California. The fighter had undergone operational evaluation with Fighter/Attack Sqn VFA-125 from February 1981.

**March** The MiG-31 *Foxhound* interceptor entered service with the Soviet Air Defence Forces.

**October** The Lockheed F-117A 'Stealth' fighter-bomber began operational evaluation with the USAF Tactical Air Command.

THE YEARS OF THE COLD WAR 1946–90

**25 October** The United States launched Operation *Urgent Fury*, the invasion of Grenada. Following initial landings by US Marines and Rangers, troops of the 82nd Airborne Division were flown in by C-141s of the 437th Military Airlift Wing. Offensive air support was provided by AC-130 Spectre gunships, together with A-6s and A-7s from the USS *Independence*. Several US helicopters were lost in the initial assault on Pearls Airport, which was guarded by Cuban troops equipped with 23-mm anti-aircraft guns. The operation was completed within a week.

# 1984

**16 January** The first McDonnell Douglas AV-8B Harrier II STOVL aircraft was handed over to Marine Training Sqn VMAT-203 at Cherry Point, North Carolina.

**26 March–21 April** The Soviet Northern Fleet carried out large-scale exercises in the Norwegian

*A Panavia Tornado GR.1 of the Tri-National Tornado Training Establishment takes off from RAF Cottesmore. The TTTE's function was to train Tornado crews from Britain, Germany and Italy.*

Sea. Air activity during the exercises was substantial and included simulated attacks by Tu-22M *Backfire* bombers against Soviet warships.

**July** The *Mirage* 2000 tactical fighter-bomber was delivered to EC1/2 *Cigognes* at Dijon.

**September** The Sukhoi Su-27 *Flanker* all-weather air superiority fighter entered service with the Soviet Tactical Air Forces.

# 1985

**February** The MiG-29 air superiority fighter became operational with the Soviet Tactical Air Forces.

*7 July* The first Rockwell B-1 supersonic variable-geometry bomber was delivered to the 96th Bomb Wing, Dyess AFB, Texas.

*1 October* Israeli Air Force F-16s, escorted by F-15s, attacked and destroyed the HQ of the Palestine Liberation Organization (PLO) at Hamman-Shatt, 21 nautical miles south-east of Tunis, capital of Tunisia. The attacking aircraft flight-refuelled from Boeing 707 tankers.

# 1986

*14/15 April* 15 General Dynamics F-111Fs of the 48th Tactical Fighter Wing, supported by three EF-111s of the 42nd Electronic Combat Sqn, took off from RAF Lakenheath and RAF Upper Heyford in the UK to attack targets in Libya in response to that nation's growing involvement with international terrorism. The F-111s flight-refuelled three times on the 2800 nautical miles journey. Ten

aircraft attacked the Libyan Air Force facility at Tripoli Airport and the Sidi Bilal port facility with Mk 20 Rockeye 500 lb (227 kg) laser-homing cluster bombs, while five attacked the Al Azzizayah military barracks and associated command centre in Tripoli with Mk 82 2000 lb (900 kg) laser-guided bombs. At the same time, 15 Grumman A-6 Intruders and Vought A-7 Corsairs, also armed with 500 lb and 2000 lb bombs attacked the Al Jumahiraya military barracks near Benghazi and the airfield at Benina. Throughout the operation, top cover was provided by US Sixth Fleet Tomcats and F-18 Hornets, directed by Grumman E-2C Hawkeye command and early warning aircraft. Effective countermeasures were provided by the EF-111s and EA-6 Prowlers. Post-strike reconnaissance by Lockheed SR-71As revealed that all the assigned targets had been hit, albeit with a

*A McDonnell Douglas F-18 Hornet is readied for launch from a carrier of the US Sixth Fleet in the Mediterranean. Hornets played a prominent part in the US attacks on Libya in April 1986.*

certain amount of collateral damage to civilian property in Tripoli, and several aircraft destroyed. One F-111F was lost in unknown circumstances.

# 1987

**1 July** The Harrier GR.5 advanced STOVL tactical support aircraft entered service with No. 233 OCU, RAF Wittering.

# 1988

**18 April** The Iranian Navy frigate *Sahand* was attacked and sunk in the Persian Gulf by A-6E intruders of VA-95 (USS *Enterprise*). The frigate *Sablan* was also attacked and crippled. This action was taken in response to Iranian attacks on US warships in the Gulf.

**28 December** The McDonnell Douglas F-15E Strike Eagle interdictor entered service with the 4th Tactical Wing at Seymour-Johnson AFB, North Carolina.

# 1989

**4 January** Two Grumman F-14 Tomcats from the carrier USS *John F. Kennedy* shot down two Libyan Air Force MiG-23 *Flogger*s over the Mediterranean. The MiGs were armed and approaching units of the US Sixth Fleet.

**July** The Tupolev Tu-160 *Blackjack* supersonic variable-geometry strategic bomber became operational with the Soviet Long-Range Aviation.

**December** In support of a US invasion to rescue American citizens, Lockheed F-117A aircraft of the 37th Tactical Fighter Wing carried out their first operational mission – an attack on a military barracks in Panama with 2000 lb (900 kg) laser-guided bombs.

# 1990

**2 August** Iraqi forces launched an invasion of Kuwait. Two of the principal objectives were the Kuwait Air Force bases of Ali al Salin (Nos. 18 and 61 Sqns, *Mirage* F.1CK) and Ahmad al Jabir (Nos. 9 and 25 Sqns, A-4KU Skyhawk). Fifteen *Mirage*s were flown to safety in Bahrain; the Skyhawks continued operations from a road site until 4 August, when 19 aircraft were flown to Saudi Arabia.

*The air strikes on Libya were directed by Grumman E-2C Hawkeye command and control aircraft, indispensable in modern air warfare.*

# Operation Desert Shield
# August–December 1990

In response to a request for assistance from Saudi Arabia following the invasion of Kuwait, the United States and Great Britain began the deployment of combat aircraft to the Middle East. Spearheading the US deployment were units of the 82nd Airborne Division, equipped with UH-60 Black Hawk helicopters armed with TOW anti-tank missiles, and the 1st Tactical Fighter Wing with F-15C Eagles, the Wing's 27th Tactical Fighter Sqn arriving at Dhahran on 8 August. Other F-15 units subsequently deployed were the 33rd TFW and a squadron of the 36th TFW, the F-15 force being supported by E-3 Sentry AWACS aircraft. Also deployed at an early stage were the F-117As of the 37th TFW. While USAF F-15s assured superiority over the battle area, Royal Saudi Air Force F-15s and RAF Tornado F.3s were tasked with the defence of the Coalition air bases; the Tornado F.3s of No. 5 (Composite) Sqn arrived at Dhahran on 11 August.

The largest deployment involved F-16 aircraft, the USAF deploying elements of five wings (the 50th, 347th, 363rd, 388th and 401st) and the Air National Guard two (the 169th and 174th). Some of the F-16s were based in Turkey. For all-weather interdiction the USAF deployed the F-15E Strike Eagles of the 4th TFW, F-111Fs of the 48th TFW and F-111Es of the 20th TFW. The task of defence suppression was assigned to the F-4G Phantoms of the 35th and 52nd TFWs. The RAF's contribution to the interdiction/strike role was the Tornado GR.1, composite squadrons being rotated to the Middle East to operate alongside Tornado IDS units of the RSAF and an eight-aircraft unit of the Italian Air Force.

For anti-armour and close support operations the USAF deployed A-10A Thunderbolt IIs of the 10th, 23rd and 345th TFWs, together with aircraft drawn from the Air Force Reserve, with OV-10 Broncos providing forward air control. RAF tactical operations were undertaken by the Jaguar GR.1As of Nos. 6, 41 and 54 Sqns, operating in conjunction with Jaguars of the *Armée de l'Air*'s EC11. The Kuwait Air Force's surviving A-4

Skyhawks also operated in the tactical role. For local air defence, and air cover of Allied warships in the Gulf, the Canadian Armed Forces positioned a composite squadron of CF-18 Hornets at Qatar; also positioned in the Emirates, apart from aircraft of their own air forces, were French *Mirage* F.1s and *Mirage* 2000s, supported by C-135F tankers. For the main combat forces, massive tanker support was provided by USAF KC-135s and KC-10s, and RAF Victor K.2s and VC.10s.

US Naval Air support in the Gulf was provided by the carriers USS *Independence* and USS *Dwight D. Eisenhower* (both of which were withdrawn before the UN deadline expired), the USS *Midway*, USS *Ranger* and USS *Theodore Roosevelt*. In addition, the USS *Saratoga*, USS *America* and USS *John F. Kennedy* were on station in the Red Sea. The carriers' air groups comprised squadrons of F-14s, F/A-18s, A-6Es and SA-3s, supported by E-2C Hawkeyes, EA-6B Prowlers and SH-3H Sea Kings. The *John F. Kennedy* also had two squadrons of A-7E Corsair IIs. The US Marine Corps deployed squadrons of F/A-18A Hornets and AV-8B Harrier IIs to the Gulf, as well as attack and assault helicopters. The principal attack helicopter used by the USMC was the AH-1W SuperCobra; the AH-1F version was deployed by the US Army, as was the AH-64A Apache.

Finally, Strategic Air Command committed the B-52s of the 42nd and 93rd Bomb Wings to the operation. The initial deployment was to the island of Diego Garcia in the Indian Ocean, but later deployments were to Saudi Arabia, Egypt, Spain and the United Kingdom. All aircraft were the B-52G version.

In opposition, the Iraqi Air Force possessed, on paper at least, a formidable force of about 800 combat aircraft, including *Mirage* F.1s, MiG-21s, MiG-23s, MiG-29s, Su-7/20s, Su-25s, MiG-25s and Su-24s, together with a massive array of SAMs, AAA systems and surface-to-surface missiles, mostly of Soviet and French origin.

# Operation Desert Storm
# January–February 1991

**16/17 January** The air assault phase of Operation *Desert Storm* began with an attack by eight AH-64A Apache helicopters on two radar stations on the approaches to Baghdad, using Hellfire ASMs, 70 mm rockets and 30 mm gunfire. The mission, involving a round trip of 950 nautical miles, was completely successful and both stations were destroyed. Initial attacks on Baghdad were made by Tomahawk cruise missiles launched by US warships in the Gulf and F-117As, directed at command and control centres, ministries, barracks and individual targets such as the Presidential Palace. Outside the capital, airfields and air defence radars and SAM/AAA sites were attacked, as were NBC and conventional armament plants, oil refineries, and *Scud* launching sites. Missile production and rocket propellant factories were also attacked. All types of strike aircraft were used in these operations, supported by tankers, surveillance and countermeasures aircraft. Airfield attacks were carried out by RAF, Italian AF and Royal Saudi AF Tornados. One Tornado (No. 15 Sqn) was shot down during a low-altitude toss-bombing attack on Ar Rumaylah AB shortly after dawn; the crew ejected and were taken prisoner.

**17 January** Attacks against enemy installations continued throughout the day. During counter-air operations, three MiG-29s were shot down by F-15Cs of the 33rd TFW, which also destroyed two *Mirage* F.1s. Another *Mirage* was shot down by an F-15C of the 1st TFW, and two MiG-21s were destroyed by F-18 Hornets of VFA-81 (USS *Saratoga*). One Hornet of VFA-18 was shot down by a SAM and its pilot killed; a Kuwaiti A-4KU was also lost to ground fire, its pilot being taken prisoner.

**17/18 January** Attacks on airfields and other key installations continued. F-111Fs of the 48th TFW, supported by EF-111 Raven countermeasures aircraft, attacked airfields and chemical weapons storage bunkers. RAF Tornado attacks were supported by aircraft fitted with ALARM defence-suppression missiles. One RAF Tornado was shot down and its crew killed; an Italian Air Force Tornado was also shot down and its navigator killed, the pilot being taken prisoner. The USAF lost an F-15E Strike Eagle and the USN an A-6 Intruder.

**18 January** RAF and *Armée de l'Air* Jaguars attacked Iraqi munitions depots in Kuwait and Ras-al-Qulayah using AS.30 laser-guided missiles. The first attack destroyed hardened shelters containing *Scud* missiles, the second installations containing *Exocet*-firing equipment.

**19 January** RAF Tornado GR.1A reconnaissance aircraft with thermal imaging equipment, and F-15E Strike Eagles similarly equipped, began searching for mobile *Scud* missiles, particularly those in western Iraq. For the first time, Iraqi troop positions in Kuwait and southern Iraq were attacked by AV-8Bs and A-10s, targets being marked by OV-10s using white phosphorus rockets. Royal Saudi Air Force Northrop F-5Es and British Aerospace Hawk 65s were also used on ground-attack operations. F-15 Eagles of the 33rd TFW shot down two MiG-25s and two MiG-29s, while F-15s of the 36th TFW destroyed two *Mirage* F.1s.

**20–22 January** The air offensive against Iraq continued to follow a similar pattern, with high emphasis on the location and destruction of *Scud* sites. Three more RAF Tornados were lost during this period. The airfield neutralization programme was now well advanced and Coalition aircraft had achieved air superiority, so the Tornado GR.1s were switched to low-level toss-bombing attacks against other targets. F-15E aircraft were particularly successful against mobile *Scud* launchers, being directed by Special Forces units operating inside Iraq.

**22–23 January** The USAF carried out its first successful combat search and rescue missions, using MH-53H and MH-60G helicopters escorted by A-10s to rescue the crews of an A-6E, F-14A and F-16 shot down over Iraqi territory.

**23/24 January** Tornado GR.1s, each carrying eight 1000 lb (450 kg) bombs, carried out medium-level attacks on Iraqi airfields found to be still operational. One Tornado was lost, and its crew taken prisoner, when one of its bombs exploded prematurely.

**24 January** The first anti-surface vessel combat of the war took place when Lynx helicopters from HMS *Cardiff* detected three Iraqi naval vessels and called up A-6E strike aircraft. The Intruders sank a patrol boat and landing craft, and a minesweeper was scuttled to avoid capture. Three Iraqi *Mirage* F.1EQ aircraft, armed with *Exocet* sea-skimming missiles, were detected by the radar picket ships HMS *Gloucester* and HMS *Cardiff*. The formation was intercepted by two RSAF F-15Cs, one of which shot down two *Mirage*s. The third turned back.

**26 January** During the day's operations, three MiG-23s were shot down by F-15Cs of the 33rd TFW. It was now observed that Iraqi aircraft were being flown to air bases in Iran. Flights to Iran by both military and civil aircraft continued at intervals for almost a month, until eventually 148 were positioned there. They included some of the Iraqi Air Force's most modern types, such as the Su-24 *Fencer*.

**27/28 January** F-111s of the 48th TFW used GBU-15 infra-red-guided glide bombs to destroy two pumping stations at Mina al Ahmadi in Kuwait, where the Iraqis had been pumping millions of gallons of crude oil into the Gulf.

**29 January** 17 Iraqi small craft, detected by an SH-60B helicopter off the island of Maradin, were attacked by Lynx helicopters from the frigate HMS *Brazen* and the destroyers HMS *Gloucester* and HMS *Cardiff*. Using Sea Skua missiles, the Lynx sank four vessels; 12 more were damaged in attacks by A-6Es and AH-1 Cobras.

**29/30 January** The 48th TFW opened the campaign to destroy strategic bridges in Iraq with an attack on those over the Hawr al Hammar lake, north-west of Basra. Thereafter, bridge attacks accounted for much of the 48th TFW's nightly effort. Tornados and F-15Es continued attacks on airfields and oil storage facilities. Almost all of Iraq's 30 major air bases had now been subjected to heavy attacks.

**30 January** A Lynx helicopter from HMS *Gloucester* hit an Iraqi T43-class mine warfare vessel with Sea Skuas, leaving the ship dead in the water and burning. The Lynx also disabled an ex-Kuwait Navy TNC-45 fast attack craft armed with *Exocets*, and damaged another Type 43. Four out of eight Iraqi fast patrol boats were sunk outside Kuwait harbour by A-6Es and F/A-18s, while RAF Jaguars and USN A-6Es attacked and sank three *Polochny*-class tank landing craft.

**31 January** A Lynx engaged an *Osa*-class missile boat near Bubiyan Island, again using Sea Skuas. The craft returned fire before exploding and sinking. An AC-130H Spectre gunship, engaged on clandestine operations, was shot down off the Kuwait coastline.

**1/2 February** RAF Tornado GR.1s attacked the oil refinery at Al Azziziyah, causing extensive damage and large fires.

**2 February** Buccaneer S.2 aircraft of the Lossiemouth Strike Wing, deployed to the Gulf, went into action for the first time with Pave Spike laser-designating pods, illuminating bridge targets for Tornado GR.1s using Mk 84 laser-guided bombs.

**3 February** Iraqi SAM sites and long-range artillery positions on Faylaka Island, off Kuwait City, were destroyed by RAF Jaguars. A B-52G returning to Diego Garcia after attacking Iraqi troop concentrations crashed in the Indian Ocean; three crew members were rescued.

**5 February** Strategic Air Command began deploying more B-52 bombers to overseas bases in support of Desert Storm; the first of eight aircraft arrived at RAF Fairford, Gloucestershire. Reinforcement B-52s were drawn from the 2nd, 379th and 416th Bomb Wings.

**5/6 February** F-111Fs of the 48th TFW began attacks on Republican Guard armoured units using GBU-12 laser-guided bombs. The main weight of the Allied air offensive now switched to attacks on enemy troop concentrations, in particular dug-in armoured fighting vehicles.

**6 February** USAF F-15s of the 36th TFW intercepted two Su-25 *Frogfoot* aircraft and two MiG-21s fleeing to Iran and shot down all four. An Iraqi helicopter was shot down in a gun engagement by an A-10A of the 926th Tactical Fighter Group, and another was destroyed by an F-14A Tomcat of VF-1 (USS *Ranger*).

**7–10 February** Intensive air bombardments of Iraqi troops in Kuwait, and in fortified positions to the north, continued. Fuel-air explosive bombs were dropped to clear enemy minefields by blast and heat effect, while B-52Gs carrying bomb loads of 50 000 lb (22 680 kg) carried out heavy attacks on Republican Guard positions.

**10 February** Tornado GR.1s equipped with TIALD thermal-imaging and laser-designating pods carried out their first operation, a strike on hardened aircraft shelters thought to contain mobile *Scuds* at the H-3 Southwest airfield in western Iraq. By this time many *Scuds* had been launched at Saudi Arabia and Israel, and the possibility that Israel might take retaliatory action – possibly even in the form of a nuclear strike – made the '*Scud* hunt' a matter of highest priority.

**11 February** Four Tornado GR.1s from Muharraq, each carrying eight 1000 lb (450 kg) bombs, carried out a high-level attack on the Al Jarrah barracks west of Kuwait City, causing many casualties.

**13 February** During an attack on the Fallujah highway bridge by Tornados using laser-guided bombs, one weapon suffered a guidance failure and exploded in a built-up area, killing 130 people and injuring 78.

**13/14 February** A bunker at Amiriya, western Baghdad, believed to be a command centre, was attacked by an F-117A with laser-guided bombs. The bunker was being used as an air-raid shelter; 314 people were killed. RAF Tornados and USAF Strike Eagles continued their attacks on hardened aircraft shelters; 46 F-111Fs of the 48th TFW, each carrying four GBU-12 bombs, destroyed 132 tanks and armoured vehicles in dug-in desert positions.

**14 February** During a medium-level attack by Tornado/Buccaneer teams on Al Taqaddum air base, one Tornado was shot down by SA-3 *Goa* SAMs. The pilot ejected; his navigator was killed. This was the sixth and last RAF Tornado GR.1 lost in combat.

**15–23 February** Attacks on Iraqi troop concentrations in and around Kuwait intensified with the approach of D-Day for the land offensive. Interdiction of bridges, highways and rail communications meant that the battlefield was now virtually isolated.

**24 February** More than 2000 troops of the US 101st Airborne Division were airlifted to Cobra Base, set up in the desert inside Iraq, by 115 helicopters (CH-47 Chinooks and UH-60 Black Hawks) flying in rotation. The operation was supported by over 300 AH-64 Apache and AH-1G Cobra helicopters. A further 2000 troops arrived at the base by surface transport to spearhead the ground offensive.

**25–27 February** All available Allied aircraft operated in support of the ground offensive to eliminate the Iraqi Army in Kuwait. Enemy forces retreating from Kuwait were heavily attacked by US Navy and Marine Corps aircraft in the Mutlah Ridge area.

**27/28 February** In a final attempt to eliminate Iraq's top military leadership, two F-111Fs of the 48th TFW each dropped a GBU-28 'bunker buster' laser-guided bomb on the underground command centre at Al Taji, near Baghdad.

**28 February** On the orders of US President George Bush, offensive operations against Iraq ended at 5 a.m., local time. During the whole of the conflict, the Coalition air forces had lost 68 aircraft, not all due to enemy action; Iraqi Air Force losses were estimated at 141, of which 42 were destroyed in air combat.

# 1993

**13 January** In response to the movement of surface-to-air missile batteries into the Air Exclusion Zones imposed by the United Nations in the north and south of Iraq, 110 American, British and French aircraft carried out the first of a series of air strikes on the SAM sites and their associated air defence control centres. Naval aircraft – A-6 Intruders, F-14 Tomcats and F/A-18 Hornets – from the USS *Kitty Hawk* were joined by land-based F-15s, F-16s, F-117As, RAF Tornados and French *Mirage* 2000s. Earlier, Allied aircraft had been fired on and intruding MiG-23s shot down by F-16s. On 17 January, 40 Tomahawk cruise missiles were fired from US warships at a factory south of Baghdad, said to be a nuclear facility.

# Previous Works by Robert Jackson

Aerial Combat: the World's Great Air Battles
  (*Weidenfeld, 1976*)
Air Heroes of WW2 (*Barker, 1978*)
Airships in Peace and War (*Cassell, 1973*)
Air War over France, May–June 1940 (*Ian Allan,
  1974*)
Air War over Korea (*Ian Allan, 1974*)
Avro Vulcan (*Patrick Stephens, 1984*)
At War with the Bolsheviks: the Allied Inter-
  vention in Russia, 1918–20 (*Stacey, 1972*)
Before the Storm: RAF Bomber Command,
  1936–42 (*Barker, 1974*)
Bomber! Famous Bomber Missions of WW2
  (*Barker, 1980*)
Combat Aircraft Prototypes Since 1945 (*Airlife,
  1985*)
Douglas Bader: a biography (*Barker, 1983*)
The Dragonflies: Story of helicopters and
  autogiros (*Barker, 1971*)
Dunkirk: The British Evacuation, 1940 (*Barker,
  1976*)
The Fall of France: May–June 1940 (*Barker, 1975*)
Fighter Pilots of WW1 (*Barker, 1977*)
Fighter Pilots of WW2 (*Barker, 1975*)
Fighter! The story of air combat, 1936–45
  (*Barker, 1979*)
Flying Modern Jet Fighters (*Patrick Stephens,
  1986*)
Hawker Hunter (*Ian Allan, 1982*)
Israeli Air Force Story (*Stacey, 1970*)
The Jet Age: True Tales of the Air Since 1945
  (*Barker, 1981*)
NATO Air Power (*Airlife, 1987*)
Operation Musketeer: Suez, 1956 (*Ian Allan,
  1980*)
RAF in Action (*Blandford, 1985*)

The Red Falcons: Soviet Air Force, 1919–69
  (*Clifton Books, 1970*)
The Secret Squadrons: Special Duties Units of
  WW2 (*Robson Books, 1983*)
The Sky their Frontier: pioneer airlines (*Airlife,
  1983*)
Storm from the Skies: the strategic bombing
  offensive, 1943–45 (*Barker, 1974*)
Strike Force: The USAF in Britain Since 1948
  (*Robson Books, 1986*)
Strike from the Sea: British Naval Air Power
  (*Barker, 1970*)
V-Bombers (*Ian Allan, 1981*)
World Military Aircraft Since 1945 (*Ian Allan,
  1980*)

**Non-fiction published in 1988:**
Aces' Twilight – Air War 1918 (*Sphere*)
The Berlin Airlift (*Patrick Stephens*)
The Hawker Hurricane (*Blandford*)
Sea Harrier (*Blandford*)
The Hawker Tempest (*Blandford*)

**Non-fiction published 1989–91:**
Air Force: The RAF in the 1990s (*Airlife*)
Canberra – The Operational Record (*Airlife*)
The Forgotten Aces (WW2) (*Sphere*)
High-Tech Warfare (*Eddison Sadd Editions*)
Hunter – The Operational Record (*Airlife*)
The Malayan Emergency, 1948–60 (*Routledge*)

**Current projects:**
Arnhem – the Battle Remembered (*Airlife*)
Mustang – the Operational Record (*Airlife*)
F-86 Sabre – the Operational Record (*Airlife*)

## About the author

Born in 1941 in the North Yorkshire village of Melsonby, Robert Jackson was educated at Richmond School, Yorkshire. He is a full-time writer, mainly on aerospace and defence issues, and is defence correspondent for North of England Newspapers. He is the author of more than 60 books on aviation and military subjects, including *Air War over France, 1940, Air War over Korea* and the widely acclaimed *Air Force: the RAF in the 1990s*. His writings also include operational histories of individual aircraft types such as the Avro Vulcan and Sea Harrier. A former pilot and navigation instructor, he was a squadron leader in the Royal Air Force Volunteer Reserve. His principal recreation is Rugby Football, and he is an official of Durham County Rugby Union.

* Note; Because of the size and
complexity of United States air
operations worldwide,
establishments/units etc are
indexed under general headings
only. For more precise details of
designations etc, see appropriate
sections of main text.